Think Again

That is why double standards are inevitable and right, and why favoritism is good and moral: double standards are invoked when you prefer the beliefs you hold to the beliefs others hold and distribute rewards accordingly; favoritism occurs when you are loyal to those who are loyal to you because they share the same values, which are local, not universal. The alternative is to award your loyalty by consulting an independent measure unattached to anyone's preferences. My message in these columns is that there is no such measure.

This might sound like relativism, but it's the reverse. It's standing up for your commitments and for your comrades rather than standing up for a principle no one has seen and whose shape is always in dispute. It's politics, and that is the theme of part 4 ("Reflections on Politics"). The rap against politics has always been that its judgments are partial; to label a decision "political" is to say that it is suspect because it proceeds not from an overarching and universal principle but from a local calculation of interest. "It's all spin," is the complaint. But the complaint has force only if there is an alternative to spin, if one could persuade simply by sticking to the facts as they exist apart from any particular point of view that might distort them. But facts are known *as* facts only within a particular point of view in relation to which they are obvious and perspicuous; to those who are ignorant of, or have rejected, that point of view, they will not be facts or even be visible. Knowledge is irremediably perspectival, and perspectives are irremediably political. Spin is not an obstacle to thought; it is the engine of thought. To hold out for a decision procedure that has not been spun is to hold out for the God's-eye point of view in which things are known face-to-face; perhaps someday, but now, as mortals, we see through a glass darkly, and the only question—not to be answered by an algorithm or a "decision procedure"—is through which dark glass we shall be seeing. It follows then that the perpetual search for a common ground, for an apolitical politics, is a fool's errand, an impossible dream; and in the absence of a common ground—despite the triumphant cries of those who claim to have found one (never the same one)—identity politics, the whipping boy of every self-righteous liberal, makes perfect sense, makes the same sense as preferring the beliefs you think to be right to the beliefs you think to be wrong. (Why would anyone do anything else?)

The unhappy (to many) consequence of this train of thought is that it makes unavailable any principled way of labeling an action for critics of both actors to linger on their impressive surfaces and fail to see the sensitivity and inward fragility that marked their best performances.

In part 3 ("Cultural Reflections") I myself turn political, in a way. The politics is antiliberal. Liberalism, as a form of thought and a mode of political organization, privileges impartiality. The idea is to develop procedures that are to the side of or above or below partisan agendas, procedures the implementation of which will neither advance nor exclude anyone's vision of the good and the good life. My argument (somewhat in tension with the argument of part 2) is that there are no such procedures and that the talismanic values that supposedly accompany them—fairness, objectivity, neutrality—are either empty or filled with the substantive claims they supposedly exclude. The world of liberal abstractions has efficacy and relevance in the pages of theorists like John Rawls, but in the everyday world of local choices and decisions, one acts on the basis of what one believes and desires. There is no road from the precepts of high philosophy to the solution of any real-world problem. Your account of truth or evidence may be right or it may be wrong, but whichever it is, it will not generate recipes for action.

This is what I mean when I declare that philosophy doesn't matter, and this is also the lesson deconstructive or postmodernist thought (otherwise known as "French Theory") preaches when it debunks the idea of a master narrative from the vantage point of which undoubted facts and universally compelling values come clearly into view. That promise, forever renewed and forever unredeemed, has recently taken a new form in the digital computer: the limitations that attend the partial perspective inhabited by all mortal men can be overcome, we are told, if we harness ourselves to an engine that knows no perspective and delivers undistorted (because unselected) data. The problem is that data randomly gathered—gathered, that is, under the impetus of no purpose or point except to have more—remains inert, and the addition to it of purpose or point will always be arbitrary. A computer (like IBM's Watson) can count things and perform calculations on what it counts, and even reach "conclusions" about what does and does not match, but it cannot produce meaning; that is the province of human beings who begin with (and within) purposes and reach conclusions not on the basis of "impartial" evidence—evidence that sits, unsituated, in an abstract space—but on the basis of commitments and beliefs already in place and internalized.

no strong assertions; only that what I assert doesn't take the form "affirmative action is right" or "affirmative action is wrong" but rather, the form "this particular argument (for or against) doesn't prove what it claims to prove." After I'm done with saying that, the substantive issue remains unaddressed, or at least unresolved, and my readers are no more in the know about where I come down than they were at the beginning. One might say, then, that although I am writing in plain sight, I'm in hiding.

But not always. A number of columns are autobiographical and even confessional. A selection of these is presented in part 1 ("Personal Reflections") of this collection. There readers will learn about my anxieties, my aspirations, my eccentricities, my foibles, my father, and my obsessions—Frank Sinatra, Ted Williams, basketball, and Jews. What links the columns, even when their subject matter is disparate, is a relentless internality, a tendency to live "in my head," a preference for activities that are absorptive, an affinity for enclosures and closure, and a fear of anything new and open.

In part 2 ("Aesthetic Reflections"), I (inadvertently) reveal more of myself in a series of meditations on movies, television, art, and music. Not surprisingly, my affinity is for self-contained, highly structured artifacts that refuse political engagement and celebrate craft. Author Colm Toibin is, in effect, my spokesman when he refuses to ground his art in autobiography. Writing is "not therapy," he declares, and I would add that writing is not self-expression or a call to justice or a thousand other things. Writing is the effort to make something out of words, and the political or sociological significance of the thing made is finally of less value than the process of making. Art, of course, must make use of political and social themes, but it is not in service to them; rather, it is the other way around. This is true even of country music, which, though it wears its politics (family values, patriotism, low-church Christianity) on its sleeve, is not aggressively political. The politics is just part of the package; it's not the message. The message is the unity and coherence of the country music vision of life, a vision that may or may not be true to the everyday experiences of actual people but is relentlessly true to the fictive world it ceaselessly elaborates. My admiration for country music is of a piece with my admiration for Charlton Heston, whose work as an actor is often dismissed by those who dislike his politics. What does one thing have to do with the other? Heston, like Kim Novak, was the victim (as well as the beneficiary) of a God-given physical beauty; it was all too easy

INTRODUCTION

The essays collected here are culled from the three hundred or so columns I wrote for the *New York Times* from 1995–2013. The order in which they appear is intended to bring out connections and themes that were perhaps not evident in their serial publication over a long period. One theme, often repeated, is that although the columns were published in the Opinion section of the newspaper, they are not, for the most part, opinion pieces. That is, they are less likely to declare a position on a disputed matter than to anatomize, and perhaps critique, the arguments deployed by opposing constituencies. There are two judgments one might make on a position: (1) the arguments put forward in support of it are weak and incoherent, and (2) it is wrong. These judgments, I contend, are logically independent of each other: it is quite possible that you could find the case being made for a position unpersuasive and still be persuaded of its rightness. Well, yes, you would be saying, I think those guys have it right, but the reasons they give for their conclusion (with which I agree) are contradictory and don't hold together. And conversely, you might be impressed by the elegance of the reasons put forward in defense of a point of view you nevertheless reject; you would be saying, yes, they have the better of it if the measure is logical cogency, but nevertheless, they're wrong.

Because I separate these two kinds of judgment—formal and substantive—a reader of these columns will often not know where I stand on the issue being discussed. The fact, for example, that I excoriate and ridicule the reasoning of professional atheists Richard Dawkins, Christopher Hitchens, and Sam Harris does not mean that I am myself a theist; it just means that I find their arguments slipshod and even silly. I might well be of their mind at bottom and still think that they are poor advocates for the conviction we share. Many readers found my refusal to lay my substantive cards on the table infuriating and agreed with Larry, who sent in this comment on November 2, 2010: "Could you do us all a favor and state in a simple declaration what you believe, because, man, you're killing me."

Sorry, Larry, that's not what I am doing in these columns. If what you want are opinions and protestations of belief, there are plenty of places to find them, but not here. This is not to say that I make

CONTENTS

To my brothers, Ron and Peter,
and in memory of my sister Rita
who was surprised to find that
her brother could be funny

Published by Princeton University Press
41 William Street, Princeton, New Jersey 08540

In the United Kingdom: Princeton University Press
6 Oxford Street, Woodstock, Oxfordshire OX20 1TW

press.princeton.edu

Jacket design by Chris Ferrante

All of the essays in this volume, with the exception of the introduction,
were originally published by the *New York Times*.

ISBN 978-0-691-16771-8

British Library Cataloging-in-Publication Data is available

This book has been composed in ITC Cheltenham Std
and ITC Franklin Gothic Std

Printed on acid-free paper. ∞

Printed in the United States of America

10 9 8 7 6 5 4 3 2 1

THINK AGAIN

Contrarian Reflections on Life, Culture,
Politics, Religion, Law, and Education

STANLEY FISH

PRINCETON UNIVERSITY PRESS
Princeton & Oxford

as either obviously right or obviously wrong. Take "hate speech," so called. I say "so called" because in order to identify something as hate speech, you would have to be in possession of a baseline rationality in relation to which some statements could be judged as resting on nothing but malignant ill will; those statements, then, could be said to proceed from no motive but the motive to inflict harm; they would be hate speech rather than political speech or nationalistic speech or religious speech. The problem is that no one accused of spewing hate speech would accept that description of his words; he would say, in fact, does say (read the websites of Holocaust deniers), "I am only speaking the truth, however difficult it may be for some to hear it; indeed, they contrive not to hear it by stigmatizing it as hate speech." This doesn't mean that there is no such thing as hate speech but that the determination of what is or is not hate speech can never be independent of the commitments and values of the person who is making the determination. Hate speech *is* a category, but it is an unstable category whose content varies with politics.

Of course, "hate speech" is a legal category, and the most significant political issues sooner or later become legal issues, at which point the politics of the matter is supposedly left behind (hence the title of part 5, "Reflections on the Law"). But since a legal issue must be framed, and the framing is never an innocent act but one fraught with ideological implications, politics is in the mix at every stage of the legal process. Consider, for example, the vexed topic of affirmative action. If affirmative action is defined as "reverse racism" (as it is by Justice Clarence Thomas and others), the issue immediately becomes one of fairness, and the question is, "Is it fair that those who did not cause the harms of past discrimination must now pay for it simply because of the color of their skin?" The question is rhetorical and the answer is directed. If, however, affirmative action is defined as an effort to remedy the deplorable consequences of state-produced wrongs, the questions put to it are quite different: "Does it work?" "Are the inconveniences experienced by some outweighed by an increase in the general good, or do the costs exceed the benefits?" These questions are linked to the calculation of empirical effects. The question, "Is it fair?" turns its back on empirical calculations and insists on applying the standards of formal, abstract concepts. It is the history of philosophy not the history of race relations in the United States that controls the discussion. It is as if racism were a concept that came down with the Ten Commandments rather than a category that emerged in the wake of the historical acts that led men first to give it a name and then to propose remedies for it.

Much the same tension—between history and principle—structures disputes that arise under the rubric of the First Amendment. Is the infusion of enormous sums into the political process to be understood as an extension of the right to free speech (money talks) or is it to be understood as an impediment to the workings of democracy and as a dilution of the right of every citizen to have a vote that counts as much as the vote of any other citizen? Must the production of "crush videos" in which kittens are brutally killed (the video-makers are not doing the killings, just filming them) to be protected as an instance of artistic expression or should it be criminalized because it encourages the acts it depicts and contributes to the coarsening of society? Should the action of militantly antigay "Christians" who show up at soldiers' funerals with signs proclaiming "Thank God for dead soldiers" be classified as a contribution to the marketplace of ideas where the moral status of homosexual acts remains a live issue, or should it be regarded as an intentional infliction of emotional distress on fathers, mothers, sisters, and brothers who are already experiencing more pain than they can bear? Is the First Amendment a theology, a veritable deity that brooks no rivals and refuses to bend to circumstances, or should the First Amendment value of free expression be weighed in the balance with other values that occasionally trump it?

One value that can (at least potentially) trump First Amendment values is enshrined in the amendment itself—the free exercise of religion. The religion clause is anomalous in that it singles out a form of speech for both special privilege and special suspicion in a context that declares all forms of speech equal. The free exercise clause says that religious expression deserves special solicitude; the establishment clause says that religious expression harbors a special danger if it is allowed to influence the public sphere; yet the First Amendment says that all speech (except treason, libel, and incitement to violence) is to be held in the same positive regard. If we live in a liberal state—a state that in Ronald Dworkin's words is neutral between competing visions of the good—the special attention paid to religion in the state's primary document is a problem, a dilemma with two horns: if the free exercise clause is read strongly and "exercise" is understood to include religiously inspired action as well as religiously inspired speech, the state is compelled to protect activities (like discriminatory hiring practices, the refusal to serve in the military, and the ending of education at the eighth grade) that are not allowed to the general population; if the establishment clause is read weakly and aid to religious institutions is justified on the basis of "even-handedness," the danger feared by James Madison and Thomas Jefferson—the danger that the state and religion will become "entangled" and the civil sphere eroded—will be actively courted. And, conversely, if the free exercise clause is read weakly and is extended only to thoughts and expression (i.e., no peyote in religious rituals), and the establishment clause is read strongly to exclude religious participation in public life (i.e., no prayers in the schools), strong religionists will regard themselves as victims of discrimination. All these permutations, and several more, are on display in the cases discussed in part 6, "Reflections on Religion."

For many *Times* readers, these dilemmas are artifacts of a mistake, the mistake of taking religion seriously. They agree with Richard Dawkins, Christopher Hitchens, and Sam Harris, who dismiss religion as a relic of the Dark Ages, as a form of mystical thinking, as a fairy tale that has led to the deaths of millions, if not billions. These "New Atheists" ridicule a form of thought anchored not by empirical evidence but by faith, which, they complain, is nebulous, subjective, and incapable of falsification. They are the apostles (irony intended) of the religion of science in its most reductionist form: all phenomena are either available to a materialist explanation or they are chimera, figments of a primitive, outmoded imagination. In a series of columns, I explore these New Atheists' arguments, not in order to prove that there is a God or that faith-based reasoning is "better" than data-based reasoning, but to suggest (as many others have) that these oppositions are too simple, even simple-minded, and that the conundrums the atheists triumphantly display as if they thought them up yesterday have always been a part of the tradition they deride but do not know.

In parts 7 and 8, I return to concerns closer to home: higher education generally and academic freedom specifically. These columns are written under the shadow of the (perennial) "crisis of the humanities," a crisis to which humanists have responded by mounting ever more elaborate (and unconvincing) justifications of the humanities as a practice that will save democracy, if not the world. These justifications, wittingly or unwittingly, have the effect of implying that the humanities have nothing to say for themselves, that any defense of them can only be instrumental. An instrumental defense of the humanities is a defense that rests everything on the humanities' usefulness to some other project—a robust economy, the realization of democratic principles, a peaceful world. The question posed to the humanities is "What are you good for?," and the answer is assumed to issue from a measure of "good" that the humanities do not contain. The answer given in the columns reprinted here is that the humanities are good for nothing, for that is the only answer that preserves the humanities' distinctiveness. If humanistic work is valued because of what it does politically or economically or therapeutically, it becomes an appendage to these other projects, and in a pinch it will always be marginalized and perhaps discarded when its instrumental payoff fails to arrive, as it always will. The paradox is that the stronger the case made for the utility of the humanities, the weaker the case for their support. In order to be truly healthy, at least in an internal way, the humanities must be entirely disassociated from the larger world of political/social/economic consequences, must, that is, be appreciated for their own sake and for no other reason.

Although the phrase "ivory tower" is often used in derision, it is one that humanists should embrace, for it is only by embracing it that the humanities, and liberal arts education in general, can be distinguished from the forces that are always poised to turn them to foreign purposes, to purposes not their own. The distinctiveness of the humanities and liberal arts education rests on their inutility, on their fostering a mode of thought that does not lead (at least by design) to the "practical" solution of real-world problems but to a deeper understanding of why they are problems in the first place and why they may never be resolved. That distinctiveness is compromised whenever the liberal arts dance to the tunes of politics, economics, citizenmaking, or anything else.

Moreover, it is only in the context of an enforced purity of motive—we do contemplative analysis; that's our job, and we don't do anyone else's—that a defensible account of academic freedom can be formulated. If the work of the liberal arts is narrowly conceived as the search for knowledge, the freedom to pursue that work in a manner unimpeded by external constituencies that want inquiry to reach predetermined conclusions is an obvious and necessary good. But if the work of the liberal arts is expansively conceived to include the alteration of worldly conditions in the direction of prosperity or justice or peace, academic freedom becomes the freedom of academics to do what they think is right irrespective of what academic protocols, traditionally understood, allow. The limiting force of the adjective "academic" is no longer felt, and academic freedom means nothing because it means everything. Both academic work and academic freedom thrive only if they are attached to precisely defined core activities; to open them up is not only to distort them but to lose them, to make them disappear, which is exactly what happens when academic institutions join the boycott of Israeli universities; the academy ceases to be what it is—a space for disinterested contemplation—and becomes an arm of someone's ideological agenda.

It might seem, as I noted earlier, that there is a tension, if not a contradiction, between my assertion that politics inflects every form of human organization despite liberalism's claim to be wholly procedural and my insistence that the liberal arts project hold itself aloof from politics and maintain a purity of motive and performance lest its distinctiveness be entirely lost. But the contradiction is only apparent. The argument that politics is everywhere and cannot be expelled or bracketed is made on a very general level: short of revelation or absorption into eternity, any action taken will always be challengeable from an alternative perspective; there is no hope, in this vale of tears, of escaping perspective altogether, and perspective is another name for politics. Yet within this condition (the human condition) marked by the pervasiveness of politics, there are differences that make a difference. The politics that is appropriate to the academy involves decisions about personnel, curricula, requirements, class size, and the like. Those involved in those decisions surely have conflicting views as to what is the right thing to do, and it is fair to label those conflicts political. But if a party to such a conflict were to take a position on an academic matter because in his or her judgment it furthered the interests of the Democratic Party or of social justice or economic equality, he or she would be importing the concerns of partisan politics—where the goal is to get someone elected or to implement a policy—into the context of academic politics, where the goal is to establish a matter of fact or verify an experimental hypothesis or come up with a better account of a social or physical phenomenon. Such an admixture, I contend, would have the effect not of enriching academic work but of corrupting it by attaching it to the wrong kind of politics. In saying that, I once again display the preference for enclosures, boundaries, and internal spaces to which I confessed in part 1. What goes around comes around.

Personal Reflections

My Life Report

OCTOBER 31, 2011

Last week my colleague David Brooks made a request I couldn't refuse. He asked people over seventy to "write a brief report on your life so far, an evaluation of what you did well, of what you did not do well, and what you learned along the way." Well, here I am, reporting in.

My father was an immigrant from Poland, a taciturn, massive man who began with nothing and became a major force in the plumbing and heating industry. Once when I locked myself in the bathroom because I had done something bad—I had either set a fire under the gas tank of a car parked in a vacant lot or pushed my baby sister's carriage off the porch with her in it, I can't remember which—he knocked down the door with a single blow of his fist. My mother was a volatile woman with a fierce but untutored intelligence and a need to control everything. She and I were engaged in a contest of wills until the day she died after having, willfully, refused treatment for congestive heart failure.

We were far from well off—I still remember the eight-dollar secondhand bike I got as a birthday present; I loved it—but we were, like everyone else we knew, upwardly mobile, and that meant college, even though no one in my family had ever been there. I was not bookish; I spent most of my time playing sports badly, playing cards a little better, and lusting after girls and cars. But I was lucky, and that, I believe, made all the difference.

My first and decisive bit of luck (in addition to having parents who wanted their children to succeed) was to have had Sarah Flanagan as an English teacher in high school. It was the time when adults were asking me a terrifying question: "What are you going to be?" or, in another version, "What are you going to do with your life?" The implication was that I was not yet anything and that, unless something happened quickly, my life would come to naught.

What happened was that Miss Flanagan told me, not in so many words, that writing papers about poems was something I was good at, and since I was desperate to be good at something, I took what she said to heart and began to think of myself as someone who could at least do that.

My next bit of luck was to have had Maurice Johnson as an English teacher at the University of Pennsylvania (one of only two schools that admitted me). Johnson was an urbane man of dry wit who offered me a model of what the academic life might be like, if I could only learn to dress better and develop a taste for irony. (To this day I never get it.)

Luck followed me to Yale graduate school (where I was admitted, I was told, as an experiment; Penn was a bit below Yale's standards) in the form of three of my classmates, A. Bartlett Giamatti, Richard Lanham, and Michael O'Loughlin, men of enormous learning and literary sophistication who gave the gift of their friendship to a rube from Providence, Rhode Island. Many years later, when I met another classmate at a professional meeting, she exclaimed, "Who would have thought back then that you of all people would make it?"

The crowning piece of luck—I am still speaking only of my professional life—was to enter the job market in 1962, when higher education was expanding and everyone I knew had at least three offers at good schools. (We thought this moment would go on forever, but it never came again.) I chose UC Berkeley, in large part because my first wife was willing to go there, and found myself in a department becoming more prominent by the day; all I had to do was go along for the ride.

So that's what I did well. I arrived at places at the right time and had enough sense to seize the opportunities that were presented to me; and that continued to be the case in a succession of appointments, book projects, administrative positions, even the opportunity to write for this newspaper, which came about one day in 1995 when out of the blue someone from the op-ed page called and asked if I would write something. As usual, I didn't have the slightest idea of what to do, but I said yes anyway to this newest piece of luck.

What I didn't do so well, and haven't yet done, was figure out how to be at ease in the world. I noticed something about myself when I was married to my first wife, an excellent cook and hostess who knew how to throw a party. My main job was to dole out the drinks, which I liked to do because I could stand behind the bar and never have to really talk to anyone. ("Do you want ice with that?") My happiest moment, and the moment I was looking forward to all evening, was when the party was over and failure of any number of kinds had been avoided once again.

If you regard each human interaction as an occasion for performance, your concern and attention will be focused on how well or badly you're doing and not on the people you're doing it with. This turned out to be true for me in the classroom, on vacations, at conferences, in department meetings, at family gatherings, at concerts, in museums, at weddings, even at the movies. Always I have one eye on the clock and at least a part of the other on whether I'm doing my part or holding my own; and always there is a sigh of relief at the end. Whew, got through that one!

It may be unnecessary to say so, but this way of interacting or, rather, not interacting does not augur well for intimate relationships. If you characteristically withhold yourself, keep yourself in reserve, refuse to risk yourself, those you live with are not going to be getting from you what they need. So my first wife didn't get what she needed and neither, in her early years, did my daughter. Typically, I escaped to work and a structured environment where the roles are prepackaged and you can ride the rails of scripted routines without having to display or respond to actual feelings.

I've tried to do better in my second marriage, and I have done better with my daughter now that she is an adult who draws sustenance from other sources and doesn't need everything I don't have to give. But I'm still overscheduling myself and trying as hard as I can to make sure that I have absolutely no time for thinking seriously about life, never mind reporting on it.

And what have I learned along the way? Three things, closely related. The first is that people are often in pain; their lives are shadowed by memories and anticipations of inadequacy, and they are always afraid that the next moment will bring disaster or exposure. You can see it in their faces, and that is especially true of children who have not yet learned how to pretend that everything is all right and who are acutely aware of the precariousness of their situations.

The second thing I have learned is that the people who are most in pain are the people who act most badly; the worse people behave, the more they are in pain. They're asking for help, although the form of the request is such that they are likely never to get it.

The third thing I have learned follows from the other two. It is the necessity of generosity. I suppose it is a form of the golden rule:

if you want them to be generous to you, be generous to them. The rule acknowledges the fellowship of fragility we all share. In your worst moments—which may appear superficially to be your best moments—what you need most of all is the sympathetic recognition of someone who says, if only in a small smile or half-nod, yes, I have been there too, and I too have tried to shore up my insecurity with exhibitions of pettiness, bluster, overconfidence, petulance, and impatience. It's not, "But for the grace of God that could be me"; it's, "Even with the grace of God, that will be, and has been, me."

'Tis the Season

DECEMBER 21, 2009

For a time now I have been engaging in two activities I find it hard to think clearly about. I give talks and I give money.

I give talks about a dozen times a year, mostly at colleges and universities. I speak on a variety of topics—literature, literary theory, political theory, legal theory, First Amendment law, academic freedom, the teaching of writing, television drama. The event itself comes at the end of a lengthy process beginning with an invitation that is followed by negotiations, the fixing of a date, the making of travel arrangements, and the setting up of a schedule. By the time the talk occurs, all the parties to it have quite a bit at stake. The host institution must worry about getting up an audience, securing a room of the appropriate size, making sure that the sound system is working, coordinating transportation, finding venues for lunches and dinners.

The speaker must worry about doing a good job.

With that in mind he or she will try to learn something about the nature of the institution, the likely makeup of the audience—some audiences will regard a basic introduction of the topic as an insult while others will welcome it—the names of previous speakers in the series, the special concerns that may be animating university conversations. (Even with a lot of preparation, you never really know what you're walking into.)

The occasion is, by definition, make or break. You only get one shot. The visit is short but you leave behind an impression that will last for quite a while. You will be judged by multiple measures. Did you seem well prepared? Were you attentive to the needs of the audience? Did you present a coherent thesis supported by the relevant evidence? Did you speak clearly? Did you handle yourself well and honorably in the question-and-answer session? Were you responsive and courteous to everyone, even to those audience members who rose with the hope of handing you your head in a basket? Did you remember to thank everyone many times?

It is clearly a pressure situation, and when it is over and you are heading out of town, you will be busily assessing your own performance and asking yourself, "How did I do?"

Now comes the curious part. If I have done badly, I feel bad. No surprise there. But if I've done well (at least in my estimation), I feel worse.

Why is that? I'm not quite sure, but I have a few notions. It may be a feeling that if I had stayed around for another twenty minutes, the jig would have been up; everyone would have seen through me; I got away just in the nick of time. It may be a feeling that my success was merely a piece of theater; there was nothing of substance in it. It may be a revulsion against hearing myself say the same old thing once again; someday—maybe tomorrow—I'll run out of audiences. It may be a suspicion (actually more than that) that I am less interested in doing justice to my subject than in bringing glory to myself.

Of course, I could avoid all this by simply declining invitations; but if I did that and the word got around, I wouldn't get any more, and I would lose the sense of myself that depends on professional recognition.

It doesn't seem that I can get into a good relationship with this scene.

This is even more true of the scene of generosity. For the past three years I have spent November and part of December in New York City, where I have an appointment as a visiting scholar. In the western Catskills and Delray Beach, Florida, where I am in residence for the rest of the year, there are no homeless people (at least none you see) sitting behind makeshift signs and asking for money. Now I encounter them on every corner, and so I am always having to decide what to do.

If I don't do anything, I feel guilty. If I reach into my pocket and hand over a few dollars, I feel guiltier. I thought for a while that the problem was the amount, so I started giving more, sometimes significantly more; but that only felt like an effort to buy my way out of an imbalance between what I had and what the objects (that's the problem; I was making them into objects) of my largesse either lacked or had lost.

The accounts could never be squared. They would always be behind in resources, I would always be behind in the obligation to care for those less fortunate than I. I could just stop giving altogether, but that would seem even worse. Or I could give away all my earthly goods, but the hook of material possessions is too deeply in me for that. I could do more, but I could never do enough.

The literature I have been teaching these many years generalizes my discomfort as a performer and a giver by explaining it as a product of original sin. No deed a fallen man or woman might perform is free of what George Herbert called the "tincture of the private." Apparently selfless acts are always done in the service of the ego's enhancement. Herbert tries to write a poem that celebrates God purely, but leaves off the effort when he realizes that the object of celebration is himself: "So did I weave my self into the sense" ("Jordan II"). Andrew Marvell makes the same effort and, midway, finds it disfigured "with wreaths of fame and interest" woven by "The Serpent old" ("The Coronet"). William James delivers the secular version of the same unhappy insight when he says, famously, "the trail of the human serpent is over everything."

In short, however much you try—indeed, because you try—you can't be good or do good. A hard lesson, especially in this season.

Max the Plumber

My father, Max Fish, was a plumber. His uncle Frank, to whom he apprenticed, was a plumber. My brother Ron was a plumber until he retired at an early age to build villas in Saint Kitts. And, as the oldest son, I was supposed to have been a plumber; my father never did quite understand what I chose to do instead.

Given these pieces of autobiography, you can understand why I have been more than slightly bemused to find that another plumber—Joe by name (although his name isn't Joe and he's not a licensed plumber)—has become a storied figure in a national election.

Max's was a better story. He emigrated from Poland with his mother and brother in 1923, at the age of fifteen. (His father, a house painter, had preceded them and sent back the money for passage.) They settled in Providence, Rhode Island, and he went to work for his uncle, carrying bathtubs three stories up on his back. In the early 1930s he married the vivacious daughter of a successful furrier. His in-laws disdained both his profession and his lack of education (he never went back to school), but in the years that followed, when the fortunes of the fur trade declined, he many times came to the rescue of my mothers' parents and siblings. He never spoke of it, but his mother was upset by this generosity. "They're bleeding my poor Max dry," she would say. My father's relationship with his uncle was always strained, and after a stint in the naval shipyards as a steamfitter in World War II, he and another plumber struck off on their own, fixing toilets and unclogging drains for other lower-middle-class householders. At some point he saw that the real money was to be found in being a plumbing contractor (the status to which Joe the plumber aspires), and he began to bid on small jobs. In 1948 he landed a (relatively) big job—$60,000—remodeling the bathrooms and heating system of a synagogue.

One thing led to another, and in the next twenty years he became one of the largest (if not the largest) plumbing and heating contractors in three states—Rhode Island, Massachusetts, and Connecticut. The brisk narrative of the preceding sentence glosses over years of struggle and the effort of learning how to draft, how to bid (an arcane art made up of equal parts of mathematics and luck), and how to deal with contracts that require work to be completed on time but withhold payment until the state is satisfied that every detail of its myriad codes has been complied with.

Over the years, Max the plumber became Max the contractor and Max the industry leader and even Max the statesman when, as president of the plumbing contractors' association, he negotiated agreements with the union of which he was always a member. He was a commanding presence, a massive man, not tall but broad and radiating force; when he entered a room he drew attention to himself without effort. (I have unsuccessfully tried to imitate this ability; of course, trying was the problem.) He had icy blue eyes and a manner that told you he did not suffer fools gladly or in any other way. People came to him with problems, with requests for help and advice and, sometimes, money. He was not quite a Godfather figure, but he had the makings. I can't imagine him seeking out the company of a presidential candidate, much less confiding to the world the state of his ambitions and disappointments.

He didn't confide much at all. At home he was usually silent, sitting in an easy chair reading the newspaper. He seemed content with his own company. But out in public, a remarkable transformation occurred. He became a mesmerizing raconteur, holding the attention of everyone at the table. His stories varied, but the plot line was always the same: the world fails to get the better of Max Fish once again.

There is one story I shall never forget; nor shall the others who heard it one evening in Carrboro, North Carolina, when my wife and I, my parents, and her parents (cultivated, literate people) were having dinner in a restaurant. Because the restaurant was housed in a former railway car, the passage was narrow and the tables close together.

My father told the story of his last night in Europe (he was to sail for America the next day). A week or so before, a gang of anti-Semitic toughs had surrounded my father and his brother and beat them up. That night he went out alone, carrying a stick the size of a baseball bat. He found one of his tormentors and cornered him in an alley. (Everyone in the restaurant is now silent.) He gave no account of what happened in that alley, except to say in an absolutely matter-of-fact tone of voice, "When I left him, I didn't know whether he was dead or alive." You can imagine the collective gasp.

In the summer of 1989, my father fell ill and was taken to the hospital. Before flying down to Florida to see him, I talked to him on the phone for a few seconds. All he could say—and these were the last words I ever heard him speak—was, "I wish it were over." I didn't know whether by "it" he meant his illness or his life. I suspect it was the latter and that in these last moments he was once again telling the world that he was going to exit on his own terms. A true American life for which the flat descriptive "Max the plumber" is wholly inadequate.

1.4

Is It Good for the Jews?

MARCH 4, 2007

When I was growing up in the '40s and '50s, a single question was asked in my neighborhood of every piece of news, large or small, local or national: "Is it good for the Jews?" We have now learned to identify this question in all of its versions—Is it good for the Catholics? Is it good for the Latinos? Is it good for the gays? and on and on—as the paradigmatic question of identity politics, the politics that is derived not from some general, even universal, assertion of what is good but from a particularized concern with insular interests. Is it good for *us*, for those of our kind, for our tribe?

A community in which this question is central and even natural will be a community with a sense of its own precariousness. (No one ever asks, "Is it good for the white, male, Anglo-Saxon graduates of Princeton?" It's always good for them.) Its members will think of themselves as perpetually under assault (even if the assault never comes) and as the likely victims of acts of discrimination and exclusion. ("No Irish need apply.") As a result it will turn inward and present to the outside world a united and fiercely defensive face. It will be informed and haunted by a conviction that no matter how well things may seem to be going, it is only a matter of time before there is a knock on the door and someone comes in and takes it all away.

By all the available evidence, formal and informal, precariousness does not mark the situation of the Jewish community today, at least not in this country. Whether the measure is education, wealth, ownership of property, influence in the corridors of power, prominence in the professions, or accomplishments in the arts, Jews in the United States are visible and successful to a degree that is remarkable given their relatively small numbers (around 2 percent of the population). Yet as Professor Charles Small of Yale University reports, "Increasingly, Jewish communities around the world feel under threat,"[1] and there are some Jews in this country who share this feeling, not because they are themselves threatened (although that does occasionally happen), but because they fear—in the spirit of Sinclair Lewis's

It Can't Happen Here or Philip Roth's *The Plot Against America*—that what is happening elsewhere may soon happen here.

Why should they think that? Part of the answer is to be found in the relationship between three words—Israel, Iraq, and anti-Semitism. Much of the world has been opposed to the Iraq war from its beginning, and now, after four years, 70 percent of Americans share the world's opinion. Some who deplore the war believe that those who got us into it and cheered it on did so, at least in part, out of a desire to improve Israel's position in the Middle East. Those who hold this view (and of course there are other analyses of the war's origins) fear that the same people—with names like Wolfowitz, Pearle, Feith, Abrams, Kristol, Kagan, Krauthammer, Wurmser, Libby, and Lieberman—are pushing for a strike against Iran, arguably a greater threat to Israel than Iraq ever was. Why, they ask, should our foreign policy be held hostage to the interests of a small country that is perfectly capable of defending itself and is guilty of treating the Palestinians, whose land it appropriated, in ways that are undemocratic and even, in the opinion of many, criminal?

A now famous answer to this question was given a year ago in the title of an article in the *London Review of Books* written by John Mearsheimer and Stephen Walt: "The Israel Lobby."[2] Mearsheimer and Walt contend that American Middle East policy "derives almost entirely from domestic politics, and especially the activities of the 'Israel Lobby,'" which they describe as an incredibly powerful "coalition of individuals and organisations who actively work to steer US foreign policy in a pro-Israel direction." The goal of the coalition, they assert, is to get "America to help Israel remain the dominant regional power," and so successful has it been that "the United States has become the de facto enabler of Israeli expansion in the Occupied Territories, making it complicit in the crimes perpetrated against the Palestinians."

So there you have it. The war was a huge mistake and is causing us no end of trouble at home and in the world at large. The lobby that led us into it is "a de facto agent for a foreign government"—Israel. Members of that lobby are largely, though not exclusively, Jewish. And that's where the anti-Semitism comes in. Or does it? One reason the lobby is "immune from criticism," Mearsheimer and Walt explain, is that criticism, when it appears, is always redescribed as anti-Semitism, and "anti-Semitism is something no one wants to be accused of." Their point, and it has been made by many, is that there is no reason to assume that those who criticize Israel and argue that America's uncritical support for a flawed state is strategically unwise and morally wrong are anti-Semitic.

Maybe so, but there is some empirical evidence to the contrary. Charles Small and his Yale colleague Edward Kaplan have recently published an article in the *Journal of Conflict Resolution*, the title of which also tells its own story: "Anti-Israel Sentiment Predicts Anti-Semitism in Europe."[3] What Small and Kaplan find is that "those with extreme anti-Israel sentiment are roughly six times more likely to harbor anti-Semitic views than those who do not fault Israel on the measures studied, and among those respondents deeply critical of Israel, the fraction that harbors anti-Semitic views exceeds 50 percent." The authors conclude that, "even after controlling for numerous potentially confounding factors, . . . anti-Israel sentiment consistently predicts the probability that an individual is anti-Semitic" and will say things like "Jews don't care what happens to anyone but their own kind" or "Jews are more loyal to Israel than to this country" or "Jews have too much power in international financial markets."

Small and Kaplan are careful to disclaim any causal implications that might be drawn from their analysis: they are not saying that anti-Semitism produces opposition to Israel or that opposition to Israel produces anti-Semitism, only that the two attitudes will more often than not be found in the same individual: scratch an opponent of Israel and you are likely—56 percent of the time—to find an anti-Semite. This does suggest that if opposition to Israel increases, there will be an increase in anti-Semitism because the population of the 56 percenters will be larger. Is this something Jews, even Jews living in the United States, should be apprehensive about?

The answer to that question will depend on whether you think that there is a meaningful distinction to be made between the "old" and the "new" anti-Semitism. Old anti-Semitism, according to Brian Klug of Oxford University, is based on a hostility to and fear of "the Jew" as an alien and demonic figure. In this ancient and much retailed story, Klug tells us, in an article in *Catalyst* magazine in 2006, subhuman Jews wander from country to country and "form a state within a state, preying on the societies in whose midst they dwell."[4] This is the anti-Semitism that came to full and disastrous flower in Nazi Germany.

The new anti-Semitism, in contrast, Klug continues, is rooted not in a hostility to "the Jew" as a vampire-like destroyer of cultures, but "in the controversial nature of the State of Israel and its policies." As such, "it is not a mutation of an existing 'virus,' but a brand new 'bug.'" That is to say, its origin is political rather than racial, and there is at least a chance that if its political source were removed—if Israel's policies were to change—its force would abate.

So there you have two stories: anti-Semitism is on the rise, and it's time to get out those "Never Again" signs. Or, it's not anti-Semitism in the old virulent sense, but a rational, if problematic, response by Middle East actors and their supporters in the West to what they see as "an oppressive occupying force"; don't take it personally. I understand this second story, and appreciate its nuance, but I can't bring myself to accept it, if only because I believe that the viral version of anti-Semitism is always capable of regaining its full and deadly form even when it is apparently dormant or weakened. All it needs is a pretext, and any pretext will do. If the Israeli-Palestinian conflict didn't exist, it would attach itself to something else; but it does exist, and anti-Semitism couldn't be happier.

Because I think this way, I can imagine a time in the not-so-distant future when American Jews might feel precarious once again. There is a certain irrationality to this imagining, given that at this moment, I am sitting in a very nice house in Delray Beach, Florida, and taking advantage of the opportunity afforded me by the *New York Times* to have my say on anything I like every Monday. And in a few months I will repair to an equally nice house in the upstate New York town of Andes, where I will be engaging in the same pleasurable activity. Sounds like a good life, and it is. So why am I entertaining fantasies of being dispossessed or discriminated against or even threatened?

Part of the answer lies in the fact that I spend much of my time in colleges and universities, where anti-Israel sentiment flourishes and is regarded more or less as a default position. And I have seen (with apologies to Shelley) that when hostility to Israel comes, anti-Semitism is not far behind. But the deeper explanation of my apprehension is generational. One of my closest friends and I agree on almost everything, but we part company on this question. He tells, and believes, the "criticism of Israel is one thing, anti-Semitism another" story. I hear it, but I can't buy it. He is ten years my junior. I remember World War II. By the time he was born it was history. Maybe it's that simple.

1. Charles Small, "Yale Creates Center to Study Antisemitism," *Associated Press*, September 19, 2006.

2. John Mearsheimer and Stephen Walt, "The Israel Lobby," *London Review of Books* 28, no. 6 (March 23, 2006).

3. Charles Small and Edward Kaplan, "Anti-Israel Sentiment Predicts Anti-Semitism in Europe," *Journal of Conflict Resolution* 50, no. 4 (2006).

4. Brian Klug, "Bad for Us All," a review of *The Paradox of Anti-Semitism* by Dan Cohn-Sherbok, *Catalyst* magazine, July 14, 2006.

My Life on the Court

MARCH 22, 2009

I have been playing basketball since I was seven years old. That's more than sixty years, and as March Madness moves into full swing, I find myself thinking about the game and my addiction to it.

It isn't skill. I can do two things—shoot from the outside and run. (I don't get tired.) I dribble as little as possible. I drive to the basket once a decade; I've blocked two shots in my entire life, and if white men can't jump, this white Jewish man really can't jump. Maybe twice a year my shot is on and I feel I can't miss. On days like that I think that I've finally arrived and can't wait for the next game. But when game day rolls around again and I get out on the court, I find that I have regressed to my usual level, which is several degrees south of mediocre.

In all these years I have had two triumphs. Once when I was playing on the beachside courts in Laguna Beach, every shot went in. The other players, black and Latino, started to yell, "Larry Bird, Larry Bird." I knew it was a joke, but I savored the moment anyway.

Another time, when I was living in Baltimore, I hired a tall young man to remove the leaves from my lawn. When I came back a couple of hours later I found the leaves merely rearranged. I complained and refused to pay. We got into a shouting match, and then I asked, "Do you play basketball?"

"Yes," he answered, and I said, "There's a gym up the street; let's play for it. You win, I pay you; you don't, I don't." He replied, "Are you crazy, old man?" (At the time I was in my midforties; I hate to imagine what he'd say today.)

We trekked to the gym and I beat him three times by big scores. In the first game he didn't guard me because he didn't believe I could do anything, and I hit one long shot after another. In the second game he guarded me too closely, and I went around him. In the third game he didn't know what to do, and it was all over. The whole thing took less than half an hour, which was good because in another twenty minutes, he would have figured out that I had only two moves and that both of them could easily be neutralized by someone taller, stronger, and more athletic, all of which he was.

And then there are the thousand other times when I walked off the court either feeling happy not to have embarrassed myself (although I hadn't done much) or trying to come to terms with the fact that I had indeed embarrassed myself. Whichever it was, I always knew that I would be back.

Why? Why continue to do something I wasn't any good at nine times out of ten? Well, for one thing, basketball players are by and large generous. (There are exceptions.) If you're not very skilled, if you're old and slow, they will make a place for you in the game. In his book *Give and Go: Basketball as a Cultural Practice*, Thomas McLaughlin speaks of the ethical practices that emerge in the course of a game even though no rules have imposed them: "Every time one of the players in our game says to a weak player as he is taking an open shot that he will likely miss 'Good shot,' he is weaving the ethical fabric of the game."[1]

I have often been the beneficiary of that ethical fabric, even when those weaving me into it are perfect strangers. For one of the great things about being a basketball player (or pretending to be one) is that no court is closed to you, which is why I always have a basketball in the trunk of my car. You can just show up wherever there is a hoop and a game and you will be included. (This holds also in foreign countries where there may be a language barrier but never a basketball barrier.)

At Live Oak Park in Berkeley I played with college standouts and with American Basketball Association all-star Lavern Tart. On a famous court in the West Village I played on a team that won every game. It was glorious even though I never touched the ball. In a strict sense, I didn't belong on those courts, but pickup basketball doesn't enforce any strict sense and is willing to relax the demands of competition and winning for the sake of extending its pleasures to those whose skills are minimal.

What are those pleasures? They are not, I think, pleasures that point outward to some external good. Rather, they are the pleasures of performing (however badly) within the strict parameters of a practice whose goals and rewards are entirely internal. Hans Gumbrecht, in his book *In Praise of Athletic Beauty*, links sports to Kant's account of the beautiful as the experience of "pure disinterested satisfaction."

It is a satisfaction, Gumbrecht explains, that "has no goal in everyday life" (like virtue, it is its own reward), and he quotes with admiration Olympic swimmer Pablo Morales's description of the pleasure he feels in competition as "that special feeling of getting lost in focused intensity."[2]

The marvel is that focused intensity can be achieved even in the act of failure, even by someone who knows what to do but most of the time can't quite do it. And it is for that intensity—not its object or its goal—that one plays, for in those moments of surrender to the game, all one's troubles, all one's strivings, all one's petty irritations fall away. And if, occasionally, you actually do set the hard pick or deliver the perfect pass or make the improbable shot, well, that's just icing on the cake.

And by the way, my money is on Duke to take it all. A pick from the heart.

1.   Thomas McLaughlin, *Give and Go: Basketball as a Cultural Practice* (New York: SUNY Press, 2009), 38.

2.   Hans Gumbrecht, *In Praise of Athletic Beauty* (Cambridge, MA: Harvard University Press, 2006), 51.

The Kid and Old Blue Eyes

OCTOBER 28, 2007

I once stood next to Ted Williams (I don't recall if I actually said anything to him), and on another occasion Frank Sinatra came to my table carrying a chair for my sister-in-law. (Stay with me; these apparently random memories will be linked up.)

My father had taken me to a Masonic father-and-son night when I was perhaps thirteen years old and Williams, dressed in his Red Sox uniform, was the guest of honor. What I remember is that he was very big.

I had my brief encounter with Sinatra much later. Along with my wife, one of her two sisters, and her mother, I was eating dinner at Sinatra's Cal-Neva Lodge in Tahoe. Our table was short a chair. Sinatra and a large party were at the next table. I leaned over and asked one of his party, a stunning blond, if I might borrow the empty chair next to her. She looked at me as if I were a presumptuous cockroach and said no. Sinatra had seen the exchange and immediately got up, grabbed the chair, and held it while my sister-in-law sat down. I said, "Thank you."

These small moments are on my mind these days for two reasons. The first is that Ted Williams and Frank Sinatra have been my heroes for as long as I can remember. For years I carried a newspaper picture of Williams (with the caption "Greatest American since George Washington") in my wallet until it finally disintegrated. As a teenager I played Sinatra's "In the Wee Small Hours" and "Songs for Swingin' Lovers" for hours and bored my friends with what I took to be intricate analyses of Nelson Riddle's great arrangement of "I've Got You Under My Skin."

In my study at home there are two large pictures, one (a painting) of my father, the other a 1953 photograph of Sinatra singing at a concert in London; one hand caresses a stand-up microphone, the other grabs on to it for dear life. Shadows and a dim spotlight make it seem that he is all alone (much like the album cover of *In the Wee Small Hours*), though there must have been thousands in the audience. Presiding over both these pictures and hanging above the doorway is a 1946 American League championship pennant signed by Williams. This boy has never grown up.

I know that naming Ted Williams and Frank Sinatra as your heroes might raise an eyebrow or two. Both were notorious for bad behavior. Sinatra punched out reporters, consorted with gangsters, cut old friends cold (see Mickey Rooney's autobiography), cheated on his wife, and held lifelong grudges. Williams feuded with reporters (he called them the "knights of the keyboard"), hit an old lady with a thrown bat, spat at fans, refused to tip his hat, smashed watercoolers, and was generally surly.

On the other hand, both were also known for good works. Sinatra used his clout to force Las Vegas hotels to integrate, donated large amounts to charity, helped people he barely knew, and was a favorite of the musicians he performed with. Williams spoke out early for the inclusion of Negro League players in the Hall of Fame, was a stalwart fund-raiser for the Jimmy Fund (a charity dedicated to helping cancer-stricken children), was a mentor to younger players and a loyal friend.

But it is neither their vices nor their virtues that appeal to me. It is their single-minded dedication to craft, Sinatra to saloon singing and the lyrics he articulated with such precision, Williams to the science of hitting (the title of his excellent book). They both wanted to be the best at what they did, and they were.

And then there is the drama of their lives.

In Sinatra's case, early success and increasing fame followed by a rapid decline; a tempestuous, doomed, and very public second marriage; and then the spectacular comeback, leading to even greater success and the title Chairman of the Board.

In Williams's case, even earlier success, an excess of expectations, followed by a failure to perform in the clutch, injuries, the loss of the best years of his professional life to war, and, after apparent decline, a glorious exit. He batted 388 when he was thirty-nine, famously hit a home run in his last at bat, and had the good luck to have John Updike in attendance. (Updike's essay "Hub Fans Bid Kid Adieu" is a classic.) What he didn't do is bring Boston a World Series championship, and for this some never forgave him.

And that brings me to the second reason that Sinatra and Williams, indomitable spirits who endured and ultimately did it their way, are on my mind these days. The Red Sox are in the World Series, and by the time you read this they may have won it.

Not the same Red Sox who so reliably provided heartbreak when I was growing up in Providence, Rhode Island. Those were the teams that always looked good on paper but never performed in the field. "Wait till next year" was the New England anthem. And then, in 2004, next year improbably arrived. The enormousness of the event for those who lived and died (quite literally) with the team cannot be overestimated. Just take a look at the 2004 documentary *The Reverse of the Curse of the Bambino* and listen to celebrities and ordinary citizens, young and old, speak of what it meant to them. Eighty-six years is a long time, and some fans and their children lived out their lives in unrealized hope. In the film, younger generations go to the graves of their fathers and grandfathers and tell them the good news.

But it's all different now.

Or is it? When the Red Sox fell behind 3–1 to the Cleveland Indians in the American League Championship series, all the old feelings came back, and I thought, *there they go again*. But it turned out that I was displaying too little faith and forgetting that you have to believe.

Okay, I believe, but after so many decades of disappointment, it isn't easy. Especially because for six years I lived on the north side of Chicago and, in a moment of apostasy and desperation, became a Cubs fan.

Some people never learn.

Travel Narrows

JULY 27, 2008

Most of us are good at a few things and bad at a longer list of other things. I am a bad traveler, and I wonder if others share my infirmity.

In the past couple of months I have taken two trips, one to New Zealand and another to England and Ireland. Both were the result of invitations to give a talk or participate in a conference, but in each case there was ample time left over to do the things that travelers do.

I tried, but I just couldn't get the hang of it.

The manifestations of my incapacity were physical, although its root causes were not. In the course of a week's touring of Ireland, all my usual little ills returned—mouth sores, intestinal difficulties (a euphemism), clogged nasal passages, and what one might call "strategic fatigue." Strategic fatigue sets in whenever I enter a museum (when I saw that the display case containing the Book of Kells was surrounded by other tourists, I didn't have the strength to push myself forward) or when I approach an ancient site (at Clonmacnoise, the location of an ancient abbey, I retreated immediately to the coffee shop and never saw the ruin) or when the possibility of getting out of the car to enjoy a scenic view presented itself (I protested that it would take too much time, or that we needed gas, or something equally feeble). The one time I tried to be a good sport and a good tourist was at Carrowmore Megalithic Cemetery in Sligo, which, as far as I could tell, consisted of clumps of small rocks placed at inconvenient distances from one another. These rocks were, I was told, tombs and significant stone circles. It was lost on me, but I dutifully trudged around a large circle taking pictures. The reward for my efforts was the discovery later in the day that, sometime during our exercise in archaeological reverence, a backpack containing my wife's clothing and jewelry had been stolen from our rental car. That'll teach me!

It was the fact that my wife was with me on this trip that alerted me to the extent of my problem. She was supposed to have accompanied me to New Zealand but couldn't make it at the last moment. I attributed my inability to fully respond to the considerable glories of New Zealand to her absence. Had she been here, I told myself, I could have fed off her enthusiasm and taken pleasure from her pleasure. But in Ireland both her enthusiasm and her sense of pleasure were abundantly visible and still I couldn't do much more than go through the motions. It's not that I didn't recognize the beauty of the landscape or the majesty of the monuments. I couldn't rise to the level of appreciation they deserved.

Why not? What's wrong with me? There are two answers to these questions. First, I just don't care about seeing sights. In London, I ended up at Milton's burial place by accident. I was there for a concert. Churches, famous squares, wide rivers, forests, cobbled streets, scenic vistas, castles, grand gardens . . . I go Spiro Agnew one better: when I've seen one, I've seen one too many.

But behind the lack of interest in sightseeing is something deeper and more unsettling. When I ask people what they like about traveling, they usually answer, "I enjoy encountering different cultures and seeing how other people live." I am perfectly happy with the fact of other cultures, and I certainly hope that those who inhabit them live well; but that's as far as it goes.

By definition, a culture other than yours is one that displays unfamiliar practices, enforces local protocols, and insists on its own decorums. Some of them even have different languages and are unhappy if you don't speak them. To me that all spells discomfort, and I don't see why I should endure the indignities of airplane travel only to be made uncomfortable once I get where I'm going. As for seeing how other people live, that's their business, not mine.

For a while, I tried to attach my feelings about travel to some honorable moral or intellectual tradition. I recalled some poems by Ben Jonson in which he praises Sir John Roe for the Roman virtue of being always the same no matter how extensively he traveled ("his often change of clime, though not of mind"). But I had to acknowledge that the springs of my own sensibilities had more to do with parochialism and sloth than with some noble capaciousness of mind. In the end, I just have to admit that I was born without the travel gene, which probably means that I was also born without the curiosity gene, and that I'll just have to live with it.

Or, rather, my wife will.

I Am, Therefore I Pollute

AUGUST 3, 2008

Last week, I confessed to being a bad traveler (1.7). This week, I confess to something much worse. I resist and resent the demands made on me by environmental imperatives. I don't want to save the planet. I just want to inhabit it as comfortably as possible for as long as I have.

Things reached something of a crisis point a few days ago when my wife asked me to read a communiqué from Greenpeace. (She thought, she told me, that if I read it rather than hearing about it from her, my unhappiness would be directed at the organization.) It said that Kimberly-Clark, the maker of the paper towels, facial tissue, and toilet paper we buy, does not use recycled fiber and instead "gets its virgin wood fiber clear-cut from . . . the North American Boreal . . . one of the world's most important forests." And that meant, she told me, that we would have to give those items up and go in search of green alternatives. But we had already done that once before when it turned out that the manufacturer of the paper products we used to buy—Procter and Gamble—engaged in research on animals. That's when we found Kimberly-Clark. So it seems that the pure were not so pure after all, and who's to say that the next corporation won't have an ecological skeleton in its closet, too?

What rankled me most was the toilet paper, but when I protested, my wife smiled at me with a mixture of indulgence and contempt. Some years ago, I beat back an attempt to eliminate paper towels altogether and replace them with rewashable rags. But there are too many battles to be fought and I find that I am losing most of them. I did retain the right to have a small supply of paper napkins in an out-of-the-way cupboard. (I hate cloth napkins; you always have to worry about soiling them; paper napkins you just throw away, which is, of course, the problem.) But my house is now full of environmentally approved lightbulbs. They are dim, ugly, and expensive, but I am told that they will last beyond my lifetime. (That's supposed to be reassuring?) A neighbor told me today that he is planning to stockpile incandescent bulbs in the face of a prediction that they will be phased out by 2012.

Meanwhile, by the weak light shed by the virtuous bulbs, I am eating local meat—meat from cows organically raised and humanely slaughtered (what a phrase!). It is, of course, expensive, but what is worse, it tastes bad. That is, it tastes like real meat, gamy and lean, rather than like the processed, marbled, frozen, supermarket stuff I had grown up on. I'm sure it is a better quality, and that buying it sustains the local community and strikes a blow against agribusiness, but I just don't like it. And since I hate vegetables, becoming a vegetarian is not an option.

And then there's the kitchen. A few months ago, we decided to renovate a thirty-year-old kitchen. The plans were modest; the contractor was engaged; the price was reasonable; I was happy. Then I went on a trip and when I returned, everything had changed. I was informed that the wood we had ordered for the cabinets comes from some far-off place and would have to be stored, transported, stored again, and transported again, adding scandalously to the carbon footprint of my poor small kitchen. If we were to avoid being labeled environmental criminals, we would have to de-order the wood (somehow we managed to do this without incurring a restocking fee) and we would have to find a company in a nearby locale that would send us wood from a tree that was not cut down until our order had been received. (How this would be monitored is something I never found out.) The same company would also immediately plant a tree to replace the one we were harvesting, and we would receive a certificate attesting to all this from the Forestry Stewardship Council.

It sounded like a scam to me—anyone can print certificates—but what can you do when faced with the dictates of someone else's religion? I acquiesced and didn't even put up a fight when the paint and the glue (also contraband for reasons I forget) had to be reordered, too. As a result, both the price of the job and the time it would take to do it have doubled. I am assured that the end product will look as good as it would have looked had we committed the sins we had been contemplating, but I'm not holding my breath.

And, of course, there's recycling. Recycling has been around for a long time now, and the irritation many people feel toward it has often been expressed. I would only add that the rules and requirements keep changing and becoming more severe. I had just gotten used to separating the mail from the magazines (which had already been separated from the newspapers, which had already been separated from the bottles and the garbage, a category that has survived the revolution) when I was informed that some of the mail had cellophane address windows and that those would have to be ripped out before proceeding to the next stage and the next bin.

Categorization being what it is, there is no end to the subcategories that can be devised, each of them bringing with it a new set of strictures and a new opportunity to be inadequate and delinquent. Michel Foucault made a career of observing that modern techniques of regulation are more far-reaching and consequential than the old way of keeping people in line with guns and clubs, especially when they are imposed for your own good and for the good of society. He would have had a field day with recycling and would no doubt have written a book (maybe he did and I missed it while sorting the garbage), entitled, perhaps, *The Archaeology of Waste*.

Now don't get me wrong. I am wholly persuaded by the arguments in support of the practices I resist. I believe that recycling is good and that disposable paper products are bad. I believe in global warming. I believe in Al Gore. But it is possible to believe something and still resist taking the actions your belief seems to require. (I believe that seat belts save lives, but I never wear them, even on airplanes.) I know that in the great Book of Environmentalism my name will be on the page reserved for serial polluters. But I just can't get too worked up about it, even though I began well in the '60s when I heeded Lyndon Johnson's plea to turn off lights when you leave a room, something I still do religiously (or is it obsessively?).

Meanwhile, I stand my ground when I can and try to reach compromises when I can't. We have now instituted (on the model of peace plans for the Middle East) a two-kinds-of-toilet-paper state. A friend tells me it could be worse. His wife makes him unplug an appliance immediately after it has been used. Who knows what's coming next? So far I have managed to avoid the indignity (for a sports-car lover) of owning a hybrid, but that's only because we haven't bought a new car in twenty years. It's only a matter of time, for, as usual, I am on the losing side of history.

Why We Can't Just Get Along

OCTOBER 29, 2006

If Heather Mills makes good on her threat to release the tapes of the shouting matches she (allegedly) engaged in with Paul McCartney, there is at least a chance that tabloid readers will be entertained and titillated by some bits of high or low drama. But if the domestic quarrels of ordinary people—people who are neither billionaires nor rock stars—were taped and transcribed, the response in most cases would be wonder at how a conversation that began so innocuously could so quickly escalate into a verbal conflagration. Most domestic quarrels start not when some big issue like war, homelessness, or the deficit or gay marriage is raised, but when one party says something perfectly ordinary and apparently nonprovocative—"Let's go to the movies tonight" or "Should we have dessert?" or "Did you call your mother?"—only to find that, nevertheless, a provocation has occurred.

The provoker—or, rather, the person accused of being one—will immediately claim innocence: "I was just asking a simple question." "I didn't mean anything by it beyond what the words literally say." "I certainly didn't mean what you took me to mean." "Why did you think I meant that?" "I would never mean that." The claim of innocence is itself not so innocent; it is at bottom an accusation of the other for having not only misunderstood an irreproachable intention, but for having impugned an irreproachable character. "Am I the kind of person who would mean what you took me to mean?" is the implicit (and sometimes explicit) question, and no answer given to it will put out the fire. If the answer is "No, you're not," the response will be, "So why did you think I was a minute ago?" And if the answer is "Yes, you are," the response will be anything from a demand for evidence— "Tell me, just when have I acted like that?"—to a detonating of the nuclear option: "If you think that, why did you marry me (or come to live with me) in the first place?"

It is tempting to think that domestic quarrels are the occasional eruptions that disturb the otherwise tranquil surface of a relationship, but in fact the reverse is true: strife, in progress or just around the corner, is the default condition of domesticity, and tranquillity is the anomaly. Perhaps that is why when the poet John Milton needed a plot device that would get Adam and Eve from the happy perfection of Eden to the act of disobedience and the Fall, he invented—it is not in Genesis—a domestic quarrel. Milton's Eve says to Adam (*Paradise Lost*, book 9), "This garden grows so quickly that we're always falling behind in our labors, especially when we stop to talk; maybe we'd get more done if we separate and work in different areas." Adam responds, "Does this mean you're tired of me?" Stung, Eve replies, "Why would you say that? Are you afraid I can't manage by myself?" And with that, they're off to the races, serpent waiting. Later, when the apple is eaten and they see it was a bad idea, each blames the other: he blames her for having left his side, and she blames him for having let her. The poet draws the moral, and it is one we all recognize: "Thus they in mutual accusation spent / The fruitless hours, but neither self-condemning, / And of their vain contest appeared no end" (9:1187–89).

Is there no way out of this unhappy spiral? Is mutual accusation the only possible career of a quarrel? Can't we learn from our mistakes? Well, there are three things to know about domestic quarrels. The first is that they have no beginning. There is no bell that announces the passage from ordinary and amiable conversation to conflict. You only know you're in one when it has already been going on for a while. In this genre, in medias res is all there is.

Once you do tumble to the fact that you're already in the middle of a quarrel—and this is the second thing to know—you will try to get out of it by returning to the beginning that never was; and this means that you will go back to your first remark (or what you take to be your first; a standard move in this game is to contest the moment of its non-origin) and vigorously assert its blamelessness. In short, you will try to clarify and sanitize your words by producing more words, but of course the more words you produce, the more weapons you provide the person who is sitting across from you at the breakfast table. (And who is he or she anyway? How did I ever get mixed up with anyone like that?) Every exculpation you offer for your previous utterances will be heard as evidence of a new sin, and every attempt to absolve yourself of that sin will generate another. The mathematics of these situations are exponential.

The third thing to know about domestic quarrels is the most discouraging: Even if you know the first two things and know them so well that you can write columns about them, that knowledge is of no help whatsoever when it comes to fording the rapids of your own domestic life. The Professor of Quarrelology is no better a practitioner of the art than anyone else. I just got back from a long trip, and my wife greeted me by saying how much she had enjoyed being alone in the house. And then I said . . . Well, you know.

Truth and Conspiracy in the Catskills

AUGUST 23, 2010

A small gathering of fifty or sixty people; roughly 95 percent white, 90 percent male, a few blond-haired kids, average age forty-five, all nodding in assent as a series of speakers explains that our government is conspiring against us and fabricating massive lies in order to hide its own crimes and frighten us into giving up our constitutional rights and liberties.

The Tea Party? Minutemen? Birthers? No, "Truthers," left-wing conspiracy theorists who believe (among other things) that 9/11 was an inside job, that no plane hit the Pentagon, that Ted Olson did not receive a call from his wife, Barbara, shortly before she perished in the crash of Flight 77, that the anthrax scare was also a government hoax (although the anthrax was real and deadly), and that Hurricane Katrina was the result of weather manipulation by racists or profiteers or both.

Like many others, I was aware of these theories and aware too that a significant percentage of Americans (about the same percentage that believes President Obama is a Muslim who was born in Kenya) was at least partly persuaded by them. But on August 15 I got an upclose look at the phenomenon when I attended a meeting of Truthers that just happened to be held in Livingston Manor, a small Catskill town about twenty miles from my house.

The thing about people who hold beliefs you find unbelievable (in two senses) is that they are in most other respects just like you and your friends. The parking lot of the facility housing the conference might have been a parking lot at any university: lots of Subarus and Priuses. The men and women were casually dressed, polite, and friendly. I'm sure that on any other topic—the Yankees, the Stieg Larsson novels, the latest Julia Roberts movie—they would have been all over the place, but when the topic is 9/11 and the "official story" told by the government, they all speak and think with an impressive unanimity of opinion and with an equally impressive sincerity.

I was the only insincere one in the room. I didn't announce myself as a columnist looking for something to write about. I let them think

I was one of them. When a speaker began his presentation by asking, "Is there anyone here who holds to the official story?," I didn't raise my hand. When he followed up by asking whether anyone was on the fence, I raised my hand weakly, along with one other person who, presumably, was telling the truth. Technically, I hadn't done anything wrong, but I felt dishonest, and I was certainly being duplicitous.

I distanced myself from my discomfort by regarding the event as theater and inventorying the dramatis personae. They were straight out of central casting. Sander Hicks, the master of ceremonies, looked like an amalgam of Johnny Depp, Sean Penn, and Matt Dillon; he kept things moving and implored "put your hands together" as each speaker came to the podium. Paul Zarembka played (and was) the left-leaning academic economist. He said, "The ruling class will do anything to keep in power." The Reverend Ian Alterman preached gentleness, humility, and respect. He said that those who have an investment in the official lies because that's all they've ever heard cannot be approached in a confrontational manner.

But confrontation was obviously the preferred mode of Barry Kissin, the resident rabble-rouser who harangued the audience with the sins of elites who deliberately killed three thousand of their own citizens and bullied "beleaguered countries" like North Korea and Iran. Nick Bryant tied the same elites to a massive network of pedophiles, including almost everyone you've ever heard of.

The star turn was taken by architect Richard Gage, founding member of Architects & Engineers for Truth, a group, he said, of twelve hundred experts in the area of the construction and destruction of tall buildings. It was Gage, the man of science and the scientific method (another stock character), who laid out the basic thesis from which everything else grew. The Twin Towers could not have been brought down by fire. A fire, however intense, would have left the steel girders standing, perhaps at an odd angle. The way the towers fell—in free fall, straight down, in only seven seconds—shows clearly, Gage declared, that the cause was controlled demolition by explosives placed next to the support structures and detonated in a precisely timed sequence. In short, destruction from the inside by insiders and not by a ragtag group of fanatics who were incapable of flying the planes they supposedly deployed with incredible skill.

Once this scenario is established, you have only to ask, first, who could have had the expertise to bring this off and, second, who had the motive to bring it off. Bingo! The government, which certainly had both money and materials and needed a pretext for starting two real wars and a metaphorical "war on terror" that could justify tight governmental and military control, torture, rendition, and the passage of the Patriot Act. On this rock the house of the Truthers is built. Everything that comes up in the way of an objection can be explained by extending the basic assumption, by asking the question, "How did the conspirators get away with this one and pull the wool over everyone's eyes?" It is always answered.

At the end of the afternoon and before the conference-ending dinner, I slipped away. I thought about identifying myself before leaving. I should have, but I didn't. Instead I drove home to a small dinner party: my wife and I, another couple, and a friend. I told them about what I had seen and heard. The man of the couple said that on September 11, 2001, when he heard the news, "inside job" was the first thought he had, although he hadn't bothered much with the thought since. Our other guest told us that her brother-in-law was even more a partisan of the "government did it" view than those I had listened to. I guess you never know.

Moving On

MAY 27, 2013

I have sold my books. Not all of them, but most of them. I held on to the books I might need while putting the finishing touches on a manuscript that is now with my publisher. I also kept the books I will likely need when I begin my next project in the fall. But the books that sustained my professional life for fifty years—books by and about Milton, Spenser, Shakespeare, Skelton, Sidney, Herbert, Marvell, Herrick, Donne, Jonson, Burton, Browne, Bacon, Dryden, Hobbes—are gone (I watched them being literally wheeled out the door), and now I look around and see acres of empty white bookshelves.

The ostensible reason for this de-acquisition is a move from a fair-sized house to a much smaller apartment. It is true, as Anthony Powell said in a title, that books do furnish a room, but in this case, too many books, too little room. But the deeper reason is that it was time. What I saw on the shelves was work to which I would never return, the writings of fellow critics whom I will no longer engage, interpretive dilemmas someone else will have to address. The conversations I had participated in for decades have now gone in another direction (indeed, in several other directions), and I have neither the time nor, if truth be told, the intellectual energy required to catch up. Farewell to all that. So long, it's been good to know you. I'm sure you'll do fine without me.

In the hours and days following the exodus of the books I monitored myself for a postmortem (please excuse the hyperbole) reaction. Would I feel regret? Nostalgia? Panic? Relief? I felt nothing. What should have been a momentous event barely registered as I moved on to what seemed the more important task of choosing a new carpet. I was reminded of what a colleague who had left a university after twenty-three years replied when I asked him if it was difficult to do. He said, "It was like checking out of a motel."

Actually, I've had stronger emotional responses to checking out of some motels than I had to the departure of the record of my professional life, a record that includes voluminous marginal notes in many of the volumes. I had always thought that I could return to my annotated copies of familiar texts and pick up where I left off. That fantasy, I now see, was part and parcel of the core fantasy that I would just go on forever, defending old positions, formulating new ones, attending annual conferences, contributing to essay collections, speaking at various universities, teaching the same old courses, confidently answering the same old questions.

I'm not going to go on forever. I avoid this realization, even as I voice it. I say, "I'm not going to go on forever," and at the same time I'm busily signing new contracts, accepting new speaking invitations, thinking up new courses, hungering after new accolades. My books are clearer-eyed than I am. They exited the stage without fuss and will, one hopes, take up residence in someone else's library where they will be put to better uses than to serve as items in a museum, which is what they were when they furnished my rooms.

Behind these musings is a word I can barely utter—"retirement." I thought seriously about retiring in 1998. That would have been "early" retirement. Instead I took an administrative job as dean of a college and traded in early retirement for endlessly deferred retirement. But friends and colleagues, many of them younger, are retiring all around me, and when one does I pester him or her with questions. What made you decide? Was it hard? How's it going? What do you do all day? I put the same questions to strangers in the hope that I will hear something that will persuade me that retirement is the way to go, or, alternatively, that retirement is not only the simulacrum of death, but hastens death's arrival on his pale horse.

Lately I've run out of strangers, and so I turn to you or at least to those of you who are of a certain age. Have you done it? Are you thinking about it? Have I, perhaps, taken the first step toward retiring by retiring my books? Is there a next step I should be taking? Any and all advice received gratefully.

PART 2

Aesthetic Reflections

Why Do Writers Write?

FEBRUARY 11, 2007

Last week, as I was rolling along the Florida Turnpike on the way to work, I heard Colm Tóibín, the Irish novelist and short story writer, being interviewed by Diane Rehm on *The Diane Rehm Show* on National Public Radio. Tóibín is the author of the award-winning novel *The Master*, a fictional but fact-based account of Henry James's life and art.[1] Tóibín was in the studio to talk about his new book of short stories, titled *Mothers and Sons*.[2]

Most of the stories, he said, focus on sons who have grown into manhood, but still struggle to come to terms with a childhood full of silences, rejections, and abandonments, including the abandonment of death. In one story, a portion of which Tóibín read aloud, a man whose mother left home long ago recognizes her as she sings a song in a pub. She seems to be looking straight at him, and he suspects that she knows who he is, but he leaves without saying anything, thus preserving their history of distance and nonconnection. Apparently, these stories are not uppers.

As I listened, I found myself not liking (an emotion different from disliking) the author. First of all, his reading of his own prose was overly dramatic and too elocutionist for my taste; the fine subtlety of his sentences was, I thought, being overwhelmed by the delivery. But the main source of my irritation—a mild irritation; I really didn't have much of a stake in this, or so I believed in the beginning—was his refusal to engage with questions posed to him by Rehm and listeners who called in.

Rehm began by asking him about his own mother, and he told her that his mother had now died, that his father had died much earlier, and that for most of his childhood the family consisted of his mother, himself, and his younger brother, who has, he reported, also died—in circumstances he refused to divulge, even when he was pressed on the point. Sometime during this part of the interview he said, not in response to a question, "please don't think that these stories are autobiographical; my relations with my mother weren't like that at all."

This effort to keep separate the stories as stories—that is, as verbal constructions—and the lived experience of the person who wrote them was intensified when it came time to respond to callers. They were all fervent admirers, but what they wanted to talk about and what he didn't want to talk about at all was the comfort and solace given to them by his work. They felt that he was speaking directly to them and that he wrote with at least the partial intention of helping his readers through a bad patch. They were calling in to tell him how much he had indeed helped, and they hoped, it was clear, that the bond they had formed with him at long distance would be deepened if they spoke to him in person (as it were) and told him *their* stories. This, they proceeded to do, in halting narratives sometimes punctuated by tears. They were stories of dysfunctional families, mostly Irish, and they were full of the pain produced by rejection, estrangement, and (often) alcoholism. The callers asked, implicitly, for recognition and empathy.

He wasn't giving any. He spoke to them of course, but he ran away from the emotions they were offering him, as we all do when confronted with a demand we cannot satisfy. What he could not do or was unwilling to do Rehm tried to do for him. It was she who, after he was finished speaking, said something sympathetic and consoling, something that communicated a measure of fellow feeling.

I grew more annoyed, until I heard him say something that turned his refusal of intimacy (if indeed intimacy can be achieved between a radio voice and an audience) into a stance I recognized and could admire. A caller asked (and her tone assumed an affirmative answer) whether the writing of these stories was a way of dealing with the deaths of his mother and younger brother. He replied, it's not that, "it's not therapy," and went on to explain that assuaging grief, his or someone else's, is not what writing strives to do. In fact, if there is a relationship of an act to the satisfaction of a need, it is the other way around. The act of writing makes use of grief as it might make use of anything.

Imagine a painter, he said, who suffers the loss of a family member. He might well find (involuntarily) that the darker colors of the palette seem to offer more opportunities for composition than they had before. In short, and he didn't quite say this, it's the craft that is important, not the emotions it may have appropriated along the way. What he is interested in is the telling of the story and the finding of the sentence that might best conclude it.

It was then that I saw that what I had first regarded as a suspect evasiveness was in fact a determination to be faithful to the practice he was dedicated to and a refusal to claim for that practice effects that could not or should not be its objective. If a reader feels consoled or comforted, that's all to the good, but it's not what writing is about. Writing is about crafting sentences and building them into paragraphs and building the paragraphs into arguments and narratives. What Rehm and her listeners were proffering was a rationale for the act that was not internal to its demands, a rationale that could take the form of an external justification: I write so that you will feel better or I write so that the world will become a better place.

Tóibín was saying, I write because making things out of words is what I feel compelled to do. Of course the words refer to events in the world, including events I may have witnessed or experienced, but to locate the value of the writing either in its effects or in the verisimilitude it achieves is to grab the wrong end of the stick.

It makes perfect sense that Tóibín would find his novelistic inspiration in Henry James, who remains enigmatic despite massively documented biographies by Leon Edel and others. James is often portrayed, as he is at times in Tóibín's *The Master*, as someone who turned his back (injured in some way never specified) on life and occupied himself solely with his art. Tóibín has him at one point saying, "life is a mystery and . . . only sentences are beautiful," and at another point resolving to "do the work of his life," the work of "high art."

I believe this resolve, and the stringency it requires, is generalizable. If you've found something you really like to do—say write beautiful sentences—not because of the possible benefits to the world of doing it, but because doing it brings you the satisfaction and sense of completeness nothing else can, then do it at the highest level of performance you are capable of, and leave the world and its problems to others. This is a lesson I have preached before in these columns when the subject was teaching, and it is a lesson that can be applied, I believe, to any project that offers as a prime reason for prosecuting it the pleasure, a wholly internal pleasure, of its own accomplishment. And if your project doesn't offer that pleasure (perhaps among others) you might want to think again about your commitment to it.

1. Colm Tóibín, *The Master*, reprint ed. (New York: Scribner, 2005).
2. Colm Tóibín, *Mothers and Sons*, reprint ed. (New York: Scribner, 2008).

2.2

Two Aesthetics

DECEMBER 16, 2007

I spent the month of November in New York, and for part of that time I hung out at the Museum of Television and Radio (now the Paley Center for Media), doing research for a book I'm writing on the '60s TV show *The Fugitive*. When I wasn't reading reviews and cover stories in old issues of *TV Guide*, I was going to galleries, listening to concerts, and seeking out movies that would probably not make it up to Delaware County. The movie I found was *Starting Out in the Evening*, described in the reviews as a "small film," which means not only that there are no special effects, but that almost nothing happens (a point of criticism on the part of some reviewers).

Leonard Schiller, an aging novelist (played by the always wonderful Frank Langella) whose four books are out of print, is laboring without much success to produce a fifth when a beautiful young woman enters his life and challenges the insularity of his hitherto inviolate routines. She is writing a master's thesis on him and wants to explore the relationship between his writing and his emotional history.

He resists any such probing—he says that his characters have their own lives and that he just follows them around waiting for something interesting to happen—and the tension between them reflects the ancient quarrel between those who think that art is an expression of personal experience and those, like Schiller, who think that art is its own realm and is responsible only to the demands and laws of craft.

In a parallel story, Schiller's forty-year-old daughter is also having birth pangs, but in a more literal sense. Devoted to a father who maintains a severe emotional distance from her, she wants desperately to have a child. But the man she loves is resolved not to bring anyone else into the world, and the two have been busy not negotiating this issue for a number of years.

That's it; nothing else.

Only two things in the film rise to the status of an event. Schiller has a stroke, but its effect, finally, is only further to slow down a life that was already near quiescent. And in a conversation where it seems to him that Heather Wolfe (his young admirer) is condescending to him, he slaps her. But since the slap comes across almost as a caress—perhaps even a statement of gratitude for her having made him think about what it means to write—it does not have that much force and is in no way a climax to the non-action of the non-plot. In the last moment of the movie, Schiller goes back to his typewriter—an emblem of his refusal to be connected to things outside his study—and begins anew the search for the right word.

Refusal is the film's mode, and watching it reminded me of why I am so drawn to *The Fugitive*, a series that ran on ABC from 1963 to 1967 and was the basis of a Harrison Ford–Tommy Lee Jones blockbuster in the nineties. (A new TV version, determinedly unfaithful to the original, tanked in 2000.)

It might seem that *The Fugitive* is the antithesis of *Starting Out in the Evening* because it is apparently so plot-driven. Everyone knows the story: Richard Kimble, a pediatrician, has been convicted of killing his wife. He alone knows that the real killer is a one-armed man he saw running from his house on the night of the murder. He is reprieved from execution when the train taking him and his detective-guard, lieutenant Philip Gerard, runs off the rails, allowing him to escape. Gerard pursues him relentlessly, and he, not quite as relentlessly, pursues the one-armed man.

But this double-pursuit plot does not give the drama its energy; it is merely a device for getting Kimble in and out of the many small towns where he encounters men and women in various stages of moral and psychological distress. The story really belongs to them and to the moments in which they must respond to the opportunities and dangers Kimble's presence in their midst produces. Will they betray him? Do they believe in his innocence? Do they trust in the workings of blind justice?

While the decisions they make and the actions they take often affect Kimble (who is always a second away from capture), the real significance of what they do (or fail to do) resides in the lives they will live when he is long gone. He is the catalyst who precipitates a self-examination and a taking of stock he never performs; and it is only when his work is done (or turns out to be impossible; some people are just too far gone) that the plot kicks in—someone recognizes him—and he has to get out of town, often hiding in the back of a truck or in some other ignominious posture.

In short, *The Fugitive* is about character and moral choice and not about plot, even though it is through the mechanism of plot that

Kimble moves on to the next place where people need his help more than he needs theirs. All the action, such as it is, takes place in small, usually dark rooms where a troubled soul is forced to confront his or her aspirations, doubts, and demons.

The same can be said of *Starting Out in the Evening*, in which a typical scene finds Schiller and his adversary/admirer, or Schiller and his daughter, or the daughter and her lover, giving voice to their fears and anxieties and trying to come to terms with their limitations, often in the limited spaces of an upper West Side apartment. "People talk a lot" in this movie, one reviewer complained, and added that it was all too "masturbatory," that is, self-focused.

And indeed, it is, to the exclusion of everything else: the only issues raised are the issues with which the members of the small cast are obsessed—dedication to art versus openness to the messiness of life, integrity versus connectedness, purity of purpose versus the seductions of commerce and fame (which Milton famously called "that last infirmity of noble mind"). You would never know, while watching this movie, that there was a whole lot going on in the world—wars, famines, international crises, presidential elections, environmental disasters. We are allowed to assume that the setting is contemporary—2007—but the scene could be shifted to 1907 or 1607 without any loss whatsoever.

This is part of what I meant when I said earlier that the mode of the film is refusal. First, it refuses cinematic virtuosity. No intricate cutting, no clever camera angles, no hallucinations, no flashbacks, no disruptions of sequence, no tricks. Just a straight-ahead representation of one conversational scene after another in "real time." Second, it refuses excitement, except of a quiet, psychological kind. And third, it refuses relevance. Politics is referenced only once, when the daughter's boyfriend (who is black, a fact of which, praise be, absolutely nothing is made) says that he would like to start a magazine that would be a forum for left-wing views.

But there are no left-wing views expressed; indeed, there are no views expressed at all, except for the ones that relate to the existential plights of the characters. (In its determined austerity, the film sides with Schiller against the women who would draw him out of his aesthetic cocoon.)

And so it is with *The Fugitive*, too. Although the period 1963–67 saw world-shaking events, none of them takes center stage in the series' 120 episodes. Kimble and those he encounters can be presumed to have political views and partisan identifications, but we hear nothing about them, for they are no part of the moral deliberations that lead the characters to see what they have become and to consider what they might become were they to make this choice rather than that.

The day after I saw *Starting Out in the Evening*, I had another, instructively different cultural experience. I went to the opening of the New Museum at 235 Bowery (not the VIP opening, to which for some reason I wasn't invited, but the free-to-the-public opening). Where I loved every moment of the movie (too much identification with the lead character, I suspect), I hated every moment in the museum, which is all drama, surprise, flash, effect, and politics.

I know that I'm supposed to admire the structure of stacked-slightly-off-kilter boxes, but it didn't do anything for me. The interior irritated me, starting with the pretentious-because-it-declares-itself-to-be-unpretentious concrete floor (complete with cracks). Then there were the harsh, industrial-style lights; the gift shop behind a mesh curtain of the kind you find in pawn shops; the cattle-car elevator; and the tiny café, intended, it would seem, to be inadequate to any conceivable occasion. Everything was making a statement and issuing a challenge: Do you get it? (Obviously I didn't.)

But it was the art that told me how hopelessly retro I am. Here is a description from a reviewer who loved it: "Looking at the New Museum of Contemporary Art's inaugural . . . exhibition is like visiting the crash pad of a favorite friend, the one that's creative and stays up all night and leaves dirty dishes piled up in the sink and doesn't have any real furniture and what's in their place came from the stuff people threw out on the sidewalk."[1]

I couldn't have said it better myself. The idea is to find bits and pieces of detritus and put them together in surprising and sometimes shocking ways. There's a picture of Mel Gibson suspended from a long pole attached to a bicycle. There's an arc of old chairs perched on what looks like broken mattress springs. There is an auditorium in which I sat watching a home movie featuring a pack of barking dogs.

At least you can sit in the auditorium. There are no chairs or benches in the rest of the building, a warning to museum-goers that they are not here to gaze reverently at timeless and monumental works of art. This inaugural exhibition is titled *Unmonumental*; the items in it, the museum's website tells us, are "conversational, provisional, at times even corroded and corrupted . . . unheroic and manifestly unmonumental."[2] These works do not attempt to defeat time, but embrace it, and with it impermanence and decay.

They also embrace politics, as the (vaguely postmodern) aesthetic that produces them demands. If art is not an autonomous discipline obeying internal laws but is responsive to and constitutive of the contingent events of history, it is already political, and offering itself as anything else would be a lie. What lies, the exhibit implies, is the illusion of depth and profundity. Here, everything is surface and perspective; no meanings are stable; no interpretations are authoritative. The largest piece in the exhibit is a multimedia installation—seven channels of ever-changing text messages flashing on rectangular shapes—"that tells a chilling story of abduction and assassination from seven separate points of view, set to an eerily laid-back bossa nova score." (You can't make these things up.)

But although randomness and chance are themes of this installation and of other pieces in the exhibit, there is nothing random in either the concepts or their implementation. I cannot deny the museum's coherence, its (playful) seriousness. I just don't like it. What it embraces—the ephemeral and the insubstantial—I shun, and what I embrace—work that aspires to permanence—it pokes fun at.

I cannot help wondering what Leonard Schiller, in search of formal perfection (he wears a tie and jacket in his study), or Richard Kimble, in search of perfect justice even as he flees its imperfect judgment, would think if they walked through the New Museum. But then I already know.

1. Teri Tynes, "Unmonumental at the New Museum: Just like Your Favorite Messy Friend's Place (A Review)," from the blog Walking Off the Big Apple, http://www .walkingoffthebigapple.com/2007/12/unmonumental-at-new-museum-just-like.html?q =Unmonumental+at+the+New+Museum.

2. History of the New Museum, http://www.newmuseum.org/history.

Norms and Deviations: Who's to Say?

JUNE 1, 2008

A letter published in the May 26 issue of *Time* magazine protests the inclusion, in *Time*'s list of the world's one hundred most influential people, of two researchers allied with the organization Cure Autism Now (a name that speaks for itself). The letter writer declares himself to be "outraged" because, in his view, "Autistic spectrum disorders are not diseases, but rather markers of 'genetic difference' in the same vein as skin color [and] gender." He equates the search for a cure with genocide—it's "part of a campaign to wipe out ASDs [autism spectrum disorder]"—and he wants the world to know that those to whom the cure would be offered neither need it nor desire it: "I speak for many when I say we are happy the way we are."

A genetic difference is often adaptive and can be regarded as an advance in the evolutionary process; it is well known that autism sometimes brings with it remarkable powers in the areas of music, art, and mathematics. In the 2006 movie *X-Men: The Last Stand*, the augmented powers of those known as "mutants" are even more remarkable and include the ability to walk through walls, to move metal objects as large as California's Golden Gate Bridge, to autogenerate fire or ice, to be in seven places at the same time, to read minds, to assume any identity, to kill with a touch, to fly like Icarus, and to change the weather. These abilities are seen by many "normal" human beings, and a few mutants, as disabilities, as an indication that the person who possesses one of them is a freak.

From this perspective, the best thing a mutant could hope for would be a cure, and it is the discovery of one that sets the plot of the movie in motion. The response of both "centrist" and militant mutants to this "medical advance" is the same. Storm (Halle Berry) declares, "They can't cure us. You know why? Because there's nothing to cure!" A crowd of mutants rallies to the chant, "We don't need a cure." The leader of the militants, Magneto (Ian McKellen), roars his defiance: "They wish to cure us. We are the cure, the cure for an imperfect and infirm condition called Homo sapiens." Not only is he happy with the way he is; he pities and scorns those who walk another, inferior way.

It might seem meretricious and insensitive to link a serious condition like autism with the heroes and antiheroes of a comic book fantasy. But the link is encouraged by the film's director, Brett Ratner, who said on About.com that the story "has strong racial, political, and sexual aspects" and wonders, "What if . . . African American[s] could take a pill [that would] 'cure' them of being black or if a gay could take something that would alter his sexuality?"[1] That is, what if a condition scorned by the majority but prized by the minority that inhabits it could be eliminated by a simple injection? What would the minority do?

In the case of blacks and gays, the answer has already been given in the mantras "black is beautiful" and "we're queer; we're here; get used to it." In the years since these battle cries were first heard, African Americans and gay Americans have secured rights, gained in influence, and earned respect, however grudging and superficial.

And why couldn't the same thing happen to autism and mutancy or to any other mode of being that refuses the judgment of those who scorn, marginalize, and seek to destroy it? For it is a question, Ratner observes, of "the use and misuse of power." Do those labeled deviant, he asks, acquiesce and "conform" to a "prejudice," or do they "maintain their uniqueness . . . and embrace what makes them different?"

"Difference" is the key concept in these sociopolitical dramas, and difference is an inherently unstable measure. In order to mark it—in order to say where difference resides—you must first identify a baseline, a center; but any such identification will appear to those exiled to the periphery as arbitrary, a function of prejudice and an illegitimate exercise of power: *it's only because there are more of you that you can consign us to the margins and refuse us respect.* Armed with this argument (which flourishes in some versions of multiculturalist and deconstructive thought), there is no form of behavior that cannot make a case for its legitimacy and for its right to be free of external coercion, whether it takes the form of legal sanctions or a forced "cure."

For some time now, many in the deaf community—a phrase that makes an argument: we are not just persons similarly afflicted; we are a community—have resisted cochlear implants, reasoning that to accept them would be to deny their culture, their language, and their identity. "An implant," wrote the editors of *Deaf Life*, "is the ultimate invasion of the ear . . . the ultimate refusal to let deaf people be deaf."[2]

"I'm happy with who I am," Roslyn Rosen, then president of the National Association of the Deaf, declared on *60 Minutes* (through an interpreter), "and I don't want to be 'fixed.'"[3] The story of the "hearing world," writes Douglas Baynton, associate professor of history and American sign language at the University of Iowa, is that deafness is an incapacity; but, he explains, what we are dealing with are "physical differences" (exactly the point made in the letter to *Time*), and physical differences "do not carry inherent meanings." That is, they do not come labeled "normal" and "inferior," "abled" and "disabled"; these labels, Baynton contends, are fixed by "a culturally created web of meaning," a web constructed by no one and everyone, a web that those who live within it find difficult to unravel, even when they know that the meanings it delivers are false.[4]

Deafness appears, it is said, as a defect only against the background of a norm that has been put in place not by nature but by history. It follows then, argues Lennard Davis, editor of *The Disability Studies Reader*, that "the problem is not the person with disabilities; the problem is the way that normalcy is constructed to create 'the problem' of the disabled person."[5] "There is no 'handicap' to overcome," insists Tom Humphries of the University of California, San Diego.[6] Paddy Ladd, a British advocate of Deaf culture, draws the moral: "Labeling us as disabled demonstrates a failure to understand that we are not disabled in any way within our own community,"[7] and the implicit question he asks is, who is to say that your community is better than ours? I. King Jordan of Gallaudet University drives the point home: "People who come to our campus and who do not know sign language are communicatively disabled" (*PMLA*, March 2005).

The logic of that question is the logic that has driven all the antidiscrimination movements of the last 120 years. A minority (deaf activists view themselves as a linguistic minority) is regarded by the mainstream as defective, impaired, criminal (Italians and Irish in the nineteenth century), inferior (Asians and blacks), immoral (gays, polygamists, and gypsies), lacking in mental or physical resources (women until only recently), and either less or more than human (X-men and Jews).

Within the minority community, the conviction grows that its stigmatization is the result not of "natural" deficiencies but of a politically established norm that serves the interests of the powers that be. Exposing that norm as a mere artifact of history with no special claim to authority means first that it is no longer obligatory to honor it, and second, that the community's norms are worthy of both loyalty and protection. What was once seen as a deviation or something to be eradicated is recharacterized as a culture, and in a short time the culture has a lobby and is demanding respect, representation, and even reparations for opportunities denied and rights withheld. The formerly shunned but now legitimized community opens cultural centers, galleries (think of graffiti artists), museums, historical archives, and soon it is being courted by the very mainstream constituencies that for so long accorded it only a negative recognition.

This could happen to any group; for once the norm has been relativized (you have yours, we have ours; why can't we just get along), there is no obvious way to declare a way of life beyond the pale. You can of course say that the test is whether those whose lifestyle the majority finds dubious and offensive causes harm to others. But the "harm" standard (elaborated by J. S. Mill in *On Liberty*) cannot itself be neutrally applied. Smokers and pornographers say, "Leave us alone; what's it to you?" Those who want to regulate them respond that smokers drive up our medical costs and pornography erodes family values and corrupts our children. Polygamists claim that they more than any honor family values (theirs is a big love); their critics talk about forcing young children to marry long before the age of consent, and polygamists come back with the observation that the "age of consent" is a political construct and certainly wasn't honored in the Bible.

Perhaps you draw the line by marking off what is criminal from what is not. But no category is more obviously the plaything of politics and prejudice than the category of lawbreakers. Until 1967, it was criminal to engage in interracial marriage; until very recently, it was criminal to engage in sex with someone of the same sex; once, it was criminal to teach blacks how to read; rigid drug laws have made criminals out of several generations of young men; Nelson Mandela was a criminal for decades.

Maybe you apply the universal outrage test, which, one presumes, would put pedophiles and serial killers in the class of those whose actions no one could possibly appreciate or justify. But the North American Man/Boy Love Association (NAMBLA) advertises itself as fighting for personal freedom and "for the empowerment of youth in all areas." NAMBLA believes that any child, regardless of age, should have the right to say "yes" or "no" to a sexual relationship. Those who would deny them that right are guilty of "ageism." (In short, boys loved by men like the way they are.) And as for serial killers, one admiring website credits at least some of them with the desire to purify the world by killing bad people, as Dexter does in the cable TV series that bears his name (he is the cure); and the same website suggests that they are heroic individuals standing up to a repressive society: "People who become serial killers will not repress their fantasies and their true feelings just because society and morality do not accept [them]."

I am neither making nor approving these arguments. I am merely noting that they can and have been made, that they will continue to be made, that there is no theoretical way to stop them from being made, and that their structure is always the same whether the condition that asks for dignity and the removal of stigma is autism, deafness, blackness, gayness, polygamy, drug use, pedophilia, or murder.

We want to say that these are all different, that there can be no equivalence between them, and that making the case for one is not to make a case for the others. And of course as a practical matter, that is true. The distinctions that cannot be shored up by theory will be put in place, at least for a time, by history; and the degree to which they remain firm or are challenged will be a contingent matter depending on political, social, economic, and other factors that cannot be predicted or managed.

All we can be sure of is that the struggle between the impulse to normalize—to specify a center and then police deviations from it—and the impulse to repel the normalizing gaze and live securely in a community of one's own will never be resolved.

1. Rebecca Murray, "Director Brett Ratner Discusses *X-Men: The Last Stand*," *About Entertainment* on About.com, 2006.

2. Quote originally appeared in the column "For Hearing People Only" in *Deaf Life* magazine. Later it was included in a compilation of columns from *Deaf Life* in Matthew S. Moore and Linda Levitan, *For Hearing People Only*, 2nd ed. (Rochester, NY: Deaf Life, 1993).

3. Roslyn Rosen, president of the National Association of the Deaf, on *60 Minutes*, January 1999.

4. Douglas T. Bayton, "'A Silent Exile on This Earth: The Metaphorical Construction of Deafness in the Nineteenth Century," *American Quarterly* 44 (June 1992): 216–43.

5. Lennard Davis, ed., *The Disability Studies Reader (London:* Routledge, 2013).

6. Tom Humphries, "Deaf Culture and Cultures," in *Multicultural Issues in Deafness*, ed. K. M. Christensen and G. L. Delgado (White Plains, NY: Longman, 1993).

7. Paddy Ladd, *Understanding Deaf Culture: In Search of Deafhood* (Great Britain: Cromwell Press, 2003).

The Ten Best American Movies

JANUARY 4, 2009

It's Top Ten time again, and like everyone else, I have a list, in my case, a list of the ten best American movies ever. Here it is, with brief descriptions and no justifications. Only the first two films are in order. The others are all tied for third.

The Best Years of Our Lives (1946), directed by William Wyler. Regarded as producer Sam Goldwyn's masterpiece, this deeply felt study of soldiers coming home after World War II boasts career-best performances by Fredric March (who won an Oscar), Myrna Loy, Teresa Wright, Dana Andrews, Virginia Mayo, Cathy O'Donnell, Hoagy Carmichael, and the amazing Harold Russell (two Oscars), a double amputee and first- and last-time (non)actor who played a double amputee.

The movie is filled with thrilling and affecting scenes—the moment when Milly Stephenson (Loy) realizes that the person at the door is her husband, Al (March), who has come back a day before he was supposed to; the moment when Homer Parrish (Russell) waves good-bye to his two new friends and his parents see the hooks that are now his hands for the first time; the moment when Fred Derry (Andrews) hoists himself into a military plane like the one he flew in so many times and hears in his mind the engines of the other dead planes surrounding him in rows. The three intertwined stories are resolved with a measure of optimism, but with more than a residue of disappointment and bitterness. Al Stephenson is still a drunk. Fred Derry is still poor and without skills. Homer Parrish still has no hands.

Sunset Boulevard (1950), directed by Billy Wilder. Notable for Gloria Swanson's triumphant comeback performance in a movie that denies her character a comeback, the film also has William Holden doing his "morally flawed person in an attractive package" act to perfection, not to mention the ancillary pleasures of a young, boyish, and humorous (would you believe it?) Jack Webb, a self-parodying turn as a director/husband-turned-factotum by Erich von Stroheim, a silent appearance by silent star Buster Keaton, and a cameo performance by Cecil B. DeMille playing himself.

The voice-over narration of the story by a dead man floating in a swimming pool seems not bizarre but exactly right; Joe Gillis (Holden) was morally dead before he hit the water. When the movie begins, Gillis comes across as a nice guy, somewhat down on his luck, and Norma Desmond (Swanson) comes across as an egomaniacal monster who pressures him into becoming her boy toy. But even before the final incredible scene of Desmond descending a staircase while the camera rolls, she has earned the sympathy we extend to the terribly needy, and he has revealed himself to be the true monster, a betrayer of Desmond, of the young girl (Nancy Olson), who sees more in him than there is, and of himself.

Double Indemnity (1944), also directed by Billy Wilder. This time Wilder's antihero—played by Fred MacMurray, who could do tall but weak with the best of them (see *The Apartment, The Caine Mutiny*, and *Pushover*)—is not dead but dying as he narrates the story into a tape recorder destined for the ears of his boss, Barton Keyes (the incomparably great Edward G. Robinson).

You know what's going to happen the moment Barbara Stanwyck—you see just her legs and an ankle-bracelet—slinks down the staircase of her house, and Walter Neff (MacMurray) probably knows it, too; but he, like us, is compelled to see the plot through the inevitable downward spiral to its ending. Phyllis (Stanwyck) predicts it all when she says, "It's straight down the line for both of us." Keyes, the indefatigable unlocker of puzzles, is even more precise: "They're stuck with each other. They've got to ride all the way to the end of the line. And it's a one-way trip; and the last stop is the cemetery." Just before that stop, the true love story of the film announces itself when, in response to Keyes's acknowledgment of the depth of his feelings for his protégé, Neff says, "I love you, too," and dies.

Shane (1953), directed by George Stevens. In this beautifully photographed western, a laconic, stoic stranger rides in out of nowhere and rides out again (perhaps mortally wounded) in the same direction, as Joey Starrett (Brandon De Wilde) implores him to "come back, Shane." In between, Shane (Alan Ladd, in the performance of his life), a man at once steely and sentimental, hard-edged and effeminate, becomes the love object of almost everyone in the movie. Joey loves

Shane; his father (a treelike Van Heflin) loves Shane; his mother (Jean Arthur, luminous in a role she disliked) loves Shane; the cowhand played by Ben Johnson learns to love Shane; and even Wilson, the gunman portrayed so memorably by Jack Palance in a breakthrough role, loves Shane in the way one can love one's mirror image.

The movie is at once clichéd—the settlers versus the cowmen; the lone, rugged individualist versus the community—and elegiac. Like the pastoral, the western caresses a landscape it knows to be already lost and alive only in the imagination; and in *Shane* the caress is lingering, loving, and sad.

Red River (1948), directed by Howard Hawks, is not elegiac but looks forward to the days when western beef will supply eastern tables. But before that can happen, there has to be the first cattle drive, and its adventures and obstacles provide the plot for this film. The real center, however, is once again the love and hate relationships among the key characters.

There are two triangles and one dyad. The first triangle is made up of cattleman Tom Dunson (John Wayne in the role he should have won an Oscar for), Dunson's adopted son Matthew Garth (Montgomery Clift, matching Wayne's screen power despite the disparity in their physical presences), and family retainer Groot Nadine (Walter Brennan, playing the irascible, principled old coot to perfection). Garth and Groot love Dunson; Dunson loves Garth and Groot; Groot loves Dunson and Garth.

None gives his love unconditionally. Groot tells Dunson at a crucial moment, "You was wrong, Mr. Dunson." Garth leads a mutiny against his father. Dunson vows vengeance against his son and promises to kill him. He is prevented from doing so (although it is unlikely that he would have ever really gone that far) by Tess Millay (Joanne Dru), who makes up a third of another triangle with Dunson and Garth. Garth, in turn, forms a dyad with Cherry Valance (John Ireland, in his best role except for his bravura turn in *All the King's Men*), a fast gun who competes with him but is devoted to him, and risks his life to protect him. Brooding over all these characters is the cattle drive itself, a force both of nature and history and a generator of excitement and purpose all on its own.

Raging Bull (1980), directed by Martin Scorsese. Tom Dunson, in *Red River*, almost brings everything he has fought for and loved down on his head, but is redeemed at the last moment. Nothing redeems Jake LaMotta (Robert De Niro, in an Oscar-winning performance), who can find the worm in any apparently happy situation and who systematically drives away everyone who cares for him with the same relentless brutality he displays in the ring. Anything can set him off, even a steak that may or may not be overdone; and if there is nothing in view, he can make up the provocation, as he does when he accuses his brother (Joe Pesci) of betraying him with his wife (Cathy Moriarty). For LaMotta, rage is the default condition, the ordinary, everyday emotion; anything else is an anomaly he cannot abide, and he soon removes it.

Most boxing movies trace the classic pattern of rise, fall, and redemption (*Somebody Up There Likes Me*, *Cinderella Man*), or tell a moral tale about the corruption of the sport (*The Harder They Fall*, *The Set-Up*), or detail the corruption of the protagonist (*Champion*, *Body and Soul*). *Raging Bull* offers no triumph and no moral. It just exhibits the self-destructiveness of its central figure again and again; even the depiction of LaMotta's later career as a nightclub entertainer extends rather than ends the pain. The wonder is that Scorsese was able to make something lyrical out of a polluting self-destructiveness, but that is what he did.

Vertigo (1958), directed by Alfred Hitchcock. Here again is a love that destroys, not in the form of rage, but in the form of obsession and control. Hitchcock was one of two directors (the other was Anthony Mann in, for example, *The Man from Laramie*) who saw that Jimmy Stewart's nice-guy persona could have a dark side.

This is a movie about manipulation and the fabrication of reality. Scottie (Stewart) is manipulated by his friend Gavin, who also manipulates the woman (Kim Novak, brilliant in a dual role) who in turn manipulates Scottie. When the deception is complete and Scottie believes that the woman he loves has died, he is lost until he sees a girl who resembles her. (She is her, but not her, at the same time.) He then does to her what had been done to him—he manipulates her, denies her her own identity, and makes her over until she is the simulacrum of a woman who never was. When he discovers how he had been fooled by a theatrical illusion, he hisses, "Did he train you? Did he rehearse you? Did he tell you what to do and what to say?"—apparently not realizing that he is furious and indignant about the very behavior he has been exhibiting.

There is an abstract, geometrical quality to the relationships in this film and they work themselves out in the space of a strangely abstract San Francisco, empty, dreamy, and in brilliantly enameled Technicolor. There's no getting to the bottom of this movie; it's vertiginous.

Groundhog Day (1993), directed by Harold Ramis. Another Pygmalion story, but this time the material the sculptor works on is himself. Phil Connors (Bill Murray) is a jaded, dyspeptic, arrogant, cynical, and obnoxious TV weatherman who on February 2 finds himself covering the emergence of the groundhog in Punxsutawney, Pennsylvania. When he wakes up the next morning, he finds that it is not the next morning, but Groundhog Day all over again and all over again and all over again. (His own spring will be late.)

His responses to being trapped eternally in the same day include disbelief, despair, excess, and hedonism before he settles down to make the best of the situation, which, it turns out, means making the best of himself—a self-help project that takes forever, but forever is what he has. (It is as if he were at once the ghosts of Christmas past, present, and future, and the object of their tutelary attention.) By bits and pieces, fits and starts, he makes himself into the most popular fellow in town and wins the love of his producer, the beautiful Rita (a perfectly cast Andie MacDowell). The miracle is that as the movie becomes more serious, it becomes funnier. The comedy and the philosophy (how shall one live?) do not sit side by side but inhabit each other in a unity that is incredibly satisfying. This is a "feel-good" movie in at least two senses of the word "good."

Meet Me in St. Louis (1944), directed by Vincente Minnelli. When the calendar finally turns a page in *Groundhog Day* and Phil and Rita walk out of the bed and breakfast to start their new life together, Phil says, "Let's live here," which means let's live in small-town America, where everyone knows everyone else and everyone takes care of everyone else. In *Meet Me in St. Louis*, the characters already live there (yes, St. Louis is a city, but in this movie it's a neighborhood), and the plot centers on the question (not exactly burning) of whether or not they will be able to stay.

The real center of the film is the loving depiction of a loving family, four sisters, a son, a mother and a father, a grandfather, and a cook (the redoubtable Marjorie Main). To be sure, there are tensions, but they are the innocent tensions found in every family—between teenage sisters, between husband and wife—and as viewers we know that they will be dispelled. A film in which the inability of a young man to find a tuxedo for an important party counts as a crisis isn't ever going to disturb your equanimity. It is only when Esther (a glorious Judy Garland) sings the achingly sad "Have Yourself a Merry Little Christmas" to her sister Tootie (a scene-stealing Margaret O'Brien) that a sense of the pains life often brings intrudes; but not long after, their father (Leon Ames) renounces his plan to move to New York (the only real villain of the story), and everything is once again well.

This is a woman's movie. Only the grandfather (Harry Davenport) is a fully drawn male character. The strength belongs to the sisters, the cook, and the mother, excellently played by Mary Astor. And, of course, there is the music, with Garland at the top of her form, especially in the "Trolley Song" sequence, perhaps the three most exhilarating musical minutes in film history. Despite the lavishly beautiful production, this is not a big movie—no grand ideas, no moral dilemmas, no transformations of character, no deep insights. All it is is perfect.

A Tree Grows in Brooklyn (1945), directed by Elia Kazan. Another happy family, but this one maintains its closeness despite the obstacles of poverty and a father given to drink who has trouble keeping his job as a singing waiter. In his first directorial effort, Kazan draws incredible performances from Dorothy McGuire as the wife and mother who is so beaten down by life's hardships that she cannot afford the luxury of emotions; from James Dunn (who won an Oscar) as the dreamer who has nothing to give but love; from Peggy Ann Garner (special Oscar) as the daughter for whom his love is enough; and from Joan Blondell as the slightly disreputable but warmhearted Aunt Sissie.

What is said of many movies is true of this one: it will break your heart, not once but many times—when you witness Francie's beautiful faith in her father despite the evidence of his failures ("faith is the evidence of things not seen"); when her mother is unable to sustain her feelings for a husband who cannot be a provider; when mother and daughter reach an understanding as they wait for the birth of a child who will never know its father. But the heart it breaks—in the film and in the audience—is made whole again by the strength of the family that refuses to bend in the face of a world that offers it little. A tearjerker, to be sure, but so what?

So there they are, ten movies marked by sentiment and cynicism in equal doses, but with sentiment winning out more often than not. There were, of course, others I would like to have included, and I list a Second Ten here, without comment and in no particular order: *Quiz Show*, *The Wild Bunch*, *Nashville*, *My Darling Clementine*, *How Green Was My Valley*, *The Night of the Hunter*, *Lonely Are the Brave*, *Detective Story*, *All About Eve*, and *Ace in the Hole*.

Of course, expanding the list to twenty rather than warding off criticism affords it even more scope. Let the disagreements begin.

Giving Kim Novak Her Due

AUGUST 17, 2008

Even these days, when it is sometimes hard to tell the difference between a general-release motion picture and soft pornography, two of the most erotic moments one can find on film feature no nudity and bodies just touching.

Both are '50s movies. The first, the 1951 *A Place in the Sun*, pairs a ravishing eighteen-year-old Elizabeth Taylor with Montgomery Clift. In a scene where the two are dancing and declaring their love for each other, Taylor sets up a rendezvous. "I'll pick you up outside the factory," she tells Clift, and then she breathes into his ear: "You'll be my pickup." Moments later the emotional intensity is raised even higher when Clift exclaims, "If I could only tell you how much I love you. If I could only tell you all." In response, she draws him closer and in a voice that could ignite fires implores him, "Tell mamma, tell mamma all."

"Sexy" doesn't even begin to describe it.

In the second movie, 1955's *Picnic*, the sparks fly between Kim Novak, then twenty-two, and William Holden. Again the context is a dance, although it would be more accurately characterized as a mating ritual. To the music of George Duning's and Morris Stoloff's brilliant arrangement of "It Must Have Been Moonglow," a radiant Novak, clapping her hands in rhythm, sways down a bank toward Holden, who then joins her in a dance of such sensuality that the observers can only gape, each betraying the emotion he or she involuntarily feels—envy, nostalgia, frustration, longing, wonder.

Picnic was not one of the films shown last Tuesday when the Turner Classic Movies (TCM) network devoted a day to Novak, a recognition some might think she does not deserve. They would be wrong.

Novak was the top box office star three years running in the '50s. Still, she is not usually mentioned in the same breath with the other major actresses of the period—Taylor, Marilyn Monroe, Grace Kelly, Ava Gardner. She was not earthy like Gardner or icy like Kelly or Rubenesque like Monroe or raunchy like Jane Russell or perky like Doris Day. She was something that has gone out of fashion and even become suspect in an era of feminist strictures: she was the object of a voyeuristic male gaze.

This is true of her first movie with a speaking role, 1954's *Pushover*, a film noir in the *Double Indemnity* mode featuring, along with Novak, Fred MacMurray, E. G. Marshall, Philip Carey, and Dorothy Malone. (In her best work, Novak is often surrounded by powerful costars, and to her credit she plays off them, not against them.) Malone could do a sultry turn of her own (*Warlock*, *Written on the Wind*), but she is no match for Novak. MacMurray plays a cop assigned to ingratiate himself to her in the hope that she will lead him to her gangster boyfriend. But, as TCM host Robert Osborne observed, one look at Novak and he's lost. When he's not watching her, the camera is, for the plot consists largely of a surveillance operation; a team of detectives spends endless hours looking at Novak through binoculars, as do we. It is voyeurism from a distance, and emphasizes her status as a glittering something beheld from afar.

This, of course, is what Jimmy Stewart does for much of the first part of *Vertigo*. Hired by a friend to monitor her activities, he follows Novak (Judy pretending to be Madeleine) from place to place, and in one extended scene stares at her as she stares at a portrait of a woman in a museum. What he doesn't know is that the object of his desire is a confection, a fantasy created by his employer, who has made her up to look like the wife he plans to kill.

When the scheme succeeds and the Stewart character believes her to be dead, he falls into a depression until he spots a young girl who bears a physical resemblance to his lost love, but is nothing like her. Rather than being refined, austere, and aloof, she is coarse, over-made-up, even common. In what remains of the movie, he works at turning her into the simulacrum of his beloved (he strips off her makeup and then applies his own), transforming her from an all-too-flesh-and-blood woman into an ever more abstract representation of an image—itself an illusion—that lives only in his memory. When the last stage of the reconstruction is complete, his restored love emerges as if from a mist—this is a close-up that actually distances—and he is once again happy to have an object to look at rather than an actual human being who has weaknesses and needs.

The characters Novak plays know and resent the fact that those who pursue them are drawn only to their surfaces and have no idea of, or interest in, what lies beneath. Betty in *Middle of the Night*, Madge in *Picnic*, Lona in *Pushover*, Linda in *Pal Joey*, Molly in *The Man with the*

Golden Arm, Polly the Pistol in *Kiss Me, Stupid*, Judy in *Vertigo*—all are the prisoners of their beauty and its effect. One critic speaks of Novak's "passive carnality."[1] Her characters draw men in, but not willfully. That is not who they are or what they want, although no one cares to know.

Madge in *Picnic* complains of being the "pretty one." Betty in *Middle of the Night* yearns to be just a housewife. Polly in *Kiss Me, Stupid* lives out her real fantasy—domesticity—for a single night. Judy in *Vertigo* begs, "Can't you just love me for who I am?" Gillian in *Bell, Book and Candle* longs to be a human and not a seductive witch. Molly in *The Man with the Golden Arm* wants nothing more than to stand by her man. Even Mildred in *Of Human Bondage* projects a vulnerability that seems more genuine than the sexual voraciousness she seems driven to display.

Of the men who become entangled with the child-women Novak repeatedly portrays, only Jerry in *Middle of the Night* (played in a towering performance by Fredric March) gets it right when he says that despite her provocative and voluptuous appearance, Betty is really a little girl, insecure and in need of someone who will protect her.

It is possible that the men who directed her—Alfred Hitchcock, Billy Wilder, Otto Preminger, Joshua Logan, Richard Quine, Delbert Mann—saw her in the same way and made her into a projection of their fantasies. She seems to think so. The *Washington Post* writer Tom Shales asked (in 1996) if the women she played were "reluctant sex symbols" and if she were one too. In response, she recalled Joshua Logan's remarking that in *Picnic* she played Madge "like she was wearing a crown of thorns"; and, she adds, Madge's "looks were definitely a handicap and it was that way for me . . . too. . . . You could really get lost in that kind of image."[2]

At any rate, "that kind of image"—of the inwardly fragile beauty dependent on the men who wish only to possess her—was no longer what the moviegoing public was looking for after the early '60s, and that model of female behavior has not come into favor again (although Scarlett Johansson comes close to reviving it in some of her movies, especially Woody Allen's *Match Point*). But however retrograde it may be, that role was performed to perfection by Kim Novak, who, after all these years, can still break your heart.

1. MovieDiva website, http://www.moviediva.com/MD_root/reviewpages/MD Vertigo.htm.
2. Tom Shales, "Kim Novak: No Fear of Falling," *Washington Post*, October 14, 1996.

Larger than Life:
Charlton Heston

APRIL 13, 2008

One day more than thirty-five years ago, I pulled into the parking lot of the massive Del Coronado hotel in San Diego when an equally massive figure walked in front of my car, blocking my view because his body filled the entire windshield. It was Charlton Heston, and he strode toward the tennis courts with a purposive authority that brought to mind Moses and Ben Hur, albeit dressed this time in shorts. This was the closest I ever got to Heston in the flesh, although, like hundreds of millions of other moviegoers, I saw a great deal of him, sometimes barely clothed (*Planet of the Apes*), on the big screen.

"Big" is an appropriate word. Heston was physically imposing and he was a big movie star, someone who for several decades was the very definition of the phrase "leading man." With his passing on April 5, and the passing of Richard Widmark ten days earlier, there are no leading men of a certain kind left, even as living mementos of a bygone era. John Wayne, Anthony Quinn, Rock Hudson, Gary Cooper, Henry Fonda, William Holden, Jimmy Stewart, Burt Lancaster, Robert Mitchum, Joel McCrea, Randolph Scott, Glenn Ford, Gregory Peck. They're all gone; the only ones still alive are Clint Eastwood, who now sits behind the camera most of the time, and Kirk Douglas, in his nineties and slowed down by a stroke.

What all these fallen stars (with the exception of Widmark) shared was a physicality that radiated energy and demanded attention. They were "compelling screen presences," in part because they literally filled the screen, just as Heston filled the smaller screen of my windshield. (Lancaster often acted with his back to the camera; power emanated from it; his back was the expressive counterpart of Douglas's chest, which was bared in almost every movie he made.) It was no accident that all these guys were identified (some more than others) with the western, a genre that foregrounds the glories and trials of masculinity as they are captured in a line from Louis L'Amour's

Heller with a Gun (1955): "It was a hard land and it bred hard men to hard ways."

But Heston wasn't hard (many have testified to how genuinely nice he was), and it showed in his best performances. The fact is that Heston's size, his monumentality, was an obstacle he had to overcome in order to become the actor he wanted to be. When you saw him, it was all too easy to agree with Pauline Kael's summary assessment: "With his perfect, lean-hipped, powerful body, Heston is a god-like hero; built for strength, he is an archetype of what makes Americans win."[1] Mike LaSalle, film critic for the *San Francisco Chronicle*, remarked just after the star's death, "By size, disposition and world-view, Heston was incapable of playing a small man."[2]

But that's not right. Not only was Heston capable of playing a small man; the tension between the inner smallness he was portraying and his physical mass added strength and poignancy to the performance. A good example is the 1958 movie *The Big Country*, a powerful western directed by William Wyler (who would direct Heston in *Ben Hur* the next year and who was the director of the best American movie ever made, *The Best Years of Our Lives*).

The Big Country is a really big movie in every way—scope, landscape, music, performances, and bodies. Heston's coactors include Gregory Peck, Charles Bickford, Chuck Connors, and Burl Ives, each a large man exuding power. In this company, Heston is at best the sixth lead (although he got fourth billing), behind Peck, Bickford, Ives, and the two female stars, Carroll Baker and Jean Simmons. The key to his role is that he is not his own man. His character is in love with his boss's daughter (Baker) and he hopes that his loyal service to "the Major" (Bickford) will someday be rewarded by a piece of the ranch. These aspirations are upset by the arrival of Peck as the daughter's successful suitor. A retired sea captain entirely out of water, the Peck character nevertheless navigates quite confidently in his new surroundings. Even when he makes mistakes, and he makes more than a few, he always displays an inner ease in contrast to Heston's Leech, who is anxious, ambitious, jealous, and frustrated.

The plot gives Leech an opportunity to redeem himself, or rather to be himself, and he almost takes it but doesn't. The Major is about to storm the ranch house of his hated rival, played by Ives (they are feuding over a water source called, what else, the Big Muddy), and set off a battle that can only end with the death of almost everyone.

Leech sees the folly of the enterprise, and tells the Major that for the first time he cannot stand with him. But when the Major starts out on his own, Leech simply cannot abandon him, and he joins him, riding down the canyon to the rousing cadences of one of the best movie scores ever written. In a more conventional western, this would have come across as an act of heroism (going down with your friend despite the odds), but *The Big Country* is an attack on the code of the West, and Leech here displays his inability to break free of it. Heston is magnificent in his willingness to be small, a man of great outward strength who cannot summon the inner strength to break free of his subservience to another. (It is a tribute to his performance that Bosley Crowther's review in this newspaper barely mentioned him.)[3]

What *The Big Country* demonstrates is that Heston was really a character actor in a leading man's body, and that his basic character was not Moses or Ben Hur or El Cid but the weak and flawed inhabitant of a physical frame he could not live up to. In some of his finest films, he plays that role even when he is the leading man. *Will Penny* (Heston's favorite among his own movies) is the best example. He plays the title character, an illiterate, limited cowhand who just tries to hang on over the winter, and has no future. A future opens up to him in the form of a woman and her son, but (like Leech) he can't take it because he knows that he's not up to it, or up to much of anything else. In the end he rides away, not in the splendid isolation that marks the exit of the classic western hero who has cleaned up the town or saved the valley, but just in isolation. A reviewer at Reel. com draws the right moral: "Heston, so often required to play larger-than-life characters, delivers a sublime performance in a role that is the exact opposite."

He does it again in *Soylent Green* (1973), a film graced by the great Edward G. Robinson's final performance as on old man ready to die. (Robinson died nine days after the film was completed.) The time is a future in which overpopulation and environmental disaster have led to a dystopia ruled over by the mysterious Soylent Corporation, which distributes a food source of questionable origin. Heston plays Thorn, a police detective investigating the death of a member of the board with the help of researcher Sol Roth (Robinson). He is bitter, venal, exploitative, and thoroughly unattractive, but as he pursues his investigation, despite the attempts of his superiors to close it down, he grows into someone who is ready to risk his life in order to bear witness to the terrible truth of a society that is literally eating itself ("Soylent green is people"). Thorn is a reluctant protagonist, again a small man in a body too big for him. Reviewer Tamara Hladick, writing for Scifi.com, calls him a "dubious, ambiguous hero" and names Robinson's Roth, a big man in a small body, the film's "conscience and soul."[4]

The conscience (in a weird sense) and soul of *Touch of Evil* is Orson Welles's Hank Quinlan, a very big man in a very big body whose zeal for justice had led him to acts of corruption, including murder. Heston plays Mike Vargas, a Mexican policeman no less self-righteous than Quinlan, but much less effective. He runs around a lot and manages to place his sexy new wife (Janet Leigh) in danger while repeatedly misreading the situation he has gotten himself into. In the end, Quinlan dies because his trusted assistant tricks him into a confession, an act not of betrayal but (he explains) of fidelity to the lessons his mentor has taught him. Vargas is technically victorious; he brings down the bad guy and gets to ride out of town with Janet Leigh; but the camera lingers on the fallen bulk of Quinlan, who, even in death, receives a famous tribute from Marlene Dietrich: "He was some kind of man." Vargas may be a man someday, but not in this movie. He just looks the part. Quinlan, barely able to move and spectacularly unattractive, is the real thing. Once again, Heston uses his movie-star profile and body as foils to set off something more substantial. It is a performance of great generosity, as he yields the spotlight to the actor/director he so much admired.

It was a generosity he displayed off-screen as well as on. He supported Welles in his battles against the studio, as he would later support Sam Peckinpah, to the extent of forfeiting his salary when the famously erratic director's funding was cut off because of cost overruns incurred in the filming of *Major Dundee* (1965). He stood and marched with Martin Luther King Jr. He lobbied for the National Endowment for the Arts despite disliking some of the projects it funded. He served as the president of the Screen Actors Guild and was chairman of the American Film Institute. He was active in politics, first as a liberal democrat, before following his friend Ronald Reagan down the path of conservatism. Again like Reagan, he announced to the public that he was suffering from what appeared to be an early stage of Alzheimer's disease, ending his announcement with these famous lines from Shakespeare's *The Tempest*: "We are such stuff / As dreams are made on, and our little life / Is rounded with a sleep" (lines 4.1.148–58). When he went to his final sleep, his wife of sixty-four years was by his bedside.

And, oh yes, he was a passionate (some said fanatic) advocate of gun rights and the president of the National Rifle Association. Many on the other side of this controversy were unable to forgive him for what they considered a moral as well as a political failing, and they vilified both the man and the career. They were wrong to do so. He was some kind of man.

1. Pauline Kael, *5001 Nights at the Movies* (New York: Henry Holt, 1991).

2. Mike LaSalle, "Remembering Charlton Heston, Mr. Confidence," *San Francisco Chronicle*, April 8, 2008.

3. Bosley Crowther, "*The Big Country* (1958): War and Peace on Range in *Big Country*; Gregory Peck Stars in Wyler's Western Action-Packed Film Scores Violence," *New York Times*, October 2, 1958.

4. Tamara I. Hladik, science fiction film critic, SciFi.com, 2008.

Vengeance Is Mine

DECEMBER 28, 2009

The *New York Post* includes among its ten best movie lines of 2009 a speech delivered by Liam Neeson in *Taken* (released in 2008 in England and France): "If you're looking for ransom, I don't have any money. But what I do have are a very particular set of skills, skills I have acquired over a very long career, skills that make me a nightmare for people like you. If you let my daughter go now, that will be the end of it; I will not look for you, I will not pursue you. But if you don't, I will look for you. I will find you. And I will kill you."

No one who has seen even a few movies in the "revenge and avenge" tradition will be surprised to learn that the *Taken* script follows the Neeson character's speech exactly. The bad guys pay no attention. The hero springs into action, finds the first of his targets in less than sixteen hours, and in the following eighty or so hours, he dispatches everyone in sight (a body count of at least twenty) before a confrontation with the man behind his daughter's kidnapping brings the story to its inevitable end.

The movie also follows its predecessors in being efficient (ninety-three-minute running time); after a setup—divorced father trying too hard to please a spoiled child—there are no wasted minutes. The avenging father is on the clock—he is told that after ninety-six hours his daughter will disappear into the world of international prostitution—and so is the movie. It's bang, bang, bang, and with each bang at least one body.

The formula is surefire and fits nicely into many movie genres: the literary classic—the Richard Chamberlain *Count of Monte Cristo*, the best of many versions; westerns—Gregory Peck's *The Bravados*, Steve McQueen's *Nevada Smith*, Burt Lancaster's *Valdez Is Coming*, Charles Bronson's *Chato's Land*, Robert Redford's *Jeremiah Johnson*, Clint Eastwood's *The Outlaw Josey Wales*; lawman on a mission—Steven Seagal's *Out for Justice* and *Under Siege*, Joe Don Baker's *Walking Tall*, Bruce Willis's *Die Hard* (maybe); ex-cons/gangsters with a moral code—Michael Caine's *Get Carter*, Terence Stamp's *The Limey*, Gary Busey's *Eye of the Tiger*, Denzel Washington's *Man on Fire*, Lee Marvin's

Point Blank, Mel Gibson's *Payback*; kick-ass feminism—Uma Thurman's *Kill Bill*, Jennifer Lopez's *Enough*, Jodie Foster's *The Brave One*; and the sturdiest category of all, the worm turns or (apparently) ordinary man transformed into a killing machine—Dustin Hoffman's *Straw Dogs*, Cole Hauser's *Paparazzi*, Charles Bronson's *Death Wish* and *Mr. Majestyk*, Mel Gibson's *Mad Max* and *Braveheart*, Patrick Swayze's *Road House*, Kevin Bacon's *Death Sentence*, Viggo Mortensen's *A History of Violence*, and the comic version, Kevin James's *Mall Cop*. Gibson, who specializes in sanctified violence and the enduring of pain, has another one coming out next month, *Edge of Darkness*.[1]

The formula's popularity stems from the permission it gives viewers to experience the rush violence provides without feeling guilty about it. The plot gives the hero the same permission when a wife or daughter or brother or girlfriend (in Jodie Foster's case a boyfriend) is abducted, injured, or killed. Liam Neeson's Bryan Mills declares that he would tear down the Eiffel Tower to get at the men who have taken his daughter. He doesn't do that, but he does shoot (but not kill) the entirely innocent wife of a former colleague just to make the point that he means business. Of course, cars, buildings, airplanes, and entire towns are destroyed without a backward glance, and also without any legal repercussions. (Law enforcement officers are often secretly and sometimes openly sympathetic with the vigilante, as in *Death Wish*, *Eye of the Tiger*, and *Paparazzi*.)

Once the atrocity has occurred, the hero acquires an unquestioned justification for whatever he or she then does; and as the hero's proxy, the audience enjoys the same justification for vicariously participating in murder, mayhem, and mutilation. In fact, the audience is really the main character in many of these films. You can almost see the director calculating the point at which identification with the hero or heroine will be so great that the desire to see vengeance done will overwhelm any moral qualms viewers might otherwise have. The trick, raised to high (or low) art in *Straw Dogs*, is to have audience members thinking, and sometimes shouting, "Yes, yes, yes" in response to actions they would never countenance, never mind perform, in real life.

Or would they?

The question of violence's relationship to morality (a question debated in the arguments over "just war" theory) is raised explicitly in many of these films, often in a manner as exploitative as the films themselves, but sometimes almost seriously. In both *The Brave One* and *Death Sentence*, much is made of the fact that the victimized everyman (or -woman) has now become indistinguishable from those who inflicted the initial injuries. After hunting down and dispatching those he holds responsible for his wife's death, Gregory Peck's Jim Douglass, in *The Bravados*, discovers that they weren't the ones, although they did enough terrible things to warrant punishment. Viggo Mortensen's Tom Stall, in *A History of Violence*, tries to escape violence, but finds that he can't get far away enough; it will always return, and he must return to it in order to protect his family.

In *Gran Torino*, Eastwood's most recent attempt to have his violence and renounce it too, the protagonist neutralizes violence by becoming its self-sacrificing recipient. He makes the world pure (or at least a little better) by taking everything on himself in an obvious imitation of Christ. But in the genre's purest film, *Point Blank*, neither moral anxiety nor semireligious cleansing is anywhere in sight. The antihero Walker just wants the $93,000 his ex-partner and betraying wife stole from him. That is his only motive, although those he encounters and assaults can't believe it. They reason that there must be something behind what he's doing; but there is nothing behind him and nothing inside him. There is no point except the trivial one of getting what he's owed. It's a point that's blank.

And the ten best of these guilty pleasures? Here's my list in alphabetical order. *Death Wish, Get Carter, A History of Violence, The Limey, Mad Max, Out for Justice, Point Blank, Straw Dogs, Taken, Valdez Is Coming.*

What's yours?

1. *Edge of Darkness*, starring Mel Gibson and directed by Adrian Grunberg, was released in January 2010.

Little Big Men

MARCH 1, 2010

Not long ago at some ungodly hour of the morning, I saw an early Charles Bronson movie (*Showdown at Boot Hill*) in which the tough-guy actor played a bounty hunter driven by the fact that he was very short. Bronson (Luke Welch) spends some time explaining to his love interest that his entire life, including his decision to strap on a gun, has been a response to the humiliations visited on him because of his diminutive stature. Synopses of the movie on the Internet either do not mention this prominent aspect of the plot or touch on it only in passing, perhaps because it seems so much at odds with the figure Bronson cut (often seminaked) in a series of famous movies— *The Magnificent Seven*, *The Great Escape*, *Hard Times*, *Chato's Land*, *Mr. Majestyk*, and, of course, in what sometimes seemed to be a series of innumerable and increasingly violent *Death Wish* movies.

Bronson is by no means the only action star whose larger-than-life screen persona was or is at odds with his "real-life" statistics. (Just what those statistics are is often debated on websites where there may be a three-inch variation in the height assigned to a particular actor.) The pattern was set in the 1930s and '40s by Edward G. Robinson (*Little Caesar*), James Cagney, George Raft, Humphrey Bogart, and Paul Muni—all small men who usually played tough and cruel. Sometimes camera angles obscured the physical facts—Robinson looks absolutely huge as Wolf Larsen in *The Sea Wolf* in what can be called, without irony, a towering performance—and sometimes the camera just didn't care, as when, for example, Cagney regularly beat up men obviously twice his size.

Slightly later came John Garfield, and the smallest of them all, Alan Ladd, who played big in *The Blue Dahlia*, *The Glass Key*, and *The Badlanders*, and who more than holds his own against Ben Johnson and Van Heflin in *Shane*. (This is slightly more plausible than a slender Montgomery Clift trading blows in *Red River* with John Wayne who, it must be said, had just been shot by John Ireland.)

Famously slight Paul Newman displayed his chest and pugilistic abilities in movies like *Somebody Up There Likes Me*, *Hud*, *The Long,*

Hot Summer, and *Cool Hand Luke*. James Dean would have made the list had he lived longer. Now aging tough guy-short guys (by short I mean under five foot nine) include Jack Nicholson, Dennis Hopper, Robert De Niro, Harvey Keitel, Al Pacino, Mel Gibson, Jean-Claude Van Damme, and Sylvester Stallone, who created not one but two iconic American males, Rocky and Rambo.

And these days we have a bumper crop of undersized super-heroes—Tom Cruise, Tobey Maguire, Mark Wahlberg, and Robert Downey Jr., along with the occasionally macho Johnny Depp and Sean Penn.

So what? Who cares? Well, I care because I used to be five foot eight and now am something less. (I don't know how much less because when I'm measured at the doctor's office, I close my eyes.) And so I'm always on the lookout for celluloid he-men no taller than I am. When I find a new one, I run home to my wife and ask, "How tall do you think Mel Gibson is?" or "Who do you think is taller, Sylvester Stallone or me?" (I know it should be "I.")

The other question I delight in asking my wife is, "Did you know that (fill in the blank) is Jewish?" This is part of my effort to convince her that she is the only non-Jew in the world. Recently I have made progress in this aim by bringing home names like Kate Hudson, Helena Bonham Carter, John Houseman, Hedy Lamarr, Laurence Harvey, Daniel Radcliffe, Jennifer Connelly, Ginnifer Goodwin, Douglas Fairbanks, Harrison Ford, Bronco Billy Anderson, Mae West, Zsa Zsa Gabor, Minnie Driver, Scarlett Johansson, Jake and Maggie Gyllenhaal, Leslie Howard—yes, Scarlett O'Hara's Ashley—and my personal favorite, another Ashley, the late, great anthropologist Ashley Montagu, née Israel Ehrenberg. (Some of these are disputed because the father, not the mother, is Jewish.)

The psychology that links my two obsessions is rather obvious. Small men feel (as does Bronson's character in *Showdown at Boot Hill*) that the world belongs to big men. Seeing men you know to be small playing big on the silver screen is comforting, even though the comfort depends on a very suspect transference. Jews—at least Jews of my generation—feel that the world is always ready to blame them for its ills and that at any moment the virulent anti-Semitism that flowered in the Third Reich could erupt again. Discovering that Jews already rule some worlds and wield influence far out of proportion to their numbers is again comforting, although the comfort is somewhat diminished by the realization that it is just this overprominence that often fuels anti-Semitism. But you take your comfort where you can get it, and for me, comfort at the highest level would be identifying with a short, tough guy who is also Jewish. That means Edward G. Robinson, John Garfield, James Caan (perhaps a bit too tall), Paul Newman, and maybe Robert Downey Jr. (the Jewish father thing again). A short list, but in times of need, big enough.

Narrative and the Grace of God: The New *True Grit*

DECEMBER 27, 2010

Movie critic Dan Gagliasso doesn't like the Coen brothers' remake of the Henry Hathaway-John Wayne *True Grit*. He is especially upset because the moment he most treasures—when Wayne, on horseback, takes the reins in his teeth and yells to Lucky Ned Pepper (Robert Duvall), "Fill your hand, you son-of-a-bitch"—is in the Coens' hands just another scene. "The new film," Gagliasso complains, "literally throws that great cinematic moment away."[1]

That's right; there is an evenness to the new movie's treatment of its events that frustrates Gagliasso's desire for something climactic and defining. In the movie Gagliasso wanted to see—in fact the original *True Grit*—we are told something about the nature of heroism and virtue and the relationship between the two. In the movie we have just been gifted with, there is no relationship between the two; heroism, of a physical kind, is displayed by almost everyone, "good" and "bad" alike, and the universe seems at best indifferent, and at worst hostile, to its exercise.

The springs of that universe are revealed to us by the narrator-heroine Mattie in words that appear both in Charles Portis's novel and the two films, but with a difference. The words the book and films share are these: "You must pay for everything in this world one way and another. There is nothing free with the exception of God's grace." These two sentences suggest a world in which everything comes around, if not sooner then later. The accounting is strict; nothing is free, except the grace of God. But free can bear two readings—distributed freely, just come and pick it up; or distributed in a way that exhibits no discernible pattern. In one reading grace is given to anyone and everyone; in the other, it is given only to those whom God chooses for reasons that remain mysterious.

A third sentence, left out of the film but implied by its dramaturgy, tells us that the latter reading is the right one: "You cannot earn that [grace] or deserve it." In short, there is no relationship between the bestowing or withholding of grace and the actions of those to whom it is either accorded or denied. You can't add up a person's deeds—so many good ones and so many bad ones—and on the basis of the column totals put him on the grace-receiving side (you can't earn it); and you can't reason from what happens to someone to how he stands in God's eyes (you can't deserve it).

What this means is that there are two registers of existence: the worldly one in which rewards and punishment are meted out on the basis of what people visibly do; and another one, inaccessible to mortal vision, in which damnation and/or salvation are distributed, as far as we can see, randomly and even capriciously.

It is, says Mattie in a reflection that does not make it into either movie, a "hard doctrine running contrary to the earthly ideals of fair play" (that's putting it mildly), and she glosses that hard doctrine—heavenly favor does not depend on anything we do—with a reference to 2 Timothy 1:9, which celebrates the power of the God "Who hath saved us, and called us with an holy calling, not according to our works, but according to his own purpose and grace, which was given us in Christ Jesus before the world began."

This and other pieces of scripture don't emerge from the story as a moral kernel emerges from a parable; they hang over the narrative (Mattie just sprays them), never quite touching its events and certainly not generated by them. There are no easy homiletics here, no direct line drawing from the way things seem to have turned out to the way they ultimately are. While worldly outcomes and the universe's moral structure no doubt come together in the perspective of eternity, in the eyes of mortals they are entirely disjunct.

Mattie gives a fine (if terrible) example early in the novel when she imagines someone asking why her father went out of his way to help the man who promptly turned around and shot him. "He was his brother's keeper. Does that answer your question?" Yes it does, but it doesn't answer the question of why the reward for behaving in accord with God's command is violent death at the hands of your brother, a question posed by the Bible's first and defining post-Edenic event, and unanswered to this day.

In the novel and in the Coens' film, it is always like that: things happen, usually bad things (people are hanged, robbed, cheated, shot, knifed, bashed over the head, and bitten by snakes), but they don't have any meaning, except the meaning that you had better not expect much in this life because the brute irrationality of it all is always waiting to smack you in the face. This is what happens to Mattie at the very instant of her apparent triumph as she shoots Tom Chaney, her father's killer, in the head. The recoil of the gun propels her backward and she falls into a snake-infested pit. Years later, as the narrator of the novel, she recalls the moment and says: "I had forgotten about the pit behind me." There is always a pit behind you and in front of you and to the side of you. That's just the way it is.

Reviewers have remarked that the new *True Grit*—bleak, violent, unrelenting—is just like *No Country for Old Men*. Yes it is, but not quite. *No Country for Old Men* is a movie I could barely stand seeing once. I watched *True Grit* twice in a single evening, not exactly happily (it's hardly a barrel of fun), but not in revulsion, either.

The reason is that while the Coens deprive us of the heroism Gagliasso and others look for, they give us a better heroism in the person of Mattie, who maintains the confidence of her convictions even when the world continues to provide no support for them. In the end, when she is a spinster with one arm who arrives too late to see Rooster once more, she remains as judgmental, single-minded, and resolute as ever. She goes forward not because she has faith in a better worldly future—her last words to us are "Time just gets away from us"—but because she has faith in the righteousness of her path, a path that is sure (because it is not hers) despite the absence of external guideposts. That is the message Iris Dement proclaims at the movie's close when she sings "Leaning on the Everlasting Arms":

> Oh how sweet to walk in this pilgrim way
> Leaning on the everlasting arms
> Oh how bright the path goes from day to day
> Leaning on the everlasting arms
> What have I to dread, what have I to fear
> Leaning on the everlasting arms.

The new *True Grit* is that rare thing—a truly religious movie. In the John Wayne version religiosity is just an occasional flourish not to be taken seriously. In this movie it is everything, not despite but because of its refusal to resolve or soften the dilemmas the narrative delivers up.

1. Dan Gagliasso, "*True Grit* Review: Talented Cast and Crew Bite Off More than They Can Chew," Breitbart B website, December 8, 2010, http://www.breitbart.com /big-hollywood/2010/12/08/true-grit-review-talented-cast-and-crew-bite-off-more-than -they-can-chew/.

Les Misérables and Irony

JANUARY 28, 2013

I may have missed it, but I don't recall *USA Today* devoting a full one and three-quarters pages to a movie, never mind a movie that's been out for some time now. But there in the Life section of the Weekend edition was a lengthy discussion of *Les Misérables*, or, more precisely, a discussion of the furiously negative responses the musical epic has evoked from a gaggle of critics who simultaneously trash the film and express an incredulity verging on outrage at fellow moviegoers who don't share their view.

David Denby, writing in the *New Yorker*, after declaring that the movie is not "just bad," but "dreadful," goes on to report himself "deeply embarrassed because all around me . . . people were sitting rapt, awed, absolutely silent, only to burst into applause after some of the numbers."[1] What embarrasses Denby is the decline in "the taste of my countrymen" in the face of something that is to him so obviously "overbearing, pretentious, madly repetitive"; and he seconds the judgment of Anthony Lane, also a *New Yorker* reviewer, who dismisses the film as "inflationary bombast."[2] (Something a bit inflationary about that phrase, perhaps.)

And then there is Matt Walsh, who was dragged to the movie by his wife and found it "a thousand times worse than I could have imagined . . . [v]apid, shallow, self-indulgent and emotionally manipulative."[3] All that crying, you know.

After reading the full versions of these diatribes and a bunch more, I decided that I just had to go see for myself. So I saw the movie twice, last Friday and Saturday. The first time I liked it, the second time I loved it. Part of the reason for my increased enthusiasm was that I could better understand what the director, Tom Hooper, was up to when he employed two techniques every reviewer comments on: (1) the actors do not lip-synch the songs, but perform them "live" (what is and is not real and authentic is always a difficult question) as the camera rolls, and (2) that camera is literally "in your face"; the close-ups are so close up that, as a viewer, you are almost inside the singer's larynx. As Dana Stevens explains (not in admiration) in

Slate, while many movies "cram ideas and themes down our throats," this one may be the first "to do so while also cramming us down the throats of its actors."[4]

The key to what is intended by these technical choices was provided for me by Hooper himself when he remarked in an interview (also printed in *USA Today*) that while "we live in a postmodern age where a certain amount of irony is expected, [t]his film is made without irony."[5] Irony is a stance of distance that pays a compliment to both its producer and consumer. The ironist knows what other, more naive, observers do not: that surfaces are deceptive, that the real story is not what presents itself, that conventional pieties are sentimental fictions.

The artist who deploys irony tests the sophistication of his audience and divides it into two parts, those in the know and those who live in a fool's paradise. Irony creates a privileged vantage point from which you can frame and stand aloof from a world you are too savvy to take at face value. Irony is the essence of the critical attitude, of the observer's cool gaze; every reviewer who is not just a bourgeois cheerleader (and no reviewer will admit to being that) is an ironist.

Les Misérables defeats irony by not allowing the distance it requires. If you're looking right down the throats of the characters, there is no space between them and you; their perspective is your perspective; their emotions are your emotions; you can't frame what you are literally inside of. Moreover, the effect—and it is an effect even if its intention is to trade effect for immediacy—is enhanced by the fact that the faces you are pushed up against fill the screen; there is no dimension to the side of them or behind them; it is all very big and very flat, without depth. The camera almost never pulls back, and when it does so, it is only for an instant.

By means of these devices, Hooper manages to create on the screen something like what the Color Field painters (Mark Rothko, Helen Frankenthaler, Barnett Newman, Jules Olitski, Kenneth Noland, Morris Louis) were always striving for: "We are for flat forms because they destroy illusion and reveal truth."[6] In Color Field painting, "figure and ground are one, and the space of the picture, conceived as a field, seems to spread out beyond the edges of the canvas."[7] As a result you are not encouraged to engage in higher-order thoughts about what you are viewing; it's all very elemental; it hits you straight on. Rothko declared that "the fact that a lot of people break down and cry when confronted by my pictures shows that I communicated . . .

basic human emotions." Newman echoed the point: "I present no dogma, no system . . . I work only out of high passion."[8]

Endless high passion and basic human emotions indulged in without respite are what *Les Misérables* offers in its refusal to afford the distance that enables irony. Those who call the movie flat, shallow, sentimental, and emotionally manipulative are not wrong; they just fail to see that what appear to them to be bad cinematic choices (in addition to prosaic lyrics that repel aesthetic appreciation, and multiple reprises of simple musical themes) are designed to achieve exactly the result they lament—an almost unbearable proximity to raw, unironized experience. They just can't go with it. And why should they? After all, the critic, and especially the critic who perches in high journalistic places, needs to have a space in which he can insert himself and do the explicatory work he offers to a world presumed to be in need of it. *Les Misérables*, taken on its own terms, leaves critics with nothing to do except join the rhythms of rapt silence, crying, and applause, and it is understandable that they want nothing to do with it.

Understandable but not admirable, if what you desire from criticism is some kind of affirmation. Irony—postmodern or any other—is a brief against affirmation, against the unsophisticated embrace of positive (unqualified) values. No one has seen this more clearly than David Foster Wallace, who complains that irony "serves an exclusively negative function" but is "singularly unuseful when it comes to replace the hypocrisies it debunks."[9] Irony, he adds, is "unmeaty"; that is, it has nothing solid inside it and is committed to having nothing inside it. Few artists, Wallace says, "dare to try to talk about ways of redeeming what's wrong, because they'll look sentimental and naive to all the weary ironists." But perhaps there is hope. "The next real . . . 'rebels' . . . might well emerge as some weird bunch of 'antirebels,' born oglers who dare to back away from ironic watching, who have the childish gall actually to endorse single-entendre values. Who treat old untrendy human troubles and emotions with reverence and conviction." Enter *Les Misérables*.

1. David Denby, "There's Still Hope for People Who Love *Les Mis*," *New Yorker*, January 3, 2013.

2. Anthony Lane, "Love Hurts," *New Yorker, January 7, 2013.*

3. Matt Walsh, "*Les Misérables* Taught Me How to Hate Again," The Matt Walsh Blog, December 28, 2012, http://themattwalshblog.com/2012/12/28/les-miserables -taught-me-how-to-hate-again/.

    4. Dana Stevens, "*Les Misérables,*" *Slate*, December 27, 2012, http://www.slate
.com/articles/arts/movies/2012/12/les_mis_rables_reviewed.html.
    5. "Tom Hooper 'Confused' by Criticism of *Les Mis,*" *USA Today*, January 24, 2013.
    6. Mark Rothko and Adolph Gottlieb, "Manifesto," *New York Times*, June 13, 1943.
    7. Ibid.
    8. Selden Rodman, *Conversations with Artists* (New York: Devin-Adair, 1957), 93;
reprinted as "Notes from a Conversation with Selden Rodman, 1956," in Mark Rothko,
Writings on Art, ed. Miguel López-Remiro (New Haven, CT: Yale University Press, 2006).
    9. David Foster Wallace, "E Unibus Pluram," *Review of Contemporary Fiction*,
June 22, 1993, 151; subsequent quotes are from this source.

No Way Out: *12 Years a Slave*

NOVEMBER 25, 2013

Last week I went to see *12 Years a Slave* a second time in search of more ammunition for my conclusion, reached after an initial viewing, that it's not a very good movie. That conclusion did not survive the second viewing, and, in fact, I was completely turned around long before the midpoint of the narrative.

What had bothered me the first time is that the movie is basically an anthology of beatings and whippings, each one more severe than the last, culminating in a moment of deep horror when the hero-victim—Solomon Northup, a free black man shanghaied into slavery—takes the whip himself and administers skin-flaying lashes to a young girl (Patsey) whose only crime is wanting a bar of soap. It's like the special-effects films that come out every other day where there is an escalation of mayhem: bodies and buildings blown up in ever more ingenious ways, leading to a last scene in which everything in sight is blasted to kingdom come. In *12 Years a Slave*, the escalation is not technical—brutal realism, not video-game pyrotechnics, is the mode—but a ratcheting up of the level of pain for both the characters and the audience.

That's still my take on the movie, but I now see, and experience, the point of it. Where the point of the *Thor-Transformers-War of the Worlds* movies is to top each eye-popping scene with a scene even more spectacular lest the audience be bored and sated, the point of the relentless sequence of physical and psychological degradation in *12 Years a Slave* is to withhold from the audience an outlet for either its hope or its sympathy.

Outlets for hope come to nothing when the apparently humane and kindly William Ford, Solomon's first master, sells him to a man he knows to be hard; when his success at figuring out a way to transport lumber cheaply and efficiently is recognized warmly by his master but received by an overseer as an affront for which the uppity slave must pay; when after having been lent out to a benevolent plantation owner who allows him to keep the money earned by playing the violin at formal dances, he is returned to the Bible-spewing but pathological Edwin Epps and subjected to more of his irrational cruelty; when, having offered his earnings to a white laborer named Armsby in exchange for an agreement to mail a letter, and having been assured that the matter would remain confidential, he is immediately betrayed. In each of these moments (and there are others) a door is opened for a second, but then slammed shut. As Northup says in his memoir, "Hopes sprang up in my heart only to be crushed and blighted."[1] No way out.

Outlets for sympathy are denied the audience when, aside from the slaves who evoke sympathy by virtue of their condition, no one, except for the ineffectual first master, displays compassion, courage, or a moral sense. This is especially true of the women, who might be expected, if only because of novelistic and filmic conventions, to be the "natural" bearers of warmth and empathy. Instead, they are, if anything, more callous than their husbands. The wife of William Ford seems moved by the wailing of a newly arrived female slave; but it turns out that she is merely annoyed, and when she is told that the woman is crying because she has been forcibly separated from her son and daughter, she tells the grieving mother that after a little food and rest, she'll forget all about her children. (She never does.) Edwin Epps's wife is even crazier than he is and alternates between displaying a gross parody of Southern hospitality, when she offers baked goods to her "property" as if they were her guests, and physically assaulting the slave girl who is too much her husband's favorite. So powerful is the image of plantation mistresses who wear beautiful clothes while presiding over an appalling ugliness, that when Northup plays his fiddle at a masked ball, we cannot help seeing the young ladies who dance and simper to his tunes as petticoated tyrants-in-waiting. Even Alfre Woodard, playing a former field hand who has "ascended" to a position of being served rather than serving, emits the stench of corruption. Sitting on a veranda and taking tea with the unfortunate Patsey, who will in minutes be returned to a life of beatings and sexual violations, she says, "This is nice." A deadly moment.

The most indifferently cruel woman is Nature. The contrast between attractive surfaces and the awful reality of what goes on beneath them is underscored by the film's visual imagery. The landscape is beautiful—mossy trees, wetlands, streams, filtered light—but it takes no notice of the horrors that fill it. This is one of the oldest tropes in the pastoral tradition, which stretches from the complaint by the Greek poet Moschus (in his "Lament for Bion") that while nature has a rebirth every spring, men once dead remain forever in the cold ground, to the black worker's lament in Jerome Kern's and Oscar Hammerstein II's *Show Boat*, that while folks like us sweat and strain, "old man river, he just keeps rolling along." We would like to think that the natural world responds to human misfortunes as it does in the Gospel of Luke when at the moment of Jesus's death the sun darkens. This is called the "pathetic fallacy"—the attributing of human emotions to nature—and its "false surmise" (John Milton's phrase) can sometimes provide a moment of consolation, however fleeting. But not in *12 Years a Slave*, where consolation of any kind is absent.

Not even the consolation of religion is offered, although Epps spouts religious talk all the time and presides over mandatory services. He does so, however, to justify to himself his ownership of men and women—God, he says, has given them to me. As a result, the words of the Bible, even when they announce hope and salvation, are received by the audience as tainted vessels that have been put to the use of rationalizing man's inhumanity to man. Occasional mention is made of God's mercy and deliverance is prayed for, but there is no sign of either.

Except, it would seem, for the rescue at the end. Northup is freed when Bass, a Canadian carpenter (Brad Pitt) with strong antislavery sentiments, agrees to do what the betrayer Armsby had agreed to do and actually does it. Almost immediately a sheriff appears at Epps's door accompanied by a storekeeper from Saratoga who recognizes and vouches for Northup. The next time we see him, he is back in the bosom of his family.

That, however, is not the way it happens in the memoir on which the movie is based. Five months elapse between the time when Northup gives Bass the letter and the time when the sheriff arrives at the plantation, and it is another month before the now-ex-slave once again sees his wife and children. In those months documents are prepared, petitions are made, and governors, senators, and Supreme Court justices are recruited for the cause. Because responsibility for the outcome is distributed among these persons and the institutions they work in, when success is finally achieved, it seems to follow from a legal process that readers are implicitly invited to trust in; if it worked for Northup, it well might work for others. But in the film version, the redress of injustice is so abrupt and so quickly achieved that it is made to seem miraculous and the audience is not invited to generalize from it to any optimistic conclusion about the merits of the liberal state informed by the rule of law.

By staging the denouement this way, by presenting it as anomalous in relation to what has preceded it, the director, Steve McQueen, deprives it of any affirming power. It seems to drop from nowhere, as does Brad Pitt, who seems to have popped in for a moment from another movie (*Amistad*? *Judgment at Nuremberg*?). Unlike those films, which leave the viewer with a reconfirmed faith in the ultimate triumph of the moral order even when it has been compromised, *12 Years a Slave* leaves the viewer with a bad moral taste in his mouth.

This can hardly be an accident, given the meticulous craftsmanship of the movie's structure, the scene-by-scene attending to detail and nuance. I think what McQueen is doing is remedying the defect Northup detected in his own narrative. "If I have failed in anything," Northup writes in his final paragraph, "it has been in presenting to the reader too prominently the bright side of the picture." McQueen has carefully removed the bright sides. He gives us no reason to conclude, as Northup does, that there "was much in [Mistress Epps's] character to admire." He does not suggest, as Northup does, that "it is not the fault of the slaveholder that he is cruel so much as it is the fault of the system in which he lives." (In the movie they are one and the same.) He omits the lyrical passage in which Northup marvels at the beauty and gentleness of Miss Mary McCoy, an owner of hundreds of slaves who treats them all fairly and is "beloved" by them in return. (This is Northup's *Gone with the Wind* moment.)

And, most tellingly, he adds a detail. At a particularly low moment, Northup smashes his violin, the instrument that had brought him whatever diversion and solace he managed to have in those long years. In pastoral poetry, the breaking of the pastoral pipe (as in Spenser's "January" Eclogue, lines 71–72) signifies a loss of faith in the moral intelligibility of the universe. What's the use? Why bother? Why go on? "What boots it with incessant care to tend the homely, slighted shepherd's trade and meditate the thankless muse?" (Milton, "Lycidas," lines 64–76). These are the questions McQueen's movie poses in another vocabulary and the question Patsey flings at the world when she begs Northup to kill her. Hers is the perspective that rules the film even after its hero is returned to middle-class life, where he is again denied justice when those who captured him, sold him, and tortured him go free. Compared with *12 Years a Slave*, the darkest of the Coen brothers' movies is a walk in the park.

1. Solomon Northup, *Twelve Years a Slave* (Mineola, NY: Dover Publications, 2000).

Stand Your Ground, Be a Man

JULY 22, 2013

The Florida Stand Your Ground law is often characterized as an expansion of the venerable "castle doctrine"—because a man's home is his castle, he is justified in repelling intruders with force if necessary—but, as many have observed, it may be more accurate to see it as the return to the contemporary American landscape of the "shoot first" ethic of the Old West, at least as it has been portrayed in dozens of movies.

The opposite of standing your ground is to retreat, and in many states the rule still is that if you are confronted outside your home and violent conflict seems imminent, you have a duty to retreat (provided that an avenue of retreat is available) before resorting to deadly force. Stand Your Ground laws remove that duty; your home is now any place you happen to be as long as you are there lawfully. Wherever you are, you have the right to be there, and no one has the right to push you around.

In fact, "stand your ground" is more than a declaration of a right; it is an injunction—stand your ground, be a man. Retreating in order to avoid violence is not the commendable act of a prudent man, but the act of a coward, of someone who runs away. It is this aspect of the Stand Your Ground laws—their implicit affirmation of a code of manliness—that links them to the novelistic and filmic representations of the Old West.

Recall two iconic moments in the tradition. Early in Owen Wister's 1902 novel *The Virginian*, the hero is playing cards and one of the other players, Trampas by name, says to him, "Your bet, you son of a ____." The response is immediate—"The Virginian's pistol came out"—and the act is followed by words: "When you call me that, smile." That is, if you smile, I'll know you don't mean it, and if I know that, I'll put my gun away. An observer explains to the narrator what's going on. "He has handed Trampas the choice to back down or draw his steel," or, in other words, to back down or stand his ground.

Trampas backs down and is thereby the loser in the encounter. A loss more final is suffered by "Stonewall Torrey," a character in

George Stevens's *Shane* (1953) played by Elisha Cook Jr. Torrey is making his way to a saloon on a muddy street. Looming above him on the wooden porch is Jack Wilson (Jack Palance), a professional gunfighter who menacingly follows—we might say stalks—the nervous homesteader ("Where do you think you're going?") while serially insulting his Southern heritage. Provoked, Torrey lashes out verbally: "You're a low-down lyin' Yankee!" "Prove it," says Wilson, and when Torrey, in obedience to the code of the West, draws, he kills him. Later, Shane takes over Torrey's role, and when Wilson says "prove it," Shane does, with fatal results. Standing your ground is a good idea if you're the fastest.

In *Shane*, as in many westerns, the plot pits the forces of civilization, represented by the agricultural activities of the homesteaders, against the forces of, well, force, represented by the rancher Ryker, who is a law unto himself. The conflict is emblematized, both physically and metonymically, by the gun on one hand and women on the other. Marian, the wife of Joe Starrett (played, respectively, by Jean Arthur and Van Heflin) exclaims that "we'd all be better off if there wasn't a single gun in this valley." Of course, if there were no guns, there could be no shootings, no showdowns, and no opportunity to stand your ground. Manhood would have to be demonstrated in other ways, by tilling the ground, raising a family, running a general store.

Just what it is that constitutes manhood is debated endlessly in the genre that (at least rhetorically) wants to be on the side of civilization and peace, but can't quite ever make it, even in its revisionist period, a period that seems to begin at the beginning. Again and again, women like Amy Fowler (Grace Kelly) in *High Noon* ask their men to back away, retreat, give ground rather than stand their ground; and again and again men respond by saying, "This is a hard land" or "If we run now we'll be running forever" or "Someone has to stand up to them."

As civilization advances, and the law book replaces the gun, these rationales for violence sound increasingly hollow, and more and more westerns are self-consciously elegiac—*High Noon*, *The Gunfighter*, *Ride the High Country*, *The Magnificent Seven*, *Lonely Are the Brave*, *The Wild Bunch*, *Monte Walsh*, *The Big Country*, *Butch Cassidy and the Sundance Kid*, *The Man Who Shot Liberty Valance*—caressing the lonely figures at their center even as they say farewell to the values they embody. Outright satirical comedies like *Cat Ballou* (1965) and *Blazing Saddles* (1974) announce loudly and without nuance what the genre as a whole had already implicitly proclaimed: the reign of what Bosley Crowther (in a review of *Shane*) called "legal killers under the frontier code" was over.[1]

Stand Your Ground laws bring it all back. That is what President Obama meant when he said on Friday that such laws seem "designed in such a way that they encourage the kinds of altercations and confrontations . . . that we saw in the Florida case rather than defuse potential altercations."[2] Do Stand Your Ground laws, he asked, really contribute to "the kind of peace and security and order that we'd like to see?" The answer is that not everyone wants to see them. There are some who imagine themselves as the modern-day Wyatt Earp or Will Kane or Shane—bravely seeking out malefactors, confronting them in the main street, and shooting them down to the applause and gratitude of less heroic citizens. Stand Your Ground laws are for them.

1. Bosley Crowther, "*Shane* (1953): The Screen in Review," *New York Times* online, April 24, 1953, http://www.nytimes.com/movie/review?res=9D06EEDF143EE53BBC4C 51DFB2668388649EDE.

2. Remarks by President Obama on Trayvon Martin, James S. Brady Press Briefing Room, July 19, 2013.

Country Roads

JULY 1, 2007

"I'd like to check you for ticks."

I was taking three days to drive from Florida to upstate New York last week when I heard that line coming out of the radio on the second day. On the first day I had done the respectable thing and searched the dial for NPR and classical music; but they were nowhere to be found after I left Savannah behind, and I was free to go where I always wanted to go anyway—to a country music station. You're not going to come across a line like "I'd like to check you for ticks" anywhere else, and the same goes for an earlier line in the same Brad Paisley song ("Ticks"), "You press that bottle to your lips and I wish I was your beer."

At first I had an academic thought: this is Petrarchism updated, a modern-day turn on the convention—perfected by Francis Petrarch and passed on to John Donne and many others—of putting yourself in the place of an inanimate object that enjoys an envied proximity to your beloved. But I shook off the pseudointellectualism (at least for the moment) and surrendered to a pleasure that gets along quite nicely without the support of hallowed antecedents.

What is the pleasure? First of all, there is the sheer delight—self-indulgent, but earned—in the cleverness of the lyrics: "If I said you have a beautiful body, will you hold it against me?" (It's hard to imagine a neater instance of a purposefully ambiguous pronoun.) Where I'd like to be is "sitting next to you sitting next to me." (The repetitions and alliterations mime the closeness the singer desires.) "I turn your picture to the wall when I'm lying next to her." (Lying and lying.)

The lyrics, arresting as they are, do not stand alone. Usually they anchor a story—the motto of one station I had on was "A story in every song"—and that story typically unfolds in a three-act drama marked at the end of each act by a refrain that changes meaning with every repetition. A recent example is Emerson Drive's "Moments."[1]

In act 1, the speaker tells us that at the end of a long walk, he was about to cross a bridge when an old homeless man asks him for change. He complies—he wouldn't need it anyway, he remarks in an aside—and, clearly ashamed, the recipient of his charity declares, "I haven't always been this way / I've had my moments"—some of which he then recalls in a longish verse.

In act 2, it becomes clear (although it is never explicitly stated) that our narrator wasn't going to cross the bridge; he intended to jump. But the homeless man, recognizing "that look in my eyes" just "kept hanging around"; and it is now the singer's turn to be ashamed and to say, "You know I haven't always felt this way / I've had my moments."

In act 3, the singer, who has obviously lived to tell his tale, imagines the old man sitting "round a trash can fire" and once again rehearsing his moments . . . to which has now been added the moment "When a young man almost ended it / I was right there, wasn't scared a bit / And I helped him to pull through / . . . I've had my moments."

Not startlingly original, and a bit O. Henryish, but nicely satisfying. After all, where else can you get wordplay, narrative structure, pathos, morality, and a small dose of social consciousness in three minutes or less?

You also get an entire culture or, rather, two. There is the culture of the country music industry itself, complete with a capital city (Nashville), a famous venue (the Grand Ole Opry), a roster of legends, several dynasties, celebrity marriages, nasty divorces, innumerable rags-to-riches stories, ostentatious displays of wealth—clothes, cars, jewels, mansions, theme parks. Then there is the culture country music describes and from which its stars all claim to have emerged—hardscrabble, hard-drinking, hard-playing, and hard-praying.

The emphasis is on family values and also on the many ways family values are eroded—by neglect, cheating, crime, poverty, illness, death. The dominant tone is an unapologetic celebration of country—life virtues (honesty, loyalty, friendship, piety) in the company of a nostalgia for the days, now vanished, when those virtues really flourished: in Montgomery Gentry's "Gone," she's gone, "gone like a '59 Cadillac, like all the good things that ain't never coming back." (You could say, if you were of a mind, that country music is a version of pastoral, a genre that foregrounds a landscape that is understood no longer to exist.)

But if you enter, if only vicariously, into the country music culture, you have to swallow, along with your enjoyment, some stances and attitudes that might give you pause (or might not, depending on who you are).

It's a man's world, even though a large number of the stars and superstars are women. In this world it is men who have the responsibilities and therefore the opportunities to default on them and then write a song about it. In those songs women, especially wives and mothers, are venerated, but it is the kind of veneration reserved for forms of behavior—patience, forbearance, steadfastness, chastity—the singer can't quite get the hang of. Songs sung from the perspective of a woman are often angry; they are about betrayal and the hard road every woman will inevitably travel: "Sometimes it's hard to be a woman" (Tammy Wynette, from the song "Stand by Your Man"); "Here's to the liars and the cheaters and the cold mistreaters" (from Danielle Peck's "Here's to Findin' a Good Man").

It's a Christian world (and for "Christian" read "low-church Protestant"), where invocations of Jesus come as naturally as waking up in the morning. Think of it as Christian radio with all the sin left in. The religion is fierce and deep, and its consolations acknowledge the pain and trouble to which they are a not-always-adequate response: "God is great, but sometimes life ain't good."

It's a white world. Not racist; there is no minority bashing; there are just no minorities. (Yes, I know about Charley Pride and Cowboy Troy. Point made.)

It's a patriotic world, given to flag-waving militarism, and distrustful of foreigners and their ways of life.

It's a world without ethnicity (except for the Southern trailer-trash kind), and everyone's name sounds like two or three bitten-off Anglo-Saxon syllables: George Strait, Clint Black, Travis Tritt, Johnny Cash, Randy Travis, Vince Gill, Trent Tomlinson. Many of the names could be reversed and they'd still work fine: Travis Randy, Tritt Travis, Paisley Brad, Gill Vince, Tomlinson Trent.

It's a "classist" world, with the favored class being lower middle and the disfavored class being any with pretensions. "They raised her up a lady / But there's one thing they couldn't avoid, / Ladies love country boys" (Trace Adkins—or is it Adkins Trace?—in "Ladies Love Country Boys").

And it is a world that knows everything I have just said about it, revels in it, and puts it all into the songs. Never has a popular music scene been so self-referential. The singers caress the history they spring from, rehearsing the litany of the great singers—Hank, Dolly, Patsy, Waylon, Loretta, Willie, Tammy—whose ranks they hope to join. (Another link to the pastoral: a pastoral poet always begins by invoking a long list of predecessors.)

Of course, I wasn't thinking about any of this while I was driving. I was listening to the music and accepting its pleasures, one of which was hearing Vince Gill and Dolly Parton sing Parton's gloriously sentimental "I Will Always Love You" just as I crossed the Mason-Dixon line.

1.   This was the most played country music song of 2007 in Canada; it reached the number one spot on US Billboard Hot Country Songs charts 2006–7.

PART 3

Cultural Reflections

Professor Sokal's Bad Joke

MAY 21, 1996

When the editors of *Social Text* accepted an essay purporting to link developments in quantum mechanics with the formulations of postmodern thought, they could not have anticipated that on the day of its publication the author, Alan Sokal, a physicist at New York University, would be announcing in the pages of another journal, *Lingua Franca*, that the whole thing had been an elaborate hoax.[1]

He had made it all up, he said, and gloated that his "prank" proved that sociologists and humanists who spoke of science as a "social construction" didn't know what they were talking about. Acknowledging the ethical issues raised by his deception, Professor Sokal declared it justified by the importance of the truths he was defending from postmodernist attack: "There is a world; its properties are not merely social constructions; facts and evidence do matter. What sane person would contend otherwise?"

Exactly! Professor Sokal's question should alert us to the improbability of the scenario he conjures up: scholars with impeccable credentials making statements no sane person could credit. The truth is that none of his targets would ever make such statements.

What sociologists of science say is that of course the world is real and independent of our observations but that accounts of the world are produced by observers and are therefore relative to their capacities, education, training, and so on. It is not the world or its properties but the vocabularies in whose terms we know them that are socially constructed—fashioned by human beings—which is why our understanding of those properties is continually changing.

Distinguishing fact from fiction is surely the business of science, but the means of doing so are not perspicuous in nature—for if they were, there would be no work to be done. Consequently, the history of science is a record of controversies about what counts as evidence and how facts are to be established.

Those who concern themselves with this history neither dispute the accomplishments of science nor deny the existence or power of scientific procedure. They just maintain and demonstrate that the nature of scientific procedure is a question continually debated in its own precincts. What results is an incredibly complex and rich story, full of honor for scientists, and this is the story sociologists of science are trying to tell and get right.

Why then does Professor Sokal attack them? The answer lies in two misunderstandings. First, Professor Sokal takes "socially constructed" to mean "not real," whereas for workers in the field, "socially constructed" is a compliment paid to a fact or a procedure that has emerged from the welter of disciplinary competition into a real and productive life where it can be cited, invoked, and perhaps challenged. It is no contradiction to say that something is socially constructed and also real.

Perhaps a humble example from the world of baseball will help make the point. Consider the following little catechism:

Are there balls and strikes in the world? Yes.

Are there balls and strikes in nature (if by nature you understand physical reality independent of human actors)? No.

Are balls and strikes socially constructed? Yes.

Are balls and strikes real? Yes.

Do some people get $3.5 million either for producing balls and strikes or for preventing their production? Yes.

So balls and strikes are both socially constructed and real, socially constructed and consequential. The facts about balls and strikes are also real but they can change, as they would, for example, if baseball's rule makers were to vote tomorrow that from now on it's four strikes and you're out.

But that's just the point, someone might object. "Sure the facts of baseball, a human institution that didn't exist until the nineteenth century, are socially constructed. But scientists are concerned with facts that were there before anyone looked through a microscope. And besides, even if scientific accounts of facts can change, they don't change by majority vote."

This appears to make sense, but the distinction between baseball and science is not finally so firm. On the baseball side, the social construction of the game assumes and depends on a set of established scientific facts. That is why the pitcher's mound is not four hundred feet from the plate. Both the shape in which we have the game and the shapes in which we couldn't have it are strongly related to the world's properties.

On the science side, although scientists don't take formal votes to decide what facts will be considered credible, neither do they present their competing accounts to nature and receive from her an immediate and legible verdict. Rather, they hazard hypotheses that are then tested by other workers in the field in the context of evidentiary rules, which may themselves be altered in the process. Verdicts are then given by publications and research centers whose judgments and monies will determine the way the game goes for a while.

Both science and baseball then are mixtures of adventuresome inventiveness and reliance on established norms and mechanisms of validation, and the facts yielded by both will be social constructions and be real.

Baseball and science may be both social constructions, but not all social constructions are the same. First, there is the difference in purpose—to refine physical skills and entertain, on the one hand, and to solve problems of a theoretical and practical kind, on the other. From this difference flow all the other differences, in the nature of the skills involved, the quality of the attention required, the measurements of accomplishment, the system of reward, and on and on.

Even if two activities are alike social constructions, if you want to take the measure of either, it is the differences you must keep in mind.

This is what Professor Sokal does not do, and this is his second mistake. He thinks that the sociology of science is in competition with mainstream science—wants either to replace it or debunk it—and he doesn't understand that it is a distinct enterprise, with objects of study, criteria, procedures, and goals all of its own.

Sociologists of science aren't trying to do science; they are trying to come up with a rich and powerful explanation of what it means to do it. Their question is, "What are the conditions that make scientific accomplishments possible?" and answers to that question are not intended to be either substitutes for scientific work or arguments against it.

When Professor Sokal declares that "theorizing about 'the social construction of reality' won't help us find an effective treatment for AIDS," he is at once right and wrong. He is right that sociologists will never do the job assigned properly to scientists. He is wrong to imply that the failure of the sociology of science to do something it never set out to do is a mark against it.

My point is finally a simple one: A research project that takes the practice of science as an object of study is not a threat to that practice because, committed as it is to its own goals and protocols, it doesn't reach into, and therefore doesn't pose a danger to, the goals and protocols it studies. Just as the criteria of an enterprise will be internal to its own history, so will the threat to its integrity be internal, posed not by presumptuous outsiders but by insiders who decide not to play by the rules or to put the rules in the service of a devious purpose.

This means that it is Alan Sokal, not his targets, who threatens to undermine the intellectual standards he vows to protect. Remember, science is above all a communal effort. No scientist (and for that matter, no sociologist or literary critic) begins his task by inventing anew the facts he will assume, the models he will regard as exemplary, and the standards he tries to be faithful to.

They are all given by the tradition of inquiry he has joined, and for the most part he must take them on faith. And he must take on faith, too, the reports offered to him by colleagues, all of whom are in the same position, unable to start from scratch and therefore dependent on the information they receive from fellow researchers. (Indeed, some professional physicists who take Professor Sokal on faith report finding his arguments plausible.)

The large word for all this is "trust," and in his *A Social History of Truth*, Steven Shapin poses the relevant (rhetorical) question: "How could coordinated activity of any kind be possible if people could not rely upon others' undertakings?"[2]

Alan Sokal put forward his own undertakings as reliable, and he took care, as he boasts, to surround his deception with all the marks of authenticity, including dozens of "real" footnotes and an introductory section that enlists a roster of the century's greatest scientists in support of a line of argument he says he never believed in. He carefully packaged his deception so as not to be detected except by someone who began with a deep and corrosive attitude of suspicion that may now be in full flower in the offices of learned journals because of what he has done.

In a 1989 report published in the Proceedings of the National Academy of Science, fraud is said to go "beyond error to erode the foundation of trust on which science is built."[3] That is Professor Sokal's legacy, one likely to be longer lasting than the brief fame he now enjoys for having successfully pretended to be himself.

1. Alan D. Sokal, "Transgressing the Boundaries: Towards a Transformative Hermeneutics of Quantum Gravity," November 28, 1994. Printed in *Social Text*, nos. 46/47

(Spring/Summer 1996): 217–52; Alan D. Sokal, "A Physicist Experiments with Cultural Studies," *Lingua Franca* (May/June 1996): 62–64. Subsequent quotes in the text are from these articles.

2.   Steven Shapin, *A Social History of Truth (Chicago: University of Chicago Press, 1995).*

3.   "On Being a Scientist," Committee on the Conduct of Science, *Proceedings of the National Academy of Science*, National Academy Press, 1989.

French Theory in America

APRIL 6, 2008

It was sometime in the '80s when I heard someone on the radio talking about Clint Eastwood's 1980 movie *Bronco Billy*. It is, he said, a "nice little film in which Eastwood deconstructs his 'Dirty Harry' image."

That was probably not the first time the verb "deconstruct" was used casually to describe a piece of pop culture, but it was the first time I had encountered it, and I remember thinking that the age of theory was surely over now that one of its key terms had been appropriated, domesticated, and commodified. It had also been used with some precision. What the radio critic meant was that the flinty masculine realism of the "Dirty Harry" movies—it's a hard world and it takes a hard man to deal with its evils—is affectionately parodied in the story of a former New Jersey shoe salesman who dresses and talks like a tough cowboy but is the good-hearted proprietor of a traveling Wild West show aimed at little children. It's all an act, a confected fable, but so is Dirty Harry; so is everything. If deconstruction was something that an American male icon performed, there was no reason to fear it; truth, reason, and the American way were safe.

It turned out, of course, that my conclusion was hasty and premature, for it was in the early '90s that the culture wars went into high gear and the chief target of the neoconservative side was this theory that I thought had run its course. It became clear that it had a second life, or a second run, as the villain of a cultural melodrama produced and starred in by Allan Bloom, Dinesh D'Souza, Roger Kimball, and other denizens of the right, even as its influence was declining in the academic precincts this crew relentlessly attacked.

It's a great story, full of twists and turns, and now it has been told in extraordinary detail in a book to be published next month: *French Theory: How Foucault, Derrida, Deleuze, & Co. Transformed the Intellectual Life of the United States.*[1] The book's author is François Cusset, who sets himself the tasks of explaining, first, what all the fuss was about, second, why the specter of French theory made strong men tremble, and third, why there was never really anything to worry about.

Certainly mainstream or centrist intellectuals thought there was a lot to worry about. They agreed with Alan Sokal and Jean Bricmont, who complained that the ideas coming out of France amounted to a "rejection of the rationalist tradition of the Enlightenment" even to the point of regarding "science as nothing more than a 'narration' or a 'myth' or a social construction among many others."[2]

This is not quite right; what was involved was less the rejection of the rationalist tradition than an interrogation of its key components: an independent, freestanding, knowing subject, the "I" facing an independent, freestanding world. The problem was how to get the "I" and the world together, how to bridge the gap that separated them ever since the older picture of a universe everywhere filled with the meanings God originates and guarantees had ceased to be compelling to many.

The solution to the problem in the rationalist tradition was to extend man's reasoning powers in order to produce finer and finer descriptions of the natural world, descriptions whose precision could be enhanced by technological innovations (telescopes, microscopes, atom smashers, computers) that were themselves extensions of man's rational capacities. The vision was one of a steady progress with the final result to be a complete and accurate—down to the last detail—account of natural processes. Francis Bacon, often thought of as the originator of the project, believed in the early seventeenth century that it could be done in six generations.

It was Bacon who saw early on that the danger to the project was located in its middle term—the descriptions and experiments that were to be a window on the reality they were trying to capture. The trouble, Bacon explained, is that everything, even the framing of experiments, begins with language, with words; and words have a fatal tendency to substitute themselves for the facts they are supposed merely to report or reflect. While men "believe that their reason governs words," in fact "words react on the understanding"; that is, they shape rather than serve rationality. Even precise definitions, Bacon lamented, don't help because "the definitions themselves consist of words, and those words beget others" and as the sequence of hypotheses and calculations extends itself, the investigator is carried not closer to but ever further way from the independent object he had set out to apprehend.[3]

In Bacon's mind the danger of words going off on their own unconstrained-by-the-world way was but one example of the deficiencies we have inherited from the sin of Adam and Eve. In men's love of their own words (and therefore of themselves), he saw the effects "of that venom which the serpent infused . . . and which makes the mind of man to swell." As an antidote he proposed his famous method of induction, which mandates very slow, small, experimental steps; no proposition is to be accepted until it has survived the test of negative examples brought in to invalidate it.

In this way, Bacon hopes, the "entire work of the understanding" will be "commenced afresh" and with better prospects of success because the mind will be "not left to take its own course, but guided at every step, and the business done as if by machinery." The mind will be protected from its own inclination to err and "swell," and the tools the mind inevitably employs, the tools of representation—words, propositions, predications, measures, symbols (including the symbols of mathematics)—will be reined in and made serviceable to and subservient to a prior realm of unmediated fact.

To this hope, French theory (and much thought that precedes it) says "forget about it"; not because no methodological cautions could be sufficient to the task, but because the distinctions that define the task—the "I," the world, and the forms of description or signification that will be used to join them—are not independent of one another in a way that would make the task conceivable, never mind doable.

Instead (and this is the killer), both the "I" or the knower, and the world that is to be known, are themselves not themselves but the unstable products of mediation, of the very discursive, linguistic forms that in the rationalist tradition are regarded as merely secondary and instrumental. The "I" or subject, rather than being the freestanding originator and master of its own thoughts and perceptions, is a space traversed and constituted—given a transitory, ever-shifting shape—by ideas, vocabularies, schemes, models, and distinctions that precede it, fill it, and give it (textual) being.

The Cartesian trick of starting from the beginning and thinking things down to the ground can't be managed because the engine of thought, consciousness itself, is inscribed (written) by discursive forms that "it" (in quotation marks because consciousness absent inscription is empty and therefore nonexistent) did not originate and cannot step to the side of no matter how minimalist it goes. In short (and this is the kind of formulation that drives the enemies of French theory crazy), what we think *with* thinks us.

It also thinks the world. This is not to say that the world apart from the devices of human conception and perception doesn't exist "out there"; just that what we know of that world follows from what we can say about it rather than from any unmediated encounter with it in and of itself. This is what Thomas Kuhn meant in *The Structure of Scientific Revolutions* when he said that after a paradigm shift— after one scientific vocabulary, with its attendant experimental and evidentiary apparatus, has replaced another—scientists are living in a different world; which again is not to say (what it would be silly to say) that the world has been altered by our descriptions of it; just that only through our descriptive machineries do we have access to something called the world.[4]

This may sound impossibly counterintuitive and annoyingly new-fangled, but it is nothing more or less than what Thomas Hobbes said three hundred years before deconstruction was a thought in the mind of Derrida or Heidegger: "True and false are attributes of speech, not of things." That is, judgments of truth or falsehood are made relative to the forms of predication that have been established in public/institutional discourse. When we pronounce a judgment— this is true or that is false—the authorization for that judgment comes from those forms (Hobbes calls them "settled significations") and not from the world speaking for itself. We know, Hobbes continues, not "absolutely" but "conditionally"; our knowledge issues not from the "consequence of one thing to another" but from the consequence of one name to another.[5]

Three centuries later, Richard Rorty made exactly the same point when he declared, "where there are no sentences, there is no truth . . . the world is out there, but descriptions of the world are not."[6] Descriptions of the world are made by us, and we, in turn, are made by the categories of description that are the content of our perception. These are not categories we choose—were they not already installed there would be nothing that could do the choosing; it would make more sense (but not perfect sense) to say that they have chosen or colonized us. Both the "I" and the world it would know are functions of language. Or in Derrida's famous and often vilified words: *There is nothing outside the text.*[7] (More accurately, there is no outside-the-text.)

Obviously, the rationalist Enlightenment agenda does not survive this deconstructive analysis intact, which doesn't mean that it must

be discarded (the claim to be able to discard it from a position superior to it merely replicates it) or that it doesn't yield results (I am writing on one of them); only that the progressive program it is thought
to underwrite and implement—the program of drawing closer and
closer to a truth independent of our discursive practices, a truth that,
if we are slow and patient in the Baconian manner, will reveal itself
and come out from behind the representational curtain—is not, according to this way of thinking, realizable.

That's a loss, but it's not a loss of anything in particular. It doesn't
take anything away from us. We can still do all the things we have
always done; we can still say that some things are true and others
false, and believe it; we can still use words like "better" and "worse"
and offer justifications for doing so. All we lose (if we have been persuaded by the deconstructive critique, that is) is a certain rationalist
faith that there will someday be a final word, a last description that
takes the accurate measure of everything. All that will have happened is that one account of what we know and how we know it—one
epistemology—has been replaced by another, which means only that
in the unlikely event you are asked, "What's your epistemology?" you'll
give a different answer than you would have given before. The world,
and you, will go on pretty much in the same old way.

This is not the conclusion that would be reached either by French
theory's detractors or by those American academics who embraced
it. For both what was important about French theory in America was
its political implications, and one of Cusset's main contentions—and
here I completely agree with him—is that it doesn't have any. When
a deconstructive analysis interrogates an apparent unity—a poem,
a manifesto, a sermon, a procedure, an agenda—and discovers, as it
always will, that its surface coherence is achieved by the suppression of questions it must not ask if it is to maintain the fiction of its
self-identity, the result is not the discovery of an anomaly, of a devi-
ance from a norm that can be banished or corrected; for no structure
built by man (which means no structure) could be otherwise.

If "presences"—perspicuous and freestanding entities—are made
by discursive forms that are inevitably angled and partial, the announcement that any one of them rests on exclusions it (necessarily)
occludes cannot be the announcement of lack or error. No normative
conclusion—this is bad, this must be overthrown—can legitimately
be drawn from the fact that something is discovered to be socially
constructed; for by the logic of deconstructive thought everything is;

which doesn't mean that a social construction cannot be criticized, only that it cannot be criticized for being one.

Criticizing something because it is socially constructed (and thus making the political turn) is what Judith Butler and Joan Scott are in danger of doing when they explain that deconstruction "is not strictly speaking a position, but rather a critical interrogation of the exclusionary operations by which 'positions' are established."[8] But those "exclusionary operations" could be held culpable only if they were out of the ordinary, if waiting around the next corner of analysis was a position that was genuinely inclusive. Deconstruction tells us (we don't have to believe it) that there is no such position. Deconstruction's technique of always going deeper has no natural stopping place, leads to no truth or falsehood that could then become the basis of a program of reform. Only by arresting the questioning and freeze-framing what Derrida called the endless play of signifiers can one make deconstruction into a political engine, at which point it is no longer deconstruction but just another position awaiting deconstruction.

Cusset drives the lesson home: "Deconstruction thus contains within itself . . . an endless metatheoretical regression that can no longer be brought to a stop by any practical decision or effective political engagement. In order to use it as a basis for subversion . . . the American solution was . . . to divert it . . . to split it off from itself." American academics "forced deconstruction against itself to produce a political 'supplement' and in so doing substituted for 'Derrida's patient philological deconstruction' a 'bellicose drama.'"[9]

That drama features deconstruction either as a positive weapon or as an object of attack, but the springs of the drama are elsewhere (in the ordinary, not theoretical, world of economic/social interest) because deconstruction neither mandates nor authorizes any course of action. Participants in the drama invoke deconstruction as a justification for reform or as the cause of evil, but the relationship between what is either celebrated or deplored will be rhetorical, not logical. That is, deconstruction cannot possibly be made either the generator of a politics you like or the cause of a politics you abhor. It just can't be done without betraying it.

But, Cusset observes, "Americans do not take kindly to things being impossible," and even though the "very logic of French theoretical texts prohibits certain uses of them," they have not refrained from "taking a criticism of all methods of putting texts to work and trying to put them to work." The result is the story Cusset tells about the past forty years. A bunch of people threatening all kinds of subversion by means that couldn't possibly produce it, and a bunch on the other side taking them at their word and waging cultural war. Not comedy, not tragedy, more like farce, but farce with consequences. Careers made and ruined, departments torn apart, writing programs turned into sensitivity seminars, political witch hunts, public opprobrium, ignorant media attacks, the whole ball of wax. Read it and laugh or read it and weep. I can hardly wait for the movie.

1. François Cusset, *French Theory: How Foucault, Derrida, Deleuze, & Co. Transformed the Intellectual Life of the United States* (Minneapolis: University of Minnesota Press, 2008).

2. Alan Sokal and Jean Bricmont, *Fashionable Nonsense* (New York: Picador, 1999).

3. Francis Bacon, *The New Organon*, book 1, aphorism 59, in *Philosophical Works*, ed. John M. Robertson (London, 1905).

4. Thomas Kuhn, *The Structure of Scientific Revolutions*, 3rd ed. (Chicago: University of Chicago Press, 1996).

5. Thomas Hobbes, *Of Man, Being the First Part of Leviathan* (1588–1679). Harvard Classics, vol. 34, part 5 (New York: P. F. Collier and Son, 1909–14).

6. Richard Rorty, *Contingency, Irony, and Solidarity* (New York: Cambridge University Press, 1989), 5.

7. Jacques Derrida, *Of Grammatology* (Baltimore, MD: Johns Hopkins University Press, 1967), 158.

8. Judith Butler and Joan Scott, *Feminists Theorize the Political* (London: Routledge, 1992).

9. François Cusset, *French Theory* (Minneapolis: University of Minnesota Press, 2008).

Dorothy and the Tree:
A Lesson in Epistemology

APRIL 25, 2011

At one point in *The Wizard of Oz*, Dorothy (Judy Garland) picks an apple and the tree she picks it off protests: "Well, how would you like to have someone come along and pick something off of you?" Dorothy is abashed, and she says, "Oh, dear—I keep forgetting I'm not in Kansas," by which she means she's now entered an alternate universe where the usual distinctions between persons and objects, animate and inanimate, human beings and the natural world that is theirs to exploit, do not hold. In Kansas and, she once assumed, everywhere else, trees are things you pick things off (even limbs) and persons are not. Persons have an autonomy and integrity of body that are to be respected; trees do not. A person who is maimed has a legal cause of action. A tree that has been cut down has no legal recourse, although there may be a cause of action (not, however, on behalf of the tree) if it was cut down by someone other than the owner of the property it stood on.

All this seems obvious, but what the tree's question to Dorothy shows is that the category of the obvious can be challenged and unsettled. I thought of this scene on the last day of my jurisprudence course when we came to the chapter on animal rights and the rights of objects. The question of the day was posed by Christopher Stone's landmark article "Should Trees Have Standing? Toward Legal Rights for Natural Objects" (1972),[1] and was answered, it would seem, in Genesis 1:26, when God gave man "dominion over the fish of the sea, and over the fowl of the air, and over the cattle and over all the earth and over every creeping thing that creepeth upon the earth."

The dominion of man over animals and nature is established theologically, and it is established again in the modern period by classical liberalism's privileging of individual rights exercised by beings endowed (by either God or nature) with the capacity of choice. From Locke to Mill to Berlin to Rawls, the centrality of the freestanding deliberative individual actor is an article of faith; and if there is a center, there must be a periphery where entities that are neither freestanding nor deliberative live out their marginalized, dependent, objectified lives.

The fact that this realm of the less than fully enfranchised has at times included children, women, blacks, Native Americans, Asians, homosexuals, and Jews as well as animals and trees tells us that there is a counternarrative in which standing has been extended in an ever-more-generous arc. Stone quotes Charles Darwin observing that while man's sympathies were at an early stage confined to himself and his immediate family, over time "his sympathies became more tender and widely diffused, extending to men of all races, to the imbecile, maimed and other useless members of society, and finally to the lower animals."[2] In the same spirit, the philosopher Richard Rorty urges that "We should stay on the lookout for marginalized people—people whom we still instinctively think of as 'they' rather than 'us.'" Indeed, we should "keep trying to expand our sense of 'us' as far as we can."[3]

And how do we do that? Rorty's exhortation suggests that it's just a matter of will; just keep trying. But that advice underestimates the difficulty Dorothy gives voice to when she chides herself for forgetting she's no longer in Kansas. Hers is not a failure of memory. Hers is not a failure at all, but the inevitable and blameless consequence of having a consciousness informed by certain assumptions about the classification of items in the world, assumptions that deliver those items already cataloged and labeled, exactly in the manner Darwin labels those to whom sympathy is being extended "lower animals" and drops the adjective "useless" ever so casually, that is, without thinking. Rorty is no less limited (not a criticism, but a description) in his vision of things when he restricts the category of the unjustly marginalized to "people." What about cats, trees, stones, streams, and cockroaches?

The obvious answer to this not entirely frivolous question is, "you can't think of everything," and that's the right answer. Despite imperatives like "broaden your thinking" or "extend your horizons" or "widen your sense of 'us,'" thought is not an expandable muscle that can contain or comprehend an infinite number of things. Thought is a structure that at once enables perception—it is within and by virtue of thought's finite categories that items emerge and can be pointed to—and limits perception; no structure of thought can enable the seeing of all items, a capacity reserved for God. It follows that when you have a change of mind (of the kind the tree is trying to provoke when it addresses Dorothy), you won't see more; you will see differently. A system of distinctions (and that is what thought is) will always privilege some categories of being and devalue others, sometimes even to the extent of not recognizing them. And when one system is succeeded by another and new things come into view, some old things will have been consigned to the category of chimera and, except for histories of error, will have vanished from sight. (Thomas Kuhn's *The Structure of Scientific Revolution* is a primer on the process.)

Another way to put this is to say that changes of mind tend to be local and piecemeal, not systemic. Wholesale conversions like Paul's on the road to Damascus do occur, but more often a change will affect only a small corner of one's conceptual universe. After her conversation with the tree, Dorothy may no longer place trees and persons in completely different compartments, but much that she used to think, she will still think.

So what? Say we have been persuaded to the thesis that the things we see and the categories we place them in and the value judgments that come along with those categories are functions of ways of thinking that have their source in culture rather than nature, what follows? Is there a new tool in our arsenal?

"Nothing" and "no" are the answers to the two questions. A realization that what we see depends on cognitive structures that could change doesn't change them. Knowing that there are things you haven't thought of and couldn't think of (unless the furniture of your consciousness were transformed) doesn't give you the slightest hint of what those things might be. The every-thing-is-socially-constructed thesis, however exciting and powerful (or dreadful) it might seem as a revolution in epistemology, cannot itself initiate a revolution in any other realm; it has no political implications whatsoever.

And I say this even though each movement on the intellectual left— feminism, postmodernism, critical race theory, critical legal studies— believes that the thesis generates a politics of liberation. It doesn't; it doesn't generate anything. Consciousness-raising has always been a false lure, although changes in consciousness are always possible. It is just that you can't design them or will them into being; there is no method that will free us from the conceptual limitations within which we make invidious distinctions and perform acts of blindness. The best we can do is wait for a tree to talk to us.

1. Article appears in Christopher Stone, *Should Trees Have Standing? Law, Morality, and the Environment*, 3rd ed. (Oxford: Oxford University Press, 2010).

2. Charles Darwin, *The Descent of Man* (1871).

3. Richard Rorty, *Contingency, Irony, and Solidarity*, 1st paperback ed. (New York: Cambridge University Press, 1989).

Does Philosophy Matter?

AUGUST 1, 2011

In a recent essay about moral relativism ("The Maze of Moral Relativism," 2011) in the *Times'* philosophy series The Stone, Paul Boghossian cites a 2001 op-ed of mine ("Condemnation without Absolutes") as an example of the contradictions relativists fall into. At one moment, he says, I declare the unavailability of "independent standards" for deciding between rival accounts of a matter, and in the next moment I am offering counsel that is "perfectly consistent with the endorsement of moral absolutes." I don't regard that as a contradiction, and I would say that to think of it as one is to fail to distinguish between relativism as a philosophical position—respectable, if controversial—and relativism as a way of life, something no one recommends and no one practices.

Boghossian defines relativism (and I'll go along with his definition for the purposes of this column) as the denial of moral absolutes. But the definition is insufficiently nuanced because there are (at least) two ways of denying moral absolutes. You can say, "I don't believe there are any," or you can say, "I believe there are moral absolutes, but (a) there are too many candidates for membership in that category and (b) there is no device, mechanical test, algorithm, or knockdown argument for determining which candidates are the true ones."

The person (and I am one) who takes this second position denies nothing except the possibility (short of force or torture, and they don't count) of securing universal assent. You might say that he or she is a moral absolutist but an epistemological relativist—someone who doesn't think that there is a trump card that, when played, will bring your interlocutor over to your side, but does think that there are any number of cards (propositions, appeals, examples, etc.) that might, in particular circumstances and given the history and interests of those in the conversation, produce a change of mind.

But does any of this matter outside the esoteric arena of philosophical disputation? Let's suppose that either of two acts of persuasion has occurred in that arena: a former moral absolutist is now a relativist of some kind, or a former relativist is now a confirmed believer in moral absolutes. What exactly will have changed when one set of philosophical views has been swapped for another? Almost nothing. To be sure, you will now give different answers than you once would have when you are asked about moral facts, objective truths, irrefutable evidence, and so on; but when you are engaged in trying to decide what is the right thing to do in a particular situation, none of the answers you might give to these deep questions will have any bearing on your decision. You won't say, "Because I believe in moral absolutes, I'll take this new job or divorce my husband or vote for the Democrat." Nor will you say, "Because I deny moral absolutes, I have no basis for deciding since any decision I make is as good or bad as any other." What you will say, if only to yourself, is "Given what is at stake, and the likely outcomes of taking this or that action, I think I'll do this." Neither "I believe in moral absolutes" nor "I don't" will be a reason in the course of ordinary, nonphilosophical deliberation.

Now it could be said (and some philosophers will say it) that the person who deliberates without self-conscious recourse to deep philosophical views is nevertheless relying on or resting in such views, even though he is not aware of doing so. To say this is to assert that doing philosophy is an activity that underlies our thinking at every point, and to imply that if we want to think clearly about anything we should either become philosophers or sit at the feet of philosophers. But philosophy is not the name of, or the site of, thought generally; it is a special, insular form of thought and its propositions have weight and value only in the precincts of its game. Points are awarded in that game to the player who has the best argument going ("best" is a disciplinary judgment) for moral relativism or its opposite or some other position considered "major." When it's not the game of philosophy that is being played, but some other—energy policy, trade policy, debt reduction, military strategy, domestic life—grand philosophical theses like "there are no moral absolutes" or "yes there are" will at best be rhetorical flourishes; they will not be genuine currency or do any decisive work. Believing or disbelieving in moral absolutes is a philosophical position, not a recipe for living.

In short, the conclusions reached in philosophical disquisitions do not travel. They do not travel into contexts that are not explicitly philosophical (as seminars, academic journals, and conferences are), and they do not even make their way into the nonphilosophical lives of those who hold them. The fact that you might give one set of answers rather than another to standard philosophical questions will say nothing about how you will behave when something other than a point of philosophy is in dispute. When Boghossian declares that "Denial of moral absolutism leads not to relativism, but to nihilism," he could mean one of two things: Either (1) if you deny the existence of moral absolutes, you are committed, as a matter of philosophical logic, to nihilism, or (2) if you deny the existence of moral absolutes, you will behave nihilistically. If he means the first, he is claiming a consequence within the parameters of philosophical debate, and nothing more. If he means the second, he is committing what I call the theory mistake, the mistake of thinking that your philosophical convictions (if you have them; most people don't) translate directly or even indirectly into the way you will act when you are not in a seminar.

It seems that Boghossian means to say only the first and thus to limit the scope and significance of what he argues to the context of his professional discipline. But he veers toward the second when he remarks that those who "give up on absolute moral facts" will produce a world "without any normative vocabulary." This would be true, however, only if someone who holds to a philosophical position that gives up on moral absolutes loses the right to say that something is right or wrong. But the ability to make judgments of right and wrong does not depend on your holding a particular belief about morality in general; all that is required are the commonsense, on-the-wing criteria you bring to bear (without deep reflection) on everyday situations of choice and decision. There is no additional requirement that you root your decision in a high philosophical abstraction to which you are positively committed.

Boghossian seems to institute that requirement in his last sentence: "[W]hen we are in a muddle about what the answer to a hard moral question is, we are in a muddle about what the absolutely correct answer is." Why "absolutely"? Isn't "correct" good enough? (Of course, without "absolutely" the assertion is circular; you wouldn't be looking for the incorrect answer.) "Absolutely" is there to insist that the answer you arrive at and consider correct must be backed up by the conviction that it is underwritten by the structure of Truth and by the universe. This is a demand that makes sense if you are doing philosophy, but if you are doing anything else, it is a demand you can safely, and without contradiction, ignore.

3.5

What Did Watson the Computer Do?

FEBRUARY 21, 2011

Last week brought the story of a fourth grader who was suspended from school for having placed a "Kick me, please" Post-it on the backside of a classmate. The punishment, the *New York Post* reported, was delivered by the school principal, who said in a note to the boy's parents, "This incident is in violation of the Discipline Code and is classified as infraction A37—engaging in bullying behavior."[1]

The code was part of a "zero tolerance" policy adopted by the New York City school system, and its application in this case tells us what zero tolerance means. It means no deviation from a precisely and narrowly formulated rule. "Narrowly formulated" is redundant because a rule is supposed to be narrow in a way that leaves very little if any latitude for interpretation. A rule does not encourage one to ask if the fourth grader's act was bullying or teasing; if it fits the physical description of bullying, then bullying, or infraction A37, is what it is. A rule is an "all or nothing" proposition; it lays down the law and admits no exceptions that might be claimed on the basis of all the considerations it purposely excludes. When strong First Amendment types encounter an argument for regulating speech in certain circumstances, they respond by asking (rhetorically), "What part of 'make no law' don't you understand?" That's what's good about a rule; it stands as a bulwark against the instability and unpredictability that come along with making decisions case by case.

That's also why people—human beings—have trouble keeping to the rules. Human beings are always thinking, "Yes, I know the rule, but surely those who crafted it would agree that in the situation I now face, it should be relaxed" or "I know the rules of this game, but if I obey them slavishly, I'm likely to lose, so why don't I bend them creatively and see if I can get away with it." And then there are the familiar conundrums: The rule is no jaywalking, but only by jaywalking will I have a chance of saving the dog that is about to be hit by a car. Or I know the rule is don't lie, but telling the truth now might endanger an innocent person. Or the rule is don't travel at a speed above twenty-five miles per hour in the city limits, but my wife is about to give birth.

The rule we find unhelpful (or inconvenient) was written with a particular set of circumstances in mind, but circumstances not contemplated by the rule-makers will always turn up. When they do, rule aficionados will say, "Well, we can emend it and make it more supple by adding to the circumstances it covers." But you can never add enough; the proliferation of circumstances always outruns the efforts to take account of them, and after a while you've reached the point when every situation will require a rewriting of the rule, which means that there will no longer be a rule at all.

If you have followed the argument so far, you will have anticipated its next turn, which is to say that the inability or unwillingness of human beings to follow rules or be content with their guidance is not a weakness but a strength; it is the strength of being able to adjust when the rules have nothing helpful to say or produce absurd results in a situation the rule-makers did not anticipate. Only a fool will persist in adhering to a rule or set of directives when its application is clearly counterintuitive and even disastrous. Those who are not fools will think that this is a new game—a new situation—and it calls for new strategies, different calculations of what will and will not work.

The computer I am writing this column on is a fool. It has a program that directs it to finish words before I do by "consulting" a database of words I have used that begin with the letters I have already typed. "Consulting" is in quotation marks because the computer isn't doing anything that requires intelligence as opposed to calculation; it is sorting through data and matching the data it has stored with the data of my initially chosen letters. It is almost always wrong because its procedures do not track my practice. I am not self-consciously generating a pattern of statistical frequencies. I am producing words that have been chosen because they contribute to the realization of a governing idea or a compositional plan. In fact, to say that the computer is wrong is to give it more credit than it deserves; for right and wrong are not what it does; what it does is count (faster than I or anyone else could) and match. What it doesn't do is begin with an awareness of a situation and an overall purpose and look around for likely courses of action within that awareness. That is because, as the philosopher Hubert Dreyfus explained almost forty years ago, a "computer is not in a situation";[2] it has no holistic sense of context and no ability to survey possibilities from a contextual perspective; it doesn't begin with what Wittgenstein terms a "form of life," but must build up a form of life, a world, from the only thing it has and is, "bits of context-free, completely determinate data." And since the data, no matter how large in quantity, can never add up to a context and will always remain discrete bits, the world can never be built.

What computers can't do, we don't have to do, because the worlds we live in are already built; we don't walk around putting discrete items together until they add up to a context; we walk around with a contextual sense—a sense of where we are and what's at stake and what our resources are—already in place; we inhabit worldly spaces already organized by purposes, projects, and expectations. The computer inhabits nothing and has no purposes, and because it has no purposes, it cannot alter its present (wholly predetermined) "behavior" when it fails to advance the purposes it doesn't have. When as human beings we determine that "the data coming in make no sense" relative to what we want to do, we can, Dreyfus explains, "try a new total hypothesis," begin afresh. A computer, in contrast, "could at best be programmed to try out a series of hypotheses to see which best fit the fixed data."

That's what Watson—the IBM-built computer that won a game of *Jeopardy* last week over two human opponents—does. It's just a bigger and fancier version of my laptop's totally annoying program. It decomposes the question put to it into discrete bits of data and then searches its vast database for statistically frequent combinations of the bits it is working with. The achievement is impressive but it is a wholly formal achievement that involves no knowledge (the computer doesn't know anything in the relevant sense of "know"); and it does not come within a million miles of replicating the achievements of everyday human thought.

Watson's builders know this; when they are interviewed they are careful to stay away from claims that their creation simulates human mental processes (although they also murmur something about future hopes). But those in charge of the artificial intelligence hype are not so careful, and they delight in exciting us and frightening us with the fiction of a machine that can think. It's great theater, or in Watson's case, great television, but that's all it is.

---

1. Jamie Schram, "9-Year-Old Suspended for 'Kick Me' Sign," *New York Post*, February 18, 2011.

2. Hubert Dreyfus, *What Computers Can't Do* (Cambridge, MA: MIT Press, 1992).

None of the Answers: Charles Van Doren Finally Speaks, or Does He?

AUGUST 10, 2008

In a famous passage in the sixth book of *The Prelude* (1805, 1850), William Wordsworth recounts a walking journey in which he and a companion (Robert Jones) crossed the Alps without having been aware that they had done so. That is, they were already heading down when they believed they were still going up. The big moment they had looked forward to occurred without their noticing. What they had missed was the liminal experience of crossing a threshold, stepping across a line, passing from one state to another. One minute they're thinking about getting somewhere and the next minute they discover they're already there. They can hardly believe it and question the peasant, who has informed them:

> And all the answers which the man returned
> To our inquiries, in their sense and substance
> Translated by the feelings which we had,
> Ended in this—that we had crossed the Alps.

(lines 521–24)

I thought about these lines when I was reading Charles Van Doren's account in the July 28 issue of the *New Yorker* of his brief experience of fame and longer experience of infamy following the revelation in 1959 that his brilliant and captivating performance on the TV show *Twenty-One* was fraudulent. He had been given the answers before he was asked the questions.

It is one indication of how much things have changed that before writing this piece Van Doren had never commented on the affair. Nowadays someone who deceives the public and is found out is immediately able to make a career (in books and on talk shows) out of confession, self-analysis, and contrition. But Van Doren repeatedly refused requests for interviews and declined invitations to be a consultant either on a WGBH documentary or on Robert Redford's brilliant movie *Quiz Show*. Only now does he speak out in an essay with the promising (but artful) title, "All the Answers."

But there are no answers, at least to the questions most readers would want to ask: Why did you do it? What was going on in your mind? What about the moral issues? The moment of decision, the moment when it would seem that a university instructor might be thinking about Plato or Kant or recalling lines from great literary works ("This above all, to thine own self be true"), seems not to have occurred, or to have occurred offstage when no one, even the person most concerned, was watching.

To be sure, the moment is presented, or, rather, it is introduced and its consequences noted, but it itself never comes into focus. Van Doren has a conversation with Al Freedman, the man who had approached him about being on the show, and although nothing specific was said, he knew "that the show was fixed." He tells this to his future wife, who "didn't say much," although it is clear that "she didn't like any of it."

And then—and then it's over. Before the next sentence is delivered, the Alps had already been crossed. "My first appearance on *Twenty-One* was on November 28, 1956." How did that happen? Van Doren doesn't know: "I must have put the whole thing out of my mind, but a week after my conversation with Freedman I suddenly found myself in the studio, with the red light glowing above the camera, totally unaware that I was being watched by millions." It's as if he were sleepwalking or had been hypnotized. One minute he's wondering what to do and the next thing he (or the reader) knows, he's done it.

He then lies about it. But as he tells it, it seems that someone else is doing the lying, and he is just a spectator. When the investigations into what became known as the Quiz Show scandals begin, he is interviewed by Manhattan district attorney Joseph Stone. The interview is long, difficult, and uncomfortable, and ends with Stone saying to him, "You can lie to me, but I'm not going to let you lie to the grand jury." He lets Stone say that he lied; he doesn't say it himself. In fact, he resents the accusation: "I hated him for making me feel like a criminal; he probably saw me as an arrogant liar." Not "I was an arrogant liar," but "he saw me as one." The suggestion is that there is a disjunction between what Stone saw and what he actually was; but what he actually was—what kind of person was doing these things and for what reasons—is something we never quite find out because when he describes his behavior, it is always in the context of some situation that screens it and casts a narrative haze over it.

Immediately after telling the Stone story, he wonders "what would have happened if I had told the truth." He gets another chance when he is to appear before a grand jury, but upon entering the room he sees "that the foreman was a senior professor at Columbia, a man I knew by sight." He panics and lies again; but he has a reason that makes the lie a response to a particular situation and not a revelation of character. "If I told him the truth, I would in effect be telling everyone in the university. So I lied. This was, of course folly, since I had to tell the story anyway—to everyone, not just to him."

Folly it may have been, but it was folly that makes a kind of sense given Van Doren's relationship to Columbia University. Its community—genteel, rarified, respectable—defines his world, most especially in the figures of his famous father, poet and critic Mark Van Doren, and uncle, historian, and biographer Carl Van Doren. He would rather confess to a vast impersonal audience than humiliate himself before one of his father's senior colleagues who, on this occasion, is obviously a stand-in for his father.

The conversation he has with his father a year before the rumors of fraud become public is marked by the same combination of reticence and circumlocution (in which everything is said, but nothing is said) that marks the essay as a whole. Mark Van Doren begins by remarking that he has never asked his son about "this whole experience." But he suspects that all this fame is not good for Charles, and he urges him to "wipe the slate clean, start over." Hearing this, Charles nudges into dangerous territory. "'You think the slate is dirty?' I couldn't look at him." His indirection is then matched by his father's (this is like reading a Henry James novel; the truth of things is always entering sideways), "It's none of my business. Dirty or not—and I don't know what 'dirty' would be—the fact is you're caught up in something you may not really want." The son comments: "That was as direct as he got that day." Or any other day. ("Dad and I never talked about the quiz shows.")

The younger Van Doren got very direct in his testimony before the congressional investigating committee, but even as he admitted all, he withheld the crucial piece of information, for the very good reason that he probably didn't have it. He rehearses the arguments Freedman made to him—it's just entertainment; you will increase the public's respect for the life of the mind—but he indicates that they really weren't really persuasive. Then why did he give in? "Perhaps I wanted to believe him," he speculates, not exactly engaging in introspection, just indicating one place it might have gone. The closest he gets to the bottom of it all is a sentence that once again has a hole at its center: "Whenever I hesitated or expressed uneasiness at the course events were taking during my time on the program the same sort of discussion ensued, and foolishly and wrongly, I persuaded myself that it was all true."

How exactly did that self-persuasion occur? In his testimony, Van Doren gets right up to the edge of that question and then draws back, in deference, he says, to his audience's sensibilities: "I will not bore this committee by describing the intense moral struggles that went on inside me. I was sick at heart." "Moral struggles" names a territory that is not visited in the exposition, and "sick at heart" raises a question that is not answered. If one is sick at heart at a prospective action, why take it? We never know; all we are given is the "fact," prefaced by a sad, plaintive, "Yet." "Yet the fact is that I unfortunately agreed, after some time, to his proposal." Oh how we want to know what was going on during that "some time."

The rest is history—a job with the Encyclopedia Britannica, the publishing of books both as a solo author and in collaboration with Mortimer Adler, living in rural Connecticut, children and grandchildren, teaching Shakespeare, and now writing a piece for the *New Yorker*, the perfect venue for someone who grew up in an intellectual culture that made New York City the capital of the literary universe and Connecticut its backyard. In Redford's movie, much is made of the fact that in the world of the Van Dorens and their academic friends, television was considered vulgar. But I bet they all read the *New Yorker* and knew many who wrote for it and perhaps wrote for it themselves or were named in its columns. And I bet too that the same crowd (or their children and grandchildren) still read the *New Yorker*, which means that Van Doren has found a way of going public and speaking only in-house. (Redford implies strongly that it was Van Doren's desire to show some accomplishment of his own to his father and his father's friends that explains his actions.)

I don't intend this analysis as a criticism of Van Doren, who has undergone and survived experiences most of us have been spared and few of us could have recovered from. Quite the reverse. Whatever temptation he succumbed to in 1956, in 2008 he refuses the temptation to make an exemplary lesson out of what happened. He does not cast himself as a victim, or as a reformed villain or a misunderstood hero, three narratives that are quite popular in these days of compulsive self-discovery. Now in his eighties, Van Doren still hasn't discovered himself (do any of us?), still hasn't been able to plumb the depths of his motivations for actions that remain unfathomable, even to him, especially to him. The best thing about the essay is its refusal to claim self-knowledge while still desiring it. He imagines someone asking, "Aren't you Charles Van Doren?"—and implying by the question knowledge of what being Charles Van Doren means. Certainly it means that he is the person who did what Charles Van Doren did— "the man who cheated on *Twenty-One* is still part of me"—but it also means more, although the bearer of the name is not sure what that more is. "That's my name, I say to myself, but I'm not who you think I am—or, at least I don't want to be." It's that last bit—"at least I don't want to be"—that is so in keeping with an autobiographical writing that tells and hides all at the same time. It is what makes the essay at once maddening—because it tantalizes without finally delivering— and affecting—because you sense that the author is not playing a game or laboring to reclaim a lost honor, but trying, as best he can, to live out a life.

Can I Put You on Hold?

NOVEMBER 16, 2009

There is a class of utterances that, when encountered, produces irritation, distress and, in some cases, the desire to kill. You hear or read one of these and your heart sinks. Everyone will have his or her (non) favorites. Mine is a three-word announcement on the TV screen, "To Be Continued," which says, "I know that you have become invested in this story and are eager to find out how it ends, but you're going to have to wait for a few days or a week or a month or forever." In the great order of things, it is only a minor inconvenience, but it is experienced as a deprivation; you were banking on something and now it has been taken away.

In the same category are "Sold Out," when you've been waiting in line at a movie theater for thirty minutes (I know you can get tickets online, but sometimes you've decided to go out on the spur of the moment); "Closed for Private Party," when you've been looking forward to a meal at your favorite restaurant all day; "Back in an Hour," when you've come crosstown to buy something you need to have immediately; "Not in Service," when you've been counting on using an ATM or getting a Coke; "Use Other Door," when you've gone around a long block to get to what you thought was the main entrance; "Register Closed," when you've been waiting not-so-patiently behind a fellow customer with twenty-five items; and "The role of Violetta will be sung by the understudy," when you've spent hundreds of dollars to see Renée Fleming.

All of these messages involve something you are bent on doing or have almost done or think you have done, and then, at the threshold of success and gratification, you are stopped in your tracks. Most annoying.

Even more annoying are the messages that are instances of formal and programmatic lying. When the dentist says to you, "This may hurt a little" or "This may sting a little," you know that pain and discomfort on a massive scale are just around the corner. It would have been better had he or she said nothing. When the mechanical voice that interrupts the bad music that has been serenading you as you wait for a live person says, "Your call is important to us," everything you've already endured and anticipate enduring for many minutes more tells you that nothing could be further from the truth. When another mechanical voice says, "I'm sorry, but I don't recognize your response," you know that she's not sorry.

And when the tech specialist who has been unable to help you and seems now to be blaming you for his inability asks, ever so politely, "May I put you on hold for a minute?" you know (a) that you have no choice (b) that one minute will become five and then ten (c) that you are likely to be cut off and put in the position of starting all over again and (d) that in the event he does in fact return, you will be asked to execute still more procedures that will leave you exactly where you were when you were so foolish as to make the call in the first place.

And then there are the messages suggesting that you are either an idiot or a bad person. When you are told by a salesperson or a machine, "Your card has been denied," you feel that the bank, the merchant, and the world have made a judgment on you: deadbeat, spendthrift, bad credit risk. (This would be the case even if you had a million dollars in the requisite account.) When the prompt system intones, "If you want to make a call," you want to scream, "What do you think I've been trying to do?" When the same system says, "To return to the menu," you are being rebuked for not having a concern of the kind its universe acknowledges.

When you are admonished, "Please listen carefully as our menu options have changed," the implications are that you don't listen carefully, and that the options being offered are sufficient to your needs, and if they aren't, so much the worse for you. When your computer tells you, "This page cannot be displayed," it is as if it were saying, "What's the matter with you? Can't you even master the elementary task of getting online? Perhaps you have a five-year-old daughter who can instruct you?" And when the same computer says sternly, "Invalid user name," you wonder if you have been the victim of identity theft or are experiencing the onset of early Alzheimer's.

So there it is: a list of phrases that make you wince and say (if only to yourself), "Oh, no!," because they derail expectation or because they offer condescension and prevarication in equal measure or because they accuse you of failures and weaknesses often before you've even had a chance to do anything.

I'm sure the list could be longer, and I invite you to add to it.

I'll get the ball rolling by adding two more: "Assembly Required," which is at least honest in its advertisement and promise of frustration and humiliation; and, finally, a saying that is confined, in my experience, to the South: "We sure don't," uttered by a salesperson who is telling you not only that an item you know the store should carry is unavailable, but that she is proud and happy to be disappointing you.

So's Your Old Man

MARCH 14, 2011

In a recent column in the *Miami Herald*, Leonard Pitts criticized Mississippi governor Haley Barbour for failing to denounce the proposal to honor Ku Klux Klan founder Nathan Bedford Forrest by issuing a vanity license plate bearing his name. When pressed by the NAACP, Barbour said, "I don't go around denouncing people."[1]

"Presumably," Pitts retorted with obvious sarcasm, Barbour "would be equally non-judgmental if his state were to consider similar honors to Osama bin Laden, convicted spy Robert Hanssen or Columbine killers Eric Harris and Dylan Klebold."

Just what is Pitts demanding here? He is demanding that Barbour earn his right to be nonjudgmental with respect to Forrest by being willing to extend the same generosity to bin Laden, Hanssen, Harris, Klebold, and literally thousands of others. You can withhold judgment in this instance, he is saying, only if you would also withhold judgment in all arguably equivalent instances. What Pitts is urging (implicitly) is not the condemnation of Ku Klux Klan founders, but the principle that condemnation or the withdrawal from condemnation must be evenhanded. You get the right to say something critical of what someone of the opposite party said or did only if you would be similarly critical when members of your own party said or did something similar. And you get the right to refrain from criticizing some only if you will also refrain from criticizing others.

This is a familiar move in political argument. We saw it in spades a while ago when Democrats lamented the incivility of public discourse and blamed right-wingers for proclaiming over and over that President Obama was a foreign Islamic usurper working to undermine American values. The right replied by rehearsing the litany of things said by democrats about George Bush—he was a tool of corporate interests, a warmonger and an enemy of civil liberties. So what gives you the high moral ground, those on the right asked, when you were equally vile in your accusations?

I want to say that this is a bad move (and a cheap trick) because it deflects attention from the substantive claims being made and puts the spotlight instead on propositional consistency. The better move (by either party) would have been to insist that Obama or Bush was in fact those things and to back up the assertion with the marshaling of evidence. The better move, in short, would have been to take a stand on truth rather than shifting the focus to a calculation of reciprocal fairness. What gives someone the high moral ground is that he or she is right, not that he or she is fair.

Back in the heyday of the culture wars, conference organizers were often faulted if those invited to participate did not represent the full variety of views in the field. Many responded by adding a token something or other to every panel. Again, the better move would have been just to say that we've gathered here to elaborate what we believe to be the right position, and to require us to give time and space to positions we reject and think worthless is to require us to value process over substance; and we won't do that.

Of course, valuing process over substance is the essence of liberalism, a form of thought and political organization that begins with a strong sense of the intractability of disputes at the level of belief and proceeds to turn everything it can into a question of procedure: Were all voices heard? Was the decision made on neutral grounds and without taking into consideration matters of race, gender, economic status, ethnicity, and so on? (Sounds good, doesn't it?) Kant showed the way when he observed that "men have different views on the empirical ends of happiness . . . and their will cannot be brought under any common principle . . . harmonizing with the freedom of everyone."[2]

The solution? Remove beliefs from the political agenda—we're not going to vote on them or distribute goods on their basis—and come up with a formula for keeping them at bay while respecting the rights of citizens to have them. Kant again: "In order to organize a group of rational beings who together require universal laws . . . but of whom each separate individual is inclined to exempt himself from them, the constitution must be designed in such a way that the public conduct of the citizens will be the same as if they did not have such evil attitudes." And how do you do that? By making it a requirement that laws neither reflect the ideological view point of one party nor marginalize and/or stigmatize the ideological viewpoint of some other party. Only pass laws to which persons of any viewpoint could assent: "No one can put anyone else under a legal obligation without submitting simultaneously to a law which requires that he can himself be put under the same kind of obligation by the other person." This seems admirable, but what it means is that moral judgment is forever deferred and made subordinate to the supposedly greater good of allowing all viewpoints to flourish. (Why that is the greater good I have never been able to understand.)

If you thus give up the right to win the ideological battle and drive your opponent from the field, you and he can occupy a space of agonistic civility—you have your beliefs (now called opinions) and I have mine—in the marketplace of ideas; you will trade the possibility of total victory for the status of formal equality and you will thus do your part in keeping the marketplace perpetually open, which is, finally, what liberalism wants to do and is all liberalism wants to do. You say the Ku Klux Klan was and is bad; I say it speaks to some genuinely held interests (see *Birth of a Nation*); let's agree to disagree heartily without declaring either of our views beyond the pale.

Leonard Pitts thinks that the Klan and its views are beyond the pale—"a man who betrayed this country, founded a terrorist group and committed mass murder is a man unworthy of honor"—but he also thinks—this is his mistake—that it is an argument against the honoring of the Klan's founder that Haley Barbour would probably not give Osama bin Laden the same benefit of the doubt he seems willing to give to Forrest. (Of course, Barbour is just playing the familiar game of political equivocation.) To which I say, what does Osama bin Laden have to do with it? Bringing him and the other symbols of wrongdoing in just takes the pressure off the core moral question—was and is the Klan evil—and turns it into a question of formal equivalences. (Are you also willing to be fair to . . . ; the list is endless.)

At bottom, Pitts's case against honoring Forrest is that he was a bad man dedicated to realizing a bad cause. Just say that, and don't mess it up (and dilute it) by playing the "gotcha" card, by challenging Barbour to display his liberal bona fides and accord equal treatment to everybody. That's not what the moral life is about.

1. Leonard Pitts, "Debating Whether to Honor a Terrorist and Murderer. Really, Mississippi?," *Miami Herald*, February 20, 2011.

2. Immanuel Kant, *Political Writings* (New York: Cambridge University Press, 1991); subsequent quotes to Kant are from this edition.

Two Cheers for Double Standards

MARCH 12, 2012

What is a double standard? It's a double standard when you condemn an opponent for doing or saying something you would approve or excuse if it were said or done by one of your buddies. The double standard that is in the news these days concerns Rush Limbaugh, who called Sandra Fluke, a law student at Georgetown, a "slut" and "prostitute" because she told Congress that her university's health plan should cover the cost of contraceptives.

Limbaugh has not had many defenders (Mitt Romney said weakly that he wouldn't have used that language), but some on the conservative side of the aisle have cried "double standard" because Ed Schultz was only mildly criticized (and suspended for a week) for characterizing Laura Ingraham as a "right-wing slut," and Bill Maher emerged relatively unscathed after he referred to Michele Bachmann as a "bimbo" and labeled Sarah Palin with words I can't mention in this newspaper. If you are going to get on your high horse when Limbaugh says something inappropriate, shouldn't you also mount the steed when commentators on your team say the same kind of thing? Isn't what's good for the goose good for the gander?

These questions come naturally to those who have been schooled in the political philosophy of enlightenment liberalism. The key move in that philosophy is to shift the emphasis from substantive judgment—is what has been said good and true?—to a requirement of procedural reciprocity: you must treat speakers equally even if you can't abide what some of them stand for. Basically, this is the transposition into the political realm of the Golden Rule: do unto others what you would have them do unto you. Don't give your friends a pass you wouldn't give to your enemies.

So if you come down hard on Limbaugh because he has crossed a line, you must come down hard on Schultz and Maher because they have crossed the same line; and you should do this despite the fact that in general—that is, on all the important issues—you think Schultz and Maher are right and Limbaugh is horribly and maliciously wrong. (Some left-wing commentators have argued that there is a principled way of slamming Limbaugh while letting the other two off the hook, because he went after a private citizen while they were defaming public figures. Won't wash.)

The idea is that in the public sphere (as opposed to the private sphere in which you can have and vent your prejudices), you should not privilege your own views to the extent that they justify treating those with opposing views unequally and unfairly. (Fairness is the great liberal virtue.) This idea is concisely captured by the philosopher Thomas Nagel when he says that in political life we should regard our most cherished beliefs, "whether moral or religious . . . simply as someone's beliefs rather than as truths."[1] In short, back away from or relax your strongest convictions about what is right and wrong and act in a manner that grants legitimacy, at least of a formal kind, to the convictions of others, even of others you despise.

But there is an alternative way of looking at the matter, and it is represented in a scene (which I have discussed previously in *The Trouble with Principle*) from the classic western movie *The Wild Bunch*.[2] Two outlaws, played by William Holden and Ernest Borgnine, are talking about the gang of railroad detectives pursuing them. What rankles is that at the head of the gang is one of their old comrades. Borgnine's character is dismayed at what he takes to be the treachery of a former colleague. Holden's character explains that he gave his word to the railroad. Borgnine's character shoots back, "That ain't what counts! It's who you give it to." What counts is who your friends and allies are. You keep your word to them and not just to anybody. Your loyalty is to particular people and not to an abstraction.

The same disdain for choosing principle over family and friends was displayed by Chicago mayor Richard J. Daley when he was accused of nepotism for having steered the city's insurance business to his son's agency. Nonplussed, Daley asked (rhetorically), "Isn't that what fathers are supposed to do, help their children get a start in life?"[3]

Another assertion of the primacy of family loyalty is found in Milton's *Paradise Lost* when Satan describes himself as a "faithful leader." The angel Gabriel retorts, "Faithful to whom? To thy rebellious crew? / Army of fiends?" (4:952–53). Like Daley and like the character Borgnine plays, Gabriel rejects a notion of fidelity that is indifferent as to its object. Your faith is not binding simply because you have pledged it; it is binding only if it is pledged to the right people. (What counts is who you give your word to.) If you're going to be faithful, be faithful to the Father who made you and not to a bunch of ungrateful apostates. Obligations are not owed to everyone, but only to those who are of the right sort.

If we think about the Rush Limbaugh dustup from this nonliberal—that is, nonformal—perspective, the similarity between what he did and what Schultz and Maher did disappears. Schultz and Maher are the good guys; they are on the side of truth and justice. Limbaugh is the bad guy; he is on the side of every nefarious force that threatens our democracy. Why should he get an even break?

There is no answer to that question once you step outside of the liberal calculus in which all persons, no matter what their moral status as you see it, are weighed in an equal balance. Rather than relaxing or soft-pedaling your convictions about what is right and wrong, stay with them, and treat people you see as morally different differently. Condemn Limbaugh and say that Schultz and Maher may have gone a bit too far but that they're basically okay. If you do that, you will not be displaying a double standard; you will be affirming a single standard, and moreover it will be a moral one because you will be going with what you think is good rather than what you think is fair. "Fair" is a weak virtue; it is not even a virtue at all because it insists on a withdrawal from moral judgment.

I know the objections to what I have said here. It amounts to an apology for identity politics. It elevates tribal obligations over the universal obligations we owe to each other as citizens. It licenses differential and discriminatory treatment on the basis of contested points of view. It substitutes for the rule "don't do it to them if you don't want it done to you" the rule "be sure to do it to them first and more effectively." It implies finally that might makes right. I can live with that.

1. Thomas Nagel, "Moral Conflict and Political Legitimacy," *Philosophy & Public Affairs* 16, no. 3 (Summer 1987).

2. Stanley Fish, *The Trouble with Principle* (Cambridge, MA: Harvard University Press, 2001).

3. "Liberty in America," comment posted by rtbohan, June 18, 2008.

Favoritism Is Good

JANUARY 7, 2013

Of the columns I have written that have been negatively received, none has been greeted with more outrage than last March's "Two Cheers for Double Standards" (3.9 in this volume). The case for a single standard is familiar and easy to make. If you're in a position either to dispense rewards (a promotion, a bonus, an appointment) or level sanctions, you should do so impartially; that is, without being influenced in your decision by family membership, friendship, religious affiliation, ethnic solidarity, or any of the other considerations that can skew judgment. When a comrade and someone in the other camp engage in the same behavior, your praise or blame should be independent of the personal feelings you may have for either. Don't give your friends a pass you wouldn't give to your enemies. Don't give your brother the job if someone else not related to you at all is more qualified.

This single-standard standard—employ a calculus of merit rather than a calculus of consanguinity—asks you to regard ideological/ political differences as articles of clothing; they are cosmetic rather than essential; the person is what he is apart from them and it is the person, rather than the accidents of birth or belief or nationality, who merits your respect.

In contrast, the double-standard standard says that it's not only okay but positively good to favor those on your side, members of your tribe. These are the people who look out for you, who have your back, who share your history, who stand for the same things you do. Why would you not prefer them to strangers? In this way of thinking, personhood is not what remains after race, gender, ethnicity, and filial relationships have been discounted; rather, personhood is the sum of all these, and it makes no sense to disregard everything that connects you to someone and to treat him or her as if the two of you had never met.

Favoritism—giving more than an even break to your own kind—is not a distortion of judgment, but the basis of judgment. And being impartial to those who are a part of you—through blood or creed or association or profession (think of the thin blue line)—is not to be virtuous but to be ungrateful and disloyal, more concerned with hewing to some abstract principle of respect for all than with discharging the obligations that come along with your most intimate relations. The particularism that in the one vision is an impediment to right action is, in the other, the key to right action.

I have been making arguments like this since 1979, when I inveighed against "blind submission," the policy of erasing from submissions for publication all the identifying marks that tell the editors of a journal exactly who has produced the essay they are judging— what position he holds, what graduate program he attended, what mentors fashioned him, what school of thought he belongs to, what work he has produced, what influence he has exerted on the field. The idea is that after knowledge of these things has been put behind a veil (much like John Rawls's "veil of ignorance"), the editors will be able to make their decisions on the basis of "intrinsic merit"—a merit that can display itself, shine through, without being obscured by the distractions of a professional résumé.

I contended that there was no such thing as intrinsic merit and that merit could be calculated only in relation to those factors the policy of blind submission forbids us from considering. The "pure" or cleansed judgment the policy supposedly fosters, I wrote, "is never available," not because editors cannot distance themselves from the biases attendant upon their professional histories—biases that incline them to value submissions congenial to their scholarly convictions, much as an employer might value the job application of a relative—but because without those biases, "there would be nothing either to see or to say."

Over the years I have made essentially the same argument in a variety of contexts—when I wrote against interdisciplinarity and for disciplinary narrowness, against openness of mind and for a mind closed to error, against objectivity and for discrimination, against meritocracy and for nepotism, against formal neutrality and for affirmative action, against independent voters and for partisan zeal, against a politics that is not a respecter of persons and for what I called "rational identity politics," against wind turbines and for Nimby (Not in My Backyard), against a worship of free speech and for the deployment of censorship (not, it should go without saying, a principled censorship, but a censorship tied to my judgment of the harms produced by some forms of speech).

Now, when I make these arguments, there is a book I can refer to in the hope that its author might become the target of the brick-bats usually hurled at me. The author is Stephen T. Asma, and the book is titled *Against Fairness*.[1] Asma is a professor of philosophy, and his thesis is that "in the background of our usual thinking about fairness is the assumption of the equality of all mankind—of egalitarianism," the idea that all persons, not just the persons you feel close to, are worthy of respect. Egalitarians believe that "tribal thinking is uncivilized because it draws its circles of respect narrowly, while 'higher civilizations' include the whole human species in their circle of respect."

There is a history and a teleology here: once human beings lived in a Hobbesian state of nature intent only on satisfying their own desires and, perhaps, the desires of their nearest and dearest; only later did they mature and "slowly learn to care for others," until at the highest reaches of understanding, they learn to care for everyone.

Favoritism in this story is something we outgrow. Asma tells another story (backed up by studies of biological and psychological development): favoritism is something we grow with; it may begin in the private sphere, but "favoritism can segue into the wider public sphere and do much good there as well." Asma finds an example in the civil rights heroes who are usually, he observes, celebrated as "fairness fighters," that is, as persons who oppose discrimination as an abstraction and fight for a principle, not for a particular local outcome. No, says Asma, "Rosa Parks and Susan B. Anthony were not fighting for the equality of all people per se, but for the inclusion of their in-groups."

So what has been characterized as the struggle to end favoritism and replace it with a universal brotherhood is in fact an effect of favoritism: "Some serious allegiance to one's tribe . . . is how anything gets done at the social level—including civil rights," Asma writes. Although diversity is the banner under which our modern moral crusaders often march, no one has ever fought for diversity, for universal, undiscriminating inclusion; rather, everyone fights for the inclusion of one's own kind.

Seeing everyone as an "idealized equal"—not as a particularized being, but as an abstract autonomous agent indistinguishable in essence from all other agents—may be the imperative of a philosophical line stretching from Kant to Rawls, but it is not an imperative that does the work of the world. That work is done, according to Asma, by locally situated persons who act not out of a concern for all humanity but out of a concern for that portion of humanity with which they identify: "Do many Jewish people privilege their tribe over the interests of non-Jews? Of course, they do, and why shouldn't they?"

The answer to that question is the content of the tradition Asma argues against, the liberal secular tradition that stipulates "fairness between autonomous individual agents" (agents who know nothing of one another) as "the defining feature of our morality." Against this tradition, which has had its run for more than two hundred years, Asma poses a morality found in "other cultures, immigrant groups and . . . rural cultures in the United States."

In that morality—the morality of favoritism—fairness and rights are less important than "loyalty and patriotism, sacred/profane issues of purity, temperance [and] obedience to authority." Those who subscribe to that morality or, rather, live it out, perform acts of generosity and caring for which they need give no impartial justification. "They bring you soup when you're sick; they watch your kids in an emergency; they open professional doors for you; they rearrange their schedules for you; they protect you; they fight for you; they *favor* you."

Sounds good.

1.   Stephen T. Asma, *Against Fairness* (Chicago: University of Chicago Press, 2012); subsequent quotes in the text are from this edition.

PART 4

Reflections on Politics

Condemnation without Absolutes

OCTOBER 15, 2001

During the interval between the terrorist attacks and the United States response, a reporter called to ask me if the events of September 11 meant the end of postmodernist relativism. It seemed bizarre that events so serious would be linked causally with a rarefied form of academic talk. But in the days that followed, a growing number of commentators played serious variations on the same theme: that the ideas foisted upon us by postmodern intellectuals have weakened the country's resolve. The problem, according to the critics, is that since postmodernists deny the possibility of describing matters of fact objectively, they leave us with no firm basis for either condemning the terrorist attacks or fighting back.

Not so. Postmodernism maintains only that there can be no independent standard for determining which of many rival interpretations of an event is the true one. The only thing postmodern thought argues against is the hope of justifying our response to the attacks in universal terms that would be persuasive to everyone, including our enemies. Invoking the abstract notions of justice and truth to support our cause wouldn't be effective anyway because our adversaries lay claim to the same language. (No one declares himself to be an apostle of injustice.)

Instead, we can and should invoke the particular lived values that unite us and inform the institutions we cherish and wish to defend.

At times like these, the nation rightly falls back on the record of aspiration and accomplishment that makes up our collective understanding of what we live for. That understanding is sufficient, and far from undermining its sufficiency, postmodern thought tells us that we have grounds enough for action and justified condemnation in the democratic ideals we embrace, without grasping for the empty rhetoric of universal absolutes to which all subscribe but which all define differently.

But of course it's not really postmodernism that people are bothered by. It's the idea that our adversaries have emerged not from some primordial darkness but from a history that has equipped them with reasons and motives and even with a perverted version of some virtues. Bill Maher, Dinesh D'Souza, and Susan Sontag have gotten into trouble by pointing out that "cowardly" is not the word to describe men who sacrifice themselves for a cause they believe in.

Ms. Sontag grants them courage, which she is careful to say is a "morally neutral" term, a quality someone can display in the performance of a bad act. (Milton's Satan in *Paradise Lost* is the best literary example.) You don't condone that act because you describe it accurately. In fact, you put yourself in a better position to respond to it by taking its true measure. Making the enemy smaller than he is blinds us to the danger he presents and gives him the advantage that comes along with having been underestimated.

That is why what Edward Said has called "false universals" should be rejected: they stand in the way of useful thinking.[1] How many times have we heard these new mantras: "We have seen the face of evil"; "these are irrational madmen"; "we are at war against international terrorism." Each is at once inaccurate and unhelpful. We have not seen the face of evil; we have seen the face of an enemy who comes at us with a full roster of grievances, goals, and strategies. If we reduce that enemy to "evil," we conjure up a shape-shifting demon, a wild-card moral anarchist beyond our comprehension and therefore beyond the reach of any counterstrategies.

The same reduction occurs when we imagine the enemy as "irrational." Irrational actors are by definition without rhyme or reason, and there's no point in reasoning about them on the way to fighting them. The better course is to think of these men as bearers of a rationality we reject because its goal is our destruction. If we take the trouble to understand that rationality, we might have a better chance of figuring out what its adherents will do next and preventing it.

And "international terrorism" does not adequately describe what we are up against. Terrorism is the name of a style of warfare in service of a cause. It is the cause, and the passions informing it, that confront us. Focusing on something called international terrorism—detached from any specific, purposeful agenda—only confuses matters. This should have been evident when President Vladimir Putin of Russia insisted that any war against international terrorism must have as one of its objectives victory against the rebels in Chechnya.

When Reuters decided to be careful about using the word "terrorism" because, according to its news director, one man's terrorist is another man's freedom fighter, Martin Kaplan, associate dean of the

Annenberg School for Communication at the University of Southern California, castigated what he saw as one more instance of cultural relativism. But Reuters is simply recognizing how unhelpful the word is, because it prevents us from making distinctions that would allow us to get a better picture of where we are and what we might do. If you think of yourself as the target of terrorism with a capital T, your opponent is everywhere and nowhere. But if you think of yourself as the target of a terrorist who comes from somewhere, even if he operates internationally, you can at least try to anticipate his future assaults.

Is this the end of relativism? If by relativism one means a cast of mind that renders you unable to prefer your own convictions to those of your adversary, then relativism could hardly end because it never began. Our convictions are by definition preferred; that's what makes them our convictions. Relativizing them is neither an option nor a danger.

But if by relativism one means the practice of putting yourself in your adversary's shoes, not in order to wear them as your own but in order to have some understanding (far short of approval) of why someone else might want to wear them, then relativism will not and should not end, because it is simply another name for serious thought.

1. Edward Said, "The Public Role of Writers and Intellectuals," *Nation* online, September 17, 2001, http://www.thenation.com/issue/september-17–2001.

The All-Spin Zone

MAY 6, 2007

When Aristotle comes to the topic of style and persuasion in book 3 of his *Rhetoric*, he draws back in distaste from a subject he considers "vulgar" and "unworthy." The only reason I am talking about this stuff, he says, is because men are so susceptible to artfully devised appearances. In the best of all possible worlds we would "fight our case with no help beyond the bare facts," for after all, "nothing should matter except the proof of those facts."

Unfortunately, Aristotle laments, both our political institutions and the citizens who populate them are "corrupted" by passion and partisan zeal, with the result that the manner of delivery counts more than the thought that is being delivered. It is therefore necessary to catalog the devices by means of which audiences are "charmed" rather than truly enlightened. We must know these base arts, Aristotle asserts, so that we will not be defenseless against those who deploy them in an effort to deceive us and turn us away from the truth.

Aristotle's *Rhetoric* may be the first, but is certainly not the last treatise that performs the double task of instructing us in the ways of deception and explaining (regretfully) why such instruction is necessary. The Romans Cicero and Quintilian took up the same task, and they were followed by countless manuals of rhetoric produced in the Middle Ages, the Renaissance, the eighteenth and nineteenth centuries, and down to the present day. A short version of the genre— George Orwell's *Politics and the English Language*—has been particularly influential and is still often cited sixty years after its publication.

And now in 2007 comes *unSpun* by Brooks Jackson and Kathleen Hall Jamieson.[1] The book's subtitle tells it all: *Finding Facts in a World of Disinformation*. Once again (for the umpteen-thousandth time) we are given a report on the sorry state of things linguistic—"We live in a world of spin"—and a promise that help is on the way, in this case in the form of a few brief precepts employed as section headings: "Check Primary Sources," "Know What Counts," "Know Who's Talking," "Cross-check Everything that Matters," "Be Skeptical, but Not Cynical." The idea is that while "we humans aren't wired to think very rationally" and are prone to "letting language do our thinking for us," we can nevertheless become "more aware of how and when language is steering us toward a conclusion." In this way, Brooks and Jamieson promise, we can learn "how to avoid the psychological pitfalls that lead us to ignore facts or believe bad information."

It all sounds so—well—rational: There's a world of fact out there waiting to be accurately perceived, but the distorting power of words, abetted by the psychological disorders of passion and bias, tends to obscure it and lead us astray. And the remedy? Watch your words and watch your mental processes, paying particular attention to your "existing beliefs" lest they "reject evidence that challenges them." In short, Jackson and Jamieson recommend, "practice active open-mindedness."

But some of their examples suggest that active open-mindedness (even if it could be practiced, and I don't think it could) may not be enough. The first example in the book of the spin you should be able to see through if you are sufficiently alert is a 2006 statement by Karl Rove to the effect that "real disposable income has risen almost 14 percent since President Bush took office."[2] Jackson and Jamieson regard this claim as "so divorced from reality as to seem unhinged." Why? Because the real disposable income Rove cited "was a statistic that measures the total increase in income, not how that income is distributed." That is to say, the 14 percent increase did not benefit everyone, but went largely "to those in the upper half of society"; the disposable income of the lower half had "fallen by 3.6 percent."

Does this prove spin? I don't think so. What it proves is that in Rove's view, the health of the economy is to be gauged by looking at how big investors and property owners are doing, while in Jackson's and Jamieson's view, an economy is not healthy unless the fruits of its growth are widely shared. This is a real difference, but it is a difference in beliefs about what conditions must obtain if an economy is to be pronounced healthy. It is not a difference between a clear-eyed view of the matter and a view colored by a partisan agenda. If the question of fact is "Do we have a healthy economy?," there are no independent bits of evidence that can tip the scale in favor of a "yes" or "no," because the evidence put forward by either side will only *be* evidence in the light of economic beliefs that are structuring the arena of assessment. Those beliefs (roughly, "trickle down" and "spread the wealth") tell you what the relevant evidence is and what it is evidence of. But they are not *judged* by the evidence; they generate it.

When Jackson and Jamieson declare that Rove's "upbeat picture" of the economy is divorced from reality, they think of reality—in this case the reality of economic conditions—as ready to reveal itself, so long as we adhere to the appropriate evidentiary procedures (like "cross-check everything"). But the reality of the economic situation will emerge when one of the competing accounts (Rove's or Jackson's and Jamieson's) proves so persuasive that reality is identified with its descriptions. Language (or discourse), rather than either reflecting or distorting reality, produces it, at least in the arena of public debate. The arts Aristotle reluctantly surveys are not obstacles to clear thinking but the shapers of what will, at least for a time, be seen as clear. Clarity is not a condition of unbiased vision; it is a rhetorical achievement.

It follows then that "letting language do your thinking for you"— one of the habits of mind Jackson and Jamieson warn against—is not an avoidable option; it is simply a description of the way thought inevitably occurs. Forms of language—pieces of vocabulary, proverbial aphorisms, slogans, revered examples of wisdom, metaphors, analogies, precedents, and a whole lot more—furnish our consciousness; they are what we think with, and we can't think without them (in two senses of "without").

That is why Orwell's insistence that we "let the meaning choose the word and not the other way around" is so silly. ("Politics and the English Language" is a really terrible essay.) He says that "when you think of a concrete object, you think wordlessly," and the trick is to choose the word that reflects (without adding to or overlaying) the object's concreteness. But objects appear to us only within some discursive framework—some way of talking that is then available as a way of thinking—and someone for whom that discursive framework is alien will simply not see the objects. For those of us who work in higher education, the world is populated by perspicuous entities like classrooms, faculty offices, deans, schedules, deadlines, semesters, and so on. But someone for whom the world of higher education is a complete mystery (and there are many such) will not see these entities; they will not be objects for him because he doesn't have— hasn't internalized—the discursive forms within which they appear and have an immediately perceivable shape.

Orwell's picture of a world full of independent objects ready to receive the right description from a mind that stands to the side of public linguistic forms and just chooses (with what and in relation to what norms he never says) is a commonsense one, but it rests on assumptions that will not survive the slightest scrutiny. "First think wordlessly" sounds good as an antidote to the tyranny of words; unfortunately, it's not something that any human being can do. "Active open-mindedness"—standing to one side of our beliefs and assumptions in the service of unbiased observation—is another name for having no mind at all. Open-mindedness, far from being a virtue, is a condition which, if it could be achieved, would result in a mind that was spectacularly empty. An open mind is an empty mind.

Jackson and Jamieson would reply (and do reply) that fancy philosophical accounts of fact, evidence, and language are all right in the seminar room, but what we're interested in is the fostering of habits of mind—a skepticism that falls short of cynicism, a determination to seek out all the evidence, an awareness of verbal sleights of hand—that will make it less likely that you will be taken in by the next snake-oil salesman. This pragmatic modesty is attractive and commendable, but now and then one gets a glimpse of ambitions that are less modest. As when they suggest that if we "practice the habits of mind and the fact-checking skills . . . suggested here," in time, prompted by our example, "our leaders will follow" and the quality of our public debates would improve to the point where spin had been greatly reduced if not eliminated.

But spin—the pronouncing on things from an interested angle—is not a regrettable and avoidable form of suspect thinking and judging; it is the very content of thinking and judging. No spin means no thought, no politics, no debating of what is true and what is false. The dream of improving mankind through a program of linguistic reform—a dream that dies hard and probably never will die—looks forward to a world in which everything is always and already "unspun." There is such a world; it is sometimes called heaven and it is sometimes called death. It is never called human.

1. Brooks Jackson and Kathleen Hall Jamieson, *unspun: Finding Facts in a World of Disinformation (New York: Random House, 2007).*
2. Karl Rove, White House deputy chief of staff, speaking at American Enterprise Institute, May 15, 2006, http://www.washingtonpost.com/wp-dyn/content/article/2006/05/15/AR2006051500635.html.

Against Independent Voters

JANUARY 20, 2008

We're in that season now when we hear the same things being said over and over again, and nothing is said more often by political pundits than "this election (it doesn't matter which one) will be decided by independent voters." Accompanying this announcement is the judgment—sometimes implicit, sometimes explicit—that this state of affairs is to be welcomed, even encouraged: it's good that the independent voters are making themselves heard and forcing candidates to think outside their partisan boxes. And this judgment itself implies another: independent voters are better, in the sense of being more reflective and less ideological, than voters who identify themselves strongly with one or the other of the two major parties. The assumption is that if we were all independent voters, the political process would be in much better shape.

This seems to me to be a dubious proposition, especially if the word "political" in the phrase "political process" is taken seriously. Those who yearn for government without politics always invoke abstract truths and moral visions (the good life, the fair society, the just commonwealth) with which no one is likely to disagree because they have no content. But sooner rather than later someone gives these abstractions content, and when that happens, definitional disputes break out immediately, and after definitional disputes come real disputes, the taking of sides, the applying of labels (both the self-identifying kind and the accusing kind) and, pretty soon, the demonization of the other. In short, politics, which is what independent voters hate.

They tend to agree with (and quote) George Washington. In his farewell address (1796), Washington spoke of the "baneful effects of the spirit of party," which includes "ill-founded jealousies and false alarms," "the animosity of one part against another," and the propagation of the "belief that there is a real difference of local interests and views." Parties, he concluded, "make the public administration the mirror of the ill-concerted . . . projects of faction rather than the organ of consistent and wholesome plans digested by common counsels and modified by mutual interests."

Consistent, wholesome, common versus conflicted, divided, factional. Mutual interests—interests that are shared—are what we want rather than special interests. This is the rhetoric and vocabulary of the independent voter, for whom it is an article of faith that differences are inessential and that what unites us is larger and more important than what divides us. Why can't we all just get along?

Washington himself knows why. The spirit of party, he says, "unfortunately is inseparable from our nature," from our tendency, that is, to identify our passions with what is right and true. Factionalism is not a deviation from ordinary human behavior; it *is* ordinary human behavior. (That is why checks and balances figure so prominently in *The Federalist Papers*.) Human beings are situated creatures; they see things not from a God's-eye point of view, but from the point of view of the beliefs, allegiances, aspirations, and fears they bring with them into the ballot box.

Floating independently above the fray and inhabiting the marketplace of ideas as if it were a shopping bazaar rather than a battlefield is an unnatural condition. The natural condition is to be political. To be political is to believe something, and to believe something is to believe that those who believe something else are wrong, and after all, you don't want people who believe (and would do) the wrong things running your government. So you organize with other like-minded folks and smite the enemy (verbally) hip and thigh. You join a party.

What do independent voters do? Well, most of all, they talk about the virtue of being an independent voter. When they are asked to explain what that means, they say, "I can't stand the partisan atmosphere that has infected our politics" (forgetting that politics is partisan by definition); or "we like to make up our own minds and don't want anyone telling us what to do (as if Democrats and Republicans were sheep eager to go over whatever cliff the leadership brings them to); or (and this was a favorite of those interviewed in Iowa and New Hampshire), "we vote the person rather than the party."

Now, voting the person rather than the party is about the dumbest thing you can do, for a reason I elaborated in an earlier column ("Parties Matter," April 8, 2007). The party affiliation of a candidate tells you what kind of appointments he or she is likely to make. Do you think that regulations of industry stifle productivity and damage the economy, or do you think that unregulated industries endanger the environment? Do you think that illegal immigrants are just that—illegal—and therefore should be deported when detected, or do you think that we should figure out a way to legitimize their status and make the best of what has already happened? Do you think that Iran poses a threat that must be countered before it is too late, or do you think that military action should be resorted to only after every avenue of diplomacy has been exhausted, even if it takes years or decades?

If you feel strongly about these and other matters, it is incumbent upon you to take into consideration the positions of the two major parties, for the successful candidate can be counted on to appoint to the offices responsible for answering these questions men and women whose views reflect the party's platform. Voting the person, however attractive or impressive he or she may be, could very well get you four years of policies you detest. In other words, policy differences are party differences, and it is hard to see how you could be a responsible voter if you held your nose at a whiff of party politics. If you are really interested in the way things should go in the country, come off the high pedestal and join the rest of us in the nurturing (and, yes, dirty) soil of the partisan free-for-all.

To this an independent voter might reply that the two-party structure is the problem, and if we could only elect an independent candidate, he or she wouldn't be beholden to any party and could make appointments on the basis of merit. But even if this miracle were to occur, the parties would still be in control of federal and state legislative bodies, and in order to do anything at all, an independent president would have to negotiate with the very political forces he or she beat up on in the course of getting elected. (There goes independence.) And what leverage would a president in that position have?

In the end, there is nothing to be said for independent voters and a lot to be said against them. Remember, a bunch of them voted for Ralph Nader. Case closed.

When "Identity Politics" Is Rational

FEBRUARY 17, 2008

If there's anything everyone is against in these election times, it's "identity politics," a phrase that covers a multitude of sins. Let me start with a definition. (It may not be yours, but it will at least allow the discussion to be framed.) You're practicing identity politics when you vote for or against someone because of his or her skin color, ethnicity, religion, gender, sexual orientation, or any other marker that leads you to say yes or no independently of a candidate's ideas or policies. In essence identity politics is an affirmation of the tribe against the claims of ideology, and by ideology I do not mean something bad (a mistake frequently made), but any agenda informed by a vision of what the world should be like.

An identity politics voter says, in effect, I don't care what views he holds, or even what bad things he may have done, or what lack of ability he may display; he's my brother, or he's my kinsman, or he's my lonsman, or he comes from the neighborhood, or he's a Southerner, or (and here the tribe is really big) my country right or wrong. "My country right or wrong" is particularly useful in making clear how identity politics differs from politics as many Americans would prefer to see it practiced. Rather than saying she's right on immigration or he's wrong on the war, the identity politics voter says he looks like me or she and I belong to the same church.

Identity politics is illiberal. That is, it is particularist, whereas liberalism is universalist. The history of liberalism is a history of extending the franchise to those who were once excluded from it by their race, gender, or national origin. Although these marks of identification were retained (by the census and other forms of governmental classification) and could still be celebrated in private associations like the church and the social club, they were not supposed to be the basis of decisions one might make "as a citizen," decisions about who might best lead the country, or what laws should be enacted or voted down. Deciding as a citizen means deciding not as a man or a woman or a Jew or an African American or a Caucasian or a heterosexual, but as a human being.

Stanley Crouch believes that the project of liberal universalizing is now pretty much complete and that "elements of distinction"—his phrase for the thinking that was fashionable in "the era of 'identity politics'"—"have become secondary to the power of human qualities with which anyone can identify or reject."[1] But his judgment is belied by almost everything that is going on in this campaign. As I write this I am watching the returns from the "Potomac Primary," and the news is being presented entirely in racial, ethnic, and gender terms. Every newspaper or magazine article I read does the same thing. The Obama and Clinton campaigns accuse each other of playing the race card or the gender card. A Hispanic superdelegate warns that by replacing her Latino campaign manager with a black one, Senator Clinton risks losing his vote and the vote of other Hispanic delegates he is in the process of contacting.

Christopher Hitchens looks at the scene and is disgusted by behavior that, in his view, "keeps us anchored in the past."[2] He will not, he tells us, vote for Clinton just so that we can have the "first woman president" (I don't remember that one from the past); and he won't vote for Obama, who, he says, "wants us to transcend something at the same time he implicitly asks us to give that same something as a reason to vote for him." It would seem that we are far from realizing Ken Connor's dream that we might judge "all of the presidential hopefuls on the basis of the content of their character and their qualifications to serve."[3]

But is it as bad as all that? Is it so irrational and retrograde to base one's vote on the gender or race of religion or ethnicity of a candidate? Not necessarily. If the vote is given (or withheld) only because the candidate looks like you or has the same religion, it does seem a shallow and meretricious act, for it is an act unsupported by reasons. "Because she is a woman as I am" is, of course, a reason, but it is not a reason of the relevant kind, a reason that cites goals and programs, and argues for them. But suppose what was said was something like this: "As a woman I find government-sponsored research skewed in the direction of diseases that afflict men and inattentive to the medical problems faced by women, and it is my belief that a woman president will devote resources to the solution of those problems." That's an identity politics argument that is thick, not thin; the she's-like-me point is not invoked as sufficient unto itself but as it relates to a matter of policy. The calculation may or may not pan out (successful candidates both disappoint and surprise), but it is a calculation of the right kind.

One objection to identity politics (Crouch makes it in the same column) is that groups and populations are not monolithic but display a diversity of attitudes and positions. Yes they do, but members of a group who might disagree with each other on any number of things could nevertheless come together on a matter of shared concern. American Jews, for example, have widely varying views on many important issues—tax cuts, tort reform, gay marriage, the Iraq war. Still, the vast majority believes that it is important to defend the security of Israel. This is a belief shared even by those American Jews who are strongly critical of Israel's treatment of the Palestinians. They may deplore Israel's actions and agree with Jimmy Carter when he likens them to apartheid, but if the choice is between a politician who pledges to support Israel and a politician who would withdraw support and leave the Jewish state to fend for itself, most of them would vote for the first candidate every time.

African Americans are no less heterogeneous in their views than Jewish Americans. Yet every African American—conservative or liberal, rich or poor, barely educated or highly educated—meets with obstacles to his or her success and mobility, which are all the more frustrating because they are structural (built into the culture's ways of perceiving) rather than official. To the non–African American, these obstacles will be more or less invisible, especially in a country where access to opportunity is guaranteed by law. It makes sense, therefore, that an African American voter could come to the conclusion that an African American candidate would be likely to fight for changes that could remove barriers a white candidate might not even see. A vote given for that reason would be a vote based on identity, but it would be more than a mere affirmation of fellowship (he's one of mine and I have to support him); it would be a considered political judgment as to which candidate will move the country in a preferred direction. Identity might be the trigger of the vote, but it would not be the whole of its content.

We should distinguish, I think, between two forms of identity politics. The first I have already named "tribal"; it is the politics based on who a candidate is rather than on what he or she believes or argues for. And that, I agree, is usually a bad idea. (I say "usually" because it is possible to argue that the election of a black or female president, no matter what his or her positions happen to be, will be more than a symbolic correction of the errors that have marred the country's history, and an important international statement as well.) The second form of identity politics is what I call "interest" identity politics. It is based on the assumption (itself resting on history and observation) that because of his or her race or ethnicity or gender a candidate might pursue an agenda that would advance the interests a voter is committed to. Not only is there nothing wrong with such a calculation—it is both rational and considered—I don't see that there is an alternative to voting on the basis of interest.

The alternative usually put forward is Crouch's: Vote "for human qualities" rather than sectarian qualities. That is, vote on the basis of reasons everyone, no matter what his or her identity, will acknowledge as worthy. But there are no such reasons and no such human qualities. To be sure, there are words often attached to this chimera—integrity, dedication, honesty, intellect, to name a few. But these qualities, even when they are found, will always be in the service of some set of policies you either favor or reject. It is those policies, not the probity of their proposer, that you will be voting for. (If your candidate is also a good person, that's a nice bonus, but it isn't the essential thing.) You will be voting, in short, for interests, and those who do not have an investment in those interests will be voting for someone else.

What this means is that the ritual deprecation of "special interests" makes no sense. All interests are special interests—proceed from some contestable point of view—and none is "generally human." And that is why identity interests, as long as they are ideological and not merely tribal, constitute a perfectly respectable reason for awarding your vote.

1. Stanley Crouch, "The Democratic Contest Is No Longer about Race, If It Ever Was," *Daily News*, February 10, 2008.

2. Christopher Hitchens, "The Perils of Identity Politics," *Wall Street Journal*, January 18, 2008.

3. Ken Connor, "Voters Should Reject Identity Politics," Townhall.com, January 20, 2008.

Blowin' in the Wind

AUGUST 26, 2007

When the issue of energy came up in the debate among the Democratic presidential contenders on August 7, the candidates began talking about "renewable" energy, and one of them (Chris Dodd) mentioned wind power. Seems logical. Why spend all the effort and money to build huge electricity plants when the wind is always blowing? Who could argue against a technology that promises to derive energy from a renewable, and free, resource?

Everyone I know.

For five months of the year, I live in the very small town of Andes, New York. Each year has its signature event—floods, drought, road construction, caterpillars. And 2006 to 2007 has been the year of the wind turbines.

Like many of the other towns targeted by the wind turbine industry, Andes is a rural community that over the years has lost its economic base. At one time the hills and valleys were home to many small dairy farms, but most of them are no longer in operation, and no industry, light or heavy, has taken their place. Now the area relies for its revenue on retirees and second home owners who are educated, relatively well off, and tend to be teachers, therapists, lawyers, artists, and social workers. In short, liberals. They are all soldiers in Al Gore's army, into organic foods, hybrid cars, clean air, clean water, the whole bit.

They are also against wind power.

Their reasons are the ones always given by those who wake up to find the wind interests at their door. Even if large wind farms were in place throughout the country, the electricity produced would be a very small percentage of the electricity we use. Because the turbines are huge, four hundred feet or more, installing them involves tearing up the ridges on which they are placed. Once in operation, they cast shadows and produce noise. Their blades cause a "flicker" effect, kill birds, and interfere with migration. The outsized towers ruin scenic views and depress real-estate values.

These last two reasons are seized on by wind proponents who say that a few elite newcomers are putting their aesthetic preferences ahead of both the community's welfare and the national effort to shift to green energy as a way of slowing down global warming.

It's a nice line, but it won't fly. The wind companies may advertise themselves as environmentalists, but they are really developers, which means that they do things with other peoples' money—yours. Wind farms are attractive as an investment because the combination of tax credits, tax shelters, and accelerated depreciation rates means that investors reap large profits in a few years. Meanwhile, those in the community pay twice for their electricity; once when their taxes go to subsidize the wind interests and a second time when the monthly bill arrives. And that bill will likely be larger than it would have been had the turbines never been erected.

Then there are the issues of "decommissioning." What happens when the turbines are no longer profitable and are shut down or fall into disrepair and become postmodern ruins larger than Stonehenge? Who fixes them? Who takes them down? Who repairs the ridges?

Don't ask the original developers. Before the special tax and depreciation breaks have run their course, they will be long gone, either because they have sold the project to another developer or because they have just decamped and moved on to the next town.

So what do you do? Some towns have done nothing; they think it can't happen here. Other towns take the developer's money but extract promises that the turbines will be set back so many yards or miles. (Good luck if the promises aren't kept; developers never return your calls.)

Others across the country have done what we did in Andes—organize. We formed an alliance, incorporated, raised money, sent out flyers, took polls, sponsored forums, wrote a zoning ordinance, presented it to the town council and planning board, and finally saw it pass. It was democracy in action.

But it's not over. The Spitzer administration has been working on a plan to shift the authority for land use control from local communities to a state commission. Local zoning ordinances would be countermanded and communities like Andes could get wind farms even if they didn't want them.

Perhaps the governor and his colleagues should be reminded of the company that made wind power into a big, profitable business in this country. It was called Enron.

4.6

Looking for Gas in All the Wrong Places

AUGUST 22, 2011

It was a big week in Andes, New York. Last Thursday, the *New York Post* devoted a full page to the small Catskill village, describing in some detail the Andes Hotel, the surrounding "rolling corn and hay fields," the affordable housing, the Hunting Tavern Museum, the country store, the coffee shop, the tea shop, the farmer's market, the art galleries and antique stores, the occasional celebrity resident, the extraordinary natural beauty—everything that led the *Post*, in an earlier article about great day-trip destinations, to dub Andes Woodstock-as-it-used-to-be.[1]

And then, the very next evening, there was another event that provided an ironic counterpoint to that summer valentine. One hundred sixty Andeans, including the town supervisor, members of the town board, and candidates running for a seat on the board, met in the school gym to hear a presentation on the geology of hydraulic fracturing, or "fracking" (the process of extracting natural gas by blasting underground rock formations with a huge volume of chemical-laced water pumped down at very high levels of pressure) and to express their views about what fracking would mean if it came to the town.

The first thing to say is that 160 is an enormous number given that the town's population is 1,600 and residents weren't given much notice of the meeting. Were a corresponding percentage of New Yorkers to turn up at a public hearing, there would be no place large enough to hold the more than 800,000 attendees. The second thing to say is that many stayed for the entire three hours and forty minutes, the length of a short Wagner opera.

The first hour and a quarter was taken up by a sober, pretty much evenhanded explanation of the hydraulics of fracking; the locations in New York of the most promising sites for drilling; the effects on the landscape; the dangers of leakage, explosions, contamination, and discharge of radiation; the available methods for containing or mitigating these dangers; and the effectiveness (not yet very great) of those methods. As a lifelong academic, I was amazed at the sustained and respectful attention of the audience members, many of whom (it turned out) already knew most of what they were being told. It is a rule in my profession that if you talk longer than fifty minutes, you will lose your audience. On this occasion, the patience displayed was extraordinary, and it extended into the question-and-answer period, which lasted another seventy-five minutes.

Then came the evening's centerpiece, three-minute prepared statements delivered by townspeople who had signed up in advance. It is often said that the opponents of fracking are mostly second-home-owners and weekenders who selfishly prefer their enjoyment of a bucolic landscape to the needs of the long-termers who came before them. But the speakers who stood up to have their say represented every sector of the population—farmers, small-business owners, real estate agents, six-generation natives, newcomers, artists, musicians.

As different as they were, the message was the same and it was eloquently proclaimed: "What we have here is unique and beautiful." "We have to take action to keep the town we love." "We must take our destiny into our own hands." "Andes could become the model for the country." One of the speakers was a local and a folksinger. She made up a song on the spot and taught it to everyone. The refrain was "If we work together / Then we can make it better."

Interspersed with the expressions of love, hope, and resolution were substantive points of anxiety. No one knows how much contaminated water will escape and where it will go. Even if we stop it here, other towns might surrender and we could see a truck kicking up dust and leaking sand every sixty seconds, seven days a week. The noise level will make conversation impossible; no more sitting on the porch of the hotel or the coffee shop. Property values will plummet by 50 to 75 percent (this from a longtime realtor). Banks are reluctant to write mortgages on property that is being drilled on. There might be limited short-term benefits to a few, but the boom will be followed by a bust, and when it is all over "people won't want to live here anymore."

There was agreement that regulation wasn't the answer, first because no regulation could prevent the disasters that come along inevitably with a project this large, and second because the state couldn't be counted on either to pass or enforce regulations: "I can't trust an industry that has got itself exempted from the air and clean water act." The position that emerged at the end of the evening was simple and unequivocal: "You can't regulate them but you can ban them if you are sophisticated enough legally and if you remain strong and stay the course." Every statement was greeted with loud applause. One speaker called for a straw poll. "Anyone in favor of fracking?" Not a hand was raised.

"Inspiring" is not a word I usually use, but this evening was inspiring. The devotion to community, the civic-mindedness, the sheer intelligence displayed by everyone who spoke was a more powerful argument for coming to Andes than the beauties and attractions listed by the *Post*. But the argument will come to nothing, and everything the *Post* celebrates will be no more, if the rural birthright of Andes is sold for a mess of fracking.

1. "Why Andes Is Worth a Peek," *New York Post*, August 18, 2011, http://nypost .com/2011/08/18/why-andes-is-worth-a-peek/; "The Catskills, from A to Z," *New York Post* online, June 7, 2010, http://nypost.com/2010/06/07/the-catskills-from-a-to-z/.

When Principles Get in the Way

DECEMBER 26, 1996

Suppose you were arguing for something but were told that you would have to make your case without the facts that supported it. This is the situation proponents of affirmative action face when they find themselves defending their position in terms of principle rather than policy.

A policy is a response to actual historical circumstances; it is directed at achieving a measurable result—like an increase in the representation of minorities in business and education. A principle scorns actual historical circumstances and moves quickly to a level of generalization and abstraction so high that the facts of history can no longer be seen.

Affirmative action is an attempt to deal with a real-world problem. If that problem is recharacterized in the language of principle—if you stop asking, "What's wrong and how can we fix it?" and ask instead, "Is it fair?"—the real world fades away and is replaced by the arid world of philosophical puzzles.

The recipe for making real-world problems disappear behind a smokescreen of philosophizing was given to us years ago by the legal scholar Herbert Wechsler in his enormously influential 1959 *Harvard Law Review* article "Toward Neutral Principles." Wechsler was trying to justify the Supreme Court's decision in *Brown v. Board of Education* (1954), which declared segregated schools unconstitutional. What troubled Wechsler about Brown was that the justices, in reaching their decision, seemed moved by a practical desire to secure a result they favored (integrated schools) rather than by some general principle whose application would yield that result independently.

Unable to find any such principle spelled out in the court's arguments, Wechsler was driven to provide one himself: the "right of freedom of association." But in attempting to make this case, he soon realized that the principle of freedom of association turned out not to justify Brown but to make it even more of a puzzle. "If the freedom of association is denied by segregation, integration forces an association upon those for whom it is . . . repugnant," he wrote. And "given a choice between denying the association to those . . . who wish it and imposing it on those who would avoid it," he was unable to find a principle that would justify either the one or the other.

Here in as naked a form as one might like (or not like) is the logic of neutral principle. When Wechsler characterizes the choice as being between the rights of those who wish to associate and the rights of those who wish not to, these two wishes have lost all contact with the issue that made their opposition meaningful—whether the school-house door should be open or shut. Once the historical specificity of that issue is lost, there no longer seems to be any moral difference between the two sides, although the difference was perfectly clear before Wechsler began his tortured analysis.

In other words, the puzzle of Brown is only a puzzle if you forget everything that made the case urgent in the first place—the long history of racism and its effects. You have substituted philosophical urgencies for social urgencies. This is what the demand for principle does, and what opponents of affirmative action intend it to do. After all, isn't it convenient to be able to deny a remedy for long-standing injustices by invoking the higher name of principle?

It is a very bad game, but it is alive and well in the phrase "reverse racism," which does in an instant what Wechsler needed an entire essay to do. The phrase makes the actions of college admissions officers who give preference to minority candidates equivalent to the hate crimes of the Ku Klux Klan. It does so by claiming that each is motivated by race-consciousness, an argument that makes sense only if the very thought of race, no matter the content or context, is considered the sin. Like the freedom of association in Wechsler's argument, race-consciousness invoked as an abstraction rides roughshod over history while laying claim to the noblest of motives.

That is in effect what Justice Clarence Thomas did in his concurring opinion in *Adarand v. Pena* (1995), in which the court struck down the policy of giving incentives to federal contractors who hired minority subcontractors. "It is irrelevant," he wrote, "whether a government's racial classifications are drawn by those who wish to oppress a race or by those who have a sincere desire to help those thought to be disadvantaged. In each instance, it is racial discrimination, plain and simple."

But both the plainness and the simplicity are apparent only if the complex facts of history have been suppressed or declared out of bounds. In his dissent, Justice John Paul Stevens returned to history to make the truly plain and simple point: "There is no moral or Constitutional equivalence between a policy that is designed to perpetuate a caste system and one that seeks to eradicate racial subordination."

The important word in Justice Stevens's statement is "moral," for it shows that the choice here is not between the principled and the nonprincipled. It is between neutral principles, which refuse to acknowledge the dilemmas we face as a society, and moral principles, which begin with an awareness of those dilemmas and demand that we address them.

Those who favor affirmative action are moved by moral principles—principles that recognize the reality and persistence of historical inequities. And yet those who favor affirmative action are often maneuvered into using a vocabulary designed to remove from sight the very realities on which their case depends.

Of course, you could also try to work within that vocabulary and fight over its terms, arguing that "fairness," "equality," and "color blindness" really belong on your side. But even if you got good at the game, you would be playing on your opponent's field and thus buying into his position, and why would you want to do that?

It would be far wiser to refuse the lure of "fairness," "merit," and "equality," now code words for ignoring the effects of the long history of racial oppression. Let's be done with code words and concentrate on the problems we face and on possible ways of solving them. Those who support affirmative action should give up searching for theoretical consistency—a goal at once impossible and unworthy—and instead seek strategies with the hope of relieving the pain of people who live in the world and not in the never-never land of theory.

Let's stop asking, "Is it fair or is it reverse racism?" and start asking, "Does it work and are there better ways of doing what needs to be done?" Merely asking these questions does not guarantee that affirmative action will be embraced, but it does guarantee that the shell game of the search for neutral principle will no longer stand between us and doing the right thing.

Revisiting Affirmative Action, with Help from Kant

JANUARY 14, 2007

Whenever I teach the political writings of Immanuel Kant (1724–1804), I always ask my students, would Kant have been for or against affirmative action? I thought of the answers they typically give to that question when University of Michigan spokesperson Theresa A. Sullivan announced last week that the university would comply with Proposal 2, a successful state ballot initiative banning affirmative action programs that give preferential treatment to persons and groups on the basis of race, gender, color, ethnicity, or national origin.[1]

On November 8, one day after Proposal 2 was approved by 58 percent of Michigan voters, President Mary Sue Coleman expressed disappointment at the result and vowed to continue the battle by every means possible. The university's lawyers then requested that the force of the new proposal be stayed until the present admissions cycle was complete. But when a federal appeals court denied the request, the university bowed to the ruling while reserving its right to mount legal challenges to the new law.

No one believes that this is the end of the story. Debates about affirmative action have been going on since the concept was first introduced during the Nixon administration. And in fact, the debate goes back at least as far as Kant and his ideas about how to tell the difference between principled and unprincipled policies. Kant says that correct political thinking must begin by affirming two propositions: (1) "the freedom of every member of society as a human being," and (2) "the equality of each with all the others as a subject."[2] This emphasis on freedom and equality has led some of my students to conclude that Kant would have been in favor of affirmative action because, they reasoned, it was the denial of freedom and equality to African Americans that produced the injustices affirmative action is intended to redress.

That, I tell my students, is the wrong answer, because it confuses and conflates two aspirations Kant was concerned to keep separate:

the achieving of results that many would think good, and acting in conformity with the moral law. In some philosophies—utilitarianism in some of its versions would be an example—morality and the bringing about of a desired social outcome (a more equal distribution of wealth, proportionate representation of minorities in positions of influence and power) would be one and the same. But Kant is, at least philosophically, indifferent to outcomes, in part because, as he puts it, "men have different views on the empirical end of happiness"— that is, different views about what society should look like and therefore different views about the policies that should be pursued.

A state dedicated to morality rather than to happiness will not take sides and choose one end before the others; rather, it will protect the right of every man to choose the end he prefers, provided that he in turn accords the same right to his fellows. "Each may seek his happiness in whatever way he sees fit, so long as he does not infringe upon the freedom of others to pursue a similar end which can be reconciled with the freedom of others." It is the abstract right rather than "the object in relation to which" it might be exercised, and the condition of freedom rather than any action freely performed, that Kant values. His interest is not in the particular life plan an autonomous citizen might wish to pursue, but in the ability of that citizen to pursue it without having the plan preferred by others imposed on him or realized at his expense.

Kant, in short, divorces morality from policy, and he makes the point by contrasting two maxims: "Honesty is the best policy," and "Honesty is better than any policy." The first maxim is a strategic recommendation. It says, when you want to accomplish something, you'll have a better chance if you are honest. The second—and in Kant's mind, superior—maxim takes no notice of strategy. It says, being true to your principles independently of the result they may or may not produce is the only moral way to go.

The danger the first maxim holds out is that at some point you might decide that your goal would be better served by a little deception and secrecy (just as some have said in recent years that the protection of democracy requires doing undemocratic things), and at that point morality will have given way to expediency and considerations of prudence. "The legislator may indeed err," says Kant, "in judging whether or not the measures he adopts are prudent," but he will not err in judging "whether or not the law harmonizes with the principle of right," because "he has ready to hand an infallible *a priori* standard." Honesty is to be followed not because it works or might work (a prudential judgment), but because it is right.

It is because Kant insists on distinguishing what works (at least in the short run) and what is right that he would, I believe, be against affirmative action. He would have said, as many opponents of affirmative action do say, that it is wrong to respond to past acts of discrimination by discriminating in the present, even if your intentions are good. If discrimination—the unequal treatment of inherently free and equal citizens—is to be condemned when the motives behind it (to preserve power or maintain a way of life) are suspect, it is also to be condemned when the motives behind it (to redress a historical injustice or have the student body reflect the diversity of America) are benign. Otherwise the calculation of happiness (at least by someone's lights) will have taken precedence over the upholding of principle. The two actions Kant contrasts—legislating in response to perceived social needs and legislating with an eye always to first principles—have defined the affirmative action debate from its beginning and continue to do so.

This opposition is played out in *Grutter v. Bollinger* (2003) between Justice Thomas (he is the justice most addicted to principle) and Justice Sandra Day O'Connor. O'Connor, writing for the majority that upheld the University of Michigan Law School's admission policy, speculated that "in 25 years from now the use of racial preferences will no longer be necessary to further the interest approved today." The interest she refers to is the interest in achieving a diverse student body, and in order to further it, she is willing, at least for a while, to allow the use of an otherwise suspect means.

Thomas replies in his dissent that if racial preferences of the kind the law school employs will be illegal in twenty-five years, they are "illegal now," for the Constitution, if it means anything, "means the same thing today as it will in 300 months." For Thomas, what is at stake is the question of whether the Constitution has an unchanging meaning to which we are obliged to adhere, or whether, on the other hand, the Constitution is a dynamic, living document that adjusts to circumstances and the emergence of problems the founders never contemplated. This is a very old question in the field of constitutional interpretation, and it is at heart the very same question raised by affirmative action. Do we judge policies as being more or less likely to have the consequences we seek in the present, or do we judge policies as being more or less compatible with first principles that know no time but are always applicable? Do we ask, will it work? Or do we ask, is it right?

My interest in these questions is (for once) more than academic, for I have been a participant in the affirmative action debates since the early 1990s. I have written a bunch of essays (some in this newspaper), two books (*There's No Such Thing as Free Speech . . . and It's a Good Thing, Too* and *The Trouble with Principle*),[3] done radio and television shows, participated in forums, appeared at city council meetings, and all in support of the position enunciated by Justice Stevens: that so-called principled arguments against affirmative action work by evacuating both history and morality—evacuating history by going to a level of abstraction so high that the difference between acts motivated by beneficence and acts motivated by malice disappear, and evacuating morality on the same reasoning.

Now I'm not so sure. Nor am I sure why I'm no longer so sure, although I expect it has something to do with two arguments I have been making with increasing vigor in the past several years. (My wife says that I'm just moving to the right in the manner typical of all old Jews.)

I have been arguing that the answer to the question, "What does a text mean?" is that a text means what its author intends, and that therefore it is incoherent to speak of a living Constitution with an evolving meaning. An evolving meaning—a meaning that alters with the times—is, I have insisted, not a meaning at all but a projection of the interpreter's desires. If interpretation is to be a serious activity rather than a game with no rules, it must have an object, and the only object it can intelligibly have is a meaning that is prior to anyone's efforts to determine it. In the context of that argument, affirmative action is an appropriate remedy for historical injustices only if it can be brought into line with constitutional and interpretive principles. The question is, can it be made to square with the meaning the founders intended and with the values—equality and equal treatment—the judicial process has enshrined? I'm not saying that the answer to that question is no, only that it is a different question from the one I used to ask, the pragmatic question of whether it will improve a bad situation.

The second argument I have been making is that institutions of higher education (and their faculty) have only two proper tasks: to introduce students to bodies of material and to equip them with analytical skills. Anything else, in my very strong view, is the job of some other industry or institution, and that includes fashioning character, molding democratic citizens, taking moral or political stands, and performing actions designed to make the world a better place. One reason for supporting affirmative action is that it will make the world a better place, a more democratic place. But from the perspective of my severe notion of what universities should and should not be doing, that is not a good reason. It follows then that if affirmative action is to be defended, it must be on the basis of a pedagogical goal it directly furthers. I'm not saying that there is no such goal—several have been proposed—but that it has not yet been identified in a way I find entirely persuasive.

On the other hand (or is it the third hand?), I still feel that affirmative action is a noble endeavor inspired more often than not by the best of motives, and I feel too that many who oppose it are the heirs (metaphorically) of those who have stood in the way of every advance in social justice made in the last sixty years. And there I stand, or rather, wobble. I've been thinking again and not finding it much fun.

1. "Letter to the University community from President Mary Sue Coleman and Provost Teresa A. Sullivan announcing the University's next steps with respect to Proposal 2 for admissions and financial aid," January 10, 2007, http://www.diversity .umich.edu/legal/proposal2.php.

2. Immanuel Kant, "On the Relationship of Theory to Practice in Political Right," in *Political Writings*, 2nd ed. (New York: Cambridge University Press, 1991).

3. Stanley Fish, *There's No Such Thing as Free Speech . . . and It's a Good Thing, Too* (New York: Oxford University Press, 1993) and *The Trouble with Principle* (Cambridge, MA: Harvard University Press, 2001).

Is the NRA Un-American?

MAY 13, 2013

The more militant members of the National Rifle Association (NRA) and most of its leaders may be un-American.

By "militant" I don't mean those who wish to protect recreational shooting and hunting; nor do I mean those who, like Justice Antonin Scalia, believe that there is a constitutional right to defend one's home and family with firearms. These are respectable positions (although I am deeply unpersuaded by the second). I mean those who read the Second Amendment as proclaiming the right of citizens to resist the tyranny of their own government.

The reason this view may be un-American is that it sets itself against one of the cornerstones of democracy—the orderly transfer of power. A transfer of power is orderly when it is effected by procedural rules that are indifferent to the partisan, ideological affiliations of either the party exiting power or the party taking power. A transfer is disorderly when it is effected by rebellion, invasion, military coup, or any other use of force.

Those who are engaged in a disorderly transfer believe that their actions are inspired by the highest of motives—the desire to set right what has gone terribly wrong. Somehow the forces of evil have gained the levers of power, and unless they are dislodged, the values necessary to the sustaining of everything we cherish will be overwhelmed. Violence is ugly, but if tyranny is to be defeated, it may be necessary. Given tyranny's resilience and its tendency to fill any available political space, we must always be ready; the price of liberty is eternal vigilance.

This is a familiar story; indeed, it is the story—or at least one story—of the American Revolution, and that is why it is the story Wayne LaPierre, the executive vice president of the NRA, told to a Senate committee in January: "Senator, I think without any doubt, if you look at why our Founding Fathers put [the Second Amendment] there, they had lived under the tyranny of King George and they wanted to make sure that these free people in this new country would never be subjugated again and have to live under tyranny."[1]

In 1990, Fred Romero, an NRA field representative, put the case as clearly as possible: "The Second Amendment is not there to protect the interests of hunters, sport shooters and casual plinkers."[2] Rather, the "Second Amendment is . . . literally a loaded gun in the hands of the people held to the heads of government." In response to statements like this (and there are many of them), President Obama recently said in a speech in Denver: "The government's us. These officials are elected by you."[3] Or, in other words, how can the people's enemy be the representatives elected by the people?

The NRA militants have an answer. The purpose of the American Revolution was to secure the freedom of individuals and that means a minimally intrusive government. Representatives elected to safeguard that freedom may become intoxicated by their power and act in ways that restrict rather than enhance individual choice. At that point it is the people's right and duty to rise against them. Measures limiting gun ownership are a sure sign that government is moving in the direction of central control and tyranny.

But who gets to decide that tyranny is imminent, and by what measure is the imminence of tyranny determined? That question was debated on patch.com by posters responding to a story about Baltimore County police chief James Johnson, who had called the tyranny argument of LaPierre and others "creepy" and "scary." A commenter posting under the name Sanchez explained that "Tyranny consists of many things we have experienced the last four years, the firearm issue the latest in the line of them." The point was echoed and amplified by another commenter, William Gill: "The second amendment is the only one that can assure the protection of your other rights, which are being attacked almost daily by the current administration." (In short, the Obama administration = tyranny.) A commenter posting as Steve responded, "It's not 'Tyranny' just because you were outvoted. That's Democracy."[4]

Steve is standing up for the orderly transfer of power and saying that we don't call it tyranny when the other guy's ideas have carried the political day. But he is met immediately by two responses from other commenters. First, "Steve, you're assuming that the voting process was above board! Let's face it, this election in November was by no means above board." That is, the election results did not reflect majority will but some form of corrupt manipulation. (Those conspiring to overthrow government cite a conspiracy theory as their justification.)

The second response cuts deeper: "We live in a Republic, Steve . . . majority rules is a problem indeed" (Buck Harmon). Harmon is invoking the familiar distinction between a democracy and a republic. In a democracy the majority determines what the law is and could, at least theoretically, take away the rights of individuals for the sake of the "public good." In a republic, the majority will is held in check by constitutional guarantees that forbid legislation encroaching on individual rights even if 51 percent or 95 percent of the population favors it. (For example, Congress shall pass no law abridging the freedom of expression.)

It follows from this distinction that a government elected by the majority can begin to think it can do anything it wants to, can begin to act as if we lived in a democracy rather than in a republic, and when that happens, or is in danger of happening, there is what the former Senate candidate Sharron Angle called a "Second Amendment remedy." Asked, in 2010, "Do we have enemies of the country in the halls of Congress?," Angle replied, "Certainly people who pass these kinds of policies—Obamacare, cap and trade, stimulus, bailout."[5] Off with their heads, either metaphorically, or in sufficiently dire circumstances, literally.

So for Angle and others, that's the shape of tyranny—legislation that, in their judgment, abridges constitutionally protected rights. Sanchez explains: "We are all to decide what tyranny is. Just as we decide what law we obey or not." This antinomian declaration—our inner light will tell us when and when not to obey—flies in the face of another commonplace of democracy: ours is a government of laws not men (a declaration found in the 1780 Constitution of Massachusetts). A government of men is one in which laws issue from the will and desires of those who happen to be in authority. In a government of laws the preferences of men (and women), even those holding high office, are checked by the impersonal requirements of an impersonal law.

Another version of the commonplace is, no man is above the law. The opposite view was famously declared by Richard Nixon when he said, "When the president does it, that means it is not illegal." NRA militants like Sanchez and Angle are, in effect, an army of little Richard Nixons, deciding what laws to obey, and deciding too when lawmakers have failed to obey the law as they see it. Unlike Nixon, they don't have an FBI, a Treasury Department, and a standing army; but they do have the Second Amendment and the right, or so they claim, to take arms against a government they have judged to be wayward.

In the same thread quoted earlier, poster C.P. takes the logic to its conclusion: "Secession is near. Can't wait. Which by the way is Constitutional." It's constitutional, in this view, because a government in the act of eroding constitutional values is itself unconstitutional and has become a tyranny. Therefore, to oppose it by whatever means available, including force, is not to undermine constitutionality but to affirm it. It is in this spirit that John Wilkes Booth cried, "Sic semper tyrannis" (thus always to tyrants) just after he shot Abraham Lincoln. Lincoln famously said, "A house divided against itself cannot stand." Booth's modern successors are saying that a house in the hands of tyrants does not deserve to stand, and they are ready to bring it down with their constitutionally protected guns.

As Police Chief Johnson said, this is creepy and scary, but is it—to return to my original musings—un-American? Yes and no. On the one hand, nothing can be more American than throwing off the shackles of a government that has overstepped its bounds and disregarded the rights of its citizens. That's how it all began. ("No taxation without representation.") But on the other hand, the American tradition of accepting the results of elections—even when they bring with them policies you believe to be misguided at best and disastrous at worst—is in danger of being undermined when groups of armed people decide that the present leadership is infected by unpatriotic, socialist ideas and must be resisted at all costs.

A government founded in a revolutionary moment is always vulnerable to a determination by a zealous minority that its revolutionary ideals have been compromised by itself. When that happens, each side will engage in its favored rhetoric, one proclaiming, "Watch out, they're coming for our guns," the other warning that militant right-wing nuts are preparing themselves for armed insurrection. One side will cry "tyranny"; the other will reply, "You guys are crazy." And both will claim the title of "true American." That's where we are.

1. "Some Gun Control Opponents Cite Fear of Government Tyranny," National Public Radio, April 8, 2013, http://www.npr.org/blogs/itsallpolitics/2013/04/08/176350364 /fears-of-government-tyranny-push-some-to-reject-gun-control.

2. Fred Romero, "California Gun Control Law Runs into Rebellion," *New York Times*, December 24, 1990.

3. Kasie Hunt, "Obama: 'No Conflict' between Respecting Gun Rights, Enacting Gun Controls," NBC News online, April 3, 2003, http://firstread.nbcnews.com/_news /2013/04/03/17588545-obama-no-conflict-between-respecting-gun-rights-enacting-gun -controls?lite.

4. "Johnson: NRA Exec's Tyranny Claim 'Not Based on Logic,'" comments by Sanchez, William Gill, and Steve were posted on February 1, 2013.

5. Sharron Angle, "Jonathan Karl's Campaign Notebook—Meet the New Sharron Angle," ABC News online, September 8, 2010, http://abcnews.go.com/blogs/politics/2010/09/jonathan-karls-campaign-notebook-meet-the-new-the-sharron-angle/.

All You Need Is Hate

FEBRUARY 3, 2008

I have been thinking about writing this column for some time, but I have hesitated because of a fear that it would advance the agenda that is its target. That is the agenda of Hillary Clinton–hating.

Its existence is hardly news—it is routinely referred to by commentators on the present campaign, and it has been documented in essays and books—but the details of it can still startle when you encounter them up close. In the January issue of *GQ*, Jason Horowitz described the world of Hillary haters, many of whom he has interviewed.[1] Horowitz finds that the hostile characterizations of Clinton do not add up to a coherent account of her hatefulness. She is vilified for being a feminist and for not being one, for being an extreme leftist and for being a "warmongering hawk," for being godless and for being "frighteningly fundamentalist," for being the victim of her husband's peccadilloes and for enabling them. "She is," Horowitz concludes, "an empty vessel into which [her detractors] can pour everything they detest." (In this she is the counterpart of George W. Bush, who serves much the same function for many liberals.)

This is not to say that there are no rational, well-considered reasons for opposing Clinton's candidacy. You may dislike her policies (which she has not been reluctant to explain in great detail). You may not be able to get past her vote to authorize the Iraq war. You may think her personality unsuited to the tasks of inspiring and uniting the American people. You may believe that if this is truly a change election, she is not the one to bring about real change.

But the people and groups Horowitz surveys have brought criticism of Clinton to what sportswriters call "the next level," in this case, to the level of personal vituperation unconnected to, and often unconcerned with, the facts. These people are obsessed with things like her hairstyles, the "strangeness" of her eyes—"Analysis of Clinton's eyes is a favorite motif among her most rabid adversaries"—and they retail and recycle items from what Horowitz calls "The Crazy Files": she's Osama bin Laden's candidate; she kills cats; she's a witch (this is not meant metaphorically).

But this list, however loony tunes it may be, does not begin to touch the craziness of the hardcore members of this cult. Back in November, I wrote a column on Clinton's response to a question about giving driver's licenses to illegal immigrants.[2] My reward was to pick up an e-mail pal who has to date sent me twenty-four lengthy documents culled from what he calls his "Hillary File." If you take that file on faith, Hillary Clinton is a murderer, a burglar, a destroyer of property, a blackmailer, a psychological rapist, a white-collar criminal, an adulteress, a blasphemer, a liar, the proprietor of a secret police, a predatory lender, a misogynist, a witness tamperer, a street criminal, a criminal intimidator, a harasser, and a sociopath. These accusations are "supported" by innuendo, tortured logic, strained conclusions, and photographs that are declared to tell their own story, but don't.

Compared to this, the Swift Boat Veterans for Truth campaign against John Kerry was a model of objectivity. When the heading of a section of the "Hillary File" reads "Have the Clintons ever murdered anyone?"—and it turns out to be a rhetorical question, like "Is the pope Catholic?"—you know that you've entered cuckooland.

Horowitz warns that as the campaign heats up, this "type of discourse will likely not stay on the fringes for long," and he predicts that some of it will be made use of by Republican operatives. But he is behind the curve, for the spirit informing it has already made its way into mainstream media. Respected political commentators devote precious network time to deep analyses of her laugh. Everyone blames her for what her husband does or for what he doesn't do. (This is what the compound "Billary" is all about.) If she answers questions aggressively, she is shrill. If she moderates her tone, she's just playacting. If she cries, she's faking. If she doesn't, she's too masculine. If she dresses conservatively, she's dowdy. If she doesn't, she's inappropriately provocative.

None of those who say and write these things is an official Hillary Clinton–hater (some profess to like and admire her), but they are surely doing the group's work.

One almost prefers an up-front hater (although he tells Horowitz that he doesn't like the word) like Dick Morris, who writes in a recent *New York Post* op-ed of the Clintons' "reprehensible politics of personal destruction" (does he think he's throwing bouquets?), and accuses them of invading the privacy of opponents, of blackmailing and threatening women, and of "whatever slimy tactics they felt they needed."[3] Morris calls Harold Ickes, a Clinton aide, a "hit man" for the president, and he calls the president "Hillary's hit man."

This is exactly the language of the most vicious anti-Hillary websites, and here it is baptized by its appearance in a major newspaper.

Horowitz observes that there is an "inexhaustible fertile market of Clinton hostility," but that "the search for a unifying theory of what drives Hillary's most fanatical opponents is a futile one." The reason is that nothing drives it; it is that most sought-after thing, a self-replenishing, perpetual-energy machine.

The closest analogy is to anti-Semitism. But before you hit the comment button, I don't mean that the two are alike either in their significance or in the damage they do. It's just that they both feed on air and flourish independently of anything external to their obsessions. Anti-Semitism doesn't need Jews and anti-Hillaryism doesn't need Hillary, except as a figment of its collective imagination. However this campaign turns out, Hillary-hating, like rock 'n' roll, is here to stay.

1. Jason Horowitz, "The Hillary Haters," *GQ*, January 2008.
2. Stanley Fish, "It Depends What the Meaning of 'Makes Sense' Is," *New York Times*, November 11, 2007.
3. Dick Morris, "A 'No' to Slime," *New York Post*, January 29, 2008.

How the Right Hijacked the Magic Words

AUGUST 13, 1995

When the verdict in the first Rodney King beating trial was announced, many were amazed at the acquittal of the police officers, especially since their actions had been filmed by an amateur photographer. How could a jury ignore the evidence of its own eyes? A part of the answer emerged in the account of the defense strategy.

It had two stages. First, the film was slowed down so that each frame was isolated and stood by itself. Second, the defense asked questions that treated each frozen frame as if everything in the case hung on it and it alone. Is this blow an instance of excessive force? Is this blow intended to kill or maim?

Under the pressure of such questions, the event as a whole disappeared from view and was replaced by a series of discontinuous moments. Looking only at individual moments cut off from the context that gave them meaning, the jury could not say of any of them that this did grievous harm to Rodney King.

This strategy—of first segmenting reality and then placing all the weight on individual bits of it—is useful whenever you want to deflect attention away from the big picture, and that is why it has proved so attractive to those conservative Republicans who want to roll back the regulatory state. On every front, from environmental protection to affirmative action, large questions of ecology and justice are pushed into the background by the same segmenting techniques that made it easy for the jurors in Simi Valley to forget it was a beating they were seeing.

As examples, consider two cases recently decided by the Supreme Court. In *Babbitt v. Sweet Home*, the question was whether an EPA regulation against "taking" an endangered species includes acts of "habitat modification" or whether words like "take" and "harm" refer narrowly to single assaults on single animals by single hunters.

Those taking the broader view argue that when you destroy the last remaining ground on which the piping plover broods, you make it "impossible for any piping plovers to reproduce." Those on the other side, the side of developers and logging interests, reply that no single plover will have been targeted and no living plover injured.

"Taking," they insist, describes only "acts done directly and intentionally to particular animals." One side recognizes indirect effects caused by large-scale patterns of action taking place over time. The other side recognizes only effects caused at a particular moment by the intentional behavior of individuals. Beginning from these two perspectives—not on the issue, but determinative of the way the issue will be framed and seen—the two sides come to predictably opposing conclusions.

Just about everything remains the same when the topic is affirmative action. In *Adarand v. Pena*, the question was whether the policy of giving financial incentives to prime contractors who hire minority subcontractors is constitutional. Those in favor of the incentives justify them by invoking constitutional history and the history of discrimination in the contracting industry. They remind us, in Justice John Paul Stevens's words, that the "primary purpose of the Equal Protection Clause was to end discrimination of the former slaves," and they report that even today certain groups remain entrenched in the building trades while others are virtually shut out.

Those opposed to the incentives reject arguments from history and specifically reject the argument that historical patterns of discrimination have impaired the life chances of African Americans as a group. They say it is individuals, not groups, that are protected by the Constitution, and they would allow remedies for discrimination only in cases where there has been "an individualized showing" of harm, a harm inflicted directly on a specific person by a specific agent at a specific time.

The idea is that even though different histories may have brought us here, we are now all individuals who enter life's race with equal opportunities and therefore any injury we suffer (at least if the law is going to recognize it) is injury done to us by an individual and not by impersonal forces either in the past or present. Harm in this model can only be imagined as a discrete event: you hit me over the head with a baseball bat. No Rube Goldberg accounts of cause and effect allowed.

The Rodney King beating, endangered species, affirmative action—three very different issues but all subject to the same analysis, which reaches the same conclusion: either a particular person at a particular moment did it or no one did it. Blows can only kill one by one and not in relation to other blows in a sequence. Birds can only be taken one by one and not by the destruction of the environment essential to their survival. Persons can only be discriminated against one by one and not by the massive effects of long-standing, structural racism.

One more example to clinch the point. In the first aftermath of the Oklahoma bombing, rumors of an Arab suspect were followed by the usual mutterings about an Islamic terrorist culture. But when Timothy McVeigh surfaced, talk of holding a culture responsible was strongly denounced by the very same people who had been engaging in it, because the culture now under the spotlight was their own.

Immediately, Mr. McVeigh was detached from everything and everyone surrounding him and proclaimed to be "merely an individual," and, more pointedly, an individual "kook," someone acting out of some inner and private compulsion and not in response to the values and goals of any group.

He may have worn the same clothes as those other guys, held the same views, listened to the same radio stations, read or wrote the same antigovernment pamphlets, and marched in the same woods with the same guns, but what he did (if he did it) he did entirely on his own, uninfluenced by anyone or anything. Just as we are to believe that Rodney King received each blow in isolation, and the piping plover experienced no harm when its habitat was degraded, and minority subcontractors suffered no disadvantage by centuries of exclusion from the trades they were now "free" to enter.

The question is, why do arguments like these often have so much force? At first glance it seems odd, even bizarre, to discount the cumulative effects of many blows, or to deny that habitat degradation constitutes a harm to individual birds, or to announce that massive patterns of societal discrimination leave minorities in the same position as everyone else, or to decide that while Timothy McVeigh talks like a militia member, walks like a militia member, thinks like a militia member, and hates like a militia member, what he does has nothing to do with the militia culture.

How is the trick done? Well, first of all, by a sleight of hand. The eye is deflected away from the whole—history, culture, habitats, society—and the parts, now freed from any stabilizing context, can be described in any way one likes. But why is the sleight of hand successful? Why don't more people see through it?

Because it is performed with the vocabulary of America's civil religion—the vocabulary of equal opportunity, color blindness, race neutrality, and, above all, individual rights. This was also the vocabulary of civil rights activists, anti-McCarthyites, and liberals in general, many of whom are now puzzled and even defensive when they hear their own words coming out of the mouths of their traditional opponents.

Their mistake is to assume that the words mean what they did in 1960, when in fact they have been repackaged and put in the service of the very agenda they once fought. When the goal was to end Jim Crow practices that kept blacks in the back of the bus and out of schools, "individual rights" was a powerful slogan in support of change. But now "individual rights" operates to maintain the status quo by ruling out as a consideration the very history that made the phrase a rallying cry in the first place.

When the goal was to make discrimination illegal, "color-blind" meant removing the obstacles to full citizenship, but "color-blind" now means blind to the effects of what has been done in the past to people because of their color. When the goal was to provide access to those long denied it, "equal opportunity" was a weapon against old habits and vested interests, but now those same interests have learned how to say "equal opportunity" and mean maintenance of all the conditions that still make it a myth.

Liberals and progressives have been slow to realize that their preferred vocabulary has been hijacked, and that when they respond to once-hallowed phrases, they are responding to a ghost now animated by a new machine. The point is not a small one, for in any debate, especially one fought in the arena of public opinion, the battle is won not by knockdown arguments but by the party that succeeds in placing its own spin on the terms presiding over the discussion.

That's what the conservatives in and out of Congress have managed to do with old war horses like "individual," and so long as they are allowed to get away with it, the opposition will spend its time insisting that it too is for the individual—or for color blindness or equal opportunity—and before we know it, all the plovers will be dead and all the subcontractors will once again be white.

PART 5

Reflections on the Law

Why Scalia Is Right

APRIL 9, 2006

Antonin Scalia is the most theatrical of the present Supreme Court justices. (He's also the best stylist, but that's a subject for another day.) It's not clear whether he seeks the spotlight or it seeks him, but he seems incapable of not occupying it. In the past couple of months, he has responded to a reporter's question with a gesture thought by some to be obscene—he denies this—and, in a speech given to the Federalist Society in Puerto Rico, he characterized those who disagreed with him on a point of interpretive theory as "idiots."

He was talking about the view, which he has often criticized but not yet succeeded in killing, that the meaning of the Constitution changes as society changes. Rather than being fixed in time, the Constitution (the story goes) is continually evolving in response to unforeseen circumstances and improvements in our moral and political understanding. In short, the Constitution is a living organism, not a dead letter.

In the speech in Puerto Rico, Justice Scalia rehearsed the argument—"The Constitution . . . has to change with society"—and then brusquely dismissed it: "But you would have to be an idiot to believe that."[1] The indignant bloggers and commentators who accuse him of everything from arrogance (there's something to that) to racism act as if this bit of name-calling were all Justice Scalia had to offer. But in fact he immediately offered the reasons for his severe judgment. First, he reminded his audience of the obvious: "The Constitution is not a living organism, it is a legal document." And then he explained succinctly, and in my view correctly, what it means to be a legal document or, for that matter, any kind of document at all. "It says something and doesn't say other things."

This might strike some as cryptic, so let me provide a gloss. A document (or text) is a vehicle of communication, and for communication to occur, some message, not all messages, must be conveyed. A document that said everything—that had no particular meaning but various and expanding meanings—would say nothing; it would be not a document but a kaleidoscope or a Rorschach test. The Constitution is most certainly a document, and therefore it must say something, and it is the job of interpreters to figure out what that something (which can't be everything) is.

Not only does this argument make perfect sense but the integrity and seriousness of the interpretive effort depend on it. Only if the Constitution is assumed to send a message that does not change over time can the claim of an interpretation to be right or an assertion that it is wrong be intelligible. In order to be right or wrong about something, that something must precede, and be independent of, your efforts to figure out what is. What a document is at the beginning—when it is drafted—will always be what it is. The Constitution cannot be a living organism.

Justice Scalia's critics do not respond to this chain of reasoning, but instead pose what they take to be a series of devastating questions. If the Constitution's meaning is fixed and unchanging, asks Paul Greenberg, how do you explain the fact that it has been "subject to different interpretations over the years?"[2] Easy. Justice Scalia's thesis is not that the Constitution's meaning will be perspicuous and agreed on by everyone. His thesis is that the Constitution has a meaning. The history of its interpretation is a history of successive efforts to specify what that meaning is. Each of these efforts will produce a different account of that meaning, but the meaning itself will always be the same. For if it were not, there would be no point to the history.

But isn't it true (a second question) that the meanings of words themselves change? Yes, they do, which is why it is important to determine (if you can) what the original author(s) meant by a word and not go immediately to what you mean by it or to what you might want it to mean, for you are not the author.

Is Justice Scalia saying (a third question posed by blogger Wayne Besen) that "American jurisprudence has not evolved in two centuries?" No, he is identifying the jurisprudential goal, which is to figure out what the Constitution means. In time, interpreters may draw closer to that goal or move further away from it, and in some sense their efforts are evolving, but the meaning they are in search of does not evolve (for if it did there would be nothing to search for).

In general, Justice Scalia's critics confuse a fact about the history of interpretation (it will produce different results at different times) with an interpretive mandate (the job is to produce different results as society needs them). The fact follows from the nontransparency (sometimes, not always) of language and the fallibility of interpreters.

The mandate, were it acted upon in the name of a Living Constitution, would direct us not to interpret better but to abandon interpretation altogether in favor of making the text mean what we want it to mean. Those who think we should go this route may not be idiots, but they are certainly wrong.

1. "Scalia: Non-Originalists Are 'Idiots,'" Associated Press, February 14, 2006, http://www.foxnews.com/story/2006/02/14/scalia-non-originalists-are-idiots.

2. Paul Greenberg, "Constitution: Dead or Alive?," *Washington Times*, February 27, 2006.

How Scalia Is Wrong

APRIL 11, 2006

In my article "Why Scalia Is Right" (5.1), I defended Supreme Court Justice Antonin Scalia's dismissal of those who believe that the Constitution is a living organism that changes over time in response to societal change. (In a speech in February, he called them "idiots.") The Constitution, I explained, is a document, not a Rorschach test. As a document—something intended to convey a particular message, not all messages—it has its own proper meaning distinguishable from the meanings one might prefer it to have, and it is the obligation of interpreters to figure out what that meaning is.

Justice Scalia's detractors object to his originalism—the term of art for those who propose a single fixed meaning for the Constitution—because they believe it goes hand in hand with and is in fact an engine of his conservative politics. They complain, for example, that if the Scalia doctrine were strictly adhered to, as Mel Seesholtz writes on saveourcourts.org, "one would have to conclude that 'all men are created equal' means exactly what it . . . meant . . . in the eighteenth century,"[1] and we would have to reinstate slavery, roll back women's rights, and refuse (as Justice Scalia has sometimes seemed to refuse) to recognize that homosexuals have any rights at all. This complaint is based on the mistake (made by Scalia's fans from the other direction) of thinking that originalism is a method, a thesis that not only asserts a single meaning for the Constitution but tells you exactly how to find it and thereby severely restricts what can be found.

But originalism, properly understood (and Justice Scalia himself might not understand it), is not a method; it is the answer to a question: What must you assume if you are seriously engaged in the act of interpretation? The answer is, you must assume that there is something to be interpreted. That also entails the assumption that the something to be interpreted was there before you or any other interpreter set to work. What that something is—what fixed meaning is there to be found—is neither identified nor delimited by the originalist argument. It could be anything; the only constraint is the requirement that it be the result of an honest effort to determine what the document originally meant.

Assuming that all men are created equal and that this principle (from the Declaration of Independence) finds its way into constitutional law via Amendments 14 and 15 as the doctrine of equal rights, an interpreter is still left with the task of defining equality in the context of some legal dispute. For example, in the debate over affirmative action, part of the argument has been about whether equal rights means the right to equal access (hence, no discriminatory restrictions) or the right to equal results (hence, reserving jobs and college admissions for minorities). Both sides believe that equal rights are what the Constitution guarantees; they just disagree about what the phrase means. Of course, the issue of affirmative action was not within the framers' contemplation, and some will think that we will have to choose between equal access and equal results without any help from them. But they have given us all the help we need by identifying equal rights as a constitutional concern. It is up to us to determine how that concern is to be honored in our present decisions.

That determination, however, cannot be made simply by declaring that the Constitution has a single meaning. While the originalist question—what is the meaning of the Constitution as drafted and ratified?—may be the right one, the question doesn't answer itself. Nor does it confer legitimacy on some answers or rule others out of court in advance. You still have to sift arguments, parse language, immerse yourself in historical archives, and more. You still have to do the interpretive work, and knowing that you have to do it—knowing that you have to search for a meaning that predates your effort—is not the same as doing it.

In short, Justice Scalia's originalism—his insistence that the Constitution has a fixed meaning—dictates no interpretive results, conservative or otherwise. In fact, no theory of constitutional interpretation dictates an interpretive result, for theoretical accounts do no interpretive work. Therefore, it doesn't matter whether you have the right one or the wrong one so long as you are really interpreting and not rewriting or making it up as you go along.

A Living Constitution proponent may, in practice, be trying to figure out what the Constitution actually means rather than what society now needs it to mean. There would then be no relationship between his or her theoretical account of that practice and the actual unfolding of that practice. And if the Living Constitution proponent actually did try to match his or her practice to that theory by laboring to refashion the Constitution so that it serves contemporary urgencies, he or she wouldn't be interpreting at all, so once again there would be no relationship between the interpretive practice and the theory of it (because there would be no interpretive practice).

And so in the end, I vindicate Justice Scalia again. But I part company with him when he tells us how to go about the task of specifying the original meaning either of the Constitution or of a statute. He believes that the text itself is the best key to its own meaning: if we focus on the meanings of the words as they would have been understood at the time of passage or ratification, we will be prevented from imposing the meanings we might prefer. This view is known as "textualism," and when Justice Scalia urges it, he often opposes it to "intentionalism," the view that meaning is to be identified with the author's intention. We must decide, he often says, not on the basis of what is meant, but on the basis of what is said.

But this distinction—between the intender's meaning and textual meaning—is undermined by one of the examples he cites to illustrate it. That example turns on a statute that provided for an increased jail term if a firearm was used in the commission of a crime. The defendant in a drug case offered to exchange a gun for cocaine, and the Supreme Court ruled that because he had "used" the gun in the course of performing an illegal act, he was subject to the longer sentence. (The case was *Smith v. United States*, 1993.) Justice Scalia is outraged and declares that this bad result would have been avoided if his colleagues had been "proper textualists." For then they would have been constrained by the fact that "The phrase 'uses a gun' fairly connoted uses of a gun for what guns are normally used for, that is, as a weapon."

But think again. Guns are used for many things and there are many meanings of the word "use" (more than thirty in the *Oxford English Dictionary*). The problem is how to sort through these meanings and uses in order to get to the right one. Consulting dictionaries won't do it. Dictionaries sketch out the scope of the problem; they don't solve it. Determining which use is statistically "normal" won't do it, because usages are specific to context and not all contexts are normal.

The only way to do it is to ask yourself what would these particular people—legislators charged with the duty to frame clear and fair laws and contemplating the question of enhanced penalties for criminal acts—have had in mind when they wrote the phrase "uses a firearm"? What would they have wanted to penalize, a piece of barter or a threat of violence? It is the obvious answer to that question—a question not about textual meaning or the statistics of usage, but about intention—that tells us why Justice Scalia was right to dissent from his fellow justices who, rather than failing to be "proper textualists," were illustrating the dangers of textualism. Having detached the words of the statute from the intentions of its drafters, they were free to range through the possible dictionary meanings of "use a firearm" and choose one that pleased them. This is exactly the result Justice Scalia hoped to avoid by insisting on textualism, but it is textualism that produces it.

The example also shows why one of the most often heard objections to intentionalism—it requires us to get inside the heads of interpreters and how do we do that?—is off the mark. The drafters of the statute are acting as institutional agents, and the intentions they might or might not have are the intentions appropriate to such agents. (Intentionalism is not a psychological thesis, but a rational one.) What was going on in the head of each individual congressperson— what were his or her private thoughts or motives or misgiving—is not to the point. The point is to ask, given the task they were jointly engaged in, what sense did each of them and of all of them intend for the words "use a firearm"?

This argument is likely to seem counterintuitive because it is usually assumed that the dictionary meaning of words directs us to intention rather than the other way around. But as the example demonstrates, only the specification of intention can stabilize the meanings of words because the dictionary gives you too many choices and no way of narrowing them. A dictionary, in fact, is less a list of meanings than a list of intentional uses, and more information than is provided by the text alone is required to determine which of those uses is being deployed on a particular occasion.

So Justice Scalia is right to champion originalism, but he backs the wrong version of it. Textual originalism doesn't do the job because severed from intention, the words of the text can mean too many things. In order to get at the meaning, you have to bring in—no, you have to start with—intention. That, however, is not the end of the matter but only its beginning, because intentional originalism, like originalism in general, only tells you what you're looking for; it doesn't tell you how to find it. It doesn't even tell you who the intender is—it could be Dick or Jane or God or Congress or the spirit of the age—and it certainly doesn't tell you where to find the evidence of what the intender—be it he, she, they or it—intends.

To determine that (or at least try to; interpretation doesn't always succeed) you have to do a lot of interpretive work. All I'm saying is that the point of that work will always and necessarily be the specification of intention.

1. Mel Seesholtz, "Theocracy Alert: Originalists and 'Proactive Judicial Activism,'" saveourcourts.org, May 3, 2005.

Intentional Neglect

JULY 19, 2005

Now that the speculation about who will replace Justice Sandra Day O'Connor on the Supreme Court is in full frenzy, we can look forward to debates in which words and phrases like "originalist," "strict constructionist," "textualist," "judicial activist," and "intentionalist" will figure prominently, because these labels are thought by many to stand for different styles of interpreting the Constitution. Those who think so are wrong.

If interpreting the Constitution—as opposed to rewriting it—is what you want to do, you are necessarily an "intentionalist," someone who is trying to figure out what the framers had in mind. Intentionalism is not a style of interpretation; it is another name for interpretation itself.

Think about it: if interpreting a document is to be a rational act, if its exercise is to have a goal and a way of assessing progress toward that goal, then it must have an object to aim at, and the only candidate for that object is the author's intention. What other candidate could there be?

One answer to this question has been given by Justice Antonin Scalia and others under the rubric of "textualism." Textualists insist that what an interpreter seeks to establish is the meaning of the text as it exists apart from anyone's intention. According to Justice Scalia, it is what is "said," not what is "meant," that is "the object of our inquiry."

The problem is that there is no such object. Suppose you're looking at a rock formation and see in it what seems to be the word "help." You look more closely and decide that, no, what you are seeing is an effect of erosion, random marks that just happen to resemble an English word. The moment you decide that nature caused the effect, you will have lost all interest in interpreting the formation, because you no longer believe that it has been produced intentionally, and therefore you no longer believe that it's a word, a bearer of meaning.

It may look like a word—it may even seem to be more regularly formed as such than the scratchings of someone who is lost—but in the absence of the assumption that what you're looking at is a vehicle of an intention, you will not regard it as language. It is not until you change your mind and become convinced that the formation was, in fact, designed that the marks will become language and it will be appropriate to interpret them.

Even then you are not home free; just because you're now sure that the marks spell the word "help," you still don't know what it means. It could be a message from a person in distress. It could be a direction like those on a computer screen ("Need help? Look here."). It could be a petition to God. It could be a reference to a Beatles song. Scrutinizing the word won't tell you which of these things it means.

This is why Justice Scalia has it backward: if you're not looking for what is meant, the notion of something being said or written is incoherent. Intention is not something added to language; it is what must already be assumed if what are otherwise mere physical phenomena (rocks or scratch marks) are to be experienced as language. Intention comes first; language, and with it the possibility of meaning, second. And this means that there can be no "textualist" method, because there is no object—no text without writerly intention—to which would-be textualists could be faithful.

And if there is no object—no plain and lucid text to which interpreters could be faithful—neither is there an object to which interpreters could be unfaithful. Consequently, "judicial activism," usually defined as substituting one's preferred meaning in place of the meaning the text clearly encodes, becomes the name of a crime no one could possibly commit. After all, you can't override a meaning that isn't there.

Indeed, because texts do not declare their own meanings, activism, at least of a certain kind, is inevitable. You must actively try to figure out what the author or authors had in mind when setting these marks down on paper. And while the text as written can be a piece of evidence, it cannot—just as that rock formation cannot—be self-sufficient and conclusive evidence.

It follows that any conclusion you reach about the intention behind a text can always be challenged by someone else who marshals different evidence for an alternative intention. Thus, interpretations of the Constitution, no matter how well established or long settled, are inherently susceptible to correction and can always (but not inevitably) be upset by new arguments persuasively made in the right venues by skilled advocates.

This does not mean, however, that interpreting the Constitution is a free-form activity in which anything goes. The activism that cannot be eliminated from interpretation is not an activism without constraint. It is constrained by the knowledge of what its object is—the specifying of authorial intention. An activism that abandons that constraint and just works the text over until it yields a meaning chosen in advance is not a form of interpretation at all but a form of rewriting.

Rewriting is what is being done by those who talk about the "Living Constitution" and ask, "Why should we be constrained by the dead hand of the past?" This makes no more sense than asking, "Why should we be constrained by wills and contracts?"

The answer is that without that constraint handed down by the past, law and predictability disappear and are replaced by irresponsibility and the exercise of power. If you can just make it up when interpreting the Constitution, you can also make it up when deciding whether or not to honor your contractual obligations, and so can everyone around you. In fact, if your question is "What do I want it to mean?" rather than "What did they mean by it?" you can dispense with "it" and "they" entirely and just go right to the fashioning of the meaning you prefer.

And that is why the only coherent answer to the question "What does the Constitution mean?" is that the Constitution means what its authors intended it to mean. The alternative answers just don't work: the Constitution can't mean what the text alone says because there is no text alone; and it can't mean what present-day society needs and wants it to mean because any meaning arrived at under that imperative will not be the Constitution's.

Only if the specification of the authors' intention is its goal does interpretation have a real object of inquiry; and only the goal of specifying authorial intention allows us to distinguish between what we might like the Constitution to mean and what we can show—by reasons and evidence publicly offered—that it does mean.

But is this account of interpretation at all helpful? If we keep it in mind, will it aid us in assessing the answers a president's nominee gives to the questions of the Senate Judiciary Committee? Not really. It does tell us a few things, mostly negative.

If the nominee identifies himself or herself as a textualist or a strict constructionist and pledges to be a faithful interpreter of the Constitution (as opposed to an unfaithful one?), you will know that he or she is blowing smoke and laying claim to virtues no one could practice. If the nominee promises to test the Constitution against the needs of our present situation, you will know that he or she will not be an interpreter but a rewriter, and no one on either the left or right wants that. And if the nominee says, "I am an intentionalist," the declaration will be uninformative, because every interpreter is necessarily an intentionalist—not by choice but by definition.

So, if you want to know how someone is likely to act on the bench, you will have to set all the labels aside and pay attention to the nominee's reasoning in response to the posing of hypothetical situations. What bodies of evidence does he or she cite on the way to deciding that the Constitution or a statute means this or that? What weight does he or she give to precedent? (Invoking precedent, I should add, is not interpreting, because in doing so one substitutes the meanings delivered by a judicial history for the meanings intended by an author.)

Does he or she construe intention narrowly and limit it to possibilities the framers could have foreseen, or is intention considered more broadly and extended to the positions the framers would likely have taken if they knew then what we know now? In short, what is the style of the nominee's intentionalism, and is it one you are comfortable with?

And then, if after having made that calculation you decide you are for this person, you can hope that the performance you see today predicts the performances of years to come. But don't bet on it.

What Did the Framers Have in Mind?

JULY 6, 2008

Whatever side of the Second Amendment controversy you may be on, the clear winner in *District of Columbia v. Heller* (2008; striking down a Washington, DC, ban on handguns) was intentionalism, the thesis that a text means what its author or authors intend.

The text in dispute is twenty-seven words long, and it is cited in the opening pages of each of the three opinions: "A well-regulated Militia, being necessary to the security of a free State, the right of the people to keep and bear arms, shall not be infringed." None of the words in this sentence is esoteric, and the syntax is straightforward, but if textual simplicity were sufficient to determine meaning, there would be no reason for 157 pages of close legal and linguistic argument.

What are the justices arguing about? A lot—the meaning of words, the significance of documents contemporary to the framing of the amendment, debates at constitutional conventions, regulations adopted or not adopted by various states, the court's own precedents—but basically the argument is about what the framers had in mind. As Justice Antonin Scalia, writing for the majority, observes, "The two sides in the case have set out very different interpretations of the amendment."

But the two sides do not proceed from different theories of interpretation. Both agree that the task is to read the amendment in the light of the purpose the framers would have had in writing it. They disagree about what that purpose was, and the materials they cite are meant to establish a purpose so firmly that in the light of it the words of the amendment will have one and only one obvious meaning.

For Scalia, that meaning is that Americans have "an individual right to possess a firearm unconnected with service in a militia, and to use that arm for traditionally lawful purposes, such as self-defense within the home."[1] For Justice John Paul Stevens, the Second Amendment "was adopted to protect the right of the people of each of the several states to maintain a well-regulated militia," and he finds no "evidence supporting the view that the amendment was intended to limit the power of Congress to regulate the civilian uses of weapons."

The evidence that might satisfy Stevens will not be found in the amendment itself, for as the opinions amply demonstrate, the twenty-seven words can be made to bear either interpretation. Does the first clause of the amendment govern the second propositional clause and constrain its meaning (it is only in relation to the desire to maintain a healthy militia that the right to bear arms is asserted)? Or does the first clause only establish a general, preexistent condition that does not direct the application of the second?

Scalia, who holds the latter view, declares that "a prefatory clause does not limit or expand the scope of the operative clause." But in fact it sometimes does and it sometimes doesn't. A formal, grammatical analysis will no more settle the matter than will a lexical analysis. Only by putting a background intention firmly in place can one stabilize a text that (like all texts) varies with the purpose assigned to it. That is why each side hears the other's interpretation as "grotesque" or "strained." Reading within different assumptions of the framers' intention, they see different texts and cannot understand how anyone could miss what is to each of them so differently clear. Scalia confidently concludes that nothing in the court's precedents "forecloses our adoption of the original understanding of the Second Amendment," and he is sure he knows what that understanding was.

Stevens just as strongly believes that the evidence he marshals "sheds revelatory light on the purpose of the amendment" and that he too knows what that purpose (and therefore the amendment's meaning) was. And yet, while the two jurists come to different interpretive conclusions, they are playing the same interpretive game: the game of trying to figure out what the authors of the amendment intended by its words.

For a large part of his separate dissenting opinion, Justice Stephen G. Breyer seems to be playing another game. He is less concerned with intention and purpose than with the problems faced by crime-ridden urban areas. His question, at least at first, is not "How can we be true to the framers' intention?" but "How can we read the amendment in a way that furthers our efforts to deal with a serious social problem?" He wants to focus on "the practicalities, the statute's rationale, the problems that called it into being, its relationship to those objectives—in a word, the details." He identifies as the statute's "basic objective" the saving of lives, and he cites statistics that establish, he believes, a strong correlation between the availability of handguns and crime. Handguns, he observes, "are involved in a majority of firearm deaths and injuries in the United States." And they are also, he declares, "a very popular weapon among criminals." He puts particular weight on a report from a congressional committee that found handguns "to have a particularly strong link to undesirable activities in the District's exclusively urban environment."

If that were all there was to Breyer's opinion, it would be vulnerable to Scalia's retort that even if "gun violence is a serious problem," no mere sociological finding authorizes or obligates the court "to pronounce the Second Amendment extinct." Where's the link to what the Constitution says?

Breyer claims to find it in the phrase "exclusively urban environment," which allows him to ground his support of the statute in what at least looks like an intentionalist argument. The reasoning is somewhat convoluted because it relies on a negative. The problem the statute is intended to redress, he says, is largely urban, but in thinking about the Second Amendment, the framers would have been "unlikely . . . to have thought of a right to keep loaded handguns in homes to confront intruders in urban settings," if only because in the America they knew, there were no urban settings. Therefore, they couldn't have had the intention to disallow a regulation of a kind they could not have contemplated.

Whether or not this argument is persuasive as an account of the framers' intention (and it wasn't persuasive to five of Breyer's brethren), its intention is clear—to allow Breyer to present himself as an intentionalist.

In the end, what we have in *District of Columbia v. Heller* is a unanimous decision. The vote is 5–4 on the interpretation of the amendment's intention, but it's 9–0 on the specification of intention as the interpreter's task.

---

1. All quotes throughout the essay are from *Columbia v. Heller* (2008) unless otherwise noted.

What Is the First Amendment For?

FEBRUARY 1, 2010

Citizens United v. Federal Election Commission (January 21, 2010)—the recent case in which the Supreme Court invalidated a statute prohibiting corporations and unions from using general treasury funds either to support or defeat a candidate in the thirty days before an election, and overruled an earlier decision relied on by the minority—has now been commented on by almost everyone, including the president of the United States in his State of the Union address.

I would like to step back from the debate about whether the decision enhances our First Amendment freedoms or hands the country over to big-money interests and read it instead as the latest installment in an ongoing conflict between two ways of thinking about the First Amendment and its purposes.

We can approach the conflict by noting a semantic difference between the majority and concurring opinions on the one hand and the dissenting opinion—a ninety-page outpouring of passion and anger by Justice Stevens—on the other. The word most important to Justice Kennedy's argument (he writes for the majority) is "chill," while the word most important to Stevens's argument is "corrupt."

Kennedy, along with Justices Roberts, Alito, Thomas, and Scalia (the usual suspects), is worried that the restrictions on campaign expenditures imposed by the statute he strikes down will "chill" speech, that is, prevent some of it from entering the marketplace of ideas that must, he believes, be open to all voices if the First Amendment's stricture against the abridging of speech is to be honored. ("[A] statute which chills speech can and must be invalidated.") Stevens is worried—no, he is certain—that the form of speech Kennedy celebrates will corrupt the free flow of information so crucial to the health of a democratic society. "[T]he distinctive potential of corporations to corrupt the electoral process [has] long been recognized."

When Stevens writes "has long been recognized," he is invoking the force of history and asking us to take note of the reasons why many past court decisions (including one written by then-Chief Justice Rehnquist) have acknowledged the dangers posed by corporations, dangers that provoked this declaration by Theodore Roosevelt in 1905: "All contributions by corporations to any political committee or for any political purpose should be forbidden by law."

Behind such strong statements is a twin fear: (1) the fear that big money will not only talk (the metaphor that converts campaign expenditures into speech and therefore into a matter that merits First Amendment scrutiny), but will buy votes and influence, and (2) the fear that corporations and unions, with their huge treasuries, will crowd out smaller voices by purchasing all the airtime and print space. The majority, Stevens admits, does "acknowledge the validity of the interest in preventing corruption," but, he complains, it is not an interest it is interested in, for "it effectively discounts the value of that interest to zero."

That's not quite right. Kennedy and the others in the majority make the proper noises about corruption; they just don't think that it is likely to occur, and they spend much time explaining why corporations are citizens like anyone else (a proposition Stevens ridicules) and why, for various economic and public-relation reasons, they pose no threat to the integrity of the electoral process.

But even if they thought otherwise, even if they were persuaded by the dire predictions Stevens and those he cites make, they would come down where they do, not because they welcome corruption or have no interest in forestalling it, or discount the value of being concerned with it, but because they find another interest of more value, indeed, of surpassing value. That is, the value of being faithful to what they take to be the categorical imperative of the First Amendment, which, with respect to political speech, forbids the suppression of voices, especially voices "the Government deems to be suspect" (Kennedy); for if this voice now, why not other voices later?

Even if there were substance to the charge of "undue influence" exercised by those with deep pockets, it would still be outweighed, says Kennedy, citing an earlier case, "by the loss for democratic process resulting from the restrictions upon free and full discussion." The question of where that discussion might take the country is of less interest than the overriding interest in assuring that it is full and free, that is, open to all and with no exclusions based on a calculation of either the motives or the likely actions of individual or corporate speakers. In this area, the majority insists, the state cannot act paternally.

Voters are adults who must be "free to obtain information from diverse sources"; they are not to be schooled by a government that would protect them from sources it distrusts.

Notice how general Kennedy's rhetoric has become. The specificity of Stevens's concerns, rooted in the historical record and in the psychology and sociology of political actors, disappears in the overarching umbrella category of "information." The syllogism is straightforward. Freedom of information is what the First Amendment protects; corporations and unions are sources of information; therefore their contributions—now imagined as wholly verbal not monetary; the conversion is complete—must be protected, come what may.

That, Kennedy is saying, is the court's job, to allow the process to go forward unimpeded. It is not the court's job to fiddle with the process in an effort to make it fairer or more representative, a point Chief Justice Roberts makes in his concurring opinion when he cites approvingly the court's "repudiation," in *Buckley v. Valeo* (1976), "of any government interest in 'equalizing the relative ability of individuals and groups to influence the outcomes of elections.'" Equality may be a good thing; it might be nice if no one had a disproportionate share of influence; but it's not our job to engineer it. Let the market sort it out.

The majority's reasoning reaches back to a famous pronouncement by Oliver Wendell Holmes, who acknowledges in *Gitlow v. New York* (1925) that there are forms of discourse that, if permitted to flourish, might very well bring disastrous results. Nevertheless, he says, "If in the long run the beliefs expressed . . . are destined to be accepted by the dominant forces of the community, the only meaning of free speech is that they should be given their chance and have their way."

Holmes's fatalism—let everyone speak, and if the consequences are bad, so be it—stands in contrast to the epistemological optimism of Justice Brandeis, who believes that if the marketplace is allowed to be completely open, bad speech will be exposed and supplanted by good speech (a reverse Gresham's law): "The remedy to be supplied is more speech, not enforced silence" (*Whitney v. California*, 1927). Both justices reject state manipulation of the speech market, one because he is willing to take what comes—it is Holmes who said that if his fellow countrymen wanted to go to hell in a handbasket, it was his job to help them—the other because he believes that what will come if speech is unfettered will be good.

The justices in the *Citizens United* majority are more in the Brandeis camp. They believe that free trade in ideas with as many trading partners as wish to join in will inevitability produce benign results for a democratic society. And since their confidence in these results is a matter of theoretical faith and not of empirical or historical observation—free speech is for them a religion with long-term rewards awaiting us down the road—they feel no obligation to concern themselves with short-term calculations and predictions.

Stevens also values robust intellectual commerce, but he believes that allowing corporate voices to have their full and unregulated say "can distort the 'free trade in ideas' crucial to candidate elections." In his view free trade doesn't take care of itself but must be engineered by the kind of restrictions the majority strikes down. The marketplace of ideas can become congealed and frozen; the free flow can be impeded, and when that happens the only way to preserve free speech values is to curtail or restrict some forms of speech, just as you might remove noxious weeds so that your garden can begin to grow again. Prohibitions on speech, Stevens says, can operate "to facilitate First Amendment values," and he openly scorns the majority's insistence that enlightened self-government "can arise only in the absence of regulation."

The idea that you may have to regulate speech in order to preserve its First Amendment value is called consequentialism. For a consequentialist like Stevens, freedom of speech is not a stand-alone value to be cherished for its own sake but a policy that is adhered to because of the benign consequences it is thought to produce, consequences that are cataloged in the usual answers to the question, what is the First Amendment for?

Answers like the First Amendment facilitates the search for truth, or the First Amendment is essential to the free flow of ideas in a democratic polity, or the First Amendment encourages dissent, or the First Amendment provides the materials necessary for informed choice and individual self-realization. If you think of the First Amendment as a mechanism for achieving goals like these, you have to contemplate the possibility that some forms of speech will be subversive of those goals because, for instance, they impede the search for truth or block the free flow of ideas or crowd out dissent. And if such forms of speech appear along with their attendant dangers, you will be obligated—not in violation of the First Amendment but in fidelity to it—to move against them, as Stevens advises us to do in his opinion.

The opposite view of the First Amendment—the view that leads you to be wary of chilling any speech even if it harbors a potential for corruption—is the principled or libertarian or deontological view. Rather than asking what is the First Amendment for and worrying about the negative effects a form of speech may have on the achievement of its goals, the principled view asks what does the First Amendment say and answers, simply, it says no state abridgment of speech. Not no abridgment of speech unless we dislike it or fear it or think of it as having low or no value, but no abridgment of speech, period, especially if the speech in question is implicated in the political process.

The cleanest formulation of this position I know is given by the distinguished First Amendment scholar William Van Alstyne: "The First Amendment does not link the protection it provides with any particular objective and may, accordingly, be deemed to operate without regard to anyone's view of how well the speech it protects may or may not serve such an objective."[1]

In other words, forget about what speech does or does not do in the world; just take care not to restrict it. This makes things relatively easy. All you have to do is determine that it's speech and then protect it, as Kennedy does when he observes that "Section 441b's prohibition on corporate independent expenditures is . . . a ban on speech."[2] That's it. Nothing more need be said, although Kennedy says a lot more, largely in order to explain why nothing more need be said and why everything Stevens says—about corruption, distortion, electoral integrity, and undue influence—is beside the doctrinal point.

The majority's purity of principle is somewhat alloyed when it upholds the disclosure requirements of the statute it is considering on the reasoning that the public has a right to be informed about the identity of those who fund a corporation's ads and videos. "This transparency enables the electorate to make informed decisions."

Justice Thomas disagrees. The interest "in providing voters with additional relevant information" does not, he says, outweigh "the right to anonymous speech." The majority's claim that disclosure requirements do not prevent anyone from speaking is, Thomas declares, false; those who know that their names will be on a list may refrain from contributing for fear of reprisals and thus be engaged in an act of self-censoring. The effect of disclosure requirements, he admonishes, is "to curtail campaign-related activity and prevent the lawful, peaceful exercise of First Amendment rights."

Only Thomas has the courage of the majority's declared convictions. Often the most principled of the judges (which doesn't mean that I always like his principles), he is willing to follow a principle all the way, and so he rebukes his colleagues in the majority for preferring the value of more information to the value the First Amendment mandates—absolutely free speech unburdened by any restriction whatsoever, including the restriction of having to sign your name. Thomas has caught his fellow conservatives in a consequentialist moment.

The consequentialist and principled view of the First Amendment are irreconcilable. Their adherents can only talk past one another and become increasingly angered and frustrated by what they hear from the other side. This ongoing soap opera has been the content of First Amendment jurisprudence ever since it emerged full blown in the second decade of the twentieth century. *Citizens United* is a virtual anthology of the limited repertoire of moves the saga affords. You could build an entire course around it. And that is why even though I agree with much of what Stevens says (I'm a consequentialist myself) and dislike the decision as a citizen, as a teacher of First Amendment law, I absolutely love it.

1. William W. Van Alstyne, "A Graphic Review of the Free Speech Clause," *Faculty Publications*, Paper 731, (1982), http://scholarship.law.wm.edu/facpubs/731.
2. *Citizens United v. Federal Election Commission* (January 21, 2010).

How the First Amendment Works

FEBRUARY 8, 2010

One of the respondents to my column on *United Citizens* ("What Is the First Amendment For?" [5.5]), the corporate campaign funding case, declares, "Professor Fish is obviously an apologist for this bad decision," while others are just as confident that I tip my hand in the other direction when I refer to the majority as "the usual suspects."

The truth is that, as usual, I was not (until the last sentence) coming down on one side or the other but attempting to lay out the assumptions that inform the majority and dissenting opinions, assumptions of which the justices may not be aware even as they are operating within them. I may have confused things a bit by saying at the end that I love the decision. What I meant is that I love the decision as a teacher because the number of issues it raises will keep a classroom discussion going for weeks, and that judgment is more than borne out by the wonderfully learned and spirited comments the column provoked. A very large number of those comments made two points: (1) money is not speech, and (2) corporations are not persons.

The equivalence between money and speech is established (at least legally) in *Buckley v. Valeo* (1976), where the Supreme Court insists that "a restriction on the amount of money a person or group can spend on political communication during a campaign necessarily reduces the quantity of expression by restricting the number of issues discussed, the depth of their exploration, and the size of the audience reached." So that while money is not literally speech, it enables and amplifies speech when it is used to buy political advertising and therefore, according to the court's logic, money expended for that purpose merits First Amendment protection.

That same logic informed another 1976 decision (*Virginia State Board of Pharmacy v. Virginia Citizens Consumer Council*), in which the court for the first time brought commercial speech under the umbrella of constitutional protection on the reasoning that by providing information to consumers it furthers the First Amendment goal of fostering an informed citizenry. And if speech used to sell toothpaste and potato chips can be elevated to the status of philosophical tracts, novels, and policy arguments (a development lamented by Chief Justice Rehnquist in a series of dissents), it is no trick at all to accord the same status to the efforts of a corporation to sell or sink a candidate.

The metamorphosis of corporations into persons follows a less straightforward course. Regarding corporations as persons for some legal purposes, while always being aware of the fiction involved, has been the practice for a long time, but breathing human life into corporations (in the manner of Michelangelo's God) and giving them rights enjoyed by flesh-and-blood citizens is arguably something new, and something Justice Stevens vigorously protests against, making many of the points made in the comments: A corporation does not have a conscience. Its interests are exclusively economic and do not include the health and welfare of society. It is not seeking to join and further the free flow of ideas. Its acts do not reflect the will of shareholders. Its massive funding of political advertising amounts to buying votes and cannot finally be distinguished from bribery. (Obviously not points that carried the day, but they may prevail in a day when the court's composition changes.)

Many readers expressed impatience with the history of these pro and con arguments and complained that the money-is-speech and the corporations-are-persons mantras just fly in the face of common sense. They said that lawyers and judges overintellectualize simple issues and obscure the reality of things on the ground by confining themselves to an arid, abstract vocabulary and endlessly spinning its artificial terms. "The legal system in this country works," writes Charles in a particularly incisive comment, "by forcing every issue into a preexisting conversation 'made up of magical words of power bandied about by robed wizards.'" In time, Charles adds, those magic words remake the facts of real-world situations as legal insiders "acquire the skill to fit every current problem into its preordained place and vocabulary."

This was precisely the complaint voiced by the legal realists in the early decades of the twentieth century, most memorably by Felix Cohen, who, in his classic essay "Transcendental Nonsense and the Functional Approach" (*Columbia Law Review*, 1935), mocked a jurisprudence that is revealed to be "a special branch of the science of transcendental nonsense" once you look behind its curtain.

In that science, or pseudoscience, solemn attention is paid to fictional entities that exist only in the special branch's special vocabulary, while real entities that have a real relevance to the real lives of real people are left behind. "Nobody," Cohen pointed out, "has ever seen a corporation," so "what right have we to believe in corporations if we don't believe in angels?" Legal discourse populated by such chimera, Cohen observes, floats free of the earth and negotiates its business in midair where it talks only to parts of itself. "To justify or criticize legal rules in purely legal terms is always to argue in a vicious circle."

A kinder way to put Cohen's point, without rejecting it, would be to say that the legal system is heavily invested in its autonomy, that is, in the claim, always dear to a profession, to have its own sphere of operation and its own perspective or lens through which the matters that come before it are seen. The desire for autonomy requires a machinery that is internal to the system and only makes contact with the outside world in attenuated and highly mediated ways. Otherwise, the apologists for autonomy explain, law would be an extension of some other project—morality, philosophy, psychology, sociology, and economics, all of which have had their takeover moments—and there would be no reason for it to have a separate, distinct existence.

However dubious the assertion of autonomy might seem to be, its appeal, at least to insiders, survives all assaults, and that is why the content of First Amendment law is an internally generated set of binary oppositions and tests that organizes its world and constrains the kinds of actions that can be taken within it. As Felix Cohen and Charles observe in disdain, those oppositions and tests are, for legal purposes, more real than the facts they order. What a court can do in the area of the First Amendment (or any area of the law for that matter) is largely determined by what previous courts have done in a language the present court cannot abandon and can only alter by degrees.

The basic opposition, the one without which the First Amendment could not get off the ground, is the opposition between speech and action. Absent the assumption that the two can be distinguished, the First Amendment makes no sense, as we can see by imagining the absurdity of a First Amendment that read, "Congress shall make no law abridging the freedom of action." Regulating and restricting action is what governments do; take that responsibility away and government has no scope of operation.

The positing of a distinct realm of mind and thought where speech is the main medium and expression is conceived of as an activity remote from worldly action (except in carefully defined circumstances) is not something lawyers and jurists must actively do. It comes with, and indeed marks out, the territory, and the main task of professionals in the field is to determine just where the line between speech and action should be drawn.

Although I haven't space to defend the assertion here, let me say that there is no principled way to draw that line. And while that fact, as I take it to be, is philosophically troubling, it is operationally useful; for a line that is not drawn in nature but yet is considered necessary for the game to be played can and must be drawn by the players who are in a position to do so. Once the line has been drawn authoritatively (an authority that can always be challenged but only within the terms already set by the discourse), it does the work of making legal sense out of a landscape that is more complex and fluid than the sense that has been artificially made.

It is this complexity that leads some readers to ask how there can be a principled view of the First Amendment if "we abridge freedom of speech all the time" (hinnymule) by outlawing bribes (P.g. Mulvaney), by criminalizing the solicitation of sex (Rael64) and the organizing of bank heists (Richard), and communications with terrorist organizations (ray).

The answer is that in each of these cases the speech involved has been redefined as action, or said to be so "brigaded" with action, that it loses the status of "mere" speech and can therefore be regulated without violating any First Amendment principle. (What a move!) Because the speech/action distinction is not perspicuous and is, in effect, always being constructed, activities can be moved to either side of the line so long as there is a will and a majority.

Take libel, which several posters cited as a form of speech that the state has always regulated even when its rhetoric affirmed a principled First Amendment position. But in *New York Times Co. v. Sullivan* (1964), the court extended First Amendment protection to libelous statements made about public officials because, it reasoned, while they may be erroneous and defamatory, they also contribute to "debate on public issues," and such debate "should be uninhibited, robust and wide-open." (I have always thought of this as the John Wayne theory of the First Amendment.) "[N]either factual error nor defamatory content suffices to remove the constitutional shield from criticism of official conduct."

At first glance that left the laws against libel in place if the person defamed was a private individual rather than a public official, but in subsequent decisions "public official" became "public person" (someone known to the public, "public" not quantitatively defined) and then a private person who happened to wander into a context of public discussion. (So much for libel.) If false and defamatory speech can migrate from unprotected to protected territory, any form of speech once considered injurious can at least theoretically make the same journey, as the decision in *Citizens United* demonstrates.

And the journey can be reversed. Speech once protected because the harm it has been said to cause is too remote from its production (think manuals for murder) can lose that protection if a sufficiently strong "but for" argument—but for this speech, the harm would never have occurred—can be mounted. Put this together with the wonderful categories of "symbolic speech" and "performative speech," which can turn cross-burning into speech (it conveys a message) and depictions of children into child abuse, and it becomes clear that First Amendment formulas and distinctions are infinitely malleable (not at will; the interpretive work still has to be done).

And the moral? Everything is political? Sure, but a conclusion so general and so banal is hardly helpful. Let's just give up because there isn't a principled distinction in sight? I don't think so. There is no moral except the obvious one: This is just the way the First Amendment works. It is always building the road it walks on and then declaring that the road was there all the while.

Cohen is right (except for his moralism); it's an act of prestidigitation, a magical sleight of hand, a game whose rules are continually changing, a discourse that can reach any conclusion at all, including one you would have thought impossible. It hasn't got a principled leg to stand on, and yet it keeps moving forward and producing real-world consequences. In short, it is an absolutely marvelous achievement, something to be admired as a wonder even when you are distressed by the content of what it has just produced.

What Does the First Amendment Protect?

JULY 4, 2011

In the two First Amendment cases handed down last week—one about limiting sales of violent video games to children (*Brown v. Entertainment Merchants* [June 27, 2011]), the other about Arizona's attempt to make public financing more attractive to candidates (*Arizona Free Enterprise v. Bennett* [June 27, 2011])—the dissenting justices contend that the protection of speech is not really the issue at all.[1]

In his dissent to *Brown v. Entertainment Merchants*, Justice Stephen Breyer declares that this is not a case, as the majority claims, about "depictions of violence"; rather, it is a case about "protection of children." What Breyer is doing (or attempting to do) is shift the category under which the matter of dispute is to be considered. According to Justice Antonin Scalia, writing for the majority, depictions of violence merit First Amendment protection because they are speech, not acts. Breyer replies that the video games in question are in fact acts, although they are, he acknowledges, acts "containing an expressive component." That component, he argues, does not outweigh or render irrelevant the "significant amount of physical activity" involved in playing these games, activity in the course of which players do not merely see violent things but do violent things.

The danger Breyer wants to protect children from is not the danger of being exposed to violence but the danger of being initiated into violence. This happens (or can happen) when game-players are required not merely to view violent acts passively but to perform them by making a succession of choices (with a button or joystick) that decide the fate of the characters they have created.

Justice Samuel Alito, who concurs in the result because he believes the law to have been poorly drafted but disagrees with the majority's reasoning, provides an example. Compare, he says, the reader of a novel depicting violence with a video-game player who creates an avatar that bears his own image; who sees a realistic image of the victim . . . in three dimensions; who is forced to decide whether or not to kill the victim and decides to do so; who then pretends to grasp an axe, to raise it above the head of the victim; who hears the thud of the axe hitting her head and her cry of pain; who sees her split skull and feels the sensation of blood on his face and hands.

Are these experiences the same?, Alito asks, and answers no. The difference, which Scalia labors to deny ("Certainly the *books* we give to children . . . contain no shortage of gore"), is sufficient, Alito thinks, to justify the state's interest in regulation, even though he finds the present attempt at regulation flawed.

Breyer frames the issue precisely when he declares, "This case is ultimately less about censorship than it is about education." Education is important in a democracy, he explains, because it gives us a means of raising "future generations committed cooperatively to making our system of government work." The implication is that a generation immersed in violent video games will be committed not to cooperation but to actions less helpful to the flourishing of the country.

Justice Clarence Thomas, writing another dissent disguised as a concurrence, shares Breyer's concern that children be protected from influences that might turn them into damaged citizens. He reminds us of Noah Webster's admonition that children's minds be "untainted till their reasoning faculties have acquired strength and the good principles which may be planted . . . have taken deep root"; and he cites a 1979 opinion in which Justice Lewis F. Powell declares that "the State is entitled to adjust its legal system to account for children's vulnerability." Children are vulnerable, according to this theory, because they have not yet developed the ability to distance themselves from what is put before them. Interactive video games increase this vulnerability and lead not merely to the consuming of bad images but to the possibility of becoming a bad person. This is the corruption that will follow, Alito fears, from allowing "troubled teens to experience in an extraordinarily personal and vivid way what it would be like to carry out unspeakable acts of violence."

Breyer drives the point home: "extremely violent games can harm children by rewarding them for being violently aggressive in play, and thereby often teaching them to be violently aggressive in life." Violent video games, in short, are not representations that deserve First

Amendment protection; they are acts with harmful consequences, and children deserve to be protected from *them*.

Although its subject matter could not be more different, *Arizona Free Enterprise v. Bennett* displays the same opposition between a libertarian concern for freedom and a consequentialist concern for the corruption that attends unregulated activity. In this case it is not a child but the political system that is in danger of corruption, and the source of corruption is not a violent game but the desire of private individuals to purchase the votes of officeholders.

That at least is the view of Justice Elena Kagan, writing in dissent: "Campaign finance reform over the last century has focused on one key question: how to prevent massive pools of private money from corrupting our political system." In Kagan's formulation, "private money" equals "special interests," whereas those who "rely on public, rather than private moneys, are 'beholden [to] no person.'" Therefore by "supplanting private cash, public financing eliminates the source of political corruption."

No, says Chief Justice John G. Roberts, writing for the majority. Arizona's public financing scheme, he contends, is an unconstitutional restriction on free speech because it penalizes privately financed candidates for being successful. Expenditures by privately financed candidates and the groups supporting them trigger the awarding of matching funds to candidates who have accepted the limits that come along with public funding. Roberts concludes that "any increase in speech is of one kind . . . that of publicly financed candidates." So even if "the matching funds provision did result in more speech . . . in general, it would do so at the expense of impermissibly burdening (and thus reducing) the speech of privately financed candidates."

But that parentheses—"and thus reducing"—is a little too fast. How exactly does the fact that in response to your expenditures an opponent with fewer resources will be given additional funds reduce *your* speech? You can still get to spend as much as you want and to say as much as you want. What you don't get to do is overwhelm the voices of less affluent candidates and their supporters. As Kagan points out, "what petitioners demand is essentially a right to quash others' speech . . . they would prefer the field to themselves, so that they can speak free from response." The Arizona law, she adds, can hardly be characterized as a restriction on speech.

It follows, Kagan asserts, that "public financing furthers a compelling interest"—the prevention of corruption—and does so without diminishing anyone's speech rights. The conclusion, she believes, is inescapable "[e]xcept in this Court," where the majority declares that the state interest in leveling the playing field "cannot justify undue burdens on political speech." But, to make the point again, there is no burden unless being prevented from being the only speaker with a megaphone is a burden, and it is not. In the majority decision, a compelling state interest is set aside because of a restriction on speech that has not occurred.

In some exasperation, Kagan remarks, "Only one thing is missing from the Court's response: any reasoning to support [its] conclusion." That's not quite right. The reasoning is contained in an assumption that is the reverse of Kagan's: private money, rather than being the vehicle of corruption, is the vehicle of speech, and therefore you can't have too much of it, no matter what its effects. The First Amendment, says Roberts, "embodies our choice as a Nation that, when it comes to . . . speech, the guiding principle is freedom—the 'unfettered interchange of ideas'—not whatever the State may view as fair."

Roberts does not have to reply to Kagan's points—he can even concede them—because in his view they are irrelevant. "When it comes to protected speech, the speaker is sovereign." Other considerations (like corruption and fairness) may be in play, but the rights of the speaker—in this case the rights of the spender—are paramount. They are what the First Amendment protects. Kagan disagrees: "The First Amendment's core purpose is to foster a healthy, vibrant political system full of robust discussion and debate," and the Arizona law, with its mechanism for increasing participation is, she maintains, true to that purpose.

And there you have it: a clash between the worship of freedom of speech and a concern for the quality of public life in relation to which free speech may sometimes be asked to take a backseat. It is the same clash that pits the freedom to play video games against society's interest in fostering a generation of young adults responsive to its ideals and aspirations. We have seen this before—in the pornography cases, in the crush-video case (*United States v. Stevens*, 2010; for more on this case, see 5.8, "The First Amendment and Kittens") in the case upholding the right of an antigay ministry to picket the funerals of soldiers—and we shall certainly see it again.

1. All of the quotes throughout this essay are from *Brown v. Entertainment Merchants* (June 27, 2011) and *Arizona Free Enterprise v. Bennett* (June 27, 2011) unless otherwise noted.

The First Amendment and Kittens

APRIL 26, 2010

To anyone who has been following First Amendment jurisprudence in the past forty or fifty years, the recent Supreme Court decision (*United States v. Stevens*, April 20) striking down a statute criminalizing the production and sale of videos depicting animal cruelty in a manner intended to satisfy a particular "sexual fetish" will come as no surprise.

The proverbial ordinary citizen, however, may be surprised to learn that, according to Chief Justice John Roberts's majority opinion, the First Amendment must be read to allow the production and dissemination of so-called crush videos, videos (and I quote from Roberts's opinion) that "feature the intentional torture and killing of helpless animals" often by women wearing high-heeled "spike" shoes who slowly "crush animals to death" while talking to them in "a kind of dominatrix patter" as they scream and squeal "in great pain." How has it come to this?

Part of the answer can be found in the history of First Amendment theory. (What follows is the quick and dirty version.) At the beginning of the twentieth century, the reigning theory was called "bad tendency." Speech that was thought to have a tendency to undermine authority or corrupt morals could be regulated, even in the absence of any evidence that sedition or immorality had in fact been produced.

But then, in a series of cases, Justices Oliver Wendell Holmes and Louis D. Brandeis developed a theory called the "clear and present danger" theory, which was more sensitive to actual patterns of cause and effect. It said that even speech advocating the overthrow of the government must be protected unless the danger is imminent. "The question in every case," Holmes explained, "is whether the words used are used in such circumstances and are of such a nature as to create a clear and present danger that they will bring about the substantive evils that Congress has a right to prevent" (*Schenck v. United States*, 1919).

This test was not without its problems: Some feared that waiting until the danger was almost upon us would leave too little time to prevent it; others feared that the state could too easily decide that a particular instance of speech harbored a danger it had the right and duty to forestall. But all parties to these arguments agreed that the judicial task was to assess the likely consequences of various kinds of speech before determining whether they deserve constitutional protection.

In essence, speech was regarded in this period as a form of behavior (albeit a particularly favored one), and like any form of behavior, speech could have both good and bad effects. The trick was to determine whether a particular effect was so bad that the cost to freedom of speech of regulating it was less than the cost of allowing it to flourish. The formula was given its definitive formulation by Judge Learned Hand: "In each case . . . ask whether the gravity of the evil . . . justifies such invasion of free speech as is necessary to avoid the danger."[1]

This balancing test, which measured effect, was joined (implicitly and sometimes explicitly) by a content test, which measured value. Some speech is an essential contribution to the marketplace of ideas; some speech contributes nothing to the marketplace and even pollutes it. Utterances of the latter kind, the Supreme Court said in *Chaplinsky v. New Hampshire* (1942), "have never been thought to raise any Constitutional problem," for they are "of such slight social value as a step to truth that any benefit that may be derived from them is clearly outweighed by the social interest in order and morality."

Put together speech that has deleterious effects with speech of no redeeming value and what do you have? You have videos depicting helpless kittens being tortured by leather-clad sadists. Case closed (if it ever got to the courts in the first place).

So what happened? The short answer is that *New York Times Co. v. Sullivan* (1964) happened. In that case (beloved by free-speech purists), the court decided, in the context of a libel action brought against this newspaper for publishing an advertisement containing erroneous statements, that "neither factual nor defamatory content" removed the "shield of constitutional protection" from speech even if it is false. The court's reasoning? "Debate on public issues should be uninhibited, robust and wide open," and therefore considerations of "truth" and "social utility" are no longer to the point. Nor, added Justice Arthur Goldberg in a concurrence, are considerations of effect, for the right the court now declares—"to speak one's mind about public officials and affairs"—must be upheld "despite the harm which may flow from excesses and abuses."

This is still a long way from constitutionalizing "crush videos," but the path to *United States v. Stevens* is now open because speech has been declared to be a value in and of itself, no matter what its content or effect. A new question is asked: not does this speech have any intrinsic worth or does it benefit or harm society but is it speech? Is it "expressive activity"? And if the answer is yes, the presumption of constitutional protection is very strong, and more often than not the court will find a way to save the speech in question, however meretricious it might be.

Thus, in *Hustler Magazine v. Falwell* (1988), the court decided that Jerry Falwell could not recover damages for an "ad" depicting the evangelist having sex with his drunken mother in an outhouse. At the bottom of the ad, in small print, one could (barely) read, "ad-parody—not to be taken seriously," an obvious legal strategy that was itself not to be taken seriously as Larry Flynt, *Hustler*'s publisher, demonstrated in an interview when he declared that it had been his intention to wound and indeed "kill" Falwell's reputation. After noting that there was no libel involved because the ad was a piece of fiction and therefore asserted no facts (Philip Sidney lives), the court declared that this "gross and repugnant" (its words) verbal production was nevertheless a contribution to "the free interchange of ideas and ascertainment of truth" and was a "distant cousin" of the political cartoons that exaggerated Franklin D. Roosevelt's "jutting jaw and cigarette holder." ("Distant" is too weak a word unless one means the distance between galaxies.) So the ad asserts nothing and cannot be taken seriously, but it is a serious enough assertion to merit constitutional protection. Go figure.

Decisions like *Hustler Magazine v. Falwell* exhibit a pattern. Before coming down on the side of the speech the government tries to regulate, the court declares its distaste and even revulsion in the face of what it must, according to its lights, permit, as if to say, "we are on the right moral side, we regret having to do this, but, hey, it's the First Amendment."

This "rhetoric of regret" is on display in spades in the famous Skokie case (*Smith v. Collin*, 1978), in which a seventh circuit court declares that a march by a band of neo-Nazis through a neighborhood populated by Holocaust survivors must be allowed even though, as the court concedes, emotional and mental distress would be inflicted upon elderly people who had already suffered more than enough. The court even acknowledges that the ideas put forward by the would-be marchers threaten to tear away the "thin coating" of civilization, and it feels "compelled" to express "repugnance at the doctrine which the appellees wish to profess." (Hardly a consolation.)

In another seventh circuit case (*American Booksellers v. Hudnut*, 1986), the speech at issue is pornography, and the court assents to the description of pornography as "an aspect of dominance," which, by putting certain images of women into the world, is more than an "idea" and is in fact an "injury." Nevertheless, the court rules against a city antipornography ordinance, not despite its injurious effects but because of them, for "if the fact that speech plays a role in a process of conditioning were enough to permit governmental regulation, that would be the end of freedom of speech." No, that would be the end of freedom of speech as an all-purpose get-out-of-jail card. It would not be the end of freedom of speech if forms of speech that were part of a benign "conditioning" were protected while malign forms were treated with the negative caution they deserve.

How malign or benign is flag burning? What is its value? In *Texas v. Johnson* (1989), the Supreme Court decides that the act of burning and spitting on the flag is valuable because by permitting it, we honor the history and tradition the flag symbolizes: "We do not consecrate the flag by punishing its desecration, for in so doing we dilute the freedom that this cherished emblem represents." Get it? We cherish the emblem by burning and spitting on it.

There are dissents to some of these decisions, and they tend to make the same point that Justices William H. Rehnquist and John Paul Stevens make in their dissents to *Texas v. Johnson*: "Flag burning is the equivalent of an inarticulate grunt" (Rehnquist). It has nothing do with ideas, but is simply "disagreeable conduct" (Stevens). Obviously, this attempt to deny or downplay the "expressive element" of the act does not carry the day, as it does not in the crush-video case where a version of it is put forward both by Solicitor General Elena Kagan in her brief for the government and by the lone dissenter, Justice Samuel Alito (the new odd couple).

In his majority opinion, Roberts acknowledges that in child pornography cases, the argument that the market for the "product" was integrally related to the incidence of child abuse was found "persuasive." Alito and Kagan try the same argument in response to the point that while the actions depicted in the crush videos are certainly illegal, depicting them is not, because the portrayal of illegal acts is not itself an infringement of law.

Not true, Kagan and Alito reply: the illegal acts occur in large part because there is a market for the videos that depict them; take away the traffic in videos and you will reduce the number of crimes. Indeed, says Alito, those "criminal acts . . . cannot be prevented without targeting . . . the creation, sale, and possession for sale of depictions of animal torture." Moreover, the effect of the ban "on trafficking in crush videos" would also help "to enforce the criminal laws and to ensure that criminals do not profit from their crimes." Not to mention, Kagan adds, preventing "the harm to living animals occurring in the creation of the depictions, as well as associated harms arising from the acts of violence."

But Roberts isn't having any. He simply invokes the post–*New York Times v. Sullivan* mantra and flatly rejects any "balancing of relative social costs and benefits" when it comes to speech. "The First Amendment," he declares, "reflects a judgment by the American people that the benefits of its restrictions . . . outweigh the costs," a judgment that he insists cannot be revised "simply on the basis that some speech is not worth it." In short, the balancing Roberts rejects has already occurred in the empyrean of First Amendment theory, and the conclusion, given in advance, is that, aside from a direct incitement to violence or an act of treason, no expressive activity can be worthless enough to forfeit its constitutional protection. So much for the kittens.

One often-heard objection to religion is that horrible acts are done in its name. It is an irony of history that the First Amendment, opposed by Justice Jackson in a famous passage to the establishment of any orthodoxy,[2] has itself become an orthodoxy, a religion, a veritable deity, and one that demands an absolute fidelity. And, sure enough, in its name (and under the injunction that thou shalt have no other gods before me), any number of horrible "expressive" acts—depictions of torture, marches designed to intimidate not inform, false caricatures of someone's mother, representations of women as the passive vessels of male needs—are performed and then declared constitutional. Glory be to God.

---

1. *Dennis v. United States*, 341 US 494 (1951).
2. *West Virginia State Board of Education v. Barnette*, 319 US 624 (1943).

Sticks and Stones

MARCH 7, 2011

In his new book, *Philosopher Kings? The Adjudication of Conflicting Human Rights and Social Values*,[1] law professor George C. Christie notes that with respect to the conflict between privacy rights and free expression rights, the United States and Europe seem to be going in different directions. European jurists will try, as one court put it, to strike "a fair balance . . . between the competing interests of the individual and of the community as a whole"; American courts are likely to come down strongly in favor of the individual's right to free expression even when an expressive activity arguably pollutes the community's conversational space or is intentionally hurtful to other individuals.

At the end of his book, Christie wonders how the Supreme Court will decide *Snyder v. Phelps* (March 2, 2011), a cause of action brought by the father of a dead soldier at whose funeral members of the militantly antigay Westboro Baptist Church waved signs saying (among other things), "Thank God for Dead Soldiers" and "You're Going to Hell." Lance Corporal Matthew Snyder's father alleged an injury under the tort category of the intentional infliction of emotional distress. Christie declares that he would be "disappointed if the Court were to allow recovery for [this] admittedly grossly tasteless and insensitive demonstration."

The court did not disappoint him, for, as everyone now knows, it held for Westboro and against Snyder by a vote of 8–1. Justice Samuel Alito was the lone dissenter. He was also the lone dissenter in a case decided a year ago (*United States v. Stevens*, 2010) when the court struck down a statute criminalizing the sale of videos depicting kittens being crushed to death by the high-heeled "spike" shoes of a dominatrix (see more on this case in 5.8, "The First Amendment and Kittens"). The majority opinion in both cases was written by Chief Justice John Roberts, and the result in Snyder was predictable, given Roberts's rejection in *Stevens* of "any balancing of relative social costs and benefits" when it comes to free expression rights: they trump.

A balancing of costs and benefits in the style of European courts would have involved asking questions like: Was the pain caused incidental to the production of speech—was the primary purpose to communicate an idea that just happened to be hurtful to some potential hearers—or was it the very point of the speech to bring the pain about? Was the Snyder family just caught up in a general scattershot diatribe against an America too friendly to gays or was the family the target of the diatribe, despite the fact that the young soldier had not himself been gay? If a lower court's award of monetary damages had been sustained, would the Westboro Church's message have been silenced or would it still have been able to proclaim its message in a thousand venues, just not in the venue of a private funeral where people already in pain are forced to endure more?

Roberts acknowledges the pain, but he sees it as an inevitable by-product of the fact that "speech is powerful." It can, he says, "stir people to action, move them to tears of both joy and sorrow, and—as it did here—inflict great pain." The concession gives away more than the chief justice realizes. If speech can cause joy, tears, and pain, what distinguishes it from action? The singling out of expression as a category worthy of special—even categorical—protection makes sense only if the work speech does is different from the work done by physical acts, if, for example, the effects of speech are limited to changing minds or increasing the store of information or enlarging the number of viewpoints in the marketplace of ideas and do not include bodily harms.

This is, of course, the traditional view as encapsulated in the familiar proverb "sticks and stones will break your bones, but names will never hurt you." The problem with this ditty is that it is false; names, libels, lies, defamatory statements, and harangues do hurt, and, moreover, the hurt they inflict—extending sometimes to measurable physical distress—is often what those who utter them are most invested in. That is, or should be, the question in this case: Is the expression of opinion primary and the pain just collateral damage, or is the damage what is desired and expression merely its vehicle?

Alito knows the answer. He begins his dissent by declaring, "Our profound national commitment to free and open debate is not a license for . . . vicious verbal assault," and he ends by insisting that "in order to have a society in which public issues can be openly and vigorously debated it is not necessary to allow the brutalization of innocent victims." Alito is speaking to the chief doctrinal argument made by Roberts that, distasteful as they may be, the signs held up by the Westboro Baptists speak to "broad issues of interest to society rather than matters of 'purely private concern.'" Even if the signs were viewed as containing messages related to Mathew Snyder or the Snyders specifically, that would not, says Roberts, "change the fact that the overall thrust and dominant theme of Westboro's demonstration spoke to broader public issues."

The logic is that you can be as abusive and scurrilous as you like as long as the terms of your abuse can be "related" to a matter of public concern; and given that the number of public concerns is infinitely large, it is almost impossible not to find such a relation if you are looking for it. Maybe the word "homosexual," when uttered, relates to a matter of public concern, but does that mean that its utterance indemnifies the entire speech context in which it occurs? Alito doesn't think so, and he makes the relevant distinction: "I fail to see why actionable speech should be immunized simply because it is interspersed with speech that is protected." In short, you shouldn't be able to produce speech with the intention of causing harm to a specific person and get it away with it because you slipped in a word or phrase that has or could have a more general application.

Two of Roberts's secondary arguments are even more vulnerable to challenge. He imagines a "group of parishioners standing at the very spot where Westboro stood, holding signs that said 'God bless America' and 'God loves you'"; they would not, he avers, "have been subjected to liability." Therefore, "It was what Westboro said that exposed it to tort damages." Wrong. Parishioners holding up benign signs would not have been doing the same thing; they would not have been engaged in an intentional infliction of emotional injury, and that is why they would not have been liable. It is what Westboro *did*, not what it *said*, that exposes it.

A couple of paragraphs later Roberts responds to the contention that because Snyder was attending his son's funeral, he was a "captive audience" (a term of art) and helpless in the face of Westboro's intrusive behavior. Citing a previous case, Roberts informs us that "the burden normally falls upon the viewer to avoid further bombardment of [his] sensibilities simply by averting his eyes." "Normally" (one hopes) you won't be at your young son's funeral, and if you are, is it really your obligation to react coolly to malevolent strangers who are doing their best (or, rather their worst) to add injury to injury? Give me a break! The court certainly didn't give Snyder one.

1. George C. Christie, *Philosopher Kings? The Adjudication of Conflicting Human Rights and Social Values* (New York: Oxford University Press, 2011).

The Harm in Free Speech

JUNE 4, 2012

Jeremy Waldron's new book, *The Harm in Hate Speech*, might well be called *The Harm in Free Speech*, for Waldron, a professor of law and political theory at New York University and Oxford, argues that the expansive First Amendment we now possess allows the flourishing of harms a well-ordered society ought not permit.[1]

Waldron is especially concerned with the harm done by hate speech to the dignity of those who are its object. He is careful to distinguish "dignity harms" from the hurt feelings one might experience in the face of speech that offends. Offense can be given by almost any speech act—in particular circumstances one might offend by saying "hello"—and Waldron agrees with those who say that regulating offensive speech is a bad and unworkable idea.

But harms to dignity, he contends, involve more than the giving of offense. They involve undermining a public good, which he identifies as the "implicit assurance" extended to every citizen that while his beliefs and allegiance may be criticized and rejected by some of his fellow citizens, he will nevertheless be viewed, even by his polemical opponents, as someone who has an equal right to membership in the society. It is the assurance—not given explicitly at the beginning of each day but built into the community's mode of self-presentation—that he belongs, that he is the undoubted bearer of a dignity he doesn't have to struggle for.

Waldron's thesis is that hate speech assaults that dignity by taking away that assurance. The very point of hate speech, he says, "is to negate the implicit assurance that a society offers to the members of vulnerable groups—that they are accepted . . . as a matter of course, along with everyone else." Purveyors of hate "aim to undermine this assurance, call it in question, and taint it with visible expressions of hatred, exclusion and contempt."

"Visible" is the key word. It is the visibility of leaflets, signs, and pamphlets asserting that the group you belong to is un-American, unworthy of respect, and should go back where it came from that does the damage, even if you, as an individual, are not a specific target.

"In its published, posted or pasted-up form, hate speech can become a world-defining activity, and those who promulgate it know very well—this is part of their intention—that the visible world they create is a much harder world for the targets of their hatred to live in." (Appearances count.)

Even though hate speech is characterized by First Amendment absolutists as a private act of expression that should be protected from government controls and sanctions, Waldron insists that "hate speech and defamation are actions performed in public, with a public orientation, aimed at undermining public goods."

That undermining is not accomplished by any particular instance of hate speech. But just as innumerable individual automobile emissions can pollute the air, so can innumerable expressions of supposedly private hate combine to "produce a large-scale toxic effect" that operates as a "slow-acting poison." And since what is being poisoned is the well of public life, "it is natural," says Waldron, "to think that the law should be involved—both in its ability to underpin the provision of public goods and in its ability to express and communicate common commitments." After all, he reminds us, "Societies do not become well ordered by magic."

Waldron observes that legal attention to large-scale structural, as opposed to individual, harms is a feature of most other Western societies, which, unlike the United States, have hate speech regulations on their books. He finds it "odd and disturbing that older and cruder models remain dominant in the First Amendment arena." But as he well knows, it is not so odd within the perspective of current First Amendment rhetoric, which is militantly libertarian, protective of the individual's right of self-assertion no matter what is being asserted, and indifferent (relatively) to the effects speech freely uttered might have on the fabric of society.

It was not always thus. At one time, both the content and effects of speech were taken into account when the issue of regulation was raised. Is this the kind of speech we want our children to see and hear? Are the effects of certain forms of speech so distressing and potentially dangerous that we should take steps to curtail them? Is this form of speech a contribution to the search for truth? Does it have a redeeming social value? Since *New York Times v. Sullivan* (1964), these questions, which assess speech in terms of the impact it has in the world, have been replaced by a simpler question—is it speech?—which reflects a commitment to speech as an almost sacrosanct activity. If the answer to that question is "yes," the presumption is that it should be protected, even though the harms it produces have been documented.

Waldron wants to bring back the focus on those harms and restore the reputation of *Beauharnais v. Illinois* (1952), in which the Supreme Court upheld a group libel law. The case turned on the conviction of a man who had distributed leaflets warning Chicagoans to be alert to the dangers of mongrelization and rape, which will surely materialize, he claimed, if white people do not unite against the Negro. Speaking for the majority, Justice Felix Frankfurter wrote that "a man's job and his educational opportunities and the dignity accorded him may depend as much on the reputation of the racial group to which he willy-nilly belongs as on his own merit."

With the phrase "on his own merit," Frankfurter gestures toward the view of dignity he is rejecting, the view in which dignity wells up from the inside of a man (or woman) and depends on an inner strength that asserts itself no matter how adverse or hostile external circumstances may be, including the circumstance in which the individual is confronted with signs, posters, and pamphlets demeaning his race or ethnic origin or religion or sexual preference. In this picture, the responsibility for maintaining dignity rests with the individual and not with any state duty to devise rules and regulations to protect it.

Some who take this position argue that if the individual feels victimized by expressions of hate directed at the group to which he "willy-nilly" belongs, that is his or her own choice. Waldron's example is C. Edwin Baker, who writes: "A speaker's racial epithet . . . harms the hearer only through her understanding of the message . . . and [harm] occurs only to the extent that the hearer (mentally) responds one way rather than another, for example, as a victim rather than as a critic of the speaker."[2]

In this classic instance of blaming the victim, the fault lies with a failure of resolve; self-respect was just not strong enough to rise to the occasion in a positive way. Waldron calls this position "silly" (it is the majority's position in *Plessy v. Ferguson* [1896]) and points out that it mandates and celebrates a harm by requiring victims of hate speech to grin and bear it: "It should not be necessary," he declares, "for [hate speech victims] to laboriously conjure up the courage to go out and try to flourish in what is now presented to them as a . . . hostile environment." The damage, Waldron explains, is already done by the speech "in requiring its targets to resort to the sort of mental mediation that Baker recommends." To the extent that those targets are put on the defensive, "racist speech has already succeeded in one of its destructive aims."

Notice that here (and elsewhere in the book), Waldron refuses to distinguish sharply between harm and representation. In the tradition he opposes, harm or hurt is physically defined; one can be discomforted and offended by speech; but something more than speech or image is required for there to be genuine (and legally relevant) damage. After all, "sticks and stones will break my bones, but names will never hurt me."

No, says Waldron (and here he follows Catharine MacKinnon's argument about pornography), the speech *is* the damage: "[T]he harms emphasized in this book are often harms *constituted* by speech rather than merely *caused* by speech." If the claim were that the harm is caused by speech, there would be room to challenge the finding by pointing to the many intervening variables that break or complicate the chain of causality. But there is no chain to break if harm is done the moment hate speech is produced. "The harm *is* the dispelling of assurance, and the dispelling of assurance is the speech act."

Waldron knows that the underlying strategy of those he writes against is to elevate the status of expression to an ultimate good and at the same time either deny the harm—the statistics are inconclusive; the claims cannot be proved—or minimize it in relation to the threat regulation poses to free expression. If "free speech trumps any consideration of social harm . . . almost any showing of harm resulting from hate speech . . . will be insufficient to justify restrictions on free speech of the kind that we are talking about."

In short, the game is over before it begins if your opponent can be counted on to say that either there is no demonstrated harm or, no matter how much harm there may be, it will not be enough to justify restrictions on speech. If that's what you're up against, there is not much you can do except point out the categorical intransigence of the position and offer an (unflattering) explanation of it.

Waldron's explanation is that the position is formulated and presented as an admirable act of unflinching moral heroism by white liberal law professors who say loudly and often that we must tolerate speech we find hateful. Easy to say from the protected perch of a faculty study, where the harm being talked about is theoretical and not experienced.

But what about the harm done "to the groups who are denounced or bestialized in pamphlets, billboards, talk radio and blogs? . . . Can their lives be led, can their children be brought up, can their hopes be maintained and their worst fears dispelled in a social environment polluted by those materials"?

Waldron answers "no," and he challenges society and its legal system to do something about it. But the likelihood that something will be done is slim if Waldron is right about the state of First Amendment discourse: "[I]n the American debate, the philosophical arguments about hate speech are knee-jerk, impulsive and thoughtless." Not the arguments of this book, however; they hit the mark every time.

1. All of Waldron's quotes in this essay are from Jeremy Waldron, *The Harm in Hate Speech* (Cambridge, MA: Harvard University Press, 2015).
2. C. Edwin Baker, "Harm, Liberty and Free Speech," *Southern California Law Review*, 1997.

Hate Speech and Stolen Valor

JULY 2, 2012

I was wondering whether to devote a third column (see 5.10, "The Harm in Free Speech" and 5.12, "Going in Circles with Hate Speech" in this volume) to the hate speech regulations Jeremy Waldron favors in his new book (*The Harm in Hate Speech*),[1] when the Supreme Court decided the matter for me last Thursday by striking down the Stolen Valor Act (*United States v. Alvarez*, June 28, 2012). The act reads (in part), "Whoever falsely represents himself, verbally or in writing, to have been awarded any decoration or medal authorized by Congress for the Armed Forces of the United States . . . shall be fined under this title, imprisoned not more than six months, or both." An enhanced penalty is provided for falsely representing oneself as a Medal of Honor winner, which is what Xavier Alvarez did when he introduced himself as a new member of the Three Valleys Municipal Water District Board in Claremont, California.

Convicted under the statute, Alvarez appealed, arguing that his First Amendment rights were violated when he was prosecuted for knowingly making a false statement. The plurality opinion (written by Justice Anthony Kennedy) agrees, declaring that the category of exceptions to the First Amendment's general protection of speech does not include false statements. The supporting citation is to *New York Times Co. v. Sullivan* (1964), in which it is said that because false statements are inevitable in public debate, they must be protected "if there is to be an open and vigorous expression of views."

Kennedy also points out that in those instances (perjury, fraud, defamation) in which false statements have been criminalized, the statements are part and parcel of a "legally cognizable harm." In the case of stolen valor, however, there is, Kennedy avers, no such harm; the statute "targets falsity and nothing more" and therefore could be extended to false statements "made to any person, at any time, in any context," including "personal whispered conversations within a home."

In response, Justice Samuel Alito, writing for the dissent, insists that the false statement in question—the claim to be a Medal of Honor recipient—does "inflict real harm" and serves "no legitimate interest." Furthermore, despite what the plurality contends, the act is specific in its potential application and "does not reach dramatic performances, satire, parody, hyperbole, or the like." As for the harm, it is, according to Alito, calculable and irreversible: "[T]he proliferation of false claims about military awards blurs the signal given out by the actual awards . . . and this diluting effect harms the military by hampering its efforts to foster morale and esprit de corps." The damage, Alito adds, is to "the very integrity of the military awards system."

Alito knows that the word "system" pinpoints the difference between his viewpoint and the plurality's. A systemic harm is one that is inflicted not on a targeted individual but on the social context in which all individuals necessarily operate. It is, Alito says, a "societal harm" measured not by the documented "specific harm" Kennedy requires, but by the damage done to the fabric of a culture. Nor is it a harm that can be remedied by the revelation and dissemination of the truth, "by what the plurality calls 'counterspeech.'" Counterspeech, Alito explains, produces a "steady stream of stories in the media about . . . imposters," that would "only exacerbate the harm . . . the Stolen Valor Act is meant to prevent."

Even from these brief excerpts, it should be clear that the two sides live in different conceptual universes. In one universe the individual reigns supreme and the chief value is the right to express one's views so long as they do not constitute fraud, perjury, libel, direct incitement to violence, or treason. ("Freedom of speech . . . flows not from the beneficence of the state but from the inalienable rights of the person.") In the other, views that contribute to the deterioration and dissolution of something society considers valuable and essential—like respect for the acts men and women perform in moments of extraordinary heroism in the service of their country— are subject to regulation and even criminalization.

The conflict is very old and irresolvable, and it periodically receives a dramatic rearticulation, as it did in 1989 when the court decided in *Texas v. Johnson* that burning the American flag is an expressive act that strengthens rather than weakens the values for which the flag stands. In a dissent that parallels Alito's in the present case, William Rehnquist, then the chief justice, lambasted an "uncritical extension of constitutional protection" that has the effect of frustrating "the very purpose for which organized governments are instituted." Justice John Paul Stevens, writing in a separate dissent, noted the argument that allowing flag burning will increase the amount of expression in the society, but he countered with his own example: "The creation of a federal right to post bulletin boards and graffiti on the Washington Monument might enlarge the market for free expression, but at a cost I would not pay. . . . Similarly . . . sanctioning the public desecration of the flag will tarnish its value."

Stevens's implicit concern for appearances, for the way a society looks (flags being burned versus flags being handled with respect; monuments being defaced versus monuments kept free of splenetic litter) is made explicit in Waldron's book. Under the rubric of "Political Aesthetics," Waldron argues that "the accepted vocabulary of a culture can become part of its established environment." He says that a society that permits the publication of calumnies defaming groups, especially vulnerable minority groups, will "look quite different from a society that does not," and he wonders "whether the law should be indifferent" to the impact of such publications "on what our society looks like and what it is for members of certain groups to have to try and make a life in a society that looks like that."

Waldron's idea is that "the look of a society is one of the primary ways of conveying assurances to its members of how they are likely to be treated . . . by the hundreds and thousands of strangers they encounter." If such assurances are absent or eroded by a hate-filled public landscape, some citizens can no longer walk the streets in the confidence that they are at home. This is the definition of dignity called for by many posters; it is a dignity that depends not on the absence of personal offense—a goal and standard Waldron rejects—but on the absence of freely circulating signs, suggesting that members of some groups have the special burden of demonstrating every day that they belong, in the (visible) face of the presumption that they do not.

Waldron is aware, as Rehnquist and Stevens were before him and as Alito is after him, that an emphasis on appearances, on words and images, runs counter to the classic liberal distinction between speech and action and the accompanying conviction that until words lead directly to beatings and blatant exclusions, "there is nothing to worry about" and therefore regulation is an overreaction. Waldron notes the hope (implied in commonplace bromides like "the remedy for bad speech is more speech" and "sunshine is the best disinfectant") that in time "hate speech [just] dies out, just withers away." But, he observes, "it is not at all clear how we are supposed to get there."

The two answers most often given by readers unpersuaded by Waldron are that the marketplace of ideas will sort things out and that education will do what regulation cannot. But if the marketplace is necessary because no one of us is sufficiently wise and impartial to serve as judge and arbiter, it will be up to the same fallible, biased beings to determine when the marketplace has completed its sorting-out work, and we will be right back where we started.

This, supposedly, is where education comes in. "What is needed," says poster frederickjoel, is an "informed and educated public." "Evil beliefs," declares amogin, should not be prohibited but exposed to "rational rebuttal" and "the light of reason." But if the elixir of reason is to do the job, there must first be agreement on what is reasonable, what is rational, and what is evil. And obviously there is none. Reason, rather than being an impersonal standard, is a contested category. (That's why we will have arguments forever.) The call for education as a means of purifying public discourse finally comes down to each party identifying education, as opposed to lies and indoctrination, with its own views. The appeal to education and rationality, like the appeal to the marketplace (and for the same reasons), is hopeless.

Maybe so, some posters will reply, but even if the outcome of the marketplace may not be benign (Justice Oliver Wendell Holmes acknowledged in *Gitlow v. New York* [1925] that its free operation, which he urged, could lead to the triumph of totalitarian ideas), and even if the direction education takes depends on who holds the reins of instruction, we would do better to put our faith in the marketplace and in education rather than hand over the monitoring of speech and expression to an inevitably partisan government.

Those who take this position (and there are many) ask, "Who, after all, is competent to judge what is hateful or harmful and what is not?" They assert that because no answer to that question will be generally acceptable—everyone will have his or her own candidate—judgment should be left to the workings of time. So it seems to come down in the end to a choice between two imperfect mechanisms—a free market in which bad speech may crowd out the good (the fear many feel in the wake of *Citizens United*), and a political market that could lead to ever-changing regulations on speech depending on which party happened to be in power.

Do you want to trust the tasks of separating the wheat from the chaff to the turns of a marketplace that has no mind or governing purpose or to a political process in which ideological purposes vie with one another in an endless contest? Do you want to permit the proliferation of fake Medal of Honor winners in the confidence that the real thing will be recognized by clear-eyed observers, or do you want to take steps to ensure that true honor is not besmirched or crowded out by counterfeit coin? Do you want to allow expressions denigrating vulnerable groups to flourish in the confidence that members of those groups will be able to survive and prosper despite them, or do you want to take legal notice of forms of speech that might be destructive of the very toleration that protects them? Is a society that does not regulate hateful and false speech demonstrating its strength or courting its own demise? These are real questions, and it is the merit both of Waldron's book and Alito's dissent that the usual facile and self-congratulating answers to them are given a run for their money.

1.   Jeremy Waldron, *The Harm in Hate Speech* (Cambridge, MA: Harvard University Press, 2015).

Going in Circles with Hate Speech

NOVEMBER 12, 2012

No topic is more frequently debated with less resolution than hate speech. This is made abundantly clear in a new collection of essays written by some of the leading contributors to the debate. The volume is called *The Content and Context of Hate Speech: Rethinking Regulation and Responses*, and it is edited by Michael Herz and Peter Molnar.[1]

What you learn in the course of reading this book is that there is no generally accepted account of (1) what hate speech is, (2) what it does (what its effects are), and (3) what, if anything, should be done about it. To be sure, everyone agrees that it is hate speech when words are used to directly incite violence against a specific person or group of persons. But as Arthur Jacobson and Bernhard Schlink point out in their contribution to the volume, on such occasions the words are instrumental "to an incipient assault," and it is the assault, not the words, that the state criminalizes. (It is, say the courts, "speech brigaded with action.") There need be no debate about what to do in the face of that kind of speech because it is already being done by extant laws.

The rest are all hard cases. Is it hate speech when, in a paper with scholarly trappings, someone says that the Holocaust never happened and was invented by Jews in an effort to induce guilt and gain money? Is it hate speech when a pamphlet explains how Muslim Americans plan to impose sharia law and subvert the traditions of this country? Some who consume such statements will certainly feel hatred for Jews and Muslims, and no doubt those who make such statements intended that result. But no call to violence is issued and one might say—in the United States it will always be said—that while it is hate speech disguised, the disguise is good enough to remove it as a candidate for regulation.

Then there is what we might call genteel hate speech—casually produced anti-Semitic and racial slurs in conversation and in countless British novels. It is certainly hateful speech, but it reflects less the intention of the speaker or writer than the cultural background of the society he lives in. If it is hate speech, it is so distant from any specific design to wound that a legal remedy against it seems quixotic and unenforceable. And yet, demeaning speech that flies under the legal radar because it is an extension of what people regularly say and even more regularly think may in the end be more harmful than the direct, frontal insult.

And what about hate speech that is never uttered but is implied by the structure of institutions? When the law in many states reduced black Americans to the status of property, wasn't it being said, in the most forceful way imaginable, that blacks were more like animals than humans? When women were denied the vote for so many decades, wasn't it being said that they were perpetual children and unworthy of an independent existence? And, to reference an example invoked by Peter Molnar in his essay "Responding to 'Hate Speech' with Art, Education, and the Imminent Danger Test,"[2] isn't the statue of Teddy Roosevelt in front of the American Museum of National History that shows him on a horse flanked by the figures of a Native American and an African American a form of hate speech declaring the natural subservience of the "red" man and the black man?

Let's suppose that we could sort through these versions of hate speech (and there are many more) and come up with a baseline definition of what it is; we would still have the problem of specifying its effects. You can't cogently debate whether to regulate something unless you have first identified the harms it produces. Bhikhu Parekh, political philosopher and a member of the British House of Lords, is quite confident in his account of those harms. Hate speech, he says, "lowers the tone of public debate, coarsens the community's moral sensibility, and weakens the culture of mutual respect that lies at the heart of a good society." In addition, hate speech "violates the dignity of the members of the target group" who lead "ghettoized and isolated lives with a knock-down effect on their children's education and career choices."[3]

Not necessarily, says Nadine Strossen, a professor of law and a past president of the ACLU. We are not, she insists, "automatically diminished just because some bigot says something negative about us." Indeed, we are better off knowing about the hateful things being said, first because it provides "valuable information," second because it gives the targeted individuals "an opportunity to respond," and third because it "highlights . . . issues that can be addressed in other ways, for example through education."[4]

Behind Strossen's and Parekh's assertions are two very different views of human beings. For Strossen, the hate speech recipient is (or can and should be) a resolute individual standing up for herself in the face of verbal assault and emerging stronger from the encounter. For Parekh, the hate speech recipient is the vulnerable victim of forces that rob her of dignity and deprive her of the resources necessary for human flourishing, resources that therefore must be supplied by the state in the form of hate speech laws. Strossen's view follows from a strongly libertarian reading of the First Amendment and is pretty much official doctrine in the United States. Parekh's view reflects the more communitarian concerns of other Western democracies that balance free expression rights against the right of the society to order itself in decent and humane ways.

Michel Rosenfeld draws the relevant contrast with respect to the United States and Canada: "Under the American view, there seems to be a greater likelihood of harm from suppression of hate speech . . . than from its toleration." But from a Canadian perspective, "dissemination of hate propaganda seems more dangerous than its suppression as it is seen as likely to produce enduring injuries to self-worth and to undermine social cohesion in the long run."[5]

Rosenfeld observes that the two countries "differ in their practical assessments of the consequences of tolerating hate speech." Not quite; what the two countries differ in is their respective assumptions concerning what must be protected: on the one hand, a rights-based individualism that can take care of itself and would be diminished by nanny-state intervention, on the other, a psychological and societal fragility that must be shored up by law. In one vision, hate speech is an opportunity; in the other, it is a virus. Given such two different accounts of the effects of hate speech, it is not surprising that there would be two different accounts of what to do about it, or what not to do about it, and no hope of reconciling them.

Taking note of differences like these, some contributors to the volume propose a contextual analysis sensitive to cultural and political circumstances. They say that in a country like ours, where there are strongly established democratic institutions, hate speech (short of incitement to violence) can be pretty much tolerated in the confidence that no drastic, long-term consequences will ensue. But in countries where democratic institutions are fragile or just emerging, and where tribal, sectarian conflict has been the order of the day for a long time, the state may have to move against forms of speech that threaten to rend the fabric of society. (A bit paternalistic, don't you think?)

One must also, it is said, take into account the recent history of the nation. In Germany, Parekh observes, banning Holocaust denial is "part of reparative justice, a public statement of the country's acknowledgment of and apology for its past, a way of fighting neo-Nazi trends in German society." In France, Julie Suk asserts, criminalizing Holocaust denial is not negatively directed at hate-speakers, but positively directed at publicly establishing the moral legitimacy of the state.[6] Whereas in America it is thought "that the state would be undermining its democratic legitimacy were it to discriminate against certain viewpoints"—an argument made by Ronald Dworkin in his essay—in France the state wants to make it clear that "racism has no place in collective self-determination." Thus "the fight against racism . . . becomes a collective national project" in which the state plays a major role.[7]

The contextual approach—regulation for this society, but not for that—will be resisted by those who insist that it's a matter of principle: it's just wrong to suppress and/or punish viewpoints with which the state disagrees, and it is wrong, indeed immoral, in every place and at every time. In response, pragmatic-minded commentators will say that the problem is not a moral but a managerial one. You've got to look at what you have, where you've been, and where you want to go, and figure out the best means to get there. Regulating hate speech may be one of those means, and it may not be, depending on the facts of your particular situation. Why commit yourself to either course in advance? Why not allow yourself the flexibility to devise strategies that will work on the ground?

These questions will always circle back to the original—and unanswerable—question of what is hate speech and what does it do anyway. It is unanswerable because hate speech is a category without a stable content. As Strossen says, "One person's hate speech is another person's deeply held religious belief." The response of Enlightenment liberalism to this difference—to the depth and intractability of substantive disagreement—is to seek a common, usually procedural, ground on the basis of which lines can be drawn without putting the state on the side of anyone's viewpoint. If we can all just agree on a minimalist definition of hate speech and its harms, we might get somewhere and bring everyone along. But every effort in this direction founders on the fact that you can't be minimal enough.

No matter how low the bar is set, some will feel, and feel with reason, that it has been set to exclude them.

Alon Harel, for example, proposes in his essay to draw the line demarcating protected from unprotected hate speech by according protection to arguably hurtful speech if it is part and parcel of "a comprehensive and valuable form of life"; if, that is, it is "deeply rooted" in "long-term customs, ways of life, and ideological commitments."[8] There is, however, a caveat, already more than implied in the word "valuable": the tradition to which the speech is attached must include "prominent humanistic components," a requirement that would exclude "Nazism and the Ku Klux Klan," for they are "hatred-based traditions." But who is to say that Nazism and the Ku Klux Klan are all hatred and have no humanistic components or ideological commitments? Surely members of those groups would not say so, and on what basis are they peremptorily eliminated from the roster of viewpoints accorded protection?

On the basis, obviously, of the substantive preferences (which in this case I certainly share) of the one doing the line-drawing. But from the perspective of the liberalism within which Harel writes, neither the state nor the political theorist can make in-advance substantive judgments on what does and does not have a place in the marketplace of ideas. Excluding Nazis and Ku Klux Klanners and gay bashers from the zone of speech-toleration may feel good, but it rests on no principled ground, and attempts, like Harel's, to specify such a ground are merely attempts to occlude the entirely arbitrary nature of the classification.

In the end, none of the alternative ways of dealing with hate speech is entirely satisfying. Allowing it all leaves unanswered the question of what to do about the harms it causes. Banning it all reopens the question of just what it is and what it isn't. Selectively banning this but not that only reanimates the divisiveness that hate speech regulation promises to diminish. We'll be at this for a long time, going in exactly the same circles.

1. Michael Herz and Peter Molnar, eds., *The Content and Context of Hate Speech: Rethinking Regulation and Responses* (New York: Cambridge University Press, 2012).

2. Peter Molnar, "Responding to 'Hate Speech' with Art, Education, and the Imminent Danger Test," in Herz and Molnar, eds., *The Content and Context of Hate Speech*, 183–97.

3. Bhikhu Parekh, "Is There a Case for Banning Hate Speech?" in Herz and Molnar, eds., *The Content and Context of Hate Speech*, 37–56.

4. Nadine Strossen, "Interview with Nadine Strossen," in Herz and Molnar, eds., *The Content and Context of Hate Speech*, 378–98.

5. Michel Rosenfeld, "Hate Speech in Constitutional Jurisprudence," in Herz and Molnar, eds., *The Content and Context of Hate Speech*, 242–89.

6. Julie Suk, "Denying Experience: Holocaust Denial and the Free-Speech Theory of the State," in Herz and Molnar, eds., *The Content and Context of Hate Speech*, 144–63.

7. Ronald Dworkin, "Reply to Jeremy Waldron," in Herz and Molnar, eds., *The Content and Context of Hate Speech*, 341–44.

8. Alon Harel, "Hate Speech and Comprehensive Forms of Life," in Herz and Molnar, eds., *The Content and Context of Hate Speech*, 306–28.

Our Faith in Letting It All Hang Out

FEBRUARY 12, 2006

If you want to understand what is and isn't at stake in the Danish cartoon furor, just listen to the man who started it all, Flemming Rose, the culture editor of the newspaper *Jyllands-Posten*. Mr. Rose told *Time* magazine that he asked forty Danish cartoonists to "depict Muhammad as they see him," after he noticed that journalists, historians, and even museum directors were wary of presenting the Muslim religion in an unfavorable light, or in any light at all.

"To me," he said, this "spoke to the problem of self-censorship and freedom of speech." The publication of the cartoons, he insisted, "was not directed at Muslims" at all. Rather, the intention was "to put the issue of self-censorship on the agenda and have a debate about it."[1]

I believe him. And not only do I believe that he has nothing against Muhammad or the doctrines of Islam, I believe that he has no interest (positive or negative) in them at all, except as the possible occasions of controversy.

This is what it means today to put self-censorship "on the agenda": the particular object of that censorship—be it opinions about a religion, a movie, the furniture in a friend's house, your wife's new dress, whatever—is a matter of indifference. What is important is not the content of what is expressed but that it be expressed. What is important is that you let it all hang out.

Mr. Rose may think of himself, as most journalists do, as being neutral with respect to religion—he is not speaking as a Jew or a Christian or an atheist—but in fact he is an adherent of the religion of letting it all hang out, the religion we call liberalism.

The first tenet of the liberal religion is that everything (at least in the realm of expression and ideas) is to be permitted, but nothing is to be taken seriously. This is managed by the familiar distinction—implied in the First Amendment's religion clause—between the public and private spheres. It is in the private sphere—the personal spaces of the heart, the home, and the house of worship—that one's religious views are allowed full sway and dictate behavior.

But in the public sphere, the argument goes, one's religious views must be put forward with diffidence and circumspection. You can still have them and express them—that's what separates us from theocracies and tyrannies—but they should be worn lightly. Not only must there be no effort to make them into the laws of the land, but they should not be urged on others in ways that make them uncomfortable. What religious beliefs are owed—and this is a word that appears again and again in the recent debate—is "respect"; nothing less, nothing more.

The thing about respect is that it doesn't cost you anything; its generosity is barely skin-deep and is in fact a form of condescension: I respect you; now don't bother me. This was certainly the message conveyed by Rich Oppel, editor of the *Austin (TX) American-Statesman*, who explained his decision to reprint one of the cartoons thusly: "It is one thing to respect other people's faith and religion, but it goes beyond where I would go to accept their taboos."[2]

Clearly, Mr. Oppel would think himself pressured to "accept" the taboos of the Muslim religion were he asked to alter his behavior in any way, say by refraining from publishing cartoons depicting the Prophet. Were he to do that, he would be in danger of crossing the line between "respecting" a taboo and taking it seriously, and he is not about to do that.

This is, increasingly, what happens to strongly held faiths in the liberal state. Such beliefs are equally and indifferently authorized as ideas people are perfectly free to believe, but they are equally and indifferently disallowed as ideas that might serve as a basis for action or public policy.

Strongly held faiths are exhibits in liberalism's museum; we appreciate them, and we congratulate ourselves for affording them a space, but should one of them ask of us more than we are prepared to give—ask for deference rather than mere respect—it will be met with the barrage of platitudinous arguments that for the last week have filled the pages of every newspaper in the country.

One of those arguments goes this way: It is hypocritical for Muslims to protest cartoons caricaturing Muhammad when cartoons vilifying the symbols of Christianity and Judaism are found everywhere in the media of many Arab countries. After all, what's the difference? The difference is that those who draw and publish such cartoons in Arab countries believe in their content; they believe that Jews and

Christians follow false religions and are proper objects of hatred and obloquy.

But I would bet that the editors who have run the cartoons do not believe that Muslims are evil infidels who must either be converted or vanquished. They do not publish the offending cartoons in an effort to further some religious or political vision; they do it gratuitously, almost accidentally. Concerned only to stand up for an abstract principle—free speech—they seize on whatever content happens to come their way and use it as an example of what the principle should be protecting. The fact that for others the content may be life itself is beside their point.

This is itself a morality—the morality of a withdrawal from morality in any strong, insistent form. It is certainly different from the morality of those for whom the Danish cartoons are blasphemy and monstrously evil. And the difference, I think, is to the credit of the Muslim protesters and to the discredit of the liberal editors.

The argument from reciprocity—you do it to us, so how can you complain if we do it to you?—will have force only if the moral equivalence of "us" and "you" is presupposed. But the relativizing of ideologies and religions belongs to the liberal's theology and would hardly be persuasive to a Muslim.

This is why calls for "dialogue," issued so frequently of late by the pundits with an unbearable smugness—you can just see them thinking, "What's wrong with these people?"—are unlikely to fall on receptive ears. The belief in the therapeutic and redemptive force of dialogue depends on the assumption (central to liberalism's theology) that, after all, no idea is worth fighting over to the death and that we can always reach a position of accommodation if only we will sit down and talk it out.

But a firm adherent of a comprehensive religion doesn't want dialogue about his beliefs; he wants those beliefs to prevail. Dialogue is not a tenet in his creed, and invoking it is unlikely to do anything but further persuade him that you have missed the point—as, indeed, you are pledged to do, so long as liberalism is the name of your faith.

1. Flemming Rose, *The Tyranny of Silence* (Washington, DC: Cato Institute, 2014).

2. Oppel is quoted to this effect on the AJR website, February 9, 2006, in an essay by Rem Rieder, "To Publish or Not to Publish."

PART 6

Reflections on Religion

The Three Atheists

JUNE 10, 2007

Writings against God and religion have been around as long as God and religion have been around. But every so often an epidemic of the genre breaks out and a spate of such writings achieves the status of notoriety (which is what their authors had been aiming for). This has now happened to three books published in the last three years: Sam Harris's *The End of Faith: Religion, Terror and the Future of Reason* (2004, 2005), Richard Dawkins's *The God Delusion* (2006), and Christopher Hitchens's *God is Not Great: How Religion Poisons Everything* (2007).[1] (Were this the kind of analysis performed in Lancelot Andrewes's sermons, I would note the fact that the names of all three authors end in "s," signifying, no doubt, the presence of Sin and Satan.)

The books differ in tone and emphasis. Harris is sounding a warning against the threat of Islam and inveighing against what he regards as the false hope of religious moderation. "We are at war with Islam," he announces, and he decides that, given the nature of the enemy— religious zealots informed by an absolute and terrifying faith—torture "in certain circumstances would seem to be not only permissible but necessary." (This from someone who denounces religion because it is used as a rationalization for inhumane deeds!)

Dawkins doesn't single out Islam for particular negative intention; in his eyes all religions are equally bad and equally absurd, and he wonders why obviously intelligent men and women can't see through the nonsense, especially given that so many of the questions religion can't answer have clearly been answered by the theory of natural selection.

Hitchens, the wittiest and most literate of the three, is a world traveler and will often recount the devastating arguments against religion he has made while lunching with a very important person in Belgrade, Bombay, Belfast, Beirut, the Vatican, North Korea, and Washington, DC, among other places.

Still, as distinct as the personalities and styles of the three are, they share a set of core arguments. (And they toss little bouquets to one another along the way.) First, religion is man-made: its sacred texts, rather than being the word of God, are the "manufactured" words of fallible men. Moreover (and this is the second shared point), these words have been cobbled together from miscellaneous sources, all of which are far removed in time from the events they purport to describe. Third, it is in the name of these corrupt, garbled, and contradictory texts that men (and occasionally women) have been moved to do terrible things. Fourth (and this is the big one), the commission of these horrible acts—"trafficking in humans . . . ethnic cleansing . . . slavery . . . indiscriminate massacre" (Hitchens)—is justified not by arguments, reasons, or evidence but by something called faith, which is scornfully dismissed by all three: "Faith is what credulity becomes when it finally achieves escape velocity from the constraints of terrestrial discourse—constraints like reasonableness, internal coherence, civility and candor" (Harris). "Faith is an evil precisely because it requires no justification and brooks no argument" (Dawkins). "If one must have faith in order to believe something, . . . then the likelihood of that something having any truth or value is considerably diminished" (Hitchens).

It's time for an example of the kind of thinking Harris, Dawkins, and Hitchens find so contemptible. At the beginning of John Bunyan's *The Pilgrim's Progress*, the hero, named simply Christian, becomes aware of a great burden on his back (it is Original Sin) and is desperate to rid himself of it. Distraught, he consults one named Evangelist, who tells him to flee "the wrath to come."

Flee where, he asks.

Pointing in the direction of a vast expanse, Evangelist says, Do you see the Wicket Gate out there?

No, replies Christian.

Do you see a shining light?

Christian is not sure ("I think I do"), but at Evangelist's urging he begins to run in the direction of the light he cannot quite make out. Then comes the chilling part: "Now he had not run far from his own door, but his Wife and Children perceiving it, began to cry after him to return, but the man put his fingers in his ears and ran on, crying Life! Life! Eternal Life."[2]

So what we have here is a man abandoning his responsibilities and resisting the entreaties of those who love and depend on him, and all for something of whose existence he is not even sure. And, even worse, he does this in the absence of reason, argument, or evidence. (Mark Twain's Huck Finn said of *The Pilgrim's Progress*: "About a man who left his family; it didn't say why.") At this point, Harris, Dawkins, and Hitchens would exclaim, "See what these nuts do at the behest of religion—child abandonment justified by nothing more substantial than some crazy inner impulse; remember, Abraham was going to kill his son because he thought the bloodthirsty god he had invented wanted him to."

I have imagined this criticism coming from outside the narrative, but in fact it is right there on the inside, in the cries of Christian's wife and children, in the reactions of his friends ("they thought that some frenzy distemper had gotten into his head"), and in the analysis they give of his irrational actions: he, they conclude, is one of those who "are wiser in their own eyes than seven men that can render a Reason." What this shows is that the objections Harris, Dawkins, and Hitchens make to religious thinking are themselves part of religious thinking; rather than being swept under the rug of a seamless discourse, they are the very motor of that discourse, impelling the conflicted questioning of theologians and poets (not to mention the Jesus who cried, "My God, My God, why hast thou forsaken me?" and every verse of the book of Job).

Dawkins asks why Adam and Eve (and all their descendants) were punished so harshly, given that their "sin"—eating an apple after having been told not to—"seems mild enough to merit a mere reprimand." (We might now call this the Scooter Libby defense.) This is a good question, but it is one that has been asked and answered many times, not by atheists and scoffers but by believers trying to work though the dilemmas presented by their faith. An answer often given is that it is important that the forbidden act be a trivial one; for were it an act that was on its face either moral or immoral, committing it or declining to commit it would follow from the powers of judgment men naturally have. It is because there is no reason, in nature, either to eat the apple or to refrain from eating it, that the prohibition can serve as a test of faith; otherwise, as John Webster explained ("The Examination of Academies," 1654), faith would rest "upon the rotten basis of humane authority."

Hitchens asks, "Why, if God is the creator of all things, were we supposed to 'praise' him incessantly for doing what comes naturally?" The usual answer (again given by theologians and religious poets) is, what else could we do in the face of his omnipotence and omnipresence? God is the epitome of the rich relative who has everything; thanks and gratitude are the only coin we can tender.

Or can we? The poet George Herbert reasons (and that is the word) that if it is only by the infusion of grace that we do anything admirable, praising God is an action for which we cannot take credit; for even that act is His. "Who hath praise enough?" he asks, but then immediately (in the same line) corrects himself: "Nay, who hath any?" ("Providence," line 57). Even something so minimal as praising God becomes a sin if it is done pridefully. Where does that leave us, Herbert implicitly asks, a question more severe and daunting than any posed by the three atheists.

Harris wonders why the Holocaust didn't "lead most Jews to doubt the existence of an omnipotent and benevolent God?" Behind this question is another one: Where does evil come from, and if God is all-powerful and has created everything, doesn't it come from Him? Again there is a standard answer (which does not mean that it is a satisfying one): evil proceeds from the will of a creature who was created just and upright, but who corrupted himself by an act of disobedience that forever infects his actions and the actions of his descendants. It is what Milton's God calls "man's polluting sin" (*Paradise Lost*, 10:631) that produces generations of evil, including the generation of the Holocaust, for, as Milton's Adam himself acknowledges, "from me what can proceed, / But all corrupt, both mind and will deprav'd?" (10:825).

But, Harris, Dawkins, and Hitchens object, if God is so powerful, why didn't he just step in and prevent evil before it occurred? Not judge slavery, but nip it in the bud; not cure a blind man, but cure blindness; not send his only begotten son to redeem a sinful mankind, but create a mankind that could not sin? And besides, if God had really wanted man to refrain from evil acts and thoughts, like the act and thought of disobedience, then, says Hitchens, "he should have taken more care to invent a different species."

But if he had done that, if Adam and Eve were faithful because they were programmed to be so, then the act of obedience (had they performed it) would not in any sense have been theirs. For what they do or don't do to be meaningful, it must be free: "Freely they stood who stood and fell who fell / Not free, what proof could they have given sincere / Of true allegiance?" (*Paradise Lost*, 3:102–4).

I have drawn these arguments out of my small store of theological knowledge not because they are conclusive (although they may be to some), but because they are there—in the very texts and traditions Harris, Dawkins, and Hitchens dismiss as naive, simpleminded, and ignorant. Suppose, says Hitchens, you were a religious believer; you would then be persuaded that a benign and all-powerful creator supervises everything, and that "if you obey the rules and commandments that he has lovingly prescribed, you will qualify for an eternity of bliss and repose."

I know of no religious framework that offers such a complacent picture of the life of faith, a life that is always presented as a minefield of the difficulties, obstacles, and temptations that must be negotiated by a limited creature in his or her efforts to become aligned (and allied) with the Infinite. Saint Paul's lament can stand in for many: "The good that I would, I do not; but the evil which I would not, I do. . . . Who shall deliver me?" (Romans 7:19, 24). The anguish of this question and the incredibly nuanced and elegant writings of those who have tried to answer it are what the three atheists miss, and it is by missing so much that they are able to produce such a jolly debunking of a way of thinking they do not begin to understand.

But I have not yet considered their prime objection to religious faith: that it leaves argument, reason, and evidence in the dust, and proceeds directly to the commission of wholly unjustified (and often horrific) acts. It is that issue that I will take up in 6.2.

1. Sam Harris, *The End of Faith: Religion, Terror and the Future of Reason*, reprint ed. (New York: W. W. Norton, 2005); Richard Dawkins, *The God Delusion*, reprint ed. (New York: Mariner Books, 2008); Christopher Hitchens, *God Is Not Great: How Religion Poisons Everything* (New York: Twelve, 2009).
2. John Bunyan, *The Pilgrim's Progress* (1678), part 1, section 1.

Atheism and Evidence

JUNE 17, 2007

Atheists like Sam Harris, Richard Dawkins, and Christopher Hitchens believe (in Dawkins's words) that "there is nothing beyond the natural, physical world" and that "if there is something that appears to lie beyond the natural world, we hope eventually to understand it and embrace it within the natural."[1]

In reply, believers, like the scientist Francis S. Collins (*The Language of God: A Scientist Presents Evidence for Belief*), argue that physical processes cannot account for the universal presence of moral impulses like altruism, "the truly selfless giving of oneself to others" with no expectation of a reward.[2] How can there be a naturalistic explanation of that?

Easy, say Dawkins and Harris. (Hitchens doesn't seem to have a dog in this hunt.) It's just a matter of time before so-called moral phenomena will be brought within the scientific ambit: "There will probably come a time," Harris declares, "when we achieve a detailed understanding of human happiness, and of ethical judgments themselves, at the level of the brain." And a bit later, "There is every reason to believe that sustained inquiry in the moral sphere will force convergence of our various belief systems in the way that it has in every other science."[3]

What gives Harris his confidence? Why does he have "every reason to believe" (a nice turn of phrase)? What are his reasons? What is his evidence? Not, as it turns out, a record of progress. He acknowledges that, to date "little convergence has been achieved in ethics," not only because "so few of the facts are in" but because "we have yet to agree about the most basic criteria for deeming an ethical fact, a fact."

But we will, if we are patient. The field of "the cognitive neuroscience of moral cognition" (a real mouthful) is young, and "it is clearly too early to draw any strong conclusions from this research."

Of course one conclusion that could be drawn is that the research will not pan out because moral intuitions will not be reducible to physical processes. That may be why so few of the facts are in. No, says Harris, the reason for our small knowledge in this area is the undue influence of—you guessed it—religion: "Most of our religions have been no more supportive of genuine moral inquiry than of scientific inquiry generally."

This is a remarkable sequence. A very strong assertion is made—we will "undoubtedly discover lawful connections between our states of consciousness [and] our modes of conduct"—but no evidence is offered in support of it; and indeed the absence of evidence becomes a reason for confidence in its eventual emergence. This sounds an awfully lot like faith of the kind Harris and his colleagues deride—expectations based only on a first premise (itself asserted rather than proven), which, if true, demands them, and which, if false, makes nonsense of them.

Dawkins exhibits the same pattern of reasoning. He believes, like Harris, that ethical facts can be explained by the scientific method in general and by the thesis of natural selection in particular. If that thesis is assumed as a baseline, one can then generate Darwinian reasons, reasons that are reasons within the Darwinian system, for the emergence of the behavior we call ethical. One can speculate, as Dawkins does, that members of a species are generous to one another out of a desire (not consciously held) to preserve the gene pool, or that unconditioned giving is an advertisement of dominance and superiority. These, he says, are "good Darwinian reasons for individuals to be altruistic, generous or 'moral' towards each other."

Exactly! They are good Darwinian reasons; remove the natural selection hypothesis from the structure of thought and they will be seen not as reasons but as absurdities. I "believe in evolution," Dawkins declares, "because the evidence supports it"; but the evidence is evidence only because he is seeing with Darwin-directed eyes. The evidence at once supports his faith and is evidence by virtue of it.

Dawkins voices distress at an imagined opponent who "can't see" the evidence or "refuses to look at it because it contradicts his holy book," but he has his own holy book of whose truth he has been persuaded, and it is within its light that he proceeds and looks forward in hope (his word) to a future stage of enlightenment he does not now experience but of which he is fully confident. Both in the vocabulary they share—"hope," "belief," "undoubtedly," "there will come a time"—and the reasoning they engage in, Harris and Dawkins perfectly exemplify the definition of faith found in Hebrews 11, "the substance of things hoped for, the evidence of things not seen."

What is and is not seen will vary with the faith within which observers look. In *The Pilgrim's Progress*, Bunyan glosses the scene in which the townspeople mock Christian as he flees toward a light he can barely discern and they do not discern at all: "They that fly from the wrath to come are a gazing stock to the world." The apostle Paul comments in 1 Corinthians 2:14 that to the man "without the Spirit" the things of the Spirit are "foolishness"; he simply "cannot understand them because they are spiritually discerned." Those who have not found the arguments of natural selection persuasive will not see what Dawkins and his colleagues see, not because they are blind and obstinate, but because as members of a different faith community—and remember, science requires faith too before it can have reasons—the evidence that seems so conclusive to the rational naturalists will point elsewhere.

But what about reasons? Isn't that what separates scientific faith from religious faith; one is supported by reasons, the other is irrational and supported by nothing but superstition? Not really. One of the basic homiletic practices in both the Jewish and Christian traditions is the catechism or examination of one's faith. An early nineteenth-century Jewish catechism is clear on the place of reason in the exercise: "By thinking for himself, let [the pupil] learn the sunny nearness of reason." Christian catechists regularly cite 1 Peter 3:15: "Be always ready to give an answer to every man that asketh you a reason of the hope that is in you." In short, and it is often put this way, at every opportunity you must give reasons for your faith.

The reasons you must give, however, do not come from outside your faith, but follow from it and flesh it out. They are not independent of your faith—if they were they would supplant it as a source of authority—but are simultaneously causes of it and products of it; just as Harris's and Dawkins's reasons for believing that morality can be naturalized flow from their faith in physical science and loop back to that faith, thereby giving it an enhanced substance.

The reasoning is circular, but not viciously so. The process is entirely familiar and entirely ordinary; a conviction (of the existence of God or the existence of natural selection or the greatness of a piece of literature) generates speculation and questions, and the resulting answers act as confirmation of the conviction that has generated them. Whatever you are doing—preaching, teaching , performing an experiment, playing baseball—you must always give a reason (if only to yourself) for your faith, and the reason will always be a reason only because your faith is in place.

Some respondents raised the issue of falsification. Is there something that would falsify a religious faith in the same way that some physical discoveries would falsify natural selection for Dawkins and Harris? As it is usually posed, the question imagines disconfirming evidence coming from outside the faith, be it science or religion. But a system of assumptions and protocols (and that is what a faith is) will recognize only evidence internal to its basic presuppositions. Asking that religious faith consider itself falsified by empirical evidence is as foolish as asking that natural selection tremble before the assertion of deity and design. Falsification, if it occurs, always occurs from the inside.

It follows then that the distinction informing so many of the atheists' arguments, the distinction between a discourse supported by reason and a discourse supported by faith, will not hold up because any form of thought is an inextricable mix of both; faith and reasons come together in an indissoluble package. There are still distinctions to be made, but they will be distinctions between different structures of faith, or, if you prefer, between different structures of reasons. The differences between different structures of faith are real and significant, for each will speak to different needs and different purposes.

Mine is not a leveling argument; it does not say that everything is the same (that is the atheists' claim); it says only that whatever differences there are between religious and scientific thinking, one difference that will not mark the boundary setting one off from the other is the difference between faith and reason.

This does not mean either that the case for God and religion has been confirmed or that the case against God and religion has been discredited. (Despite what some commentators assumed, I am not taking a position on the issues raised by the three books; readers of this and essay 6.1 have learned nothing about my own religious views, or even if I have any.) My point is only that some of the arguments against faith and religion—the arguments Dawkins, Harris, and Hitchens most rely on—are just not good arguments. The three atheists needn't give up the ghost, but they might think about going back to the drawing board.

1. Richard Dawkins, *The God Delusion* (London, 2006), 14.
2. Francis S. Collins, *The Language of God: A Scientist Presents Evidence for Belief*, 1st paperback ed. (New York: Free Press, 2007).
3. Sam Harris, *The End of Faith*, 175.

Is Religion Man-Made?

JUNE 24, 2007

Sure it is. Sam Harris, Richard Dawkins, and Christopher Hitchens think that this fact about religion is enough to invalidate its claims.

"[R]eligion and the churches," declares Hitchens, "are manufactured, and this salient fact is too obvious to ignore." True to his faith, Dawkins finds that the manufacturing and growth of religion is best described in evolutionary terms: "[R]eligions, like languages, evolve with sufficient randomness, from beginnings that are sufficiently arbitrary, to generate the bewildering—and sometimes dangerous— richness of diversity." Harris finds a historical origin for religion and religious traditions, and it is not flattering: "The Bible, it seems certain, was the work of sand-strewn men and women who thought the earth was flat and for whom a wheelbarrow would have been a breathtaking example of emerging technology."[1]

And, they continue, it wasn't even the work of sand-strewn men who labored in the same place at the same time. Rather, it was pieced together from fragments and contradictory sources and then had claimed for it a spurious unity: "Ever since the nineteenth century, scholarly theologians have made an overwhelming case that the gospels are not reliable accounts of what happened in the history of the real world" (Dawkins).[2]

Hitchens adds that "the sciences of textual criticism, archaeology, physics, and molecular biology have shown religious myths to be false and man-made." And yet, wonders Harris, "nearly 230 million Americans believe that a book showing neither unity of style nor internal consistency was authored by an omniscient, omnipotent, and omnipresent deity."[3]

So there's the triple-pronged case. Religions are humanly constructed traditions and at their center are corrupted texts that were cobbled together by provincial, ignorant men who knew less about the world than any high school teenager alive today. Sounds devastating, but when you get right down to it, all it amounts to is the assertion that God didn't write the books or establish the terms of worship—men did—and that the results are (to put it charitably) less than perfect.

But that is exactly what you would expect. It is God (if there is one) who is perfect and infinite; men are finite and confined within historical perspectives. And any effort to apprehend him—including the efforts of the compilers of the Old Testament, the New Testament, and the Koran—will necessarily fall short of a transparency that will be achieved (if it is achieved) only at a future moment of beatific vision. Now—any now, whether it be 2007 or 6,000 years ago—we see through a glass darkly (1 Corinthians 13:12); one day, it is hoped, we shall see face-to-face.

In short, it is the unfathomable and unbridgeable distance between deity and creature that assures the failure of the latter to comprehend or prove (in the sense of validating) the former.

O.L. (in a comment on June 11) identifies the "religion is man-made claim" as the "strongest foundation of atheism" because "it undermines the divinity of god." No, it undermines the divinity of man, which is, after all, the entire point of religion: man is not divine but mortal (capable of death), and he is dependent upon a creator who by definition cannot be contained within human categories of perception and description. "How unsearchable are his judgments and his ways past finding out! For who hath known the mind of the Lord? or who hath been his counselor?" (Romans 11:33–34). It is no wonder, then, that the attempts to contain him—in scriptures, in ceremonies, in prayer—are flawed, incomplete, and forever inadequate. Rather than telling against divinity, the radical imperfection, even corruption, of religious texts and traditions can be read as a proof of divinity, or at least of the extent to which divinity exceeds human measure.

If divinity, by definition, exceeds human measure, the demand that the existence of God be proven makes no sense because the machinery of proof, whatever it was, could not extend itself far enough to apprehend him.

Proving the existence of God would be possible only if God were an item in his own field; that is, if he were the kind of object that could be brought into view by a very large telescope or an incredibly powerful microscope. God, however—again, if there is a God—is not in the world; the world is in him; and therefore there is no perspective, however technologically sophisticated, from which he could be spied. As that which encompasses everything, he cannot be discerned by anything or anyone because there is no possibility of achieving the requisite distance from his presence that discerning him would require.

The criticism made by atheists that the existence of God cannot be demonstrated is no criticism at all; for a God whose existence could be demonstrated wouldn't be a God; he would just be another object in the field of human vision.

This does not mean that my arguments constitute a proof of the truth of religion; for if I were to claim that, I would be making the atheists' mistake from the other direction. Nor are they arguments in which I have a personal investment. Their purpose and function is simply to show how the atheists' arguments miss their mark and, indeed, could not possibly hit it.

At various points Harris, Dawkins, and Hitchens all testify to their admiration for Shakespeare, who, they seem to think, is more godly than God. They would do well to remember one of the bard's most famous lines, uttered by Hamlet: "There are more things in heaven and earth than are dreamt of in your philosophy."

1. Ibid., 45.
2. Dawkins, *The God Delusion*, 118.
3. Harris, *The End of Faith*.

God Talk

MAY 3, 2009

In the opening sentence of the last chapter of his new book, *Reason, Faith and Revolution*, the British critic Terry Eagleton asks, "Why are the most unlikely people, including myself, suddenly talking about God?"[1] His answer, elaborated in prose that is alternately witty, scabrous, and angry, is that the other candidates for guidance—science, reason, liberalism, capitalism—just don't deliver what is ultimately needed. "What other symbolic form," he queries, "has managed to forge such direct links between the most universal and absolute of truths and the everyday practices of countless millions of men and women?"

Eagleton acknowledges that the links forged are not always benign—many terrible things have been done in religion's name—but at least religion is trying for something more than local satisfactions, for its "subject is nothing less than the nature and destiny of humanity itself, in relation to what it takes to be its transcendent source of life." And it is only that great subject, and the aspirations it generates, that can lead, Eagleton insists, to "a radical transformation of what we say and do."

The other projects, he concedes, provide various comforts and pleasures, but they are finally superficial and tend to the perpetuation of the status quo rather than to meaningful change: "A society of packaged fulfillment, administered desire, managerialized politics and consumerist economics is unlikely to cut to the depth where theological questions can ever be properly raised."

By theological questions, Eagleton means questions like, "Why is there anything in the first place?," "Why what we do have is actually intelligible to us?," and "Where do our notions of explanation, regularity, and intelligibility come from?"

The fact that science, liberal rationalism, and economic calculation cannot ask—never mind answer—such questions should not be held against them, for that is not what they do.

And, conversely, the fact that religion and theology cannot provide a technology for explaining how the material world works should not be held against them, either, for that is not what *they* do. When Christopher Hitchens declares that given the emergence of "the telescope and the microscope" religion "no longer offers an explanation of anything important," Eagleton replies, "But Christianity was never meant to be an explanation of anything in the first place. It's rather like saying that thanks to the electric toaster we can forget about Chekhov."

Eagleton likes this turn of speech, and he has recourse to it often when making the same point: "[B]elieving that religion is a botched attempt to explain the world . . . is like seeing ballet as a botched attempt to run for a bus." Running for a bus is a focused empirical act, and the steps you take are instrumental to its end. The positions one assumes in ballet have no such end; they are after something else, and that something doesn't yield to the usual forms of measurement. Religion, Eagleton is saying, is like ballet (and Chekhov); it's after something else.

After what? Eagleton, of course, does not tell us, except in the most general terms: "The coming kingdom of God, a condition of justice, fellowship, and self-fulfillment far beyond anything that might normally be considered possible or even desirable in the more well-heeled quarters of Oxford and Washington." Such a condition would not be desirable in Oxford and Washington because, according to Eagleton, the inhabitants of those places are complacently in bondage to the false idols of wealth, power, and progress. That is, they feel little of the tragedy and pain of the human condition but instead "adopt some bright-eyed superstition such as the dream of untrammeled human progress" and put their baseless "trust in the efficacy of a spot of social engineering here and a dose of liberal enlightenment there."

Progress, liberalism, and enlightenment—these are the watchwords of those, like Hitchens, who believe that in a modern world, religion has nothing to offer us. Don't we discover cures for diseases every day? Doesn't technology continually extend our powers and offer the promise of mastering nature? Who needs an outmoded, leftover, medieval superstition?

Eagleton punctures the complacency of these questions when he turns the tables and applies the label of "superstition" to the idea of progress. It is a superstition—an idol or "a belief not logically related to a course of events" (*American Heritage Dictionary*)—because it is blind to what is now done in its name: "The language of enlightenment has been hijacked in the name of corporate greed, the police state, a politically compromised science, and a permanent war economy," all in the service, Eagleton contends, of an empty suburbanism that produces ever more things without any care as to whether or not the things produced have true value.

And as for the vaunted triumph of liberalism, what about "the misery wreaked by racism and sexism, the sordid history of colonialism and imperialism, the generation of poverty and famine"? Only by ignoring all this and much more can the claim of human progress at the end of history be maintained: "If ever there was a pious myth and a piece of credulous superstition, it is the liberal-rationalist belief that, a few hiccups apart, we are all steadily en route to a finer world."

That kind of belief will have little use for a creed that has at its center "one who spoke up for love and justice and was done to death for his pains." No wonder "Ditchkins"—Eagleton's contemptuous amalgam of Hitchens and Richard Dawkins, perhaps with a sidelong glance at Luke 6:39, "Can the blind lead the blind? Shall they not both fall into the ditch?"—seems incapable of responding to "the kind of commitment made manifest by a human being at the end of his tether, foundering in darkness, pain, and bewilderment, who nevertheless remains faithful to the promise of a transformative love."

You won't be interested in any such promise, you won't see the point of clinging to it, if you think that "apart from the odd, stubbornly lingering spot of barbarism here and there, history on the whole is still steadily on the up," if you think that "not only is the salvation of the human species possible but that contrary to all we read in the newspapers, it has in principle already taken place." How, Eagleton asks, can a civilization "which regards itself as pretty well self-sufficient" see any point in or need of "faith or hope"?

"Self-sufficient" gets to the heart of what Eagleton sees as wrong with the "brittle triumphalism" of liberal rationalism and its ideology of science. From the perspective of a theistic religion, the cardinal error is the claim of the creature to be "self-originating": "Self-authorship," Eagleton proclaims, "is the bourgeois fantasy par excellence," and he could have cited in support the words of that great bourgeois villain, Milton's Satan, who, upon being reminded that he was created by another, retorts,

> [W]ho saw
> When this creation was . . . ?

> We know no time when we were not as now
> Know none before us, self-begot, self-raised

> *(Paradise Lost*, 5:856–60)

That is, we created ourselves (although how there can be agency before there is being and therefore an agent is not explained), and if we are able to do that, why can't we just keep on going and pull progress and eventual perfection out of our own entrails?

That is where science and reason come in. Science, says Eagleton, "does not start far back enough"; it can run its operations, but it can't tell you what they ultimately mean or provide a corrective to its own excesses. Likewise, reason is "too skin-deep a creed to tackle what is at stake"; its laws—the laws of entailment and evidence—cannot get going without some substantive proposition from which they proceed but which they cannot contain; reason is a nonstarter in the absence of an a priori specification of what is real and important, and where is that going to come from? Only from some kind of faith.

"Ditchkins," Eagleton observes, cannot ground his belief "in the value of individual freedom" in scientific observation. It is for him an article of faith, and once in place, it generates facts and reasons and judgments of right and wrong. "Faith and knowledge," Eagleton concludes, are not antithetical but "interwoven." You can't have one without the other, despite the satanic claim that you can go it alone by applying your own independent intellect to an unmediated reality: "All reasoning is conducted within the ambit of some sort of faith, attraction, inclination, orientation, predisposition, or prior commitment." Meaning, value, and truth are not "reducible to the facts themselves, in the sense of being ineluctably motivated by a bare account of them." Which is to say that there is no such thing as a bare account of them. (Here, as many have noted, is where religion and postmodernism meet.)

If this is so, the basis for what Eagleton calls "the rejection of religion on the cheap" by contrasting its unsupported (except by faith) assertions with the scientifically grounded assertions of atheism collapses; and we are where we always were, confronted with a choice between a flawed but aspiring religious faith or a spectacularly hubristic faith in the power of unaided reason and a progress that has no content but, like the capitalism it reflects and extends, just makes its valueless way into every nook and cranny.

For Eagleton the choice is obvious, although he does not have complete faith in the faith he prefers. "There are no guarantees," he concedes, that a "transfigured future will ever be born." But we can be sure that it will never be born, he says in his last sentence, "if liberal dogmatists, doctrinaire flag-wavers for Progress, and Islamophobic intellectuals . . . continue to stand in its way."

One more point. The book starts out witty and then gets angrier and angrier. (There is the possibility, of course, that the later chapters were written first; I'm just talking about the temporal experience of reading it.) I spent some time trying to figure out why the anger was there, and I came up with two explanations.

One is given by Eagleton, and it is personal. Christianity may or may not be the faith he holds to (he doesn't tell us), but he speaks, he says, "partly in defense of my own forbearers, against the charge that the creed to which they dedicated their lives is worthless and void."

The other source of his anger is implied but never quite made explicit. He is angry, I think, at having to expend so much mental and emotional energy refuting the shallow arguments of schoolyard atheists like Hitchens and Dawkins. I know just how he feels.

1. Terry Eagleton, *Reason, Faith and Revolution* (New Haven, CT: *Yale University Press, 2010*).

Suffering, Evil, and the Existence of God

NOVEMBER 4, 2007

In book 10 of Milton's *Paradise Lost*, Adam asks the question so many of his descendants have asked: Why should the lives of billions be blighted because of a sin he, not they, committed ("Ah, why should all mankind / For one man's fault . . . be condemned?" [10:822–23])? He answers himself immediately: "But from me what can proceed, / But all corrupt, both Mind and Will depraved?" (10:824–25). Adam's Original Sin is like an inherited virus. Although those who are born with it are technically innocent of the crime—they did not eat of the forbidden tree—its effects rage in their blood and disorder their actions.

God, of course, could have restored them to spiritual health, but instead, Paul tells us in Romans, he "gave them over" to their "reprobate minds" and to the urging of their depraved wills. Because they are naturally "filled with all unrighteousness," unrighteous deeds are what they will perform: "fornication, wickedness, covetousness, maliciousness . . . envy, murder . . . deceit, malignity." "There is none righteous," Paul declares, "no, not one" (Romans 3:11).

It follows, then (at least from these assumptions), that the presence of evil in the world cannot be traced back to God, who opened up the possibility of its emergence by granting his creatures free will but is not responsible for what they, in the person of their progenitor Adam, freely chose to do.

What Milton and Paul offer (not as collaborators of course, but as participants in the same tradition) is a solution to the central problem of theodicy—the existence of suffering and evil in a world presided over by an all-powerful and benevolent deity. The occurrence of catastrophes, natural (hurricanes, droughts, disease) and unnatural (the Holocaust), always revives the problem and provokes anguished discussion of it. The conviction, held by some, that the problem is intractable leads to the conclusion that there is no God, a conclusion reached gleefully by the authors of books like *The God*

Delusion, God Is Not Great, and *The End of Faith* (see discussion in 6.1, 6.2, and 6.3).

Now two new books (to be published in the coming months) renew the debate. Their authors come from opposite directions—one from theism to agnosticism, the other from atheism to theism—but they meet, or rather cross paths, on the subject of suffering and evil.

Bart D. Ehrman is a professor of religious studies and his book is titled *God's Problem: How the Bible Fails to Answer Our Most Important Question—Why We Suffer.*[1] A graduate of Princeton Theological Seminary, Ehrman trained to be a scholar of New Testament studies and a minister. Born-again as a teenager, devoted to the scriptures (he memorized entire books of the New Testament), and strenuously devout, he nevertheless lost his faith because, he reports, "I could no longer reconcile the claims of faith with the fact of life . . . I came to the point where I simply could not believe that there is a good and kindly disposed Ruler who is in charge." "The problem of suffering," he recalls, "became for me the problem of faith."

Much of the book is taken up with Ehrman's examination of biblical passages that once gave him solace, but that now deliver only unanswerable questions: "Given [the] theology of selection—that God had chosen the people of Israel to be in a special relationship with him—what were Ancient Israelite thinkers to suppose when things did not go as planned or expected? . . . How were they to explain the fact that the people of God suffered from famine, drought, and pestilence?"

Ehrman knows and surveys the standard answers to these questions—God is angry at a sinful, disobedient people; suffering is redemptive, as Christ demonstrated on the cross; evil and suffering exist so that God can make good out of them; suffering induces humility and is an antidote to pride; suffering is a test of faith—but he finds them unpersuasive and as horrible in their way as the events they fail to explain: "If God tortures, maims and murders people just to see how they will react—to see if they will not blame him, when in fact he is to blame—then this does not seem to me to be a God worthy of worship."

And as for the argument (derived from God's speech out of the whirlwind in the book of Job [38:1]) that God exists on a level far beyond the comprehension of those who complain about his ways, "Doesn't this view mean that God can maim, torment, and murder at will and not be held accountable? . . . Does might make right?"

These questions are as old as Epicurus, who gave them canonical form: "Is God willing to prevent evil but not able? Then he is impotent. Is he able but not willing? Then he is malevolent. Is he both able and willing? Whence, then, evil."

Many books of theology and philosophy have been written in response to Epicurus's conundrums, but Ehrman's isn't one of them. What impels him is not the fascination of intellectual puzzles but the anguish produced by what he sees when he opens his eyes. "If he could do miracles for his people throughout the Bible, where is he today when your son is killed in a car accident, or your husband gets multiple sclerosis? . . . I just don't see anything redemptive when Ethiopian babies die of malnutrition."

The horror of the pain and suffering he instances leads Ehrman to be scornful of those who respond to it with cool, abstract analyses: "What I find morally repugnant about such books is that they are so far removed from the actual pain and suffering that takes place in our world."

He might have been talking about Antony Flew's *There Is a God: How the World's Most Notorious Atheist Changed His Mind.*[2] Flew, a noted professor of philosophy, announced in 2004 that after decades of writing essays and books from the vantage point of atheism, he now believes in God. "Changed his mind" is not a casual formulation. Flew wouldn't call what has happened to him a conversion, for that would suggest something unavailable to analysis. His journey, he tells us, is best viewed as "a pilgrimage of reason," an extension of his lifelong habit of "following the argument no matter where it leads."

Where it led when he was a schoolboy was to the same place Ehrman arrived at after many years of devout Christian practice: "I was regularly arguing with fellow sixth formers that the idea of a God who is both omnipotent and perfectly good is incompatible with the manifest evils and imperfections of the world." For much of his philosophical career, Flew continued the argument in debates with a distinguished list of philosophers, scientists, theologians, and historians. And then gradually, and to his own great surprise, he found that his decades-long "exploration of the Divine ha[d] after all these years turned from denial to discovery."

What exactly did he discover? That by interrogating atheism with the same rigor he had directed at theism, he could begin to shake the foundations of that dogmatism. He poses to his former fellow atheists the following question: "What would have to occur or have occurred to constitute for you a reason to at least consider the existence of a superior Mind?" He knows that a cornerstone of the atheist creed is an argument that he himself made many times—the sufficiency of the materialist natural world as an explanation of how things work. "I pointed out," he recalls, that "even the most complex entities in the universe—human beings—are the products of unconscious physical and mechanical forces."

But it is precisely the word "unconscious" that, in the end, sends Flew in another direction. How, he asks, do merely physical and mechanical forces—forces without mind, without consciousness—give rise to the world of purposes, thoughts, and moral projects? "How can a universe of mindless matter produce beings with intrinsic ends [and] self-replication capabilities?" In short (this is the title of a chapter), "How Did Life Go Live?"

Flew does not deny the explanatory power of materialist thought when the question is, how are we to understand the physical causes of this or that event or effect. He is just contending that what is explained by materialist thought—the intricate workings of nature—itself demands an explanation, and materialist thought cannot supply it. Scientists, he says, "are dealing with the interaction of chemicals, whereas our questions have to do with how something can be intrinsically purpose-driven and how matter can be managed by symbol processing." These queries, Flew insists, exist on entirely different levels and the knowledge gained from the first cannot be used to illuminate the second.

In an appendix to the book, Abraham Varghese makes Flew's point with the aid of an everyday example:

> To suggest that the computer "understands" what it is doing is like saying that a power line can meditate on the question of free will and determinism or that the chemicals in a test tube can apply the principle of non-contradiction in solving a problem, or that a DVD player understands and enjoys the music it plays.

How did purposive behavior of the kind we engage in all the time—understanding, meditating, enjoying—ever emerge from electrons and chemical elements?

The usual origin-of-life theories, Flew observes, are caught in an infinite regress that can only be stopped by an arbitrary statement of the kind he himself used to make: "[O]ur knowledge of the universe must stop with the big bang, which is to be seen as the ultimate fact." Or, "The laws of physics are 'lawless laws' that arise from the void— end of discussion." He is now persuaded that such pronouncements beg the crucial question—Why is there something rather than nothing?—a question to which he replies with the very proposition he argued against for most of his life: "The only satisfactory explanation for the origin of such 'end-directed, self-replicating' life as we see on earth is an infinitely intelligent Mind."

Will Ehrman be moved to reconsider his present position and reconvert if he reads Flew's book? Not likely, because Flew remains throughout in the intellectual posture Ehrman finds so arid. Flew assures his readers that he "has had no connection with any of the revealed religions" and no "personal experience of God or any experience that may be called supernatural or religious." Nor does he tell us in this book of any experience of the pain and suffering that haunts Ehrman's every sentence.

Where Ehrman begins and ends with the problem of evil, Flew only says that it is a question that "must be faced," but he is not going to face it in this book because he has been concerned with the prior "question of God's existence." Answering that question affirmatively leaves the other still open (one could always sever the godly attributes of power and benevolence, and argue that the absence of the second does not tell against the reality of the first).

Flew is for the moment satisfied with the intellectual progress he has been able to make. Ehrman is satisfied with nothing, and the passion and indignation he feels at the manifest inequities of the world are not diminished in the slightest when he writes his last word.

Is there a conclusion to be drawn from these two books, at once so similar in their concerns and so different in their ways of addressing them? Does one or the other persuade?

Perhaps an individual reader of either will have his or her mind changed, but their chief value is that together they testify to the continuing vitality and significance of their shared subject. Both are serious inquiries into matters that have been discussed and debated by sincere and learned persons for many centuries. The project is an old one, but these authors pursue it with an energy and goodwill that invite further conversation with sympathetic and unsympathetic readers alike.

In short, these books neither trivialize their subject nor demonize those who have a different view of it, which is more than can be said for the efforts of those fashionable atheist writers whose major form of argument would seem to be ridicule.

(In an article published Sunday—November 4—in the *New York Times Magazine*,[3] Mark Oppenheimer more than suggests that Flew, now in his eighties, did not write the book that bears his name but allowed Roy Varghese, listed as coauthor, to compile it from the philosopher's previous writings and some extended conversations. Whatever the truth is about the authorship of the book, the relation of its argument and trajectory to the argument and trajectory of Ehrman's book stands.)

1. Bart D. Ehrman, *God's Problem: How the Bible Fails to Answer Our Most Important Question—Why We Suffer*, reprint ed. (New York: HarperOne, 2009); subsequent quotes by Ehrman in the essay are from this volume.
2. Antony Flew, *There Is a God: How the World's Most Notorious Atheist Changed His Mind* (New York: HarperOne, 2008); subsequent quotes by Flew are to this volume.
3. Mark Oppenheimer, "The Turning of an Atheist," *New York Times* online, November 4, 2004, http://www.nytimes.com/2007/11/04/magazine/04Flew-t.html?pagewanted=all&_r=0.

Liberalism and Secularism: One and the Same

SEPTEMBER 2, 2007

Back in June, I wrote three columns ("The Three Atheists," "Atheism and Evidence," and "Is Religion Man-Made?" [6.1, 6.2, and 6.3]) about the recent vogue of atheist books, books that accuse religion of being empty of genuine substance, full of malevolent and destructive passion, and without support in evidence, reason, or common sense.

The authors of these tracts are characterized by Professor Jacques Berlinerblau of Georgetown University as "the soccer hooligans of reasoned discourse." He asks (rhetorically), "Can an atheist or agnostic commentator discuss any aspect of religion for more than thirty seconds without referring to religious peoples as imbeciles, extremists, mental deficients, fascists, enemies of the public good, crypto-Nazis, conjure men, irrationalists . . . authoritarian despots and so forth?"[1]

In a similar vein, Tom Krattenmaker, who studies religion in public life, wonders why, given their celebration of open-mindedness and critical thinking, secularists "so frequently leave their critical thinking at the door" when it "comes to matters of religion?"[2] Why are they closed-minded on this one subject?

An answer to these questions can be found, I think, in another publishing phenomenon: the growing number of books and articles dedicated to the rehabilitation of liberalism both as a political vision and as a self-identification of which one needn't be ashamed.

A recent example is Paul Starr's *Freedom's Power: The True Force of Liberalism* (2007).[3] Starr, a professor of sociology at Princeton, claims that what unites liberals are political principles rather than agreement "on the ultimate grounds on which these principles rest." This is the familiar (and suspect) claim that liberalism is not a substantive ideology but a political device that allows many ideologies to flourish and compete in the marketplace of ideas. Liberalism, says Starr, "is only a framework—that is, it provides a space for free development." Where there are deep "divisions over the meaning of the good life," he continues, the "neutrality" of the liberal state "furthers mutual forbearance."

But right there, in the invocation of "free development" and "mutual forbearance," Starr gives the lie to liberal neutrality. Free development (the right of individuals to frame and follow their own life plans) and mutual forbearance (a live-and-let-live attitude toward the beliefs of others as long as they do you no harm) are not values everyone endorses.

And neither are the other values Starr identifies as distinctively liberal—individualism, egalitarianism, self-realization, free expression, modernity, innovation. These values, as many have pointed out, are part and parcel of an ideology, one that rejects a form of government organized around a single compelling principle or faith and insists instead on a form of government that is, in legal philosopher Ronald Dworkin's words, "independent of any particular conception of the good life."[4] Individual citizens are free to have their own conception of what the good life is, but the state, liberal orthodoxy insists, should neither endorse nor condemn any one of them.

It follows then that the liberal state cannot espouse a particular religion or require its citizens to profess it. Instead, the liberal state is committed to tolerating all religions while allying itself with none. Indeed, Starr declares, "the logic of liberalism" is "exemplified" by religious toleration. For if the idea is to facilitate the flourishing of many points of view while forestalling "internecine . . . conflicts" between them, religion, the most volatile and divisive of issues, must be removed from the give and take of political debate and confined to the private realm of the spirit, where it can be tolerated because it has been quarantined.

Thus the toleration of religion goes hand in hand with—is the same thing as—the diminishing of its role in the society. It is a quid pro quo. What the state gets by "excluding religion from any binding social consensus" (Starr) is a religion made safe for democracy. What religion gets is the state's protection. The result, Starr concludes approvingly, is "a political order that does not threaten to extinguish any of the various theological doctrines" it contains.

That's right. The liberal order does not extinguish religions; it just eviscerates them, unless they are the religions that display the same respect for the public-private distinction that liberalism depends on and enforces. A religion that accepts the partitioning of the secular and the sacred and puts at its center the private transaction between the individual and his God fits the liberal bill perfectly. John Locke and his followers, of whom Starr is one, would bar civic authorities from imposing religious beliefs and would also bar religious establishments from meddling in the civic sphere. Everyone stays in place; no one gets out of line.

But what of religions that will not stay in place but claim the right, and indeed the duty, to order and control the affairs of the world so that the tenets of the true faith are reflected in every aspect of civic life? Liberalism's answer is unequivocal. Such religions are the home of "extremists . . . fascists . . . enemies of the public good . . . authoritarian despots and so forth."

This harsh judgment, which Berlinerblau and Krattenmaker label closed-minded, is inevitable given liberalism's founding premises. If the goal is to facilitate the free flow of ideas in a marketplace of ideas, the one thing that cannot be tolerated is the idea of shutting down the marketplace. Liberalism, if it is to be true to itself, must refuse to entertain seriously an argument or a project the goal and effect of which would be to curtail individual exploration, self-realization (except in one direction), free expression, and innovation. Closed-mindedness with respect to religions that do not honor the line between the secular and the sacred is not a defect of liberalism; it is its very definition.

This has been so from the beginning. In 1644, John Milton wrote a tract (*Areopagitica*) in defense of free expression and uncensored publication. It is considered (along with J. S. Mill's "On Liberty") a founding document of modern liberalism. But Milton exempts from his toleration Catholicism ("I mean not tolerated Popery") because, in his judgment, Catholic doctrine undermines "civil supremacies" and therefore must be "extirpate," that is, torn out at the roots.

Some 350 years later, John Rawls (in *Political Liberalism*) seeks a political framework that legitimates all "reasonable comprehensive doctrines." A reasonable comprehensive doctrine is one that would not lead its adherents to "use political power" in an effort to "decide constitutional essentials or basic questions of justice" in a manner directed by that doctrine. A reasonable comprehensive doctrine is ecumenical and tolerant. An unreasonable comprehensive doctrine, on the other hand, would display no such tolerance. It would insist on its right to be preeminent, and therefore it would not be welcome in Rawls's liberal society.

At first glance, this makes perfect sense. After all, why should we tolerate the unreasonable? But the sense it makes depends on "reasonable" having been defined as congruent with the liberal values of pluralism and moderation, and "unreasonable" having been defined as any viewpoint that refuses to respect and tolerate its competitors, but seeks to defeat them. In liberal thought, "reasonable" is a partisan, not a normative, notion. It means "reasonable" from our perspective.

In saying this, I am not criticizing liberalism, just explaining what it is. It is a form of political organization that is militantly secular and incapable, by definition, of seeing the strong claim of religion—the claim to be in possession of a truth all should acknowledge—as anything but an expression of unreasonableness and irrationality. Berlinerblau and Krattenmaker hold out the hope that secularists and strong religionists might come to an accommodation if they would listen to each other rather than just condemn each other. That hope is illusory, for each is defined by what it sees as the other's errors.

But surely, one might object, this is too categorical a statement. There are many who are liberal in their political views—they honor free expression, toleration, individual rights, free and frequent elections, and limited government—and are also people of faith. Yes there are, but the faiths they profess (at least publicly) must be the moderate and undemanding kind liberalism recognizes as legitimate.

There are two answers presidential candidates cannot give to the now obligatory (and deeply offensive) question about their religious faith. A candidate cannot say, "I don't have any," and a candidate cannot say, "My faith dictates every decision I make and every action I take." Rather, a candidate must say something like, "My faith generally informs my moral values, but my judgments and actions as president will follow from the constitutional obligations of the office, not from my religion." In other words, *I too believe in the public-private distinction and I will uphold it. I won't insist that you adopt my values and I will respect yours.* (In short, I'm a liberal.)

A candidate who didn't say something like that but instead announced a determination to reshape public institutions in accordance with the dictates of his or her faith would be seen as too closely resembling the Islamic fundamentalists who, we are told again and again, are our sworn enemies. The divide between those who subscribe to a form of politics uninflected by religious faith (except as a pious "add-on") and those who would derive their politics from faith and acknowledge no distinction between them is not simply national but global. And as Mark Lilla has recently argued,[5] it is a divide that cannot be bridged either by efforts at education or by the supposedly inexorable drift of history toward modernization and secularization. Lilla's lesson is that there is no such drift, although messianic liberals (like George W. Bush) continue to believe in it.

What Lilla calls "political theology"—a politics fueled by faith and visions of eternal life—is not going away, and the two standard liberal responses to its growing strength are inadequate. One is comical, although it has had disastrous consequences. It says, let's tell them about the separation of theology and politics (or lend them copies of Mill and Rawls and James Madison's "Remonstrance") and they'll soon come to want it, too. The second response is to demonize secularism's opponents as fanatics, fascists, and know-nothings, and resolve to stamp them out, a resolve that looks increasingly like a bad bet given the numbers. "It is we," Lilla reminds us, "who are the fragile exception."

So secularism isn't going to win by waiting for what it thinks to be its better arguments to carry the day (politics is neither rational nor Darwinian); and the military option holds out the prospect of more horror than hope. What to do?

One thing we can't do is appeal to some common ground that might form the basis of dialogue and possible rapprochement. There is no common ground, and therefore Lilla is right to say that "agreement on basic principles won't be possible." After all, it is a disagreement over basic principles that divides us from those who have been called "God's warriors." The principles that will naturally occur to us—tolerance, mutual respect, diversity—are ones they have already rejected; invoking them will do no real work except the dubious work of confirming us in our feelings of superiority. (We're tolerant, they're not.)

So again, what to do? Lilla's answer is pragmatic rather than philosophical (and all the better for that). All we can do, he says, is "cope"; that is, employ a succession of ad hoc, provisional strategies that take advantage of, and try to extend, moments of perceived mutual self-interest and practical accommodation. "We need to recognize that coping is the order of the day, not defending high principles." Now there's a principle we can live with, maybe.

1. Jacques Berlinerblau, "Secularism: Boring (Part I)," *OnFaith Blog*, July 16, 2007, http://www.faithstreet.com/onfaith/2007/07/16/secularism-boring-part-i/1576.

2. Tom Krattenmaker, "Secularists, What Happened to the Open Mind?," April 1, 2011, *USA Today* online, http://usatoday30.usatoday.com/printedition/news/20070820/opledereligion90.art.htm.

3. Paul Starr, *Freedom's Power: The True Force of Liberalism*, reprint ed. (New York: Basic Books, 2008).

4. Ronald Dworkin, "Liberalism," in *A Matter of Principle* (New York: Oxford University Press, 1985), 181, 191.

5. Mark Lilla, "The Great Separation," *New York Times Magazine*, August 19, 2007.

Are There Secular Reasons?

FEBRUARY 22, 2010

In the always-ongoing debate about the role of religion in public life, the argument most often made on the liberal side (by which I mean the side of Classical Liberalism, not the side of left politics) is that policy decisions should be made on the basis of secular reasons, reasons that, because they do not reflect the commitments or agendas of any religion, morality, or ideology, can be accepted *as* reasons by all citizens no matter what their individual beliefs and affiliations. So it's okay to argue that a proposed piece of legislation will benefit the economy, or improve the nation's health, or strengthen national security, but it's not okay to argue that a proposed piece of legislation should be passed because it comports with a verse from the book of Genesis or corresponds to the will of God.

A somewhat less stringent version of the argument permits religious reasons to be voiced in contexts of public decision-making so long as they have a secular counterpart: thus, citing the prohibition against stealing in the Ten Commandments is all right because there is a secular version of the prohibition rooted in the law of property rights rather than in a biblical command. In a more severe version of the argument, on the other hand, you are not supposed even to have religious thoughts when reflecting on the wisdom or folly of a piece of policy. Not only should you act secularly when you enter the public sphere; you should also think secularly.

Whether the argument appears in its softer or harder versions, behind it is a form of intellectual/political apartheid known as the private/public distinction: matters that pertain to the spirit and to salvation are the province of religion and are to be settled by religious reasons; matters that pertain to the good order and prosperity of civil society are the province of democratically elected representatives and are to be settled by secular reasons. As John Locke put it in 1689 ("A Letter Concerning Toleration"), the "care of men's souls" is the responsibility of the church while to the civil magistrate belongs the care of "outward things such as money, land, houses, furniture and the like"; it is his responsibility to secure for everyone, of whatever denomination or belief, "the just possession of these things belonging to this life."

A neat division, to be sure, which has the effect (not, I think, intended by Locke) of honoring religion by kicking it upstairs and out of sight. If the business of everyday life—commerce, science, medicine, law, agriculture, education, foreign policy, and so on—can be assigned to secular institutions employing secular reasons to justify actions, what is left to religious institutions and religious reasons is a private area of contemplation and worship, an area that can be safely and properly ignored when there are "real" decisions to be made. Let those who remain captives of ancient superstitions and fairy tales have their churches, chapels, synagogues, mosques, rituals, and liturgical mumbo jumbo; just don't confuse the (pseudo)knowledge they traffic in with the knowledge needed to solve the world's problems.

This picture is routinely challenged by those who contend that secular reasons and secular discourse in general don't tell the whole story; they leave out too much of what we know to be important to human life.

No they don't, is the reply; everything said to be left out can be accounted for by the vocabularies of science, empiricism, and naturalism; secular reasons can do the whole job. And so the debate goes, as polemicists on both sides hurl accusations in an exchange that has become as predictable as it is overheated.

But the debate takes another turn if one argues, as the professor of law Steven Smith does in his new book, *The Disenchantment of Secular Discourse*, that there are no secular reasons, at least not reasons of the kind that could justify a decision to take one course of action rather than another.[1]

It is not, Smith tells us, that secular reason can't do the job (of identifying ultimate meanings and values) we need religion to do; it's worse: secular reason can't do its own self-assigned job—of describing the world in ways that allow us to move forward in our projects—without importing, but not acknowledging, the very perspectives it pushes away in disdain.

While secular discourse, in the form of statistical analyses, controlled experiments, and rational decision trees, can yield banks of data that can then be subdivided and refined in more ways than we can count, it cannot tell us what that data means or what to do with it. No matter how much information you pile up and how sophisticated are the analytical operations you perform, you will never get one millimeter closer to the moment when you can move from the piled-up information to some lesson or imperative it points to; for it doesn't point anywhere; it just sits there, inert and empty.

Once the world is no longer assumed to be informed by some presiding meaning or spirit (associated either with a theology or an undoubted philosophical first principle) and is instead thought of as being "composed of atomic particles randomly colliding and . . . sometimes evolving into more and more complicated systems and entities including ourselves," there is no way, says Smith, to look at it and answer normative questions, questions like "What are we supposed to do?" and "At the behest of who or what are we to do it?"

Smith is not in the business of denigrating science and rationalism or minimizing their great achievements. Secular reason—reason cut off from any a priori stipulations of what is good and valuable—can take us a long way. We'll do fine as long as we only want to find out how many X's or Y's there are or investigate their internal structure or discover what happens when they are combined, and so forth.

But the next step, the step of going from observation to evaluation and judgment, proves difficult, indeed impossible, says Smith, for the "truncated discursive resources available within the downsized domain of 'public reason' are insufficient to yield any definite answer to a difficult issue—abortion, say, or same sex marriage, or the permissibility of torture." If public reason has "deprived" the natural world of "its normative dimension" by conceiving of it as freestanding and tethered to nothing higher than or prior to itself, how, Smith asks, "could one squeeze moral values or judgments about justice . . . out of brute empirical facts?" No way that is not a sleight of hand. This is the cul de sac that Enlightenment philosophy traps itself in when it renounces metaphysical foundations in favor of the "pure" investigation of "observable facts." It must somehow bootstrap or engineer itself back up to meaning and the possibility of justified judgment, but it has deliberately jettisoned the resources that would enable it do so.

Nevertheless, Smith observes, the self-impoverished discourse of secular reason does in fact produce judgments, formulate and defend agendas, and speak in a normative vocabulary. How is this managed? By "smuggling," Smith answers.

> [T]he secular vocabulary within which public discourse is constrained today is insufficient to convey our full set of normative convictions and commitments. We manage to debate normative

matters anyway—but only by smuggling in notions that are formally inadmissible, and hence that cannot be openly acknowledged or adverted to.

The notions we must smuggle in, according to Smith, include "notions about a purposive cosmos, or a teleological nature stocked with Aristotelian 'final causes' or a providential design," all banished from secular discourse because they stipulate truth and value in advance rather than waiting for them to be revealed by the outcomes of rational calculation. But if secular discourse needs notions like these to have a direction—to even get started—"we have little choice except to smuggle [them] into the conversations—to introduce them incognito under some sort of secular disguise."

And how do we do that? Well, one way is to invoke secular concepts like freedom and equality—concepts sufficiently general to escape the taint of partisan or religious affiliation—and claim that your argument follows from them. But, Smith points out (following Peter Westen and others), freedom and equality—and we might add justice, fairness, and impartiality—are empty abstractions. Nothing follows from them until we have answered questions like "fairness in relation to what standard?" or "equality with respect to what measures?"—for only then will they have content enough to guide deliberation.

That content, however, will always come from the suspect realm of contested substantive values. Is fairness to be extended to everyone or only to those with certain credentials (of citizenship, education, longevity, etc.)? Is it equality of opportunity or equality of results (the distinction on which affirmative action debates turn)? Only when these matters have been settled can the abstractions do any work, and the abstractions, in and of themselves, cannot settle them. Indeed, concepts like fairness and equality are normatively useless, except as rhetorical ornaments, until they are filled in by some partisan or ideological or theological perspective, precisely the perspectives secular reason has forsworn. Therefore, Smith concludes, "conversations in the secular cage could not proceed very far without smuggling."

Smith does not claim to be saying something wholly new. He cites David Hume's declaration that by itself "reason is incompetent to answer any fundamental question," and Alasdair MacIntyre's description in *After Virtue* of modern secular discourse as consisting "of the now incoherent fragments of a kind of reasoning that made sense on older metaphysical assumptions."[2]

And he might have added Augustine's observation in "De Trinitate" that the entailments of reason cannot unfold in the absence of a substantive proposition they did not and could not generate; or Roberto Unger's insistence in *Knowledge and Politics* that "as long as formal neutrality is strictly maintained, the standards it produces will be . . . empty shells . . . incapable of determining precisely what is commanded or prohibited in particular situations of choice."[3] (In *The Trouble with Principle*, I myself argue that "there are no neutral principles, only principles that are already informed by the substantive content to which they are rhetorically opposed.")[4]

But no matter who delivers the lesson, its implication is clear. Insofar as modern liberal discourse rests on a distinction between reasons that emerge in the course of disinterested observation—secular reasons—and reasons that flow from a prior metaphysical commitment, it hasn't got a leg to stand on.

1. Steven Smith, *The Disenchantment of Secular Discourse* (Cambridge, MA: Harvard University Press, 2010).
2. Alasdair MacIntyre, *After Virtue*, 3rd ed. (Notre Dame, IN: University of Notre Dame Press, 2007).
3. Roberto Unger, *Knowledge and Politics* (New York: Free Press, 1976).
4. Stanley Fish, *The Trouble with Principle* (Cambridge, MA: Harvard University Press, 2001).

Serving Two Masters: Sharia Law and the Secular State

OCTOBER 25, 2010

A few weeks ago, the Cardozo School of Law mounted a conference marking the twentieth anniversary of *Employment Division v. Smith* (1990), a case in which the Supreme Court asked what happens when a form of behavior demanded by one's religion runs up against a generally applicable law—a law not targeted at any particular agenda or point of view—that makes the behavior illegal. (The behavior at issue was the ingestion of peyote at a Native American religious ceremony.) The answer the court gave, with Justice Antonin Scalia writing for the majority, was that the religious believer must yield to the law of the state so long as that law was not passed with the intention of curtailing or regulating his or anyone else's religious practice. (This is exactly John Locke's view in his "Letter Concerning Toleration.")

"To make the individual's obligation to obey . . . a law contingent upon the law's coincidence with his religious beliefs" would have the effect, Scalia explains, of "permitting him, by virtue of his beliefs, 'to become a law unto himself.'" And if that were allowed, there would no longer be a single law—universally conceived and applied—but multiple laws each of which was tailored to the doctrines and commands of a particular faith. In order to have law in the strong sense, Scalia is saying, you can have only one. ("No man can serve two masters.")

The conflict between religious imperatives and the legal obligations one has as a citizen of a secular state—a state that does not take into account the religious affiliations of its citizens when crafting laws—is an old one (Scalia is quoting *Reynolds v. United States*, 1878); but in recent years it has been felt with increased force as Muslim immigrants to Western secular states evidence a desire to order their affairs, especially domestic affairs, by sharia law rather than by the supposedly neutral law of a godless liberalism. I say "supposedly" because of the obvious contradiction: How can a law that refuses, on principle, to recognize religious claims be said to be neutral with respect to those claims? Must a devout Muslim (or orthodox Jew or fundamentalist Christian) choose between his or her faith and the letter of the law of the land?

In February 2008, the Right Reverend Rowan Williams, archbishop of Canterbury, tried in a now-famous lecture to give a nuanced answer to these questions by making what he considered a modest proposal. After asking "what degree of accommodation the laws of the land can and should give to minority communities with their strongly entrenched legal and moral codes," Williams suggested (and it is a suggestion others had made before him) that in some areas of the law a "supplementary jurisdiction," deriving from religious law, be recognized by the liberal state, which, rather than either giving up its sovereignty or invoking it peremptorily to still all other voices, agrees to share it in limited areas where "more latitude [would be] given in law to rights and scruples rooted in religious identities."[1]

Williams proceeded immediately to surround his proposal with cautionary safeguards—"no 'supplementary' jurisdiction could have the power to deny access to the rights granted to other citizens or to punish its members for claiming those rights"—but no safeguards would have satisfied his many critics, including Prime Minister Gordon Brown, who declared roundly that there is only one common law for all of Britain and it is based squarely on "British values."

Prompted by Williams's lecture and the responses it provoked, law professors Rex Ahdar and Nicholas Aroney have now put together a volume, to be published in 2011, under the title *Shari'a in the West*, a collection of learned and thoughtful essays by some of the world's leading scholars of religion and the law.[2] The volume's central question is stated concisely by Erich Kolig, an anthropologist from New Zealand: "How far can liberal democracy go, both in accommodating minority groups in public policy, and, more profoundly, in granting official legal recognition to their beliefs, customs, practices and worldviews, especially when minority religious conduct and values are not congenial to the majority," that is, to liberal democracy itself?[3]

This is exactly the question posed by John Rawls in a preface to the second edition of *Political Liberalism*, his magisterial account and defense of liberal political principles: "How is it possible for those affirming a religious doctrine that is based on religious authority . . . also to hold a reasonable political conception that supports a just democratic regime?"[4] The words to stumble on are "reasonable" and "just," which at once introduce the requirement and indicate how hard, if not impossible, it will be to meet it: "reasonable" means confirming to rational, not religious, principles; "just" means respecting the equality of all, not just male or faithful, individuals.

With these concepts as the baseline of "accommodation," accommodation is going to fall far short of anything that will satisfy the adherents of a religion that "encompasses all aspects of public and private law, hygiene, and even courtesy and good manners."[5] In liberal thought, these areas are the ones in which the individual reigns supreme and the value of individual choice is presupposed; but, as Ann Black explains, "Muslims do not conceptualize Islam in terms of the Westernized sociological categorization of religion which places the individual at the centre of all analyses."[6]

And so, perhaps predictably, the essays in sharia in the West tack back and forth between the uneasy alternatives Williams names in his lecture—"an assumption on the religious side that membership of the community . . . is the only significant category," and on the other side secular government's assumption of a "monopoly in terms of defining public and political identity." These assumptions seem to be standing obstacles to the ability of secular Western states to think through the problem presented by growing Muslim populations that are sometimes militant in their demand to be ruled by their own faiths and traditions.

On the one hand, there is the liberal desire to accord one's fellow human beings the dignity of respecting their deepest beliefs. On the other hand, there is the fear that if those beliefs are allowed their full scope, individual rights and the rule of law may be eroded beyond repair. It would seem, at least on the evidence of most of these essays, that there is simply no way of "finding a viable path that accommodates diversity with equality,"[7] that is, accommodates tolerance of diverse religious views with an insistence that, in the last analysis, the rights of individuals cannot be trumped by a theological imperative. No one in this volume quite finds the path.

Except perhaps theologian and religious philosopher John Milbank, who puts forward, the editors tell us, "the striking argument that only a distinctly Christian polity—not a secular postmodern one—can actually accord Islam the respect it seeks *as a religion*."[8] The italicized phrase is key: the respect liberalism can accord Islam (or any other strong religion) is the respect one extends to curiosities, eccentrics, the backward, the unenlightened, and the unfortunately deluded. Liberal respect stops short—and this is not a failing of liberalism, but its very essence—of taking religious claims seriously, of considering them as possible alternative ways of ordering not only private but public life.

Christianity, says Milbank, will be more capable of deeply respecting Islam because the two faiths share a commitment to the sacred and to a teleological view of history notably lacking in liberalism (again, this is not a criticism but a definition of liberalism): A "Christian polity can go further in acknowledging the integral worth of a religious group as a group than a secular polity can." Christianity can acknowledge the worth of Islam not merely in an act of tolerance but in an act of solidarity in the same way that Christian sects can acknowledge each other. If you are a Catholic, Milbank explains, "and you do not agree with the Baptists you can nevertheless acknowledge that, relatively speaking, they are pursuing social goals that are comparable with, and promote a shared sense of human dignity" as defined by a corporate religious identity. Liberalism can acknowledge individual Muslims or individual Baptists or individual Catholics, but the liberal acknowledgment detaches these religious believers from their community of belief and turns them into citizens who are in the things that count (to liberalism) just like everyone else.

"Liberal principles," declares Milbank, "will always ensure that the rights of the individual override those of the group." For this reason, he concludes, "liberalism cannot defend corporate religious freedom." The neutrality liberalism proclaims "is itself entirely secular" (it brackets belief; that's what it means by neutrality) and is therefore "unable to accord the religious perspective [the] equal protection" it rhetorically promises. Religious rights "can only be effectively defended pursuant to a specific and distinctly religious framework." Liberal universalism, with its superficial respect for everyone (as long as everyone is superficial) and its deep respect for no one, can't do it.

If that is so, then the other contributors to this volume are whistling "Dixie," at least with respect to the hope declared by Rawls that liberalism in some political form might be able to do justice to the strongly religious citizens of a liberal state. Milbank's fellow essayists cannot negotiate or remove the impasse he delineates, but what they can do, and do do with considerable ingenuity and admirable tact, is find ways of blunting and perhaps muffling the conflict between secular and religious imperatives, a conflict that cannot (if Milbank is right, and I think he is) be resolved on the level of theory, but which can perhaps be kept at bay by the ad hoc, opportunistic, local, and stopgap strategies that are at the heart of politics.

1. Rowan Williams, "Civil and Religious Law in England: A Religious Perspective," February 2008, http://rowanwilliams.archbishopofcanterbury.org/articles.

2. Rex Ahdar and Nicholas Aroney, *Shari'a in the West* (Oxford: Oxford University Press, 2011).

3. Erich Kolig, "To Shari'atize or Not to Shari'atize: Islamic and Secular Law in Liberal Democratic Society," in *Shari'a in the West*, 255–77.

4. John Rawls, preface to *Political Liberalism*, 2nd ed. (New York: Columbia University Press, 2005).

5. Abdullahi Ahmed An-Na'im, *Toward Islamic Reformation: Civil Liberties, Human Rights, and International Law* (New York: Syracuse University Press, 1996), 11.

6. Ann Black, "In the Shadow of Our Legal System: Shari'a in Australia," in *Shari'a in the West*, 239.

7. Ayelet Shachar, "State, Religion, and the Family: The New Dilemmas of Multicultural Accommodation," in *Shari'a in the West*, 125.

8. John Milbank, "The Archbishop of Canterbury: The Man and the Theology behind the Shari'a Lecture," in *Shari'a in the West*, 43. Also see Milbank, "Shari'a and the True Basis of Group Rights" in the same volume.

Religion and the Liberal State Once Again

NOVEMBER 1, 2010

Nothing gets the juices and the comments flowing better than a column on religion and the liberal state. But before attempting a response to the issues raised by readers of my previous column (6.8), I would like to offer a couple of clarifications.

First, by "liberal" and "liberalism" I do not mean, as some posters assumed, a position on the political continuum at the other end of which would be "conservative" and "conservatism." Liberalism is the name of an enlightenment theory of government characterized by an emphasis on procedural rather than substantive rights: the law protects individual free choice and is not skewed in the direction of some choices or biased against others; the laws framed by the liberal state are, or should be, neutral between competing visions of the good and the good life; the state intervenes aggressively only when the adherents of one vision claim the right to act in ways that impinge upon the rights of others to make their own choices.

You are free to believe that salvation comes only through faith in Jesus Christ and to order your behavior accordingly. You are not free to coerce others, either by physical force or the force of law, to share your faith and behave as you do. Adherence to the primacy of individual choice and to the idea that law should not enshrine any orthodoxy is compatible with any politics (except an avowedly racial, sexual, or religious politics). Barack Obama and Ronald Reagan are both classical liberals.

The key distinction underlying classical liberalism is the distinction between the private and the public. This distinction allows the sphere of political deliberation to be insulated from the intractable oppositions that immediately surface when religious viewpoints are put on the table. Liberalism tells us that religious viewpoints should be confined to the home, the heart, the place of worship, and the personal relationship between oneself and one's God.

When the liberal citizen exits the private realm and enters the public square, he or she is supposed to leave religious commitments behind and function as a stripped-down entity, as an abstract-not-full personage, who makes political decisions not as a Jew or a Christian or a Muslim but as what political scientist Michael Sandel calls an "unencumbered self," a self unencumbered by ethnic, racial, gender, class or religious identities.[1] (Some theorists allow the liberal citizen to think politically through a religious lens as long as the policies advocated can be stated in secular terms; other insist that the liberal citizen should not even have religious thoughts when operating in the public sphere.) The basic notion is captured nicely (if hostilely) by Jeffrey: "A human being is first a human being before he or she becomes infected with the virus of religious ideology and superstition."

Now some religions—notably forms of Lockean Protestantism—reflect in their doctrines the private-public split liberalism requires. Others—some versions of Christian fundamentalism, some versions of Orthodox Judaism, some versions of Islam—don't. Such a religion, as Dave points out, "cannot be separated from its role as an entire political/governmental system." That is, it won't respect the private-public distinction; its adherents want to see its strictures and regulations enacted in every corner of daily life, not just in the privacy of the home or chapel.

The question is what does the liberal state do with those religious believers—the popular answer in the comments is "tell them to go back where they came from"—and my contention, and the only one I make (in agreement with John Milbank), is that the liberal state is incapable of doing anything with them except regard them, as many of the posters do, as fanatical, medieval, crazy, dictatorial, and downright dangerous. As I point out, liberalism's inability to regard strong religious claims—claims that spill out into public life—as anything but a mistake and a transgression is not something liberalism can correct or get beyond; it is the inevitable (and blameless) reflection of what liberalism is and must be if it is to sustain its particular, not to say peculiar, brand of universalism, a universalism that operates by reducing persons to formal entities, all of which are, in the essential political respect, exactly the same. (It's universalism writ small.)

When I say that is the only contention I put forward, I am responding to these readers who chided me for recommending a surrender of legal jurisdiction in at least some areas to religious courts and tribunals. Chris protests that "this article's message is that we should alter our current system to adhere to [sharia] law." I offer no such message and, in fact, I offer no message at all. I am certainly not implying "that stoning a woman for adultery is something a liberal state ought to allow" (glennvirt). I'm just foregrounding an issue, reporting on its having been raised controversially by the archbishop of Canterbury, and alerting readers to a new volume (*Shari'a in the West* [see 6.8]) that takes up the matter in depth, and includes, let me add, full and detailed discussions of the dangers to women's rights associated with the legitimization of sharia or other comprehensive religious codes in Western democracies.

The danger is not theoretical or far away. Dean Jamison alerts us to a 2010 decision by a judge in New Jersey that a Muslim man from Morocco accused of sexually abusing his wife did not have criminal intent because he "was operating under his belief that . . . his desire to have sex when . . . he wanted to was something consistent with his [religious] practices"—according to testimony he had said, "You are my wife, I can do anything to you"—and was therefore "not prohibited." In other words, "I was merely acting on the basis of and at the behest of my Muslim faith and committed no wrong."

An appellate court overturned the judge's ruling, declaring that what the husband believed was irrelevant to the question of whether he had acted criminally; but the principle invoked—this is the way we do it where I come from and so I shouldn't be punished for doing it here—is not foreign to US courts, where it has had some success, more often in the penalty or sentencing phases than in the determination of innocence or guilt.

The name of the principle is the "cultural defense"—the argument by a defendant, often but not always an immigrant, that his or her allegedly criminal behavior should be excused or subject to a lesser penalty because in the culture of origin that behavior is an accepted and even commanded norm. The cultural defense is obviously distinct from the issue of establishing religious tribunals alongside the tribunals of the sovereign state. In a way, the person pleading the cultural defense is saying that he has brought the tribunal of his religious faith with him by virtue of having deeply internalized its precepts and imperatives. The question raised by the cultural defense is, "When people come to America [do] they have to give up their way of doing things?"[2]

The answer divides social and legal commentators in a way that mirrors the division produced by the specter of "supplementary" religious courts: The "larger debate," explains legal scholar Doriane Lambelet Coleman, "concerns whether there is and should be a unifying American culture that guides our institutions, including the justice system, or whether the United States is and should be a culturally pluralistic nation in all respects, including in the law."[3] Or, if I may rephrase slightly, does the (undoubted) fact that the United States is very much a pluralistic nation provide a normative basis for plural legal orders? Does multiculturalism as a demographic reality demand multiculturalism as a principle of legal decision making?

There are three responses one might give to these questions and to the cultural defense when it is invoked. (1) I see your point; you were acting in the grip of a sincere belief; go and sin no more; (2) That may be the way they do it back home, but you're here now and our laws trump your culturally acquired beliefs; and (3) That may be the way they do it back home, but here we do it differently, and the way we do it here is the right way and should be the way it's done in the culture you came from.

Response #1 (not often given in its strong form by US courts) acknowledges the legal relevance of deep religious beliefs to the question of culpability and is in synch with the spirit of multiculturalism. Response #2 says, no, in the United States, the legal system operates independently of anyone's religious beliefs and is undergirded by neutral procedural norms. The interesting thing is that both #1 and #2 accept the logic of multiculturalism—different strokes for different folks. It's just that the first would apply the logic to individuals and the second to nations: yes, there are different forms of law in different cultures, but you're in ours now.

The problem with this stance is that it makes law's shape a matter of political power and has nothing positive to affirm in case the political winds shift and bring with them a new kind of law. Response #3, on the other hand, is genuinely universal; it recognizes cultural difference and the existence of many legal systems but insists that there is only one right way to conceive of law, and that nations that conceive of law differently—by, for example, encoding male supremacy or corporal punishment for female adultery—are not just different; they're wrong.

Multicultural deference, procedural neutrality as a local norm, procedural neutrality as a norm every nation should embody in its laws. These three alternative conceptions of law are in play in every advanced society on earth, including ours. More than a few posters were amazed that the question of plural legal jurisdictions was being debated in this day and age and wondered why the *Times* would devote its coveted space to matters settled long ago. The truth is that they are by no means settled and, given patterns of migration and what C. S. Peirce called the "tenacity of belief," they never will be.

1. Michael Sandel, "The Procedural Republic and the Unencumbered Self," *Political Theory* 12, no. 1 (February 1984): 81–96.

2. Cathy Young, "Feminists' Multicultural Dilemma," *Chicago Tribune*, July 8, 1992.

3. Doriane Lambelet Coleman, "Individualizing Justice through Multiculturalism: The Liberals' Dilemma," *Columbia Law Review*, June 1996.

Religion without Truth

MARCH 31, 2007

In 1992, at a conference of Republican governors, Kirk Fordice of Mississippi referred to America as a "Christian nation." One of his colleagues rose to say that what Governor Fordice no doubt meant is that America is a Judeo-Christian nation. If I meant that, Fordice replied, I would have said it.

I thought of Fordice when I was reading *Time* magazine's April 2 cover story, "The Case for Teaching the Bible," by David Van Biema, which also rehearses the case for not teaching the Bible.[1] The arguments are predictable.

On the one side, knowledge of the Bible "is essential to being a full-fledged, well-rounded citizen"; also, if you get into a debate with a creationist, it would be good if you knew what you're talking about.

On the other side: bring the Bible into the schools and you are half a step away from proselytizing; and besides, courses in the Bible typically play down the book's horrific parts (dashing children against stones and the like), and say little about the killings done in its name.

As the *Time* article reports, the usual response to those who fear that allowing the camel's nose under the tent will sooner or later turn the tent into a revival meeting is to promise that the Bible will be taught as a secular text. Students will become familiar with the Bible's stories and learn how to spot references to them in works of literature stretching from Dante to Toni Morrison.

There may be a bit of instruction in doctrine here and there, but only as much as is necessary to understand an allusion, and never to a degree that would make anyone in the class uncomfortable.

Stephen Prothero of Boston University, who is cited several times by Van Biema, describes the project and the claim attached to it succinctly: "The academic study of religion provides a kind of middle space. . . . It takes the biblical truth claims seriously and yet brackets them for purposes of classroom discussion." But that's like studying the justice system and bracketing the question of justice. (How do you take something seriously by putting it on the shelf?)

The truth claims of a religion—at least of religions like Christianity, Judaism, and Islam—are not incidental to its identity; they *are* its identity.

The metaphor that theologians use to make the point is the shell and the kernel: ceremonies, parables, traditions, holidays, pilgrimages—these are merely the outward signs of something that is believed to be informing them and giving them significance. That something is the religion's truth claims. Take them away and all you have is an empty shell, an ancient video game starring a robed superhero who parts the waters of the Red Sea, followed by another who brings people back from the dead. I can see the promo now: more exciting than *Pirates of the Caribbean* or *The Matrix*. That will teach, but you won't be teaching religion.

The difference between the truth claims of religion and the truth claims of other academic topics lies in the penalty for getting it wrong. A student or a teacher who comes up with the wrong answer to a crucial question in sociology or chemistry might get a bad grade or, at the worst, fail to be promoted. Those are real risks, but they are nothing to the risk of being mistaken about the identity of the one true God and the appropriate ways to worship him (or her). Get that wrong, and you don't lose your grade or your job, you lose your salvation and get condemned to an eternity in hell.

Of course, the "one true God" stuff is what the secular project runs away from, or "brackets." It counsels respect for all religions and calls upon us to celebrate their diversity. But religion's truth claims don't want your respect. They want your belief and, finally, your soul. They are jealous claims. Thou shalt have no other God before me.

This is what Fordice meant. He understood that if he prefaced Christian with "Judeo," he would be blunting the force of the belief he adhered to and joining the ranks of the multiculturalist appreciators of everything. Once it's Judeo-Christian, it will soon be Judeo-Islamic-Christian, then Judeo-Islamic-Native American-Christian and then. . . . Teaching the Bible in that spirit may succeed in avoiding the dangers of proselytizing and indoctrination. But if you're going to cut the heart out of something, why teach it at all?

1. David Van Biema, "The Case for Teaching the Bible," *Time*, March 22, 2007.

Is the Establishment Clause Unconstitutional?

MARCH 11, 2007

The question in my title sounds odd, even silly, because as everyone knows, the establishment clause is a *part* of the Constitution. It is the first clause of the First Amendment: "Congress shall make no law respecting an establishment of religion." At this point I am tempted to begin a sentence with "that is" and follow it with a gloss on the clause. But just what these apparently simple words mean has been debated by the courts with increasing vociferousness and little resolution since *Everson v. Board of Education* (1947), often referred to as the first modern establishment clause case, was decided in February 1947.

The issue in Everson was whether the use of public funds to transport students to and from parochial schools was an establishment of religion because religion's interests would be advanced by the expenditure of state monies. Now, sixty years later on March 6, the Supreme Court of California has considered and ruled on the issue of whether a municipal agency (the California Statewide Communities Development Authority), may provide tax-exempt bonds to avowedly sectarian schools for the purpose of constructing cafeterias, athletic facilities, and other campus buildings. The facts are different—in 2007 it is buildings rather than buses that pose the problem—but the basic question is the same: When can it be said that a government action amounts to an establishing of religion?

Everyone agrees that a good place to look for an answer to this question is James Madison's "Memorial and Remonstrance Against Religious Assessments" (1785), in which one finds this oft-cited rhetorical question: "Who does not see," Madison asks, "that the same authority which can force a citizen to contribute three pence only of his property for the support of any one establishment, may force him to conform to any other establishment in all cases whatsoever?" (Madison was writing against a proposed order by the General Assembly of Virginia to provide funds to "Teachers of the Christian Religion.")

After quoting and discussing "Memorial and Remonstrance," Justice Hugo Black, who delivered the majority opinion in Everson, declared roundly that if the establishment clause means anything, it means "at least" that "No tax in any amount, large or small, can be levied to support any religious activities." When Black added to this statement an endorsement of Thomas Jefferson's metaphor (not in the Constitution, but a part of constitutional tradition) of "a wall of separation between church and State," the case would seem to have been closed.

And indeed it was, but not in the direction one might have anticipated, for Black concluded that the state (in this case New Jersey) did not violate the establishment clause when it reimbursed parents for the expense of transporting their children to and from parochial schools. How was this reversal managed and justified? By changing the subject and varying the question. Instead of asking, does the state's reimbursement program have the effect of supporting a religious institution (the answer to that question surely would be yes), Black asked, what did the legislature have in mind? And he found that it had in mind nothing more than to "provide a general program to help parents get their children, regardless of their religion, safely and expeditiously to and from accredited schools." The First Amendment, he added, requires only that "the state be neutral in its relations with . . . religious believers; it does not require the state to be their adversary."

The reasoning here was at best disingenuous; it more than implied that if the state were not to reimburse parents of parochial school students it would be discriminating against them—denying them a *general* benefit—on the basis of their religion. But the discrimination would not be against religious believers but against religious institutions as the possible recipients of public funds, and that discrimination is what the establishment clause enjoins, at least as James Madison would read it. The point was made by Justice Robert Jackson in his dissent when he insisted on "a difference which the Constitution sets up between religion and almost every other subject matter of legislation."

Those who oppose a strict application of the establishment clause often argue that religion shouldn't be "singled out" for hostile attention. But the special status of religion is the *reason* for the establishment clause (if religion was to be treated like everything else, there would be no establishment clause), and that special status, Jackson observed, is both positive and negative: "it was intended not only to keep the state's hand out of religion, but to keep religion's hands off the state," an intention that would be flouted if religion's hands were allowed to dip into the state's pocket.

This plain fact is occluded by the trick of running two inquiries at the same time and assuming (or pretending) that they are the same. One inquiry (proper to the establishment clause) asks, is the state expending public monies in a way that advances religion? The second inquiry (more philosophical then juridical) asks, is the state being fair and evenhanded to religion? The first inquiry is responsive to the establishment clause's nervousness about religion, and alert, in the spirit of Madison, to the slightest ("three pence only") breach of the wall of separation. The other inquiry is responsive to the demand of impartiality, and its rule is, if the public schools receive aid from the state, the parochial schools should too. As Justice Wiley Rutledge noted in his dissent, by generalizing away from establishment concerns and moving to "larger" concepts like "promoting the general cause of education and the welfare of the individual," the rule of impartiality "ignores the religious factor." It does more than that, for by rejecting the establishment clause's suspicion of any intersection of religious activity and state action, the rule of impartiality comes very close to discarding the establishment clause altogether.

This was pretty much the result in a later case, *Rosenberger v. Rector* (1995). The case turned on the refusal of the University of Virginia to authorize payment (from student funds) for the printing of an evangelical student newspaper, *Wide Awake*, on the grounds that it was engaged in religious rather than educational activity, and therefore fell afoul of the establishment clause. Justice Anthony Kennedy, writing for the majority, ruled against the university's position on the reasoning that its action amounted to "viewpoint discrimination." That is, by setting up a student activities fund with the purpose of encouraging the presentation of diverse views, the university had established a forum open to all forms of expression, and now it was trying to exclude one kind of expression, the expression of the "Christian viewpoint."

This argument works by moving the dispute out of the establishment clause context and into the context of the free expression clause. The free expression clause depends on a distinction between speech and action: it says that while action can be regulated (that, after all, is what government and laws do), expression, no matter what its content, must be freely allowed. (It's the fairness or evenhanded requirement again.) The establishment clause, in contrast, is uninterested in expression except when it turns into, or is a component of, an action of the kind it polices—state action that has the effect of furthering the interests of religion. This difference is marked by the university's characterization of *Wide Awake* as "religious activity" rather than as religious expression. What triggered an establishment clause concern is what Justice David Souter, writing in dissent, called the "hortatory" nature of the newspaper's appeal. This was not, he said, "the discourse of the scholar's study," but of the evangelist's mission station and the pulpit. It was "nothing other than the preaching of the word" and a "straightforward exhortation to enter into a relationship with God."

It was "obviously crucial," Souter contended, to distinguish "between works characterized by the evangelism of *Wide Awake*" and "simply descriptive writing informing a reader about the position of a given religion." *Wide Awake*, despite the fact that it takes the form of words, was not speech; it was action—a "call" to religious behavior—and because it was an action sponsored by state funds, it fell into the category of things regulated by the establishment clause. If you take this distinction away, the establishment clause no longer has an area in which it can be applied, and this is exactly what happened when Justice Kennedy made the case turn on the question of viewpoint discrimination.

Five years later Souter was singing the same song, and again he was on the losing side. In *Mitchell v. Helms* (2000), the question was, can funds distributed by the federal government to the states for dispersion to public and private schools be used to aid religious schools? Writing for the majority, Justice Clarence Thomas restated the question as one that asks "whether any religious indoctrination that occurs in those schools could be reasonably attributed to governmental action?" In short, is government doing the indoctrinating? No, said Thomas, because the government provided funds in a neutral manner "to a broad range of groups and persons without regard to their religion." Any indoctrinating, then, was being done by the persons and groups that used the funds, not by the government.

I call this the "money laundering" strategy for getting around the establishment clause (it is often used by those in favor of school vouchers), and Souter was predictably indignant. This "conception of neutrality" as a sufficient prophylactic against an establishment clause violation "would, if adopted by the Court, eliminate inquiry into the law's effects" and would mark, Souter predicted, "the end of the principle of no aid to the schools' religious mission." This has been in the process of ending for a long time.

The day after *Everson* came down, a *Washington Post* editorial warned that if citizens can be taxed to pay for buses sent to and from parochial schools, in time "they can be taxed to pay the salaries of church teachers and the cost of buildings for religious educational purposes."[1] The California Supreme Court case decided last week demonstrates just how prophetic this warning was. The case, as I noted earlier, is about using tax-free bonds to finance buildings at Christian schools. The relevant article of the California Constitution says that neither the legislature nor any municipality "shall ever make an appropriation, or pay for any public fund whatever . . . in aid of any religious sect, church, creed or sectarian purpose, or help to support or sustain any school, college, university or other institution controlled by any religious creed, church, or sectarian denomination." (It's the establishment clause writ large.) Immediately after citing this article, Justice Joyce Kennard, writing for the majority, made the *Everson* move and declared that because funds for the building projects "will not come from any government entity but from private-sector purchasers of the bonds," the state cannot be said to be directly aiding religion. The program is "simply a mechanism by which the government extends available tax to private individuals" who may then turn around and confer a benefit on religious institutions. But that's their choice, not the government's.

It's the money laundering argument once again, and Justice Ming Chin, in dissent, gamely tried to counter it by asserting that the "key question is not whether the benefit . . . is direct or incidental," but whether it results in the support of sectarian schools. Justice Chin was saying, let's remember that, after all, this is an establishment clause case, and what we're supposed to be worried about is the diversion of public funds for religious purposes. But it's too late in the day for that, and if this case goes up to the Supreme Court, I doubt the result will be any different. The establishment clause may still be on the books, but it is honored more in the breach than in the observance.

1. The date of the editorial was February 11, 1947.

The Religion Clause Divided against Itself

MARCH 18, 2007

My last column (6.11) told the story of the diminishing scope of the establishment clause of the Constitution. Once understood as prohibiting state actions that endorse, benefit, or advance religion, the clause has in recent decades been reread in ways that permit, among other things, taxpayer financing of evangelical student newspapers and the construction of buildings at sectarian (mostly Christian) schools. This result has been accomplished by shifting the inquiry from the traditional establishment clause question—does this amount to government funding of religious activities?—to a free expression clause question—would denying the religious institution this benefit or subsidy be an unfair instance of viewpoint discrimination? By substituting the requirement of fairness for an investigation of a law's effects, the courts have moved dramatically away from James Madison's insistence that not even three pence of public funds should be spent for religious purposes and have rendered the establishment clause nugatory.

Some of those who commented on the column attributed the pattern I described to the nefarious forces of organized religion or to the machinations of the Bush administration (always the default villain for *Times* readers), but a deeper explanation might be found in a religion-clause jurisprudence so fissured that one might even call it schizophrenic. The division is between two views of the assumptions that should be kept in mind when an establishment clause case or a free exercise case is being adjudicated. One view stresses history and cultural traditions; the other embraces the iron logic of principle.

The touchstone statement for those who urge us to respect history is Justice William Douglas's declaration in *Zorach v. Clauson* (1952) that "We are a religious people whose institutions presuppose a Supreme Being." The key word is "presuppose." It says that the assumption of a supreme being and of a citizenry that believes in him (or her) hangs over this country's institutions, including its legal institutions. It is a given, and any consideration of a benefit that state action confers on religion should occur within it. One should not, therefore, regard religion clause prohibitions as categorical and without exception. Rather, as Justice Sandra Day O'Connor asserted in *County of Allegheny v. American Civil Liberties Union* (1989), "the meaning of the Clause is to be determined by reference to historical practices and understandings," and, she noted, "[g]overnment policies of accommodation, acknowledgment, and support for religion are an accepted part of our political and cultural heritage."

Religion clause purists respond to this argument by pointing out that what is accepted may not be right and by insisting that principle, not history, should be the guide. Thus Justice William Brennan contends (in *Marsh v. Chambers*, 1983) that the practice of "official invocational prayer" in many state legislatures, "is not saved . . . by its history," for it is simply "wrong." And in the same vein, Justice Harry Blackmun (again in *County of Allegheny v. American Civil Liberties Union*) maintains that the "bedrock Establishment Clause principle" must be affirmed "regardless of history."

The opposition of principle to history is complicated, however, by the fact that both sides claim to find support for their positions in history—the history of the framers' intentions. Those who argue for the primacy of the "accepted habits of our people" (Justice Stanley Reed in *McCollum v. Board of Education*, 1948) will say that the framers intended only to prevent government from favoring one sect over the others; don't establish a particular religion was their directive. Here, for example, is William Rehnquist telling us (in *Wallace v. Jaffree*, 1985), "that the framers intended the Establishment Clause to prohibit the designation of any church as a 'national' one." It was not their intention to "require government neutrality between religion and irreligion."

Yes it was, says Justice David Souter, who argued (in *Capitol Square Review v. Pinette*, 1995) that when Ohio permitted a cross and a menorah to be erected on a plaza adjacent to the statehouse, it sent the message that "The State of Ohio favors religion over irreligion," and "this message is incompatible with the principles embodied by our Establishment Clause."

Defenders of the more flexible view of the framers' intention will point out that "In the very week that Congress approved the Establishment Clause . . . it enacted legislation providing for paid chaplains for the House and Senate" (Justice Warren Burger in *Lynch v. Donnelly*,

1984). The response, implicit in the reasoning of the strict construc-tionists, is that it was a principle the framers were announcing, and although they may have not fully understood the scope of their prin-ciple, we do. So it's a standoff between those who believe that the framers historically intended that we pay attention to history and those who believe that the framers historically intended that we should not.

Notice that the cases I have cited in these two columns span more than fifty years and ten administrations. In that time, the cast of char-acters on the Supreme Court has constantly changed, and the line dividing the opposing positions (which persist unchanged) does not correlate with differences of religion, politics, interpretive philoso-phy, seniority, or judicial temperament. The arguments that emerged full-blown in 1947 are the arguments that are still being run today. There is no progress to be discerned; no clarity has emerged; no con-sistency has been achieved. Almost all of the decisions, in whatever directions they tip, are 5–4. It's a mess, and more than once the jus-tices themselves have commented that the jurisprudence in which they are engaged is incoherent and chaotic.

If there is a pattern at all, it is most assuredly not linear. Rather, it is a pendulum, or a roller coaster or, at times, a kaleidoscopic fun house, as we are told that a crèche set up in a public sphere with state funds is not an establishment of religion (*Lynch v. Donnelly*), while the delivery of a prayer carefully denuded of any sectarian content (or any content at all) at a middle school graduation—the very middle school from which I graduated in some other century—is (*Lee v. Weisman*, 1992).

That is why I said at the outset that blaming either evangelical ideologues or the administration they may be said to own for this or that decision is an oversimplification. The fault, dear readers, lies not in the players—on or off the court—but in the enterprise, an enter-prise so fundamentally divided against itself, that it will continually reproduce its built-in ambiguities and contradictions no matter what issues are brought to its bar or whose hands are, at the moment, on the wheel.

When Is a Cross a Cross?

MAY 3, 2010

Also, when is a menorah a menorah, and when is a crèche a crèche, and when are the Ten Commandments directives given to the Jews by God on Mount Sinai? These questions, which might seem peculiar in the real world, are perfectly ordinary in the wild and wacky world of establishment clause jurisprudence, where in one case (*Lynch v. Donnelly*, 1984) the Supreme Court declared, with a straight judicial face, that a display featuring the baby Jesus, Mary, Joseph, and the wise men conveyed a secular, not a religious message.

In the latest chapter of this odd project of saving religion by emptying it of its content, Justice Anthony Kennedy, writing for a plurality in *Salazar v. Buono*, ordered a district court to reconsider a ruling that Congress had impermissibly promoted religion by devising a plan designed to prevent the removal of a cross standing in the Mojave National Preserve. The cross had originally been erected in 1934 by the Veterans of Foreign Wars to commemorate American soldiers who had died in World War I. In 2002, Frank Buono, a retired Park Service employee, filed suit alleging a violation of the establishment clause and "sought an injunction requiring the government to remove the cross."

In litigation unfolding in at least four stages, the District Court and the Appellate Court of the Ninth Circuit determined that "a reasonable observer would perceive a cross on federal land as governmental endorsement of religion." In response, Congress took several actions, including designating the cross and the adjoining land a national memorial and transferring ownership of the land in question to the VFW in exchange for land located elsewhere in the preserve. Turning again to the courts, Buono asked for an injunction against the transfer; the District Court granted it, concluding that "the transfer was an attempt by the Government to keep the cross atop Sunrise Rock and so was invalid."

The issue was Congress's motive. The effect of what it had done was obvious: the cross now stood on private land, which meant, at least theoretically, that there was no longer an establishment clause violation because a private party, not the government, was speaking. But the question remained: Did the transfer "cure" the violation or did it, as Justice John Paul Stevens contended in dissent, extend and reperform it?

Now the fun and crazy stuff begins. Kennedy denies that the "emplacement" of the cross was accompanied by any intention "to promote a Christian message." It was "intended simply to honor our Nation's fallen soldiers." (At oral argument Peter Eliasberg, an ACLU lawyer, observed, "There is never a cross on a tombstone of a Jew.") Therefore, Kennedy reasoned, Congress had no "illicit" intention either; it merely sought a way to "accommodate" (a term of art in establishment clause jurisprudence) a "symbol often used to honor and respect those whose heroic acts, noble contributions and patient striving help secure an honored place in history for this Nation and its people."

Notice what this paroxysm of patriotism had done: it has taken the Christianity out of the cross and turned it into an all-purpose means of marking secular achievements. (According to this reasoning, the cross should mark the winning of championships in professional sports.) It is one of the ironies of the sequence of cases dealing with religious symbols on public land that those who argue for their lawful presence must first deny them the significance that provokes the desire to put them there in the first place.

It has become a formula: if you want to secure a role for religious symbols in the public sphere, you must de-religionize them, either by claiming for them a nonreligious meaning, as Kennedy does here, or, in the case of multiple symbols in a park or in front of a courthouse, by declaring that the fact of many of them means that no one of them is to be taken seriously; they don't stand for anything sectarian; they stand for diversity. So you save the symbols by leeching the life out of them. The operation is successful, but the patient is dead.

The game being played here by Kennedy (and many justices before him) is "let's pretend." Let's pretend that a cross that, as Kennedy acknowledges, "has been a gathering place for Easter services since it was first put in place," does not breathe Christianity. Let's pretend that Congress, which in addition to engineering a land-swap for the purpose of keeping the cross in place attached a reversionary clause requiring that the "memorial" (no cross is mentioned) be kept as it is, did not have in mind the preservation of a religious symbol. Let's pretend that after all these machinations a "reasonable observer" who knew all the facts would not see the government's hand but would only see the hands of private parties. (This is what I call the "look, ma, no hands" argument.) Let's pretend that there will be many who, if the cross were removed, would think that the government had conveyed "disrespect for those the cross was seen as honoring." (Stevens points out that Kennedy just made that one up without the support of "any legislative history or findings.")

The trouble with pretending is that it involves a strain; keeping the pretense going is hard, and the truth being occluded often peeks through, as it does when Kennedy protests that the establishment clause "does not require eradication of all religious symbols in the public realm" and adds that "the Constitution does not oblige government to avoid any public acknowledgment of religion's role in society."

But I thought that the cross was not, at least in this instance, a religious symbol and that the issue was not government acknowledging religion, but government honoring its dead. At moments like this, the mask slips and the plurality's real concern—"to foster the display of the cross" (Stevens)—is revealed for all (who had no doubt already spied it beneath the subterfuge) to see. The Christian and conservative websites that welcomed the decision as a blow for Christianity and against liberalism knew what they were looking at.

My distaste for Kennedy's opinion has nothing to do with its result. In general, and for the record, I have no problem with the state accommodating religious symbols, and I am not bothered by the thought of a cross standing in a remote part of the Mojave desert even if the land it stands on is owned by the government. I do have a problem with reasoning that is patently dishonest and protests too much about its own motives and the motives of those it defends. But that is what the religion clause drives you to when in one of its subclauses— the free exercise clause—it singles out religion for special positive treatment, and in the other subclause—the establishment clause—it places a warning label (watch out for this stuff; it's trouble) on religion. It's no wonder that the justices who try to deal with this house-divided-against-itself tie themselves in knots and produce opinions that are as unedifying as they are disingenuous.

Being Neutral Is Oh So Hard to Do

JULY 19, 2010

In the opening paragraph of his dissent in *Christian Legal Society v. Martinez* (June 28, 2010), Justice Samuel Alito names the principle he finds animating the majority opinion: "no freedom for expression that offends prevailing standards of political correctness in our country's institutions of higher learning." I have come to think he is right.

But before I say why, let me review the facts of the case.

The Christian Legal Society (CLS) is an organization with chapters at a number of law schools. The purpose of the society, according to the petitioner's brief, is to "provide opportunities for fellowship, as well as moral and spiritual guidance, for Christian lawyers," to promote "justice, religious liberty, and biblical conflict resolution" and encourage "lawyers to furnish legal services for the poor."

Anyone can attend and participate in a CLS meeting, but voting members and officers are required to "affirm their commitment to the group's core beliefs" by signing a Statement of Faith that declares a trust in Jesus as one's savior, and a belief in the Trinity as well as in the Bible as the inspired word of God. Those who sign the Statement of Faith are expected to live up to its precepts, and if they do not—if they do not refrain from "either participation in or advocacy of a sexually immoral lifestyle"—they disqualify themselves from CLS membership. "Sexually immoral" behavior includes premarital sex, adultery, and homosexual conduct.

And there's the rub, at least as far as the University of California Hastings College of the Law is concerned; for, according to its briefs, the school requires all RSOs (registered student organizations) to maintain an "all-comers" policy with regard to memberships and candidacy for group officers. In a deposition, the law school's dean explained that "in order to be a registered student organization you have to allow all our students to be members and full participants if they want to." (There is a dispute about just when this policy was put in place, the petitioners claiming that it was conveniently invented in the middle of the case, the law school claiming that it had been in force since 1990.)

Organizations that will not open their membership rolls to all-comers can still form and have a campus presence and petition to use school facilities for meetings, but they will not be granted the benefits that come along with official recognition (which is different, Hastings is careful to point out, from positive sponsorship).

So the issue is joined: must CLS's right under the First Amendment to form an association of like-minded persons around an idea or an agenda give way—at least with respect to the privilege of RSO status—to the nation's and the university's compelling interest in eliminating "invidious" discrimination? Or should the all-comers policy be relaxed in recognition of the right of an association to maintain the integrity of its declared purposes and beliefs?

CLS argues that all "expressive associations, regardless of their beliefs, have a constitutionally protected right to control the content of their speech by excluding those who do not share their essential purposes and beliefs" (petitioner's brief). Hastings responds that "the people of California, through their elected representatives, have barred discrimination based on various enumerated factors, including religion and sexual orientation 'in any program . . . conducted by any postsecondary educational institution that receives . . . state financial assistance'"; and therefore the law school is precluded "from allowing any such discrimination in its publically funded RSO program" (respondent's brief).

One more complication: the case unfolds under the Supreme Court's "limited forum" doctrine, which says (among other things) that once a state or state entity has established a forum for expressive activity, it cannot exclude from the forum speakers or groups whose viewpoints it disfavors. It may, however, impose restrictions on participation that are viewpoint-neutral, restrictions that do not flow from an official disapprobation of what is being expressed. The question, then, is does the Hastings all-comers policy involve a viewpoint-neutral restriction that only incidentally sweeps up CLS in its wake, or is the policy, as Justice Alito claims, designed to discriminate against the Christian viewpoint?

Writing for the majority, Justice Ruth Bader Ginsburg aligns herself with the first prong of my question and agrees with the district court's conclusion that the policy is "neutral and of general applicability" and "does not target or single out religious beliefs." After all, she declares, it is "hard to imagine a more viewpoint-neutral policy than one requiring *all* student groups to accept *all* comers."

However, here things get tricky. The reasoning that the all-comers policy does not single out religious beliefs depends on a distinction between belief and conduct, a distinction Ginsburg invokes several times, first when she says that all student organizations remain able to "express what they wish," as long as they do not "discriminate in membership," and later when she adds that "CLS's conduct—not its Christian perspective—is . . . what stands between the group and RSO status." But the distinction between belief and conduct, the very basis of formal neutrality, is not itself neutral because it favors religions (like the Protestantism John Locke explicates in his "Letter Concerning Toleration," 1689) that are centered on the personal relationship between adherents and the God they believe in, and disfavors religions that require, and regard as a nondetachable extension of belief, the performance of specific forms of behavior.

That is to say, the belief/conduct distinction, a close relative of the mind/body distinction and the private/public distinction, itself embodies a very specific viewpoint (one the government is not entitled to have or enforce) concerning just what a religious belief is, and as such it discriminates against religions that do not respect, indeed cannot respect, the belief/conduct distinction. The Statement of Faith CLS members are asked to sign and the canons of conduct they are asked to observe mark it as that kind of religion, one that demands not just assent to a set of doctrines but conformity to a code of behavior. CLS members must not only believe certain things; they must comport themselves in ways dictated by their belief, and so must the organization itself if it wishes to be true to the beliefs it declares, the beliefs around which it organized in the first place.

So when Ginsburg insists that the all-comers policy "aims at the *act* of rejecting would-be group members without reference to the reasons motivating that behavior," she treats the act (of requiring members to affirm and adhere to CLS's doctrinal and behavioral tenets) as if it were just a disagreeable manifestation of prejudice unrelated to the group's beliefs, as if it were distinct from the "reasons" animating the group's existence. She appears to think that, were CLS's membership rules relaxed in deference to Hastings' all-comers policy, the organization's beliefs would survive intact; for it's just an extrinsic procedural change, isn't it?

The alternative is to view CLS membership policy and the beliefs it declares as inextricable; you can't have one without the other. And this would mean, as I have already more than suggested, that the so-called viewpoint-neutral all-comers policy is not neutral at all, any more than a law that no one can sleep under bridges (a classic example) would be neutral. Only the poor and homeless would want to sleep under bridges; the "neutral" law forbidding it would obviously be directed at them. Only religions that recognize no distinction between belief and conduct would want to restrict membership to persons pledged to the performance of specific behaviors; the "neutral" all-comers requirement is obviously directed at them. The distinction on which Ginsburg relies between disapproving CLS's beliefs and disapproving its "act" won't work. If you penalize the group for its membership policies, you are penalizing it for its beliefs.

This is Alito's point in his dissent: "As written and enforced, the Policy targets solely those groups whose beliefs are based on 'religion' or that disapprove of a particular kind of sexual behavior." I would emend slightly: the policy is targeted at those religions that would be in violation of their own beliefs were they to countenance, by membership policy or any other action, particular kinds of sexual behavior. The legal doctrine to be invoked here (and Alito invokes it) is "expressive association," the idea that certain actions a group might take are so expressive of their reasons for being that those actions are inseparable from those reasons.

Alito cites Justice Sandra Day O'Connor's observation in *Roberts v. United States Jaycees* (1984) that an "association's right to define its membership derives from the recognition that the formation of an expressive association is the creation of a voice, and the selection of members is the definition of that voice." It follows that a regulation preventing the association from selecting its members narrowly, or withholding benefits if it does so, would amount to a silencing of the association's voice, an infringement on its expressive rights.

This is not an argument Justice Ginsburg pays much attention to. She pretty much dismisses it by claiming that CLS "faces only indirect pressure to modify its membership policies" and was not "compelled," as groups were in other expressive association cases, "to include unwanted members with no choice to opt out." (I guess she doesn't think the cost of the so-called opt-out choice is worth bothering about.) Ginsburg is more interested in the limited forum doctrine, which, she asserts (citing an earlier case) gives the state the right "to make distinctions in access on the basis of . . . speaker identity"; and she cites another case to the effect that "the state may not exclude speech where its distinction is not reasonable in the light of the purposes served by the forum."

This citation raises the question of the relationship between the exclusion of groups (or group; only CLS has been targeted) with selective membership policies and the purposes of the forum. Is the exclusion reasonable? What are those purposes? Or to put the question more precisely, what purposes that an educational institution might have would require it to withhold the benefits of official recognition from a group that limited its members to those who abided by the dictates of its faith?

Ginsburg answers the question by accepting a view of education and its purposes put forward by the amicus brief of the American Civil Liberties Union: "Just as 'Hastings does not allow its professors to host classes open only to those students with a certain status or belief,' so the Law School may decide, reasonably in our view, 'that the educational experience is best promoted when all participants in the forum must provide equal access to all students.'" And just what is the "educational experience" envisioned in this statement? It turns out, in Ginsburg's view, to be the experience of an environment that encourages the "development of conflict-resolution skills, toleration, and readiness to find a common ground."

Now that is a "reasonable" list of educational goals, but it is not the only one. Another might be an educational experience that encourages fidelity to correct behavior as defined by some religion or system of morality, an experience devoted less to the finding of common ground than to the finding of, and hewing to, truth.

I am not saying that this latter view of education's purposes—the view held by the Christian Legal Society—should be the official view of the law school. I am saying that no view of education's purposes, as long it is contestable (and they all are), should be the official view of the law school. Under cover of "neutrality," Hastings, with the majority's approval, is imposing the goals and ideology of liberal multiculturalism on the very diverse members of the law school's community. Justice John Paul Stevens may be right on the law when he observes in a concurring opinion that "the university need not remain neutral . . . in determining which goals the [RSO] program will serve and which rules are best suited to facilitate those goals," but he and his colleagues in the majority cannot at the same time make statements like that one and claim to be speaking in the name of neutrality.

PART 7

Reflections on Liberal Arts Education

Analyzing welfare reform in an academic context is a political action in the sense that any conclusion a scholar might reach will be one another scholar might dispute. (That, after all, is what political means: subject to dispute.) But such a dispute between scholars will not be political in the everyday sense of the word, because each side will represent different academic approaches, not different partisan agendas.

My point is not that academics should refrain from being political in an absolute sense—that is impossible—but that they should engage in politics appropriate to the enterprise they signed onto. And that means arguing about (and voting on) things like curriculum, department leadership, the direction of research, the content and manner of teaching, establishing standards—everything that is relevant to the responsibilities we take on when we accept a paycheck. These responsibilities include meeting classes, keeping up in the discipline, assigning and correcting papers, opening up new areas of scholarship, and so on.

This is a long list, but there are many in academia who would add to it the larger (or so they would say) tasks of "forming character" and "fashioning citizens." A few years ago, the presidents of nearly five hundred universities issued a declaration on the "Civic Responsibility of Higher Education." It called for colleges and universities to take responsibility for helping students "realize the values and skills of our democratic society."

Derek Bok, the former president of Harvard and one of the forces behind the declaration, has urged his colleagues to "consider civic responsibility as an explicit and important aim of college education." In January, some thirteen hundred administrators met in Washington under the auspices of the Association of American Colleges and Universities to take up this topic: "What practices provide students with the knowledge and commitments to be socially responsible citizens?" That's not a bad question, but the answers to it should not be the content of a college or university course.

No doubt, the practices of responsible citizenship and moral behavior should be encouraged in our young adults—but it's not the business of the university to do so, except when the morality in question is the morality that penalizes cheating, plagiarizing, and shoddy teaching, and the desired citizenship is defined not by the demands of democracy but by the demands of the academy.

Why We Built the Ivory Tower

MAY 1, 2006

After nearly five decades in academia, and five and a half years as a dean at a public university, I exit with a three-part piece of wisdom for those who work in higher education: do your job; don't try to do someone else's job, as you are unlikely to be qualified; and don't let anyone else do your job. In other words, don't confuse your academic obligations with the obligation to save the world; that's not your job as an academic; and don't surrender your academic obligations to the agenda of any nonacademic constituency—parents, legislators, trustees, or donors. In short, don't cross the boundary between academic work and partisan advocacy, whether the advocacy is yours or someone else's.

Marx famously said that our job is not to interpret the world, but to change it. In the academy, however, it is exactly the reverse: our job is not to change the world, but to interpret it. While academic labors might in some instances play a role in real-world politics—if, say, the Supreme Court cites your book on the way to a decision—it should not be the design or aim of academics to play that role.

While academics in general will agree that a university should not dance to the tune of external constituencies, they will most likely resist the injunction to police the boundary between academic work and political work. They will resist because they simply don't believe in the boundary—they believe that all activities are inherently political, and an injunction to avoid politics is meaningless and futile.

Now there is some truth to that, but it is not a truth that goes very far. And it certainly doesn't go where those who proclaim it would want it to go. It is true that no form of work—including even the work of, say, natural science—stands apart from the political, social, and economic concerns that underlie the structures and practices of a society. This does not mean, however, that there is no difference between academic labors and partisan labors, or that there is no difference between, for example, analyzing the history of welfare reform—a history that would necessarily include opinions pro and con—and urging students to go out and work for welfare reform or for its reversal.

This is so not because these practices are political, but because they are the political tasks that belong properly to other institutions. Universities could engage in moral and civic education only by deciding in advance which of the competing views of morality and citizenship is the right one, and then devoting academic resources and energy to the task of realizing it. But that task would deform (by replacing) the true task of academic work: the search for truth and the dissemination of it through teaching.

The idea that universities should be in the business of forming character and fashioning citizens is often supported by the claim that academic work should not be hermetically sealed or kept separate from the realm of values. But the search for truth is its own value, and fidelity to it mandates the accompanying values of responsibility in pedagogy and scholarship.

Performing academic work responsibly and at the highest level is a job big enough for any scholar and for any institution. And, as I look around, it does not seem to me that we academics do that job so well that we can now take it upon ourselves to do everyone else's job too. We should look to the practices in our own shop, narrowly conceived, before we set out to alter the entire world by forming moral character, or fashioning democratic citizens, or combating globalization, or embracing globalization, or anything else.

One would like to think that even the exaggerated sense of virtue that is so much a part of the academic mentality has its limits. If we aim low and stick to the tasks we are paid to perform, we might actually get something done.

There's No Business like Show Business

OCTOBER 15, 2006

On October 4, some Columbia University students rushed a stage during a public lecture and prevented Jim Gilchrist, the leader of the anti-immigration Minuteman Project, from speaking. Every day brings new controversies like this one and renewed complaints that the traditional mission of the liberal arts has been abandoned and replaced by partisanship and ideological zealotry, usually identified as emanating from a left-leaning faculty unchecked by weak administrators. There's something to the weak administrators bit, if only because administrators often have a weak grasp of the distinctions that would enable them to draw clear and rational lines marking off what is appropriate from what is not.

The first thing to note is that although the aborted lecture was to have been given in an academic venue, the occasion was not itself academic; it was theatrical. Any education that might have transpired had Mr. Gilchrist been allowed to give his talk would have been incidental to the shock value of his appearance before an audience known in advance to be hostile to his message. That was why he was invited—not to impart instruction but to provoke a response (and it is the response rather than the content that is always focused on in media reports), although in this instance those who brought him to campus got more than they bargained for. The spirit presiding over this occasion from the beginning was more Jerry Springer than Socrates. Jeers, catcalls, insults, and (verbal) brickbats were not intrusions on the performance but predictable ingredients of it; had they been absent, organizers and audience alike would have gone away disappointed because they would not have gotten their student-fees worth. It's just that things got a little out of hand.

When I call the occasion theatrical, I am not registering a criticism. Theater is what it is supposed to be, and theater is what it would also be were another student group to invite Noam Chomsky or Michael Moore. The intention, whoever the invitee, is not to analyze an issue but to "stir things up," a euphemism for the intention to tick somebody off. Chris Kulawick, the student president of the group sponsoring the talk, made this crystal clear when he said it was his dearest wish "to attain the cherished title of 'Most Despised Person on Campus.'"

Once one understands the true nature of the event, one understands too the scope (and limits) of the university's responsibility. In the context of what is essentially a piece of entertainment, Columbia, or any other university, does not have the responsibility to protect free speech, encourage democratic debate, or stand up for academic freedom. These resonant phrases, invoked at the drop of a hat by parties on every side, are simply too large for what is going on. The university's responsibility is, rather, to safety and (relatively) good order. Just as you don't want your rock concert to end in the destruction of property or the injury of spectators (although you do want a little unruliness; it belongs to the genre), so you don't want the provoked energies of those present at a campus spectacle to break up either the program or the furniture. After all, tomorrow is another day and a new act will be coming to town (on October 10 it was I), and it won't come if the university gets the reputation of assembling crowds that it cannot control.

It follows that the editorial page of the *New York Post* was wrong (as usual) when it demanded that the Columbia administration "expel each and every one of the guilty students." Guilty of what? Apparently no one was hurt, so the answer cannot be guilty of assault; even guilty of attempted assault would be a stretch. Guilty of a violation of Mr. Gilchrist's free speech rights? He has no constitutional right not to be shouted down or hounded off the stage. No government has abridged his freedom of expression. And he can give his talk elsewhere (no doubt he already has) or come back and give it at Columbia when the university has instituted better crowd-control measures. At most, the students are guilty of being impolite, bumptious, and rowdy, but again, this is the kind of behavior that the event—more akin to a keg party than to a reasoned discussion—was designed to elicit. If there is any discipline to be meted out here, its object should be not the students, who were doing just what they were expected and (in some sense) directed to do, but those administrators or staff members who, by virtue of their positions, were responsible for seeing that nothing went wrong, or, at least, too wrong.

Everything I have said so far is simply an unpacking of the distinction between curricular and extracurricular activities. Extracurricular means outside (the Latin *extra*) the curriculum and therefore outside the protocols and values that govern the classroom. And this means, in turn, that the norms by which extracurricular activities are to be measured belong not to morality or philosophy or constitutional law (all versions of what I call "big think") but to show business. The question to be asked is not "Did it further free speech or contribute to a robust democratic culture or provide a genuine educational experience?" Rather, the questions to be asked are: "Did it rock?" "Was it a blast?" "Was a good time had by all?"

Now one might think that if we turn from the extracurricular to the curricular—to contexts that are actually and centrally academic—the moral and philosophical questions I have just dismissed would be reinstated with full force. But in fact I don't believe that morality and philosophy have very much to do with curricular matters either, although if you are interested in knowing why I believe that, you'll have to wait for my next post (7.3).

Tip to Professors: Just Do Your Job

OCTOBER 22, 2006

In my previous post (7.2) I asserted that when protesters prevented a speaker at Columbia University from giving his talk, no issues of freedom of expression or democratic civility or any other high-sounding abstraction were raised. The event, I said, was not an academic one, even though it took place—or didn't quite take place—in an academic setting. Rather, it was a piece of theater with all parties playing their roles according to the script. The speaker brought a message he (and the organizers) knew the audience would resist. Audience members responded (as expected) by engaging in a loud and unruly protest. Counterprotestors answered in kind, and in the aftermath each side was able to accuse the other of being intolerant, fascistic, close-minded, and un-American. The only unscripted thing that happened—or at least I think it was unscripted—is that the proceedings were shut down prematurely, and that was the result not of a moral or philosophical failure but of a failure—purely administrative in nature—to exercise effective crowd control.

I made the further point that this is what extracurricular means—outside the curriculum, and therefore not subject to the imperatives usually thought to be in force in the classroom. What I want to say today is that classroom imperatives are not moral or philosophical either. While phrases like "freedom of speech" and "academic freedom" are routinely invoked whenever there is a discussion of how professors should conduct themselves, classroom performance has nothing to do with such grand abstractions and everything to do with a simple injunction: do your job.

Of course, before you can do your job, you have to know what it is. And you will not be helped by your college's mission statement, which will lead you to think that your job is to cure every ill the world has ever known—not only illiteracy, bad writing, and cultural ignorance, which are at least in the ballpark, but poverty, racism, ageism, sexism, war, exploitation, colonialism, discrimination, intolerance, pollution, and bad character. (The list could be much longer.) I call this the save-the-world theory of academic performance, and you can see it on display in a recent book by Derek Bok, the former and now once-again president of Harvard. Bok's book is titled *Our Underachieving Colleges*, and here are some of the things he thinks colleges should be trying to achieve: "[H]elp develop such virtues as racial tolerance, honesty and social responsibility"; "prepare . . . students to be active, knowledgeable citizens in a democracy"; and "nurture such behavioral traits as good moral character."[1]

I can't speak for every college teacher, but I'm neither trained nor paid to do any of those things, although I am aware of people who are: ministers, therapists, social workers, political activists, gurus, inspirational speakers, and diversity consultants. I am trained and paid to do two things (although, needless to say, I don't always succeed in my attempts to do them): (1) to introduce students to materials they didn't know a whole lot about, and (2) to equip them with the skills that will enable them, first, to analyze and evaluate those materials and, second, to perform independent research, should they choose to do so, after the semester is over. That's it. That's the job. There's nothing more, and the moment an instructor tries to do something more—tries to do some of the things urged by Derek Bok or tries to redress the injustices of the world—he or she will have crossed a line and will be practicing without a license. In response to this trespass someone will protest the politicization of the classroom, after which a debate will break out about the scope and limits of academic freedom, with all parties hurling pieties at one another and claiming to be the only defenders of academic integrity.

But the whole dreary sequence can be avoided if everyone lets go of outsized ambitions and pledges to just teach the materials and confer the skills, for then no one will be tempted to take on the job of moralist or reformer or political agent, and there will be no more outcries about professors who overstep their bounds. The *New York Post* would have nothing to write about, and organizations like Campus Watch could just disband.

There is an obvious objection to what I have just said. Any course of instruction, especially in the social sciences and humanities, will touch on deep moral and political issues. The materials students are asked to read will be fraught with them. Wouldn't it be impossible to avoid discussing these issues without trivializing and impoverishing the classroom experience? No, it's easy. You don't have to ignore or ban moral and political questions. What you have to do is regard them as objects of study rather than as alternatives you and your students might take a stand on.

That is, instead of asking questions like "What should be done?" or "Who is in the right?" you ask, "What are the origins of this controversy?" or "What relationship does it have to controversies taking place in other areas of inquiry?" or "What is the structure of argument on both sides?" I have coined an ugly word for this way of turning politically charged matters into the stuff of academic investigation. The word is academicize. To academicize a topic is to detach it from the context of its real-world urgency, where there is a decision to be made, and reinsert it into a context of an academic urgency, where there is an analysis to be performed.

Take, for example, the Terry Schiavo tragedy. There was hardly anyone in the country who didn't have an opinion about what should be done and who should do it. How might one go about academicizing something so freighted with moral, political, and theological implications? In my classroom I discuss the Terry Schiavo case as a contemporary example of a tension that has structured American political thought from the founding to this day: the tension between substantive justice—justice done in response to some vision of right and wrong—and procedural justice—justice derived from formal rules laying out the steps to be taken and specifying the people authorized to take them. On the one side were those who asked, "What is the moral thing to do here?" and on the other, those who asked, "Who is legally entitled to make the relevant decisions, irrespective of whether we find those decisions morally satisfying?"

After having identified these two ways of looking at the matter, I trace their sources in the work of political philosophers from John Locke to John Rawls. And as this line of inquiry is extended, the concern to render a moral and political judgment is replaced by the concern to fully comprehend and describe a phenomenon. The subject has been academicized.

Anything can be academicized and everything in the classroom should be, but this injunction will be resisted by those who believe that the purpose of higher education is to transform students into exemplary moral and political people (as opposed to people who simply know more). That goal is both unworkable and misguided; unworkable because it is impossible to control what students will do with the instruction they receive, and misguided because it forsakes the genuine pleasure of intellectual inquiry—the pleasure of trying to figure something out—for the hallucinogenic pleasure of trying to improve the world. Improving the world is a good thing and I would dissuade no one from the effort. Just don't do it as a substitute for what you are paid to do. Just do your job.

1.   Derek Bok, *Our Underachieving Colleges* (Princeton: Princeton University Press, 2008).

Devoid of Content

MAY 31, 2005

We are at that time of year when millions of American college and high school students will stride across the stage, take diploma in hand, and set out to the wider world, most of them utterly unable to write a clear and coherent English sentence. How is this possible? The answer is simple and even obvious: students can't write clean English sentences because they are not being taught what sentences are.

Most composition courses that American students take today emphasize content rather than form, on the theory that if you chew over big ideas long enough, the ability to write about them will (mysteriously) follow. The theory is wrong. Content is a lure and a delusion, and it should be banished from the classroom. Form is the way.

On the first day of my freshman writing class I give the students this assignment: You will be divided into groups and by the end of the semester each group will be expected to have created its own language, complete with a syntax, a lexicon, a text, rules for translating the text, and strategies for teaching your language to fellow students. The language you create cannot be English or a slightly coded version of English, but it must be capable of indicating the distinctions— between tense, number, manner, mood, agency, and the like—that English enables us to make.

You can imagine the reaction of students who think that "syntax" is something cigarette smokers pay, guess that "lexicon" is the name of a rebel tribe inhabiting a galaxy far away, and haven't the slightest idea of what words like "tense," "manner," and "mood" mean. They think I'm crazy. Yet fourteen weeks later—and this happens every time—each group has produced a language of incredible sophistication and precision.

How is this near miracle accomplished? The short answer is that over the semester the students come to understand a single proposition: a sentence is a structure of logical relationships. In its bare form, this proposition is hardly edifying, which is why I immediately supplement it with a simple exercise. "Here," I say, "are five words randomly chosen; turn them into a sentence." (The first time I did this the words were coffee, should, book, garbage, and quickly.) In no time at all I am presented with twenty sentences, all perfectly coherent and all quite different. Then comes the hard part. "What is it," I ask, "that you did? What did it take to turn a random list of words into a sentence?" A lot of fumbling and stumbling and false starts follow, but finally someone says, "I put the words into a relationship with one another."

Once the notion of relationship is on the table, the next question almost asks itself: What exactly are the relationships? And working with the sentences they have created, the students quickly realize two things: first, that the possible relationships form a limited set; and second, that it all comes down to an interaction of some kind between actors, the actions they perform, and the objects of those actions.

The next step (and this one takes weeks) is to explore the devices by which English indicates and distinguishes between the various components of these interactions. If in every sentence someone is doing something to someone or something else, how does English allow you to tell who is the doer and who (or what) is the doee; and how do you know whether there is one doer or many; and what tells you that the doer is doing what he or she does in this way and at this time rather than another?

Notice that these are not questions about how a particular sentence works, but questions about how any sentence works, and the answers will point to something very general and abstract. They will point, in fact, to the forms that, while they are themselves without content, are necessary to the conveying of any content whatsoever, at least in English.

Once the students tumble to this point, they are more than halfway to understanding the semester-long task: they can now construct a language whose forms do the same work English does, but do it differently.

In English, for example, most plurals are formed by adding an "s" to nouns. Is that the only way to indicate the difference between singular and plural? Obviously not. But the language you create, I tell them, must have some regular and abstract way of conveying that distinction; and so it is with all the other distinctions—between time, manner, spatial relationships, relationships of hierarchy and subordination, and relationships of equivalence and difference—languages permit you to signal.

In the languages my students devise, the requisite distinctions are signaled by any number of formal devices—word order, word endings, prefixes, suffixes, numbers, brackets, fonts, colors, you name it. Exactly how they do it is not the point; the point is that they know what it is they are trying to do; the moment they know that, they have succeeded, even if much of the detailed work remains to be done.

At this stage last semester, the representative of one group asked me, "Is it all right if we use the same root form for adjectives and adverbs, but distinguish between them by their order in the sentence?" I could barely disguise my elation. If they could formulate a question like that one, they had already learned the lesson I was trying to teach them.

In the course of learning that lesson, the students will naturally and effortlessly conform to the restriction I announce on the first day: "We don't do content in this class. By that I mean we are not interested in ideas—yours, mine, or anyone else's. We don't have an anthology of readings. We don't discuss current events. We don't exchange views on hot-button issues. We don't tell each other what we think about anything—except about how prepositions or participles or relative pronouns function." The reason we don't do any of these things is that once ideas or themes are allowed in, the focus is shifted from the forms that make the organization of content possible to this or that piece of content, usually some recycled set of pros and cons about abortion, assisted suicide, affirmative action, welfare reform, the death penalty, free speech, and so forth. At that moment, the task of understanding and mastering linguistic forms will have been replaced by the dubious pleasure of reproducing the well-worn and terminally dull arguments one hears or sees on every radio and TV talk show.

Students who take so-called courses in writing where such topics are the staples of discussion may believe, as their instructors surely do, that they are learning how to marshal arguments in ways that will improve their compositional skills. In fact, they will be learning nothing they couldn't have learned better by sitting around in a dorm room or a coffee shop. They will certainly not be learning anything about how language works; and without a knowledge of how language works, they will be unable either to spot the formal breakdown of someone else's language or to prevent the formal breakdown of their own.

In my classes, the temptation of content is felt only fleetingly, for as soon as students bend to the task of understanding the structure of language—a task with a content deeper than any they have been asked to forgo—they become completely absorbed in it and spontaneously enact the discipline I have imposed. And when there is the occasional and inevitable lapse, and some student voices his or her "opinion" about something, I don't have to do anything, for immediately, some other student will turn and say, "No, that's content." When that happens, I experience pure pedagogical bliss.

What Should Colleges Teach?

AUGUST 24, 2009

A few years ago, when I was grading papers for a graduate literature course, I became alarmed at the inability of my students to write a clean English sentence. They could manage for about six words and then, almost invariably, the syntax (and everything else) fell apart. I became even more alarmed when I remembered that these same students were instructors in the college's composition program. What, I wondered, could possibly be going on in their courses?

I decided to find out, and asked to see the lesson plans of the 104 sections. I read them and found that only four emphasized training in the craft of writing. Although the other one hundred sections fulfilled the composition requirement, instruction in composition was not their focus. Instead, the students spent much of their time discussing novels, movies, TV shows, and essays on a variety of hot-button issues—racism, sexism, immigration, globalization. These artifacts and topics are surely worthy of serious study, but they should have received it in courses that bore their name, if only as a matter of truth-in-advertising.

As I learned more about the world of composition studies, I came to the conclusion that unless writing courses focus exclusively on writing, they are a sham, and I advised administrators to insist that all courses listed as courses in composition teach grammar and rhetoric and nothing else. This advice was contemptuously dismissed by the composition establishment, and I was accused of being a reactionary who knew nothing about current trends in research. Now I have received (indirect) support from a source that makes me slightly uncomfortable, the American Council of Trustees and Alumni (ACTA), which last week issued its latest white paper, "What Will They Learn? A Report on General Education Requirements at 100 of the Nation's Leading Colleges and Universities."

Founded by Lynne Cheney and Jerry Martin in 1995, ACTA is "an independent, nonprofit organization committed to academic freedom, excellence, and accountability at America's colleges."[1] Sounds good, but that "commitment" takes the form of mobilizing trustees and alumni in an effort to pressure colleges and universities to make changes in their curricula and requirements. Academic institutions, the ACTA website declares, "need checks and balances" because "internal constituencies"—which means professors—cannot be trusted to be responsive to public concerns about the state of higher education.

The battle between those who actually work in the academy and those who would monitor academic work from the outside has been going on for well over a hundred years, and I am on record (in *Save the World on Your Own Time* and elsewhere) as being against external regulation of classroom practices if only because the impulse animating the effort to regulate is always political rather than intellectual.[2]

It is of course true that political motives can also inform the decisions made by academic insiders; the professorial guild is far from pure. But the cure for the politicization of the classroom by some professors is not the counterpoliticization urged by ACTA when it crusades for "accountability," a code word for reconfiguring the academy according to conservative ideas and agendas.

Nevertheless, I found myself often nodding in agreement when I was reading ACTA's new report. In it, the one hundred colleges and universities are ranked on a scale from A to F based on whether students are required to take courses in seven key areas—composition, literature, foreign language, US government or history, economics, mathematics, and natural or physical science.

It's hard to quarrel with this list; the quarrel and the criticism have been provoked by the criteria that accompany it. These criteria are stringent and narrow and have been criticized as parochial and motivated by nostalgia and politics, but in at least four of the seven areas, they make perfect sense. Credit for requiring instruction in mathematics will not be given for linguistic courses or computer literacy courses because their "math content is usually minimal." Credit for requiring instruction in the natural or physical sciences will not be given for courses with "weak scientific content" or courses "taught by faculty outside of the science departments" (i.e., the philosophy or history of science). Credit for requiring instruction in a foreign language will not be given for fewer than three semesters of study because it takes that long to acquire "competency at the intermediate level." And credit for requiring composition will not be given for courses that are "writing intensive" (there is a significant amount of writing required, but the focus is on some substantive topic), or for courses in disciplines other than English and composition (often termed "writing in the discipline" courses), courses in public speaking, or remedial courses. In order to qualify, a course must be devoted to "grammar, style, clarity, and argument."

The rationale behind these exclusions is compelling: mathematics, the natural sciences, foreign languages, and composition are disciplines with a specific content and a repertoire of essential skills. Courses that center on another content and fail to provide concentrated training in those skills are really courses in another subject. You can tell when you are being taught a mathematical function or a scientific procedure or a foreign language or the uses of the subjunctive and when you are being taught something else.

Things are not so clear when it comes to literature and history. Why should the literature requirement be fulfilled only by "a comprehensive literary survey" and not by single-author courses (aren't Shakespeare and Milton "comprehensive" enough), or by a course in the theater or the graphic novel or the lyrics of Bob Dylan (all rejected in the report)?

With respect to science, composition, foreign language instruction, and mathematics, ACTA is simply saying, "Don't slight the core of the discipline." But when the report decrees that only broad surveys of literature can fulfill a literature requirement, the organization is intervening in the discipline and taking sides in its internal debates. Why should trustees and alumni have a say in determining whether the graphic novel—a multimedia art that goes back at least as far as William Blake—deserves to represent literature? (For the record, I think it does.) This part of the report is an effort to shape the discipline from the outside according to a political vision.

This holds too for the insistence that only the study of American history "in both chronological and thematic breadth" can fulfill the history requirement. Here the politics is explicit: such courses, we are told, are "indispensable for the formation of citizens and for the preservation of our free institutions."

Indispensable I doubt (this is academic hubris), and while the formation of citizens and the preservation of our free institutions may be admirable aims, it is not the task of courses in history to achieve them. The question of how best to introduce students to the study of history should be answered not by invoking external goals, however worthy, but by arguing the merits of academic alternatives; and I see no obvious reason why a course on the Civil War or the American Revolution or the French Revolution (or both of them together) would not do the job as well as a survey stretching from the landing at Plymouth Rock to the war in Iraq. (At any rate, the issue is one for academic professionals to decide.)

But if I have no problem with alternative ways of teaching literature or history, how can I maintain (with ACTA) that there is only one way to teach writing? Easy. It can't be an alternative way of teaching writing to teach something else (like multiculturalism or social justice). It can, however, be an alternative way of teaching history to forgo a broad chronological narrative and confine yourself to a single period or even to a single world-changing event. It is the difference between not doing the job and getting the job done by another route.

This difference is blurred in the ACTA report because it is running (and conflating) two arguments. One argument (with which I agree) says "teach the subject matter and don't adulterate it with substitutes." The other argument says "teach the subject matter so that it points in a particular ideological direction, the direction of traditional values and a stable canon." The first argument is methodological and implies no particular politics; the second is political through and through, and it is the argument the authors are finally committed to because they see themselves as warriors in the culture wars. The battle they are fighting in the report is over the core curriculum, the defense of which is for them a moral as well as an educational imperative, as it is for those who oppose it.

The arguments pro and con are familiar: on one side the assertion that a core curriculum provides students with the distilled wisdom of the Western tradition and prepares them for life; on the other side the assertion that a core curriculum packages and sells the prejudices and biases of the reigning elite and so congeals knowledge rather than advancing it.

Have we lost our way or finally found it? Thirty-five years ago there was no such thing as a gay and lesbian studies program; now you can build a major around it. For some this development is a sign that a brave new world has arrived; for others it marks the beginning of the end of civilization.

It probably is neither; curricular alternatives are just not that world-shaking. The philosophical baggage that burdens this debate should be jettisoned and replaced with a more prosaic question: What can a core curriculum do that the proliferation of options and choices (two words excoriated in the ACTA report) cannot? The answer to that question is given early in the report before it moves on to its more polemical pages. An "important benefit of a coherent core curriculum is its ability to foster a 'common conversation' among students, connecting them more closely with faculty and with each other."

The nice thing about this benefit is that it can be had no matter what the content of the core curriculum is. It could be the classics of Western literature and philosophy. It could be science fiction. It could be globalization. It could be anything, so long as every student took it. But whatever it is, please let it include a writing course that teaches writing and not everything under the sun. That should be the real core of any curriculum.

1. The quote is from the ACTA website at http://www.goacta.org/.
2. Stanley Fish, *Save the World on Your Own Time* (New York: Oxford University Press, 2012).

Will the Humanities Save Us?

JANUARY 6, 2008

In the final paragraph of my column "Bound for Academic Glory?" (December 3, 2007), I observed that the report of the New York State Commission on Higher Education slights—indeed barely mentions—the arts and humanities, despite the wide-ranging scope of its proposals.[1] Those who posted comments agreed with David Small that "the arts and the humanities are always the last to receive any assistance."

There were, however, different explanations of this unhappy fact. Sean Pidgeon put the blame on "humanities departments who are responsible for the leftist politics that still turn people off." Kedar Kulkarni blamed "the absence of a culture that privileges Learning to improve oneself as a human being." Bethany blamed universities, which, because they are obsessed with "maintaining funding," default on the obligation to produce "well-rounded citizens." Matthew blamed no one, because in his view the report's priorities are just what they should be: "When a poet creates a vaccine or a tangible good that can be produced by a Fortune 500 company, I'll rescind my comment."

Although none of these commentators use the word, the issue they implicitly raise is justification. How does one justify funding the arts and humanities? It is clear which justifications are not available. You can't argue that the arts and humanities are able to support themselves through grants and private donations. You can't argue that a state's economy will benefit by a new reading of *Hamlet*. You can't argue—well you can, but it won't fly—that a graduate who is well versed in the history of Byzantine art will be attractive to employers (unless the employer is a museum). You can talk, as Bethany does, about "well-rounded citizens," but that ideal belongs to an earlier period, when the ability to refer knowledgeably to Shakespeare or Gibbon or the Thirty Years' War had some cash value (the sociologists call it cultural capital). Nowadays, larding your conversations with small bits of erudition is more likely to irritate than to win friends and influence people.

At one time justification of the arts and humanities was unnecessary because, as Anthony Kronman puts it in *Education's End: Why*

Our Colleges and Universities Have Given Up on the Meaning of Life,
it was assumed that "a college was above all a place for the training
of character, for the nurturing of those intellectual and moral habits
that together form the basis for living the best life one can."[2] It followed that the realization of this goal required an immersion in the
great texts of literature, philosophy, and history even to the extent of
memorizing them, for "to acquire a text by memory is to fix in one's
mind the image and example of the author and his subject."

It is to a version of this old ideal that Kronman would have us return, not because of a professional investment in the humanities (he
is a professor of law and a former dean of Yale Law School), but because he believes that only the humanities can address "the crisis of
spirit we now confront" and "restore the wonder which those who
have glimpsed the human condition have always felt, and which our
scientific civilization, with its gadgets and discoveries, obscures."

As this last quotation makes clear, Kronman is not so much mounting a defense of the humanities as he is mounting an attack on everything else. Other spokespersons for the humanities argue for their
utility by connecting them (in largely unconvincing ways) to the goals
of science, technology, and the building of careers. Kronman, however, identifies science, technology, and careerism as impediments to
living a life with meaning. The real enemies, he declares, are "the careerism that distracts from life as a whole" and "the blind acceptance
of science and technology that disguise and deny our human condition." These false idols, he says, block the way to understanding. We
must turn to the humanities if we are to "meet the need for meaning
in an age of vast but pointless powers," for only the humanities can
help us recover the urgency of "the question of what living is for."

The humanities do this, Kronman explains, by exposing students
to "a range of texts that express with matchless power a number of
competing answers to this question." In the course of this program—
Kronman calls it "secular humanism"—students will be moved "to
consider which alternatives lie closest to their own evolving sense of
self." As they survey "the different ways of living that have been held
up by different authors," they will be encouraged "to enter as deeply
as they can into the experiences, ideas, and values that give each its
permanent appeal." And not only would such a "revitalized humanism"
contribute to the growth of the self, it "would put the conventional
pieties of our moral and political world in question" and "bring what

is hidden into the open—the highest goal of the humanities and the first responsibility of every teacher."

Here then is a justification of the humanities that is neither strained (reading poetry contributes to the state's bottom line) nor crassly careerist. It is a stirring vision that promises the highest reward to those who respond to it. Entering into a conversation with the great authors of the Western tradition holds out the prospect of experiencing "a kind of immortality" and achieving "a position immune to the corrupting powers of time."

Sounds great, but I have my doubts. Does it really work that way? Do the humanities ennoble? And for that matter, is it the business of the humanities, or of any other area of academic study, to save us?

The answer in both cases, I think, is no. The premise of secular humanism (or of just old-fashioned humanism) is that the examples of action and thought portrayed in the enduring works of literature, philosophy, and history can create in readers the desire to emulate them. Philip Sydney put it as well as anyone ever has when he asks (in "The Defence of Poesy," 1595), "Who reads Aeneas carrying old Anchises on his back that wishes not it was his fortune to perform such an excellent act?" Thrill to this picture of filial piety in the Aeneid and you will yourself become devoted to your father. Admire the selfless act with which Sidney Carton ends his life in Charles Dickens's *A Tale of Two Cities* and you will be moved to prefer the happiness of others to your own. Watch with horror what happens to Faust and you will be less likely to sell your soul. Understand Kant's categorical imperative and you will not impose restrictions on others that you would resist if they were imposed on you.

It's a pretty idea, but there is no evidence to support it and a lot of evidence against it. If it were true, the most generous, patient, good-hearted, and honest people on earth would be the members of literature and philosophy departments, who spend every waking hour with great books and great thoughts, and as someone who's been there (for forty-five years), I can tell you it just isn't so. Teachers and students of literature and philosophy don't learn how to be good and wise; they learn how to analyze literary effects and to distinguish between different accounts of the foundations of knowledge. The texts Kronman recommends are, as he says, concerned with the meaning of life; those who study them, however, come away not with a life made newly meaningful but with a disciplinary knowledge newly enlarged.

And that, I believe, is how it should be. Teachers of literature and philosophy are competent in a subject, not in a ministry. It is not the business of the humanities to save us, no more than it is their business to bring revenue to a state or a university. What then do they do? They don't do anything, if by "do" is meant to bring about effects in the world. And if they don't bring about effects in the world, they cannot be justified except in relation to the pleasure they give to those who enjoy them.

To the question "Of what use are the humanities?," the only honest answer is none whatsoever. And it is an answer that brings honor to its subject. Justification, after all, confers value on an activity from a perspective outside its performance. An activity that cannot be justified is an activity that refuses to regard itself as instrumental to some larger good. The humanities are their own good. There is nothing more to say, and anything that is said—even when it takes the form of Kronman's inspiring cadences—diminishes the object of its supposed praise.

1. New York State Commission on Higher Education, https://www.suny.edu/files/sunynewsfiles/pdf/CHEFinalReport.pdf.

2. Anthony Kronman, *Education's End: Why Our Colleges and Universities Have Given Up on the Meaning of Life* (New Haven, CT: Yale University Press, 2008); subsequent quotes by Kronman are from this edition.

The Uses of the Humanities

JANUARY 13, 2008

In a poem titled "Matins," the seventeenth-century Anglican poet George Herbert says to God, "Teach me thy love to know; . . . Then by a sunbeam I will climb to thee." But the dynamics of the proffered bargain—if you do X, I'll do Y—are undercut by the line that proposes it, and especially by the double pun in "sunbeam."

"Sun" is a standard pun on "Son"; it refers to Jesus Christ; "beam" means not only ray of light, but a piece of wood large enough to support a structure; it refers to the cross on which a crucified Christ by dying takes upon himself and redeems (pays the price for) the sins of those who believe in him. So while "by a sunbeam" seems to specify the means by which the poem's speaker will perform a certain act—"I will climb to thee"—the phrase undercuts his claim to be able to do so by reminding us (not him) that Christ has already done the climbing and thereby prevented (in the sense of anticipating) any positive act man mistakenly thinks to be his own. If the speaker climbs to God, he does so by means of God, and cannot take any personal credit for what he "does." If he truly knows God's love, he will know that as an unconditional and all-sufficing gift, it has disabled him as an agent.

This brief analysis of a line of poetry that simultaneously reports a resolution and undermines it is an example of the kind of work and teaching I have done for almost five decades. It is the work of a humanist, that is, someone employed in a college to teach literary, philosophical, and historical texts. The questions raised in my previous column, "Will the Humanities Save Us?" (7.6), and in the responses to it are: What is the value of such work, why should anyone fund it, and why (for what reasons) does anyone do it?

Why do I do it? I don't do it because Herbert and I are coreligionists. I don't believe what he believes or value what he values. I don't do it because it inspires me to do other things, like change my religion or go out and work for the poor. If I had to say, I'd say that I do it because I get something like an athletic satisfaction from the experience of trying to figure out how a remarkable verbal feat has been achieved.

The satisfaction is partly self-satisfaction—it is like solving a puzzle—but the greater satisfaction is the opportunity to marvel at what a few people are able to do with the language we all use. "Isn't that amazing?" I often say to my students. "Don't you wish you could write a line like that?" (In the column, I used the word "pleasure" to describe the reward of discussing and unpacking literary texts, but "pleasure" is at once too narrow and too broad; it is the very particular pleasure that attends cognitive awareness of an effect you not only experience but can now explain.)

Note that what we're talking about here is the study, not the production, of humanistic texts. The question I posed in the column was not do works of literature, philosophy, and history have instrumental value, but does the academic analysis of works of literature, philosophy, and history have instrumental value. When Jeffrey Sachs comments that "in the real world" the distinction between the humanities and the sciences on the basis of utility does not hold because "philosophers have made important contributions to the sciences" and "the hard sciences have had a profound impact on the humanities," he doesn't come within a hundred miles of refuting anything I say. Whatever does or does not happen in the "real world" is not the issue; the issue is what happens in the academic world, where the distinctions Sachs dismisses do hold. It may be, as George Mobus maintains, that "only in academia where you are supposed to be a specialist . . . do we parse the world into silos," but the academic world is by definition parsed into silos, and when the utility of one of them is questioned, it is not to any point to say that in some other world everything exists in some great big mix.

In general, those who disagree with my assertions do what Sachs and Mobus do—slide (without acknowledgment or awareness) back and forth between the precincts of academia (which, to make the point again, are the precincts where the dispute is located) to the precincts, often larger, of some other enterprise. When I declare that the humanities are of no use whatsoever, I am talking about humanities departments ("the humanities" is an academic, not a cultural category), not about poets and philosophers and the effects they do or do not have in the world and on those who read them.

The funding of the humanities in colleges and universities cannot be justified by pointing to the fact that poems and philosophical arguments have changed lives and started movements. (I was surprised that no one mentioned *Uncle Tom's Cabin*, a book Lincoln is said to have credited with the starting of the Civil War.) The pertinent questions are: Do humanities courses change lives and start movements? Does one teach with that purpose, and if one did, could it be realized?

If the answers to these questions are (as I contend) "no"—one teaches the subject matter and any delayed effect of what happens in a classroom is contingent and cannot be aimed at—then the route of external justification of the humanities, of a justification that depends on the calculation of measurable results, is closed down. The fact that some commentators, including a few of my former students, report life-changing experiences as a result of their studies is heartening (although I am sure that the vast majority would report something quite different), but it hardly amounts to a reason for supporting the entire apparatus of departments, degrees, colloquia, and so on that has grown up around the academic study of humanistic texts.

Some who posted put forward a negative reason for supporting the teaching of the humanities. They say things like, if only "the cabal running or government . . . had known a bit of history, we might not be in Iraq" and "Would the neoconservatives really believe that the world is a battlefield of good versus evil were they to expand their minds to include a more complete knowledge of history and human nature?" But the neoconservatives these respondents no doubt have in mind—Wolfowitz, Pearle, Kristol, Huntington—are as widely read in history, philosophy, and the arts as anyone, and they participate in deeply intellectual discussions of important texts in the Liberty Fund seminars and elsewhere.

Assuming that if they had been schooled in the right texts (Paul Krugman rather than Milton Friedman, Cornel West rather than William Buckley) they would have devised better policies is a fantasy, and indeed, it is the same fantasy the neoconservatives buy into when they argue that if we were to introduce radical Muslims to the writings of Jefferson, Madison, and J. S. Mill, they would learn to love freedom and stop wanting to destroy us. The truth is that a mastery of literary and philosophical texts and the acquisition of wisdom (in whatever form) are independent variables.

All of this should not be taken to mean, as it was by some, that I am attacking the humanities or denigrating them or declaring them worthless. I am saying that the value of the humanities cannot be validated by some measure external to the obsessions that lead some (like me) to devote their working lives to them—measures like increased economic productivity, or the fashioning of an informed citizenry, or the sharpening of moral perceptions, or the lessening of prejudice and discrimination. If these or some other instrumental benchmarks— instrumental in the sense that they are tied to a secondary effect rather than to an internal economy—are what the humanities must meet, they will always fall short. But the refusal of the humanities to acknowledge or bow to an end they do not contemplate is, I argue, their salvation and their value. As Stacia says in words more precise than mine, "These studies are not to be used as tools to achieve something else . . . they are the achievement."

Of course, this does not mean that anyone will pay for them. In fact, as several posters observed, my argument (and it isn't only mine) that the humanities are their own good and aren't much good for anything else can be used to justify turning humanities departments into service departments and cutting funding for humanities research.

I still remember serving on an all-university committee at Johns Hopkins University and hearing one of my fellow committee members say that he would happily support the English Department because his wife very much enjoyed seeing plays. When I told him that the department never put on plays, and at that moment did not even have a faculty member who was interested in plays, he was amazed and asked the obvious question: What then do you do? When I replied that we research things like medieval astrology, Renaissance iconography, eighteenth-century political satire, and romantic theories of the imagination, and then share our findings and interpretations with students, his puzzlement grew.

Had he asked the next question—But what can you do with that?—I would have had to say, not much of anything except, perhaps, entice a few people to join the same esoteric enterprise. He was more polite than another colleague, a friend, who announced one day that members of English Departments were "parasites on the carcass of literature." A medical doctor, he was also a lover of literature and just didn't see why a world that already had poets and novelists and playwrights needed an army of people feeding off them.

His sentiments were echoed by those respondents who complained that humanities departments are narrowly professional and concerned largely with reproducing themselves. "A father" reports the "repugnant truth" that "the humanities is study of a discipline. Mastery of the discipline qualifies you to profess it." Qjiang observes that "there are Shakespeares and Shakespeare's interpreters" and "Humanities nowadays . . . largely and unfortunately refer to the latter."

That's right. What is in need of defense is not the existence of Shakespeare but the existence of the Shakespeare industry (and of the Herbert industry and the Hemingway industry), with its seminars, journals, symposia, dissertations, and libraries. The challenge of utility is not put (except by avowed Philistines) to literary artists but to the scholarly machinery that seems to take those operating it further and further away from the primary texts into the reaches of incomprehensible and often corrosive theory. More than one poster decried the impenetrable jargon of literary studies. Why, one wonders, is the same complaint not made against physics or economics or biology or psychology, all disciplines with vocabularies entirely closed to the uninitiated?

The answer is that those disciplines are understood to be up to something and to be promising a payoff that will someday benefit even those who couldn't read a page of their journals. What benefit do literary studies hold out to those asked to support them? Not much of anything except the (parochial) excitement experienced by those caught up in arcane discussions of the mirror stage, the trace, the subaltern, and the performative. (Don't ask.) The general public, which includes legislators, trustees, and parents, is on the side of my colleague at Johns Hopkins. Let them put on plays.

Of the justifications for humanistic study offered in the comments, two seemed to me to have some force. The first is that taking courses in literature, philosophy, and history provides training in critical thinking. I confess that I have always thought that "critical thinking" is an empty phrase, a slogan that a humanist has recourse to when someone asks what good is what you do and he or she has nothing to say. What's the distinction, I have more than occasionally asked, between critical thinking and just thinking? Isn't the adjective superfluous? And what exactly would "uncritical thinking" be? But now that I have read the often impassioned responses to my column, I have a better understanding of what critical thinking is.

Taking as an example the concept of IQ, William Haboush says that while a scientist will use it, a humanist "will ask what does it mean? Is it one thing or many? Who made up the questions used in measuring it?" This, then, is critical thinking—the analytic probing of formulas, precepts, and pieces of received wisdom that too often go unexamined and unchallenged. This skill, Warren Call claims, is taught in humanities courses where students "analyze ideas, differing viewpoints, justifications, opinions and accounts" and, in the process, learn how to "construct a logical assessment . . . and defend their conclusions with facts and lucid argument."

That certainly sounds like a skill worth having, and I agree that it can be acquired in courses where literary texts, philosophical arguments, and historical events are being scrutinized with an eye to seeing what lies beneath (or to the side of) their surfaces. But it also can be, and is, acquired elsewhere. Right now millions of TV viewers are acquiring it when they watch Chris Matthews, George Will, or Cokie Roberts analyze the current political moment and say things like, "It would be wrong to draw any long-run conclusion from Hillary Clinton's victory in New Hampshire because in other states the voting population is unlikely to be 57 percent female and 97 percent white," or "If we are to understand the immigration debate, we must go back to the great waves of immigration in the late nineteenth and early twentieth centuries," or "Homelessness is not a single problem, but a nest of problems that cannot be solved piecemeal."

You can hear the same kind of thinking on sports radio, where host and callers-in debate the ingredients that go to make up a successful team. And critical thinking is what tens of thousands of preachers encourage every week in their sermons when they ask parishioners to slow down and reflect on the impulses, perhaps obscure to them, driving their everyday behavior.

So two cheers for critical thinking, but the fact that you can learn how to do it in any number of contexts means that it cannot be claimed for the humanities as a special benefit only they can supply. Justification requires more than evidence that a consumer can get a desirable commodity in your shop, too; it requires a demonstration that you have the exclusive franchise.

The second justification for studying the humanities that in my view has some force speaks to those of us who have been trapped in conversations with people who, after "How about those Bears?" (the equivalent of "hello" in Chicago), can think of nothing to say. EM observes that "being exposed to great ideas from [a] variety of fields . . . and learning how to think critically all make for a more interesting and informed person" and that "lots of people want interesting and informed people as their friends, lovers and employees." Amen. Count me as one of those who would welcome an increase in the number of those who can be relied on to enliven a dinner party rather than kill it (although I have seen dinner parties killed by the most erudite and sophisticated person at the table). But it won't do as a defense society will take seriously to say, "Let's support the humanities so that Stanley Fish and his friends have more people to talk to."

One final point. Nguyen Chau Giao asks, "Dr. Fish, when was the last time you read a poem . . . that so moved you to take certain actions to improve your lot or others?" To tell the truth, I can't remember a single time. But I can remember countless times when I've read a poem (like Herbert's "Matins") and said "Wow!" or "Isn't that just great?" That's more than enough in my view to justify the enterprise of humanistic study, but I cannot believe, as much as I would like to, that the world can be persuaded to subsidize my moments of aesthetic wonderment.

The Value of Higher Education Made Literal

DECEMBER 13, 2010

A few weeks ago at a conference, I listened to a distinguished political philosopher tell those in attendance that he would not be speaking before them had he not been the beneficiary, as a working-class youth in England, of a government policy to provide a free university education to the children of British citizens. He walked into the university with little knowledge of the great texts that inform modern democracy, and he walked out an expert in those very same texts.

It goes without saying that he did not know what he was doing at the outset; he did not, that is, think to himself, *I would like to become a scholar of Locke, Hobbes, and Mill.* But that's what he became, not by choice (at least in the beginning) but by opportunity.

That opportunity—to stroll into a world from which he might otherwise have been barred by class and a lack of funds—is not likely to be extended to young men and women in England today, especially if the recommendations of the Browne report, "Securing a Sustainable Future for Higher Education," are implemented by a government that seemed to welcome them and, some suspect, mandated them.[1]

The rhetoric of the report is superficially benign; its key phrase is "student choice": "Our proposals put students at the heart of the system." "Our recommendations . . . are based on giving students the ability to make an informed choice of where and what to study." "Students are best placed to make the judgment about what they want to get from participating in higher education."

The obvious objection to this last declaration is, "No, they aren't; judgment is what education is supposed to produce; if students possessed it at the get-go, there would be nothing for courses and programs to do." But that objection would be entirely beside the point in the context of the assumption informing the report, the assumption that what students want to get from participating in higher education is money. Under the system the report proposes, government support of higher education in the form of block grants to universities (which are free to allocate funds as they see fit) would be replaced by monies given directly to matriculating students, who would then vote with their pocketbooks by choosing which courses to "invest" in.

"Invest" is the right word because the cost of courses will be indexed to the likelihood of financial rewards down the line. A course's "key selling point" will be "that it provides improved employability" and students will be asked to pay "higher charges" for a course only "if there is a proven path to higher earnings." (There is a verbal echo here, surely unintended, of the value nowhere to be found in the report, the value of higher learning.)

The result, anticipated and welcomed by the report's authors, will be that courses of study that "deliver improved employability will prosper," while those that don't "will disappear." This will hold also for universities, which will either prosper or wither on the vine depending on the agility they display in adapting themselves to student-consumer demands. "Institutions will have to persuade students that the charges they put on their courses represents [*sic*] value for money." (Adapt or die.)

It hardly need be said that under this scheme the arts and the humanities (and most of the social sciences) will be the losers: the model of rational economic (as opposed to educational) choice does not encourage investment in medieval allegory, modern poetry, or Greek history.

But the Browne report is taking no chances. Concerned that students might choose (invest) poorly and thereby threaten the viability of "priority" courses of study—science, technology, clinical medicine, and nursing—the report proposes "additional and targeted investment for those courses."

The confidence in consumer choice as a means of identifying value will be supplemented (one might say weakened) by a state subsidy that will ensure that the proper values—technological and scientific—are nourished and make it even more likely that other values, associated with art, literature, philosophy, history, anthropology, political science, and so on, are not. In addition, strict surveillance will be required to make sure that universities accepting these "targeted investment" funds actually use them for priority courses and don't divert them to frills.

Students will not only be the drivers of the new system; they will pay for it, but only after they enjoy the income they have been promised: "Students should only pay towards the cost of their education once they are enjoying the benefits of that education."

The logic is the logic of privatization. Higher education is no longer conceived of as a public good—as a good the effects of which permeate society—but is rather a private benefit, and as such it should be supported by those who enjoy the benefit. "It is reasonable to ask those who gain private benefits from higher education to help fund it rather than rely . . . on public funds collected through taxation from people who have not participated in higher education themselves." No one who has not been to a university has any stake in the health or survival of the system.

At the end of the report, the authors congratulate themselves: "We have never lost sight of the value of learning to students, nor the significant contribution of higher education to the quality of life in a civilized society." A first response to this declaration might be to describe it as either a lie or a joke. There is no recognition in the report at all of the value of learning; quality is a measure nowhere referenced; civilization, as far as one can see, will have to take care of itself.

But at second thought this paean of self-praise is merited once we remember that the report's relentless monetization of everything in sight has redefined its every word: value now means return on the dollar; quality of life now means the number of cars or houses you can buy; a civilized society is a society where the material goods a society offers can be enjoyed by more people.

One must admit that this view of value and the good life has a definite appeal. It will resonate with many, not only in England but here in the United States. And to the extent it does, the privatization of higher education will advance apace, and the days when a working-class Brit or (in my case) an immigrant's son can wander into the groves of academe and emerge a political theorist or a Miltonist will recede into history and legend.

1. Browne report, "Securing a Sustainable Future for Higher Education," October 12, 2010, https://www.gov.uk/government/uploads/system/uploads/attachment _data/file/31999/10–1208-securing-sustainable-higher-education-browne-report.pdf.

A Classical Education: Back to the Future

JUNE 7, 2010

I wore my high school ring for more than forty years. It became black and misshapen and I finally took it off. But now I have a new one, courtesy of the organizing committee of my fifty-fifth high school reunion, which I attended over the Memorial Day weekend.

I wore the ring (and will wear it again) because although I have degrees from two Ivy League schools and have taught at UC Berkeley, Johns Hopkins, Columbia, and Duke, Classical High School (in Providence, Rhode Island) is the best and most demanding educational institution I have ever been associated with. The name tells the story. When I attended, offerings and requirements included four years of Latin, three years of French, two years of German, physics, chemistry, biology, algebra, geometry, calculus, trigonometry, English, history, and civics, in addition to extracurricular activities and clubs—French Club, Latin Club, German Club, and Science Club, among many others. A student body made up of the children of immigrants or first-generation Americans; many, like me, the first in their families to finish high school. Nearly a 100 percent college attendance rate. A yearbook that featured student translations from Virgil and original poems in Latin.

Sounds downright antediluvian, outmoded, narrow, and elitist, and maybe it was (and is; the curriculum's still there, with some additions like Japanese), but when I returned home I found three new books waiting for me, each of which made a case for something like the education I received at Classical. The books are Leigh A. Bortins's *The Core: Teaching Your Child the Foundations of Classical Education*, Martha C. Nussbaum's *Not for Profit: Why Democracy Needs the Humanities*, and Diane Ravitch's *The Death and Life of the Great American School System: How Testing and Choice Are Undermining Education*.[1]

Three more different perspectives from three more different authors could hardly be imagined. Leigh A. Bortins writes as an engineer, a homeschooling advocate, and the CEO of Classical Conversations, Inc. She sees learning "as a continuing conversation that humankind has been engaged in for centuries" and believes that the decisions we must make today will be better if they are informed by "classical content," that is, by an awareness of what great thinkers of the past have made of the problems we encounter in the present. She wants her children and ours to "hear the collective wisdom of the ages" and "regularly consult the advice of wise and virtuous men and women" when faced with modern "predicaments."

To this end, she proposes a two-pronged program of instruction: "classical education emphasizes using the classical skills to study classical content." By classical skills she means imitation, memorization, drill, recitation, and, above all, grammar; not grammar as the study of the formal structure of sentences (although that is part of it) but grammar as the study of the formal structure of anything: "Every occupation, field of study or concept has a vocabulary that the student must acquire like a foreign language . . . . A basketball player practicing the fundamentals could be considered a grammarian . . . as he repeatedly drills the basic skills, of passing dribbling, and shooting." "Every student," Bortins counsels, "must learn to speak the language of the subject."

"Classical content" identifies just what the subjects to be classically studied are. They are the subjects informed and structured by "the ideas that make us human"—math, science, language, history, economics, and literature, each of which, Bortins insists, can be mastered by the rigorous application of the skills of the classical Trivium, grammar, the study of basic forms, logic, the skill of abstracting from particulars and rhetoric, the ability to "speak and write persuasively and eloquently about any topic while integrating allusions and examples from one field of study to explain a point in another." Assiduously practice, or as Bortins puts it, "overpractice" these skills, and "a student is prepared to study anything."

Notably absent from Bortins's vision of education is any mention of assessment outcomes, testing, job training (one of her subchapters is entitled "The Trivium Replaces Careerism"), and the wonders of technology. Her emphasis is solely on content and the means of delivering it. She warns against the narrowing distractions of "industrialization and technologies" and declares that "students would be better educated if they weren't allowed to use computers . . . until they were proficient readers and writers."

Martha Nussbaum, philosopher, classicist, ethicist, and law professor, starts from the same place. She critiques the current emphasis on "science and technology" and the "applied skills suited to profit making," and she argues that the "humanistic aspects of science and social science—the imaginative and creative aspect, and the aspect of rigorous critical thought—are . . . losing ground" as the humanities and the arts "are being cut away" and dismissed as "useless frills" in the context of an overriding imperative "to stay competitive in the global market." The result, she complains, is that "abilities crucial to the health of any democracy" are being lost, especially the ability to "think critically," the ability, that is, "to probe, to evaluate evidence, to write papers with well-structured arguments, and to analyze the arguments presented to them in other texts."

While not the language of the Trivium (which Nussbaum knows well), it breathes the same spirit, and we might well be reading Bortins when Nussbaum praises the kind of course that pays "attention to logical structures" and thus "gives students templates that they can then apply to texts of many different types." But this and related abilities will look "dispensable if what we want are marketable outputs of a quantifiable nature," if we embrace an "economic growth" paradigm rather than a "human development paradigm."

For Nussbaum, human development means the development of the capacity to transcend the local prejudices of one's immediate (even national) context and become a responsible citizen of the world. Students should be brought "to see themselves as members of a heterogeneous nation . . . and a still more heterogeneous world, and to understand something of this history of the diverse groups that inhabit it." Developing intelligent world citizenship is an enormous task that cannot even begin to be accomplished without the humanities and arts that "cultivate capacities for play and empathy," encourage thinking that is "flexible, open and creative," and that work against the provincialism that too often leads us to see those who are different as demonized others.

Unfortunately, at least according to Nussbaum, the trend toward a narrower and narrower vision of education is not being resisted by the Obama administration. Rather than decreasing the focus on testing and test preparation—a focus that reverses the relationship between test and content; the test becomes the content—"the administration plans to expand it." Obama and his secretary of education, Arne Duncan (who, says Nussbaum, "presided over a rapid decline in humanities and arts funding" as head of the Chicago public schools), continue to implement the assumptions driving the Bush administration's

No Child Left Behind, chiefly the assumption that "individual income and national economic progress" should be education's main goals.

Diane Ravitch, noted historian and theorist of education, writes as someone who once strongly supported the promise and goals of No Child Left Behind but underwent a deconversion in 2007: "Where once I had been hopeful, even enthusiastic, about the potential benefits of testing, accountability, choice, and markets, I now found myself experiencing profound doubts about these same ideas."

Her conclusions, backed up by exhaustive research and an encyclopedic knowledge both of the literature and of situations on the ground, are devastating. The mantra of choice produced a "do your own thing" proliferation of educational schemes, "each with its own curriculum, and methods, each with its own private management, all competing for . . . public dollars" rather than laboring to discover "better ways of educating hard-to-educate students." The emphasis on testing produced students who could "master test taking methods, but not the subject itself," with the consequence that the progress claimed on the basis of test scores was an "illusion": "The scores had gone up, but the students were not better educated." A faith in markets produced gamesmanship, entrepreneurial maneuvering and outright cheating, very little reflection on "what children should know," and very little thought about the nature of the curriculum.

Ravitch, like Nussbaum, finds little hope in the policies of President Obama, who promised change but seems to have picked up "the same banner of choice, competition, and markets that had been the hallmark of his predecessors." The result is that we continue to see "the shrinking of time available to teach anything other than reading and math; other subjects, including history, science, the arts, geography, even recess, were curtailed."

Ravitch's recommendations are simple, commonsensical, and entirely consonant with the views of Bortins and Nussbaum. Begin with "a well-conceived, coherent, sequential curriculum," and then "adjust other parts of the education system to support the goals of learning." This will produce a "foundation of knowledge and skills that grows stronger each year." Forget about the latest fad and quick fix, and buckle down to the time-honored, traditional "study and practice of the liberal arts and sciences: history, literature, geography, the sciences, civics, mathematics, the arts and foreign languages."

In short, get knowledgeable and well-trained teachers, equip them with a carefully calibrated curriculum and a syllabus filled with challenging texts and materials, and put them in a room with students who are told where they are going and how they are going to get there.

Worked for me.

1. Leigh A. Bortins, *The Core: Teaching Your Child the Foundations of Classical Education* (New York: Palgrave Macmillan, 2010); Martha C. Nussbaum, *Not for Profit: Why Democracy Needs the Humanities* (Princeton: Princeton University Press, 2012); and Diane Ravitch, *The Death and Life of the Great American School System: How Testing and Choice Are Undermining Education*, rev. and expanded ed. (New York: Basic Books, 2011).

Deep in the Heart of Texas

JUNE 21, 2010

A number of responses to my column "A Classical Education: Back to the Future" (7.9) about the education I received at Classical High (a public school in Providence, Rhode Island) rehearsed a story of late-flowering gratitude after an earlier period of frustration and resentment. "I had a high school (or a college) experience like yours," the poster typically said, "and I hated it and complained all the time about the homework, the demands, and the discipline; but now I am so pleased that I stayed the course and acquired skills that have served me well throughout my entire life."

Now suppose those who wrote in to me had been asked when they were young if they were satisfied with the instruction they were receiving? Were they getting their money's worth? Would they recommend the renewal of their teachers' contracts? I suspect the answers would have been "no," "no," and "no," and if their answers had been taken seriously and the curriculum they felt oppressed by had been altered accordingly, they would not have had the rich intellectual lives they now happily report, or acquired some of the skills that have stood them in good stead all these years.

The relationship between present action and the judgment of value is different in other contexts. If a waiter asks me, "Was everything to your taste, sir?," I am in a position to answer him authoritatively (if I choose to). When I pick up my shirt from the dry cleaner, I immediately know whether the offending spot has been removed. But when, as a student, I exit from a class or even from an entire course, it may be years before I know whether I got my money's worth, and that goes both ways. A course I absolutely loved may turn out be worthless because the instructor substituted wit and showmanship for an explanation of basic concepts. And a course that left me feeling confused and convinced I had learned very little might turn out to have planted seeds that later grew into mighty trees of understanding.

"Deferred judgment" or "judgment in the fullness of time" seems to be appropriate to the evaluation of teaching.

And that is why student evaluations (against which I have inveighed since I first saw them in the '60s) are all wrong as a way of assessing teaching performance: they measure present satisfaction in relation to a set of expectations that may have little to do with the deep efficacy of learning. Students tend to like everything neatly laid out; they want to know exactly where they are; they don't welcome the introduction of multiple perspectives, especially when no master perspective reconciles them; they want the answers.

But sometimes (although not always) effective teaching involves the deliberate inducing of confusion, the withholding of clarity, the refusal to provide answers; sometimes a class or an entire semester is spent being taken down various garden paths leading to dead ends that require inquiry to begin all over again, with the same discombobulating result; sometimes your expectations have been systematically disappointed. And sometimes that disappointment, while extremely annoying at the moment, is the sign that you've just been the beneficiary of a great course, although you may not realize it for decades.

Needless to say, that kind of teaching is unlikely to receive high marks on a questionnaire that rewards the linear delivery of information and penalizes a pedagogy that probes, discomforts, and fails to provide closure. Student evaluations, by their very nature, can only recognize, and by recognizing encourage, assembly-line teaching that delivers a nicely packaged product that can be assessed as easily and immediately as one assesses the quality of a hamburger.

Now an entire state is on the brink of implementing just that bite-sized style of teaching under the rubric of "customer satisfaction." Texas, currently in a contest with Arizona and South Carolina for the title "most retrograde," is signing on to a plan of "reform" generated by the Texas Public Policy Foundation, a conservative think tank dedicated to private property rights and limited government. Backed by Governor Rick Perry (yes, the one who thinks secession is a viable political option), the plan calls for college and university teachers to contract with their customers—that is, students—and to be rewarded by as much as $10,000 depending on whether they meet the contract's terms. The idea is to hold "tenured professors more accountable,"[1] and what they will be accountable to are not professional standards but the preferences of their students, who, in advance of being instructed, are presumed to be authorities on how best they should be taught.

A corollary proposal is to shift funding to the student-customers by giving them vouchers. "Instead of direct appropriations, every Texas high school graduate would get a set amount of state funds usable at any state university."[2] Once this gets going (and Texas A&M is already pushing it), you can expect professors to advertise: "Come to my college, sign up for my class, and I can guarantee you a fun-filled time and you won't have to break a sweat." If there ever was a recipe for non-risk-taking, entirely formulaic, dumbed-down teaching, this is it. One respondent to the June 13 story in the *Eagle* got it exactly right: "In the recent past, A&M announced that it wanted to be a top ten public university. Now it appears to be announcing it wants to be an investment firm, a pharmaceutical manufacturer, and a car dealership."

The people behind this cockamamie scheme wouldn't be fazed by this description or regard it as an accusation. They actively want their colleges and universities to be like car dealerships, with an emphasis on the bottom line, efficiency, and consumer choice. This means that the middleman has to be cut out, and in this case, the middleman is the faculty member. Jeff Sandefer, whose presentation at a 2008 meeting with Governor Perry and the university Board of Regents established the tone and contours of "reform," makes no bones about it. Professors, he complains, seem to believe "that our colleges and universities belong to them."[3] It's time, he says, to stop writing "blank checks" to faculty members who occupy themselves "writing academic journal articles that few people read."

That, of course, is an accurate description. Senior faculty members do in fact write articles that only their peers at the top of very rarefied disciplines can read. That is what academic research is all about: highly qualified scholars working on problems that may have no practical payoff except the unquantifiable payoff of advancing our understanding of something in philosophy or nature that has long been a mystery.

More than occasionally in these columns I have mocked the pretensions of those faculty members who cry "academic freedom" at the slightest infringement of what they take to be their god-given liberty. But academic freedom does in fact have a meaning and a legitimate purpose: it protects faculty members from external constituencies intent on taking over the enterprise for mercenary or political reasons. The Texas "reform plan" is just that; its so-called reforms would be funny were they not so dangerous. And it all began with student evaluations, or, rather, with the mistake of taking them seriously. Since then, it's been all downhill.

1. Vimal Patel, "A&M Regents Push Reforms," *Eagle*, June 13, 2010.
2. William Lutz, *Lone Star Report*, May 23, 2008.
3. "Public Universities Belong to the Public, Not the Faculty," Texas Public Policy Foundation, May 6, 2009.

The Digital Humanities and the Transcending of Mortality

JANUARY 9, 2012

This is a blog. There, I've said it. I have been resisting saying it—I have always referred to this space as a "column"—not only because "blog" is an ugly word (as are clog, smog, and slog), but because blogs are provisional, ephemeral, interactive, communal, available to challenge, interruption, and interpolation, and not meant to last; whereas in a professional life now going into its fiftieth year I have been building arguments that are intended to be decisive, comprehensive, monumental, definitive, and, most important, all mine.

In *Changing Places* and *Small World*, the novelist David Lodge fashions a comical/satirical portrait of a literary critic named Morris Zapp, whose ambition, as his last name suggests, is to write about a topic with such force and completeness that no other critic will be able to say a word about it.[1] The job will have been done forever. That has always been my aim, and the content of that aim—a desire for preeminence, authority, and disciplinary power—is what blogs and the digital humanities stand against.

The point is made concisely by Kathleen Fitzpatrick in her book *Planned Obsolescence: Publishing, Technology, and the Future of the Academy*: "a blog privileges immediacy—the newest posts appear first on the screen and older posts quickly lose currency. . . . This emphasis on the present works at cross purposes with much long-form scholarship, which needs stability and longevity in order to make its points."[2]

As Fitzpatrick well sees, long-form scholarship—books and articles submitted to learned journals and university presses—needs more than that. It needs the interdependent notions of author, text, and originality. In the traditional model of scholarship, a credentialed author—someone with a PhD or working toward one—gets an idea (that's the original part) and applies it to a text or a set of problems, and produces, all by himself, a new text that is offered to readers with the promise that if they follow (that is, submit to) it, they will gain an increase in understanding and knowledge. Fitzpatrick comments: "It is . . . not enough that the text be finished; it also has to be new, springing entirely from the head of the author, and always distinguishing itself from the writing of other authors."

Fitzpatrick contends, first, that authorship has never been thus isolated—one always writes against the background of, and in conversation with, innumerable predecessors and contemporaries who are in effect one's collaborators—and, second, that the "myth" of the stand-alone, masterful author is exposed for the fiction it is by the new forms of communication—blogs, links, hypertext, remixes, mash-ups, multimodalities, and much more—that have emerged with the development of digital technology.

The effect of these technologies is to transform a hitherto linear experience—a lone reader facing a stable text provided by an author who dictates the shape of reading by doling out information in a sequence he controls—into a multidirectional experience in which voices (and images) enter, interact, and proliferate in ways that decenter the authority of the author, who becomes just another participant. Again Fitzpatrick: "we need to think less about completed products and more about text in process; less about individual authorship and more about collaboration; less about originality and more about remix; less about ownership and more about sharing."

"Text in process" is a bit of an oxymoron: for if the process is not occurring with an eye toward the emergence of a finished artifact but with an eye toward its own elaboration and complication—more links, more voices, more commentary—the notion of "text" loses its coherence; there is no longer any text to point to because it "exists" only in a state of perpetual alteration: "Digital text is, above all, malleable . . . there is little sense in attempting to replicate the permanence of print [itself an illusion, according to the digital vision] in a medium whose chief value is change" (Fitzpatrick).

Nor is there any sense in holding on to the concept of "author," for as Fitzpatrick observes, "all of the texts published in a network environment will become multi-author by virtue of their interpenetration with the writings of others." Fitzpatrick insists that there will still be a place for individual authors, but with a difference: the collective, she says, should not be understood as "the elimination of individual, but rather as . . . a fertile community composed of multiple intelligences, each of which is always working in relationship with others."

But this is just like "text in process": if the individual is defined and constituted by relationships, the individual is not really an entity that can be said to have ownership of either its intentions or their effects; the individual is (as poststructuralist theory used to tell us) just a relay through which messages circulating in the network pass and are sent along. Author Mark Poster draws the moral: "[T]he shift . . . to the globally networked computer is a move that elicits a rearticulation of the author from the center of the text to its margins, from the source of meaning to an offering, a point in a sequence of a continuously transformed matrix of signification."[3]

Meaning everywhere and nowhere, produced not by anyone but by everyone in concert, meaning not waiting for us at the end of a linear chain of authored thought in the form of a sentence or an essay or a book, but immediately and multiply present in a cornucopia of ever-expanding significances.

There are two things I want to say about this vision: first, that it is theological, a description its adherents would most likely resist, and, second, that it is political, a description its adherents would most likely embrace.

The vision is theological because it promises to liberate us from the confines of the linear, temporal medium in the context of which knowledge is discrete, partial, and situated—knowledge at this time and this place experienced by this limited being—and deliver us into a spatial universe where knowledge is everywhere available in a full and immediate presence to which everyone has access as a node or relay in the meaning-producing system. In many theologies that is a description of the condition (to be achieved only when human life ends) in which the self exchanges its limited, fallen perspective for the perspective (not a perspective at all) of union with deity, where there is no distance between the would-be knower and the object of his cognitive apprehension because, in Milton's words, everyone and everything is "all in all."

The obstacle to this happy state is mortality itself. To be mortal is to be capable of dying (as opposed to going on and on and on), and therefore of having a beginning, middle, and end, which is what sentences, narratives, and arguments have: you start here and end there with the completed thought or story or conclusion (quod erat demonstrandum).

What both the religious and digital visions offer (if only in prospect) is a steady yet dynamic state where there is movement and change, but no center, no beginning and end, just all middle (as the novelist Robert Coover saw in his piece "The End of Books," *New York Times*, June 21, 1992). Delivered from linearity, from time-bound, sharply delineated meanings, from mortality, from death, everyone, no longer a one, will revel in and participate in the universal dance, a "mystical dance" of

> . . . mazes intricate,
> Eccentric, intervolved, yet regular
> Then most when most irregular they seem,
> And in their motions harmony divine
> So smooths her charming tones, that God's own ear
> Listens delighted.

(John Milton, *Paradise Lost*, 5:620, 5:622–27)

Now, no one in the digital humanities community talks like that, although they do speak, as Fitzpatrick does, of the "impoverished" medium of print (implying the availability of a medium more full and authentic), and they do predict, without very many specifics, a new era of expanding, borderless collaboration in which all the infirmities of linearity will be removed.

Chief among those infirmities are the institutions that operate to keep scholar separated from scholar, readers separate from the creation as well as the consumption of meaning, and ordinary men and women separate from the knowledge-making machinery from which they are excluded by the gatekeeping mechanisms of departments, colleges, universities, university presses, and other engines dedicated to the maintaining of the status quo.

This is the political component of the digital vision, and it is heard when Fitzpatrick writes that "access to the work we produce must be opened up as a site of conversation not just among scholars but also between scholars and the broader culture"; when "The Digital Humanities Manifesto 2.0" tells us that while the period since World War II has seen "the proliferation of ever smaller and more rigorous areas of expertise and sub-expertise and the consequent emergence of private languages and specialized jargons," the digital humanities "is about integration" and the practice of "digital anarchy"; when Matthew Kirschenbaum calls for the dissemination of scholarship apart from "the more traditional structures of academic publishing, which . . . are perceived as outgrowths of dysfunctional and out-moded practices surrounding peer review, tenure and promotion"; when Michael Shanks promotes a "deep interdisciplinarity" or "trans-disciplinarity" that is not "premised upon long-standing disciplinary borders" (Artereality).[4]

The rhetoric of these statements (which could easily be multi-plied) is not one of reform but of revolution. As Mark Sample puts it, "It's all about innovation and disruption. The digital humanities is really an insurgent humanities." The project is insurgent in relation, first, to the present exclusionary structures of access and accredita-tion and, second, to the hegemony of global capitalism of which those structures are an extension. Digital humanities, declares the "Mani-festo," "have a utopian core shaped by its genealogical descent from the counterculture-cyberculture of the '60s and '70s. This is why it affirms the value of the open, the infinite, the expansive [and] the democratization of culture and scholarship."

It is, then, a left agenda (although the digital has no inherent po-litical valence) that self-identifies with civil liberties, the elimination of boundaries, a strong First Amendment, the weakening or end of copyright, and the Facebook/YouTube revolutions that have swept across the Arab world.

The ambitions of the digital humanities are at times less grand and more local. The digital humanities is viewed by some of its propo-nents as a positive response to the dismal situation many humanists, especially younger ones, now find themselves in. The movement, Kirschenbaum reports, has been "galvanized by a group of younger (or not so young) graduate students, faculty members . . . who now wield the label 'digital humanities' instrumentally amid an increas-ingly monstrous institutional terrain defined by declining public sup-port for higher education, rising tuitions, shrinking endowments, the proliferation of distance education and the for-profit university, and underlying it all, the conversion of full-time, tenure-track academic labor to a part-time adjunct workforce."

The digital humanities, it is claimed, can help alter that "mon-strous terrain" in at least two ways. The first is to open up the con-versation to the public, whose support the traditional humanities has lost. If anyone and everyone can join in, if the invitation of open ac-cess is widely accepted, appreciation of what humanists do will grow beyond the confines of the university. Familiarity will breed not con-tempt but fellowship. "Only in this way," Fitzpatrick declares, "can we ensure the continued support for the university not simply as a credentialing center, but rather as a center of thought."

The second way the digital humanities can help, or so it is said, is it to confer on students skills that will be attractive to employers inside and outside the academy. In "The Humanities and the Fear of Being Useful," Paul Jay and Gerald Graff argue that "because students in the digital humanities are trained to deal with concrete issues related to intellectual property and privacy," they will be equipped "to enter fields related to everything from writing computer programs to text encoding and text editing, electronic publishing, interface design, and archive construction."[5] Get into the digital humanities and get a job. Not a bad slogan.

I am aware that in this decidedly abstract (and linear) discussion, I have still said nothing at all about the "humanities" part of digital humanities. Does the digital humanities offer new and better ways to realize traditional humanities goals? Or does the digital humanities completely change our understanding of what a humanities goal (and work in the humanities) might be?

The pertinent challenge to this burgeoning field has been issued by one of its pioneer members, Jerome McGann of the University of Virginia. "The general field of humanities education and scholarship will not take up the use of digital technology in any significant way until one can clearly demonstrate that these tools have important contributions to make to the exploration and explanation of aesthetic works."[6] What might those contributions be? Are they forthcoming? These are the questions I shall take up in the next column (7.12)—oops, I mean blog.

1. David Lodge, *Changing Places*, 2nd ed. (New York: Penguin Books, 1979) and *Small World* (*New York*: Penguin Books, 1995).

2. Kathleen Fitzpatrick, *Planned Obsolescence: Publishing, Technology, and the Future of the Academy* (New York: NYU Press, 2011); subsequent quotes by Fitzpatrick are to this volume.

3. Mark Poster, *What's the Matter with the Internet?* (Minneapolis: University of Minnesota Press, 2001).

4. "The Digital Humanities Manifesto 2.0," http://manifesto.humanities.ucla.edu/2009/05/29/the-digital-humanities-manifesto-20/; Matthew Kirschenbaum, "What Is Digital Humanities and What's It Doing in English Departments?," *ADE Bulletin*, no. 150, 2010.

5. Paul Jay and Gerald Graff, "The Humanities and the Fear of Being Useful," Inside Higher Education website, January 5, 2012.

6. Jerome McGann, "Ivanhoe Game Summary," 2002, http://www.speculative computing.org/ivanhoe/framework/summary.html.

Mind Your P's and B's: The Digital Humanities and Interpretation

JANUARY 23, 2012

The question I posed at the conclusion of my last post (7.11) was how do the technologies wielded by digital humanities practitioners either facilitate the work of the humanities, as it has been traditionally understood, or bring about an entirely new conception of what work in the humanities can and should be? I'm going to sneak up on that question by offering a piece of conventional (i.e., nondigital) literary analysis that deals, as the digital humanities do, with matters of statistical frequency and pattern.

Halfway through *Areopagitica* (1644), his celebration of freedom of publication, John Milton observes that the Presbyterian ministers who once complained of being censored by Episcopalian bishops have now become censors themselves. Indeed, he declares, when it comes to exercising a "tyranny over learning," there is no difference between the two: "Bishops and Presbyters are the same to us both name and thing." That is, not only are they acting similarly; their names are suspiciously alike.

In both names the prominent consonants are "b" and "p," and they form a chiasmic pattern: the initial consonant in "bishops" is "b"; "p" is the prominent consonant in the second syllable; the initial consonant in "presbyters" is "p," and "b" is strongly voiced at the beginning of the second syllable. The pattern of the consonants is the formal vehicle of the substantive argument, the argument that what is asserted to be different is really, if you look closely, the same. That argument is reinforced by the phonological fact that "b" and "p" are almost identical. Both are "bilabial plosives" (a class of only two members), sounds produced when the flow of air from the vocal tract is stopped by closing the lips.

There is more. (I know that's not what you want to hear.) In the sentences that follow the declaration of equivalence, "b's" and "p's" proliferate in a veritable orgy of alliteration and consonance. Here is a partial list of the words that pile up in a brief space: prelaty, pastor, parish, Archbishop, books, pluralists, bachelor, parishioner, private, protestations, chop, Episcopacy, palace, metropolitan, penance, pusillanimous, breast, politic, presses, open, birthright, privilege, Parliament, abrogated, bud, liberty, printing, Prelatical, people.

Even without the pointing provided by syntax, the dance of the "b's" and "p's" carries a message, and that message is made explicit when Milton reminds the presbyters that their own "late arguments . . . against the Prelats" should tell them that the effort to block free expression "meets for the most part with an event utterly opposite to the end which it drives at." The stressed word in this climactic sentence is "opposite." Can it be an accident that a word signifying difference has two "p's" facing and mirroring each other across the weak divide of a syllable break? Opposite superficially, but internally, where it counts, the same.

To my knowledge, I am the first critic to put forward this interpretation of the sequence. However, that claim, the claim of originality, brings with it its own problems, at least in the context of literary criticism as it has been practiced since the late 1930s. Doesn't the fact that for 368 years only I have noticed the b/p pattern suggest that it is without significance, an accidental concatenation of consonants? Aren't I being at best overingenious and at worst irresponsibly arbitrary?

In order to answer such questions, I would have to demonstrate that Milton self-consciously put the pattern there and made it the formal bearer of his argument. I would have to build a chain of inference that led from the undoubted, countable presence of the "b's" and "p's" in the passage to Milton's intention and back again. Were I to attempt to fashion that chain (don't worry!), I would begin by citing the last line of a Milton sonnet—"New Presbyter is but old Priest writ large"—and go on to instance other places in his poetry and prose where Milton plays with sounds in a manner he would have learned from the rhetorical manuals we know he studied at school.

The requirement I would have to satisfy illustrates the problem of formalist analysis, analysis that wants to move from the noting of formal properties to the drawing of interpretive conclusions: given that there are only twenty-six letters (and twenty-one consonants) in the alphabet, it is inevitable that in a text of any size, patterns of repetition and frequency will abound. The trick is to separate the patterns produced by the scarcity of alphabetic resources (patterns to which meaning can be imputed only arbitrarily) from the patterns designed by an author.

The usual way of doing this is illustrated by my example: I began with a substantive interpretive proposition—Milton believes that those who suffered under the tyrannical censorship of episcopal priests have turned into their oppressors despite apparent differences in worship and church structure—and, within the guiding light, indeed searchlight, of that proposition I noticed a pattern that could, I thought, be correlated with it. I then elaborated the correlation.

The direction of my inferences is critical: first the interpretive hypothesis and then the formal pattern, which attains the status of noticeability only because an interpretation already in place is picking it out.

The direction is the reverse in the digital humanities: first you run the numbers, and then you see if they prompt an interpretive hypothesis. The method, if it can be called that, is dictated by the capability of the tool. You have at your disposal an incredible computing power that can bring to analytical attention patterns of sameness and difference undetectable by the eye of the human reader. Because the patterns are undetectable, you don't know in advance what they are and you cannot begin your computer-aided search (called text-mining) in a motivated—that is, interpretively directed—way. You don't know what you're looking for or why you're looking for it. How then do you proceed?

The answer is, proceed randomly or on a whim, and see what turns up. You might wonder, for example, what place or location names appear in American literary texts published in 1851, and you devise a program that will tell you. You will then have data.

But what do you do with the data?

The example is not a hypothetical one. It is put forward by Matthew Wilkens in his essay "Canons, Close Reading, and the Evolution of Method."[1] Wilkens digitizes the corpus of mid-nineteenth-century American novels and produces a data bank ready for quarrying. And Wilkens does do something with the data. He notices that "there are more international locations than one might have expected"—digital humanists love to be surprised because surprise at what has been turned up is a vindication of the computer's ability to go beyond human reading—and from this he concludes that "American fiction in the mid-nineteenth century appears to be pretty diversely outward looking in a way that hasn't received much attention."

More international locations named than we would have anticipated; therefore, mid-nineteenth-century American fiction is outward-looking, a fact we would not have "discovered" were it not for the kind of attention a computer, as opposed to a human reader, is capable of paying.

But does the data point inescapably in that direction? Don't we have to know in what novelistic situations foreign lands are alluded to and by whom? If the international place-names are invoked by a narrator, it might be with the intention not of embracing a cosmopolitan, outward perspective but of pushing it away: yes, I know that there is a great big world out there, but I am going to focus in on a landscape more insular and American. If a character keeps dropping the names of towns and cities in Europe, Africa, and Asia, the novelist could be alerting us to his pretentiousness and admonishing the reader to stay close to home. If a more sympathetic character daydreams about Paris, Istanbul, and Moscow, she might be understood as caressing the exotic names in rueful recognition of the experiences she will never have.

The list of possible contextual framings is infinite, but some contextual framing is necessary if we are to move from noticing the naming of international locations to the assigning of significance. Otherwise we are asserting, without justification, a correlation between a formal feature the computer program just happened to uncover and a significance that has simply been declared, not argued for. (Frequency is not an argument.) Don't we have to actually read the books before saying what the patterns discovered in them mean?

No, says Wilkens (and many in the field agree with him). We have been working, he declares, with too few texts—a handful of "purportedly . . . representative works"—and we have drawn from that small sample conclusions we might radically revise were we to have in our contemplation the totality of texts produced in nineteenth-century America. The problem is that no reader could possibly process that totality, never mind discern the patterns that exist in it on a level too minute and deep for human apprehension.

This is where the computer comes to the rescue. Digitize the entire corpus and you can put questions to it and get answers in a matter of seconds. We can, says Wilkens, "look for potentially interesting features without committing months and years to extracting them via close reading." The Stanford scholar Franco Moretti calls this method of analyzing huge bodies of data "distant reading."[2] The Shakespearean scholar Martin Mueller briskly urges humanists to "stop reading."[3] So much for the old humanist program.

Wilkens acknowledges that we may "still need to read some of the texts closely," and he admits that the more humanists turn to "algorithmic and quantitative analysis of piles of texts," the "worse close readers" they will become. He sees it as a trade-off between a skill practiced on small samples by a priesthood of ivory-tower academics and a larger-scale enterprise that has the promise of encompassing all of knowledge. Wilkens thinks that's a good bargain—"a few more numbers in return for a bit less text"—and declares that "We gain a lot by having available to us the kinds of evidence text-mining . . . provides." The result, he predicts, will be "a more useful humanities scholarship."

Words like "useful" and "evidence" indicate that Wilkens is still holding out for an interpretive payoff (evidence has to be evidence of something) although he concedes that as of yet that payoff has been "pretty limited." Quite another route of success is imagined by Stephen Ramsay, perhaps the most sophisticated theorist of the burgeoning field. Ramsay is not concerned that computer-assisted analysis has not yet delivered an interpretive method, a way of pruning the myriad paths that are opened up by the generation of data. He doesn't want to narrow interpretive possibilities, he wants to multiply them.

When another scholar worries that if one begins with data, one can "go anywhere," Ramsay makes it clear that going anywhere is exactly what he wants to encourage. The critical acts he values are not directed at achieving closure by arriving at a meaning; they are, he says, "ludic" and they are "distinguished . . . by a refusal to declare meaning in any form." The right question to propose "is not 'What does the text mean?' but, rather, 'How do we ensure that it keeps on meaning'—how . . . can we ensure that our engagement with the text is deep, multifaceted, and prolonged?"[4]

The answer is not to go to the text "armed with a hypothesis" but "with a machine that is ready to reorganize the text in a thousand different ways instantly." Each reorganization (sometimes called a "deformation") creates a new text that can be reorganized in turn and each new text raises new questions that can be pursued to the point where still newer questions emerge. The point is not to get to a place you had in mind and then stop; the point is to keep on going, as, aided by the data-generating machine, you notice this and then notice that which suggests something else and so on, ad infinitum.

It is, he explains, like browsing in a store. The salesclerk asks, "Can I help you?," a question that assumes you came in with a definite purpose. You say, "No, I'm just browsing," which Ramsay glosses as "(a) I don't know what's here and (b) I don't know what I'm looking for." In effect, he concludes, "I'm just screwing around," picking up this item, and moving randomly to another and another and another. "Look at this. Then look at that." That's the method or antimethod; just try one algorithm and then another and see what the resulting numbers suggest (not prove) in the way of an interpretive hypothesis. And then do it again. Are we ready, he asks, "to accept surfing and stumbling—screwing around, broadly understood—as a research methodology?"[5] If we are ready, computer programs are ready to help us.

Ramsay accepts the criticism of those who say that readings of texts cannot "be arrived at algorithmically."[6] This incapacity, however, doesn't worry him, because the value of numbers for him is not that they produce or confirm readings, but that they provoke those who look at them to flights of interpretive imagination: "algorithmic transformations can provide the alternative visions that give rise to . . . readings." There is, he says, "no end of our understanding" of texts and concepts. There are only new noticings which . . . are practically discernible only through algorithmic means").

Ramsay presents these ideas in two tonal registers. At times he argues that however alien algorithmic criticism may seem, it is really a technologically ramped-up version of what literary criticism has always been. Although the rhetoric of traditional literary criticism emphasizes getting at the truth about a text as its end point, in practice what critics do is try out one hypothesis, and then another, and in the process recharacterize or deform the text. We say about a poem, let's look at this as an erotic poem, or a poem about markets, or a poem about literary imagination, and then, under the impetus of these various hypotheses, we rewrite the poem again and again. We produce new poems. "All criticism and interpretation is deformance." What computers do is multiply the ways in which this "readerly process of deformation," this opening up of "serendipitous paths" can be performed. We should understand computer-based criticism to be what it has always been: "human-based criticism with computers."

But in another mood, Ramsay is more messianic. By embracing rather than warding off alternative interpretive paths, algorithmic criticism "may come to form the basis for new kinds of critical acts," acts that do not merely facilitate literary analysis but "build a platform for social networking and self-expression." Prompted by the numbers, you try out something and you call across the room to a coworker or to a colleague in another country and ask, "Here is what I found, what did you find?" ("The Hermeneutics of Screwing Around"). And that colleague asks another who asks another who, well, you get the point. The antimethodology that refuses closure and insists on fecundity facilitates—no, demands—sharing, and builds an ever-expanding community of digital fellowship, an almost theological community in which everyone explores in "the inexhaustible nature of divine meaning" ("Reading Machines").

These two visions of the digital humanities project—the perfection of traditional criticism and the inauguration of something entirely new—correspond to the two attitudes digital humanists typically strike: (1) we're doing what you've always been doing, only we have tools that will enable you to do it better; let us in, and (2) we are the heralds and bearers of a new truth and it is the disruptive challenge of that new truth that accounts for your recoiling from us. It is the double claim always made by an insurgent movement. We are a beleaguered minority and we are also the saving remnant.

But whatever vision of the digital humanities is proclaimed, it will have little place for the likes of me and for the kind of criticism I practice: a criticism that narrows meaning to the significances designed by an author, a criticism that generalizes from a text as small as half a line, a criticism that insists on the distinction between the true and the false, between what is relevant and what is noise, between what is serious and what is mere play. Nothing ludic in what I do or try to do. I have a lot to answer for.

1.   Matthew Wilkens, "Canons, Close Reading, and the Evolution of Method," in *Debates in the Digital Humanities*, ed. Matthew Gold (Minneapolis: University of Minnesota Press, 2012).

2.   Franco Moretti, *Graphs, Maps, Trees: Abstract Models for Literary History* (New York: Verso, 2007).

3.   Martin Mueller, "Digital Shakespeare or Toward a Literary Informatics," Department of English, Northwestern University, Evanston, Illinois, February 13, 2009.

4.   Stephen Ramsay, "Toward an Algorithmic Criticism," *Literary and Linguistic Computing* 18, no. 2 (2003).

5.   Stephen Ramsay, "The Hermeneutics of Screwing Around; or What You Do with a Million Books," in *Pastplay: Teaching and Learning History with Technology*, ed. Kevin Kee (Ann Arbor: University of Michigan Press, 2014), 111–20.

6.   Stephen Ramsay, *Reading Machines* (Champaign: University of Illinois Press, 2011).

PART 8

Reflections on Academic Freedom

Conspiracy Theories 101

JULY 23, 2006

Kevin Barrett, a lecturer at the University of Wisconsin at Madison, has now taken his place alongside Ward Churchill of the University of Colorado as a college teacher whose views on 9/11 have led politicians and ordinary citizens to demand that he be fired.

Mr. Barrett, who has a one-semester contract to teach a course titled "Islam: Religion and Culture," acknowledged on a radio talk show that he has shared with students his strong conviction that the destruction of the World Trade Center was an inside job perpetrated by the American government. The predictable uproar ensued, and the equally predictable battle lines were drawn between those who disagree about what the doctrine of academic freedom does and does not allow.

Mr. Barrett's critics argue that academic freedom has limits and should not be invoked to justify the dissemination of lies and fantasies. Mr. Barrett's supporters (most of whom are not partisans of his conspiracy theory) insist that it is the very point of an academic institution to entertain all points of view, however unpopular. (This was the position taken by the university's provost, Patrick Farrell, when he ruled on July 10 that Mr. Barrett would be retained: "We cannot allow political pressure from critics of unpopular ideas to inhibit the free exchange of ideas.")

Both sides get it wrong. The problem is that each assumes that academic freedom is about protecting the content of a professor's speech; one side thinks that no content should be ruled out in advance, while the other would draw the line at propositions (like the denial of the Holocaust or the flatness of the world) considered by almost everyone to be crazy or dangerous.

But in fact, academic freedom has nothing to do with content. It is not a subset of the general freedom of Americans to say anything they like (so long as it is not an incitement to violence or is treasonous or libelous). Rather, academic freedom is the freedom of academics to *study* anything they like; the freedom, that is, to subject any body of material, however unpromising it might seem, to academic interrogation and analysis.

Academic freedom means that if I think that there may be an intellectual payoff to be had by turning an academic lens on material others consider trivial—golf tees, gourmet coffee, lingerie ads, convenience stores, street names, whatever—I should get a chance to try. If I manage to demonstrate to my peers and students that studying this material yields insights into matters of general intellectual interest, there is a new topic under the academic sun and a new subject for classroom discussion.

In short, whether something is an appropriate object of academic study is a matter not of its content—a crackpot theory may have had a history of influence that well rewards scholarly scrutiny—but of its availability to serious analysis. This point was missed by the author of a comment posted to the blog of a University of Wisconsin law professor, Ann Althouse: "When is the University of Wisconsin hiring a professor of astrology?" The question is obviously sarcastic; its intention is to equate the 9/11-inside-job theory with believing in the predictive power of astrology, and to imply that since the university wouldn't think of hiring someone to teach the one, it should have known better than to hire someone to teach the other.

But the truth is that it would not be at all outlandish for a university to hire someone to teach astrology—not to profess astrology and recommend it as the basis of decision making (shades of Nancy Reagan), but to teach the history of its very long career. There is, after all, a good argument for saying that Shakespeare, Chaucer, and Dante, among others, cannot be fully understood unless one understands astrology.

The distinction I am making—between studying astrology and proselytizing for it—is crucial and can be generalized; it shows us where the line between the responsible and irresponsible practice of academic freedom should always be drawn. Any idea can be brought into the classroom if the point is to inquire into its structure, history, influence, and so forth. But no idea belongs in the classroom if the point of introducing it is to recruit your students for the political agenda it may be thought to imply.

And this is where we come back to Mr. Barrett, who, in addition to being a college lecturer, is a member of a group calling itself Scholars for 9/11 Truth, an organization with the decidedly political agenda of persuading Americans that the Bush administration "not only permit-ted 9/11 to happen but may even have orchestrated these events."

Is the fact of this group's growing presence on the Internet a rea-son for studying it in a course on 9/11? Sure. Is the instructor who discusses the group's arguments thereby endorsing them? Not at all. It is perfectly possible to teach a viewpoint without embracing it and urging it. But the moment a professor does embrace and urge it, ac-ademic study has ceased and been replaced by partisan advocacy. And that is a moment no college administration should allow to occur.

Provost Farrell doesn't quite see it that way, because he is too hung up on questions of content and balance. He thinks that the im-portant thing is to assure a diversity of views in the classroom, and so he is reassured when Mr. Barrett promises to surround his "uncon-ventional" ideas and "personal opinions" with readings "representing a variety of viewpoints."

But the number of viewpoints Mr. Barrett presents to his students is not the measure of his responsibility. There is, in fact, no academic requirement to include more than one view of an academic issue, al-though it is usually pedagogically useful to do so. The true require-ment is that no matter how many (or few) views are presented to the students, they should be offered as objects of analysis rather than as candidates for allegiance.

There is a world of difference, for example, between surveying the pro and con arguments about the Iraq war, a perfectly appropriate academic assignment, and pressing students to come down on your side. Of course, the instructor who presides over such a survey is likely to be a partisan of one position or the other—after all, who doesn't have an opinion on the Iraq war?—but it is part of a teacher's job to set personal conviction aside for the hour or two when a class is in session and allow the techniques and protocols of academic re-search full sway.

This restraint should not be too difficult to exercise. After all, we require and expect it of judges, referees, and reporters. And while its exercise may not always be total, it is both important and possible to make the effort.

Thus the question Provost Farrell should put to Mr. Barrett is not "Do you hold these views?" (he can hold any views he likes) or "Do you proclaim them in public?" (he has that right no less than the rest of us) or even "Do you surround them with the views of others?"

Rather, the question should be: "Do you separate yourself from your partisan identity when you are in the employ of the citizens of Wisconsin and teach subject matter—whatever it is—rather than urge political action?" If the answer is yes, allowing Mr. Barrett to remain in the classroom is warranted. If the answer is no (or if a yes answer is followed by classroom behavior that contradicts it), he should be shown the door. Not because he would be teaching the "wrong" things, but because he would have abandoned teaching for indoctrination.

The advantage of this way of thinking about the issue is that it outflanks the sloganeering and posturing both sides indulge in: on the one hand, faculty members who shout "academic freedom" and mean by it an instructor's right to say or advocate anything at all with impunity; on the other hand, state legislators who shout "not on our dime" and mean by it that they can tell academics what ideas they can and cannot bring into the classroom.

All you have to do is remember that academic freedom is just that: the freedom to do an academic job without external interference. It is not the freedom to do other jobs, jobs you are neither trained for nor paid to perform. While there should be no restrictions on what can be taught—no list of interdicted ideas or topics—there should be an absolute restriction on appropriating the scene of teaching for partisan political ideals. Teachers who use the classroom to indoctrinate make the enterprise of higher education vulnerable to its critics and shortchange students in the guise of showing them the true way.

8.2

Always Academicize:
My Response to the Responses

NOVEMBER 6, 2006

In my post of October 22 ("Tip to Professors: Just Do Your Job" [7.3]), I argued that college and university teachers should not take it upon themselves to cure the ills of the world, but should instead do the job they are trained and paid to do—the job, first, of introducing students to areas of knowledge they were not acquainted with before, and second, of equipping those same students with the analytic skills that will enable them to assess and evaluate the materials they are asked to read. I made the further point that the moment an instructor tries to do something more, he or she has crossed a line and ventured into territory that belongs properly to some other enterprise. It doesn't matter whether the line is crossed by someone on the left who wants to enroll students in a progressive agenda dedicated to the redress of injustice, or by someone on the right who is concerned that students be taught to be patriotic, God-fearing, family oriented, and respectful of tradition. To be sure, the redress of injustice and the inculcation of patriotic and family values are worthy activities, but they are not academic activities, and they are not activities academics have the credentials to perform. Academics are not legislators, or political leaders or therapists or ministers; they are academics, and as academics they have contracted to do only one thing—to discuss whatever subject is introduced into the classroom in academic terms.

And what are academic terms? The list is long and includes looking into a history of a topic, studying and mastering the technical language that comes along with it, examining the controversies that have grown up around it and surveying the most significant contributions to its development. The list of academic terms would, however, not include coming to a resolution about a political or moral issue raised by the materials under discussion. This does not mean that political and moral questions are banned from the classroom, but that they should be regarded as objects of study—Where did they come from? How have they been answered at different times in different cultures?—rather than as invitations to take a vote (that's what you do at the ballot box) or make a life decision (that's what you do in the private recesses of your heart). No subject is out of bounds; what is out of bounds is using it as an occasion to move students in some political or ideological direction. The imperative, as I said in the earlier post, is to "academicize" the subject; that is, to remove it from whatever context of urgency it inhabits in the world and insert it into a context of academic urgency where the question being asked is not "What is the right thing to do?" but "Is this account of the matter attentive to the complexity of the issue?"

Those who commented on the post raised many sharp and helpful objections to it. Some of those objections give me the opportunity to make my point again. I happily plead guilty to not asking the question Dr. James Cook would have me (and all teachers) ask when a "social/political" issue comes up in the classroom: "Does silence contribute to the victory of people who espouse values akin to those of Hitler?" (see 7.3). The question confuses and conflates political silence—you decide not to speak up as a citizen against what you consider an outrage—with an academic silence that is neither culpable nor praiseworthy because it goes without saying if you understand the nature of academic work. When, as a teacher, you are silent about your ethical and political commitments, you are not making a positive choice—Should I or shouldn't I? is not an academic question—but simply performing your pedagogical role.

Of course the teacher who doesn't think to declare his or her ethical preferences because it is not part of the job description might well be very active and vocal at a political rally or in a letter to the editor. I am not counseling moral and political abstinence across the board, only in those contexts—like the classroom—where the taking of positions on the war in Iraq or assisted suicide or the conduct of foreign policy is extraneous to or subversive of the activity being performed. Dr. Cook, along with Dr. Richard Flanagan, Ignacio Garcia, and others accuse me of putting aside every moral issue or sterilizing issues of their moral implications or leaving my ethical sense at the door. No, I am refusing the implication that one's ethical obligations remain the same no matter where one is or what one is doing or what one is being paid to do.

In fact, my stance is aggressively ethical: it demands that we take the ethics of the classroom—everything that belongs to pedagogy, including preparation, giving assignments, grading papers, keeping discussions on point, and so on—seriously and not allow the scene of instruction to become a scene of indoctrination. Were the ethics appropriate to the classroom no different from the ethics appropriate to the arena of political action or the ethics of democratic citizenry, there would be nothing distinctive about the academic experience—it would be politics by another name—and no reason for anyone to support the enterprise. For if it's politics you want, you might as well get right to it and skip the entire academic apparatus entirely.

My argument, then, rests on the conviction that academic work is unlike other forms of work—if it isn't, it has no shape of its own and no claim on our attention—and that fidelity to it demands respect for its difference, a difference defined by its removal from the decision-making pressures of the larger world. And that finally may be the point underlying the objections to my position: in a world so beset with problems, some of my critics seem to be asking, is it either possible or desirable to remain aloof from the fray? Thus Fred Moramarco declares, "It's clearly not easy to 'just do your job' where genocide, aggression, moral superiority, and hatred of opposing views are ordinary, everyday occurrences." I take him to be saying at least two things: (1) it's hard to academicize a political/moral issue and stay clear of coming down on one side or another, and (2) it's irresponsible to do so given all that is wrong with the current state of things. As to the assertion that it's hard, it's really quite easy, a piece of cake, but the second assertion—academicizing is not what we should be doing in perilous times—has a genuine force, and if, as a teacher, you feel that force, your response should not be to turn your classroom into a political rally or an encounter group but to get out of teaching and into a line of work more likely to address directly the real world problems you want to solve. There is nothing virtuous or holy about teaching; it's just a job, and like any job it aims at particular results, not at all results. If the results teaching is able to produce when it is done well—improving student knowledge and analytical abilities— are not what you're after, then teaching is the wrong profession for you. But if teaching is the profession you commit to, then you should do it and not use it to do something else.

The issue not explicitly raised in the comments but implied by many of them is the issue of justification. If the point of liberal arts education is what I say it is—to lay out the history and structure of political and ethical dilemmas without saying yes or no to any of the proposed courses of action—what is the yield that justifies the enormous expenditure of funds and energies? Beats me! I don't think that the liberal arts can be justified and, furthermore, I believe that the demand for justification should be resisted because it is always the demand that you account for what you do in someone else's terms, be they the terms of the state, or of the economy, or of the project of democracy. "Tell me, why should I as a businessman or a governor or a preacher of the Word, value what you do?" There is no answer to this question that does not involve preferring the values of the person who asks it to yours. The moment you acquiesce to the demand for justification, you have lost the game, because even if you succeed, what you will have done is acknowledge that your efforts are instrumental to some external purpose, and if you fail, as is more likely, you leave yourself open to the conclusion that what you do is really not needed. The spectacle of departments of French or Byzantine studies or classics attempting to demonstrate that the state or society or the world order benefits from their existence is embarrassing and pathetic. These and other programs are in decline not because they have failed to justify themselves, but because they have tried to.

The only self-respecting form justification could take is internal and circular. You value the activity because you like doing it and you like encouraging others to do it. Aside from that, there's not much to say. Kathryn Jakacbin makes my point (inadvertently) when she observes that while "inquiry into the phenomena, their origins, extent, implications would be enlightening," it would, if "untethered from a basic moral base also be weightless." Just so! I'm saying that "weightless" is good, because "enlightening," without any real-world payoff, is the business we're in. And I would give the same reply to Andrea, who is worried "that what we do as academics may be irrelevant to the active/political life." Let's hope so. In a similar vein, John Dillinger (a great name) complains that, "As it is now, academia in the US couldn't be more depoliticized, and more irrelevant." Would that were true, but read any big-city newspaper and you will find endless stories about politicized classrooms, stories that would never have been written if teachers followed the injunction to always academicize. You know you're doing your job if you have no comeback at all to the charge that, aside from the pleasures it offers you and your students, the academic study of materials and problems is absolutely useless.

My mention of the pleasures of the classroom brings me to a final point and to the complaint most often voiced by the respondents to the initial post: an academicized classroom will be an arid classroom, a classroom that produces mindless robots and "cold passionless non-critical thinkers" versed only in the bare facts, a classroom presided over by a drab technician who does little but show up and could just as easily have mailed it in. Nothing could be further from the truth. Excitement comes in many forms, and not all forms of excitement are appropriate to every activity. The excitement appropriate to the activity of college and university teaching is the excitement of analysis, of trying to make sense of something, be it a poem, an archive, a historical event, a database, a chemical reaction, whatever. Analysis may seem a passionless word denoting a passionless exercise, but I have seen students fired up to a pitch just short of physical combat arguing about whether Satan is the hero of *Paradise Lost* or whether John Rawls is correctly classified as a neo-Kantian or whether liberal democracies are capable of accommodating strong religious belief. The marshaling of evidence, the framing of distinctions, the challenging of the distinctions just framed, the parsing of dense texts—these are hard and exhilarating tasks, and the students who engage in them are anything but mindless, not despite but because they don't have their minds on the next election.

Of course, there will also be excitement in your class if you give it over to a discussion of what your students think about this or that hot-button issue. Lots of people will talk, and the talk will be heated, and everyone will go away feeling satisfied. But the satisfaction will be temporary, as will its effects, for the long-lasting pleasure of learning something will have been sacrificed to the ephemeral pleasure of exchanging uninformed opinions. You can glorify that exercise in self-indulgence by calling it interactive learning or engaged learning or ethical learning, but in the end it will be nothing more than a tale full of sound and fury, signifying nothing.

A Closing Argument (for Now)

NOVEMBER 12, 2006

The conversation about what teachers should and should not be doing in a college classroom could go on forever, and I may return to it in a future post, but for now I want to take one more stab at clarifying my position. Many of those who, in their comments on my last column ("Always Academicize: My Response to the Responses" [8.2]), find fault with what I say assert what is for them an obvious and incontrovertible truth: everything is, at bottom, political, and therefore any effort to avoid politics in the classroom by "academicizing" political questions is doomed to failure. Earl Brown Jr. reports that when he told a student that "the purpose of teaching was not to inculcate students with your values," she replied, but "all acts are political acts." He wanted to respond but found that he didn't know how ("I had no ready response"). I am happy to tell him that help has arrived.

Let's first get on the table a few examples of the classroom activities said by my respondents to be politically inflected, whether the instructor is aware of it or not. Peter Gardner observes that in a class in which the texts of John Milton or John Rawls (my examples) are being taught and debated, "the instructor has selected those texts and framed those arguments," and he asks, "Are those choices apolitical?" Anthony Dimatteo makes the same point: Fish's case falls apart, he maintains, "as soon as we begin to write a syllabus," for "we select some texts for our students to read and not others" and "we choose some topics to discuss and present some opposing views, but not just any topic and not just any view." C.B. generalizes the point: "Anything, any discourse, any position, any field of study," he insists, is political "in that it advocates certain positions and points of view with certain consequences, and as such, it excludes other interpretations." Michael M. O'Hara agrees and, for good measure, accuses me of bad scholarship: "[Fish] ignores countless years of scholarly analysis of the complex web of politics that surround and undergird nearly everything in the scholarly enterprise."

Well, it would be hard for me to ignore a strain of scholarly analysis to which I have been a prominent contributor, but that is a minor, and a personal, matter, and I pass it by. It is no doubt true that a web of politics surrounds and undergirds everything that goes on in higher education. Private and public sources fund colleges and universities, and they could have chosen—and some would say should have chosen—to fund something else. Within the college, resources are given to some departments and withheld from others. Within those departments, some courses are required for the major and others are not. And the instructors of those courses focus on some issues and downplay or completely marginalize others. At every level, then, selections are made that would have been made differently by others who had different ideas of what is valuable or central to the enterprise. And one could, I suppose, regard those differences as political, if the political is defined as the realm in which competing agendas, reflecting opposing views of the way things should be, fight it out.

Defined that generally, the realm of the political is in fact coincident with the entire realm of human behavior, and no activity escapes it. If I contribute money to the campaign of a candidate for public office, I have acted politically under anyone's understanding. Under the expanded understanding of the political, I have acted politically if I enter teaching rather than advertising. And I have also acted politically if I teach and write about Milton rather than Hemingway or Toni Morrison. Merely to put it that way, however, should alert us to the fact that by stretching the notion of the political to include everything, we have fudged distinctions that will return in force the moment some simple questions are posed. Is the political act (if you want to think of it that way) of teaching one author rather than another really the same as the political act of campaigning for one candidate rather than another? Is the political act (at least by this expanded definition of the political) of teaching a theological Milton (as I do) rather than a feminist Milton or a psychoanalytic Milton really the same as the political act of using Milton as a lens through which to view the depredations or glories of the Bush administration? The answer to both questions is no. These may all be political acts if the category of the political is taken to be all-inclusive, but that only means that unless you want to equate the choice of a text to teach with the choice of whether or not to support a war—and if you want to do that, there is nothing I could say to you and no reason for you to read me—at some point you're going to have to recover the commonsense differences you have sacrificed to a slogan. (Otherwise it's all forest and no trees.)

One way to do that and still keep the slogan is to say yes, everything is political, but the politics appropriate to the academy—the politics that involve deciding what readings will serve to introduce students to the field—is different from the politics of the ballot box: the politics that involve deciding when or whether security should trump civil liberties. In each case the politics will follow from the distinctive imperatives of the enterprise—in one case the imperative of being responsive to the present state of scholarship, in the other the imperative of determining what's good for the country. Partisanship will be a feature of both contexts—fights over the next department chair can be just as vicious as fights over the next Supreme Court justice—but it will not be the same partisanship, and to pretend that it is so that you can justify using the classroom to introduce an ideological agenda is to trivialize what is at stake in either venue. And if you do decide to say the sensible thing—yes, it's all politics, but the politics, and the decorums they bring with them, are not everywhere alike—there will be no longer any point to insisting that everything is political; that mantra will not be doing any work, and you might as well stop intoning it, a directive I would write into law if I could.

But isn't my own position—that ballot-box politics has no place in the politics of the classroom—itself political? This is the question raised by Cikarmak, who asks me to realize that what I advocate "is itself eminently political and susceptible to the very criticisms" I aim at others. François Comilliat is even more direct: "The kind of teaching ethics you defend is indeed an ethics, assuming principles, an active determination of what is good." Once again, this is absolutely correct, but it does not challenge or contradict my argument. I acknowledge that my position is an ethical one replete with values. And because it is a position contested by others, it is, by definition, political. But the politics it participates in will be the politics of the academy, where one debates approaches to knowledge (should we teach quantitative or qualitative methods in the social sciences?) rather than the politics of election campaigns where one debates courses of action (should we be isolationist or Wilsonian in our foreign policy?). The two kinds of politics are not only distinct; they can come apart in the behavior of a single person. Someone might disagree with me about what should and should not be done in the classroom and yet share my views about the environment or the deficit or the Iraq war. And conversely, an ally of mine in the curricular wars might part company with me when it comes to the question of the minimum wage.

In short, academic political allegiances and "real world" political allegiances are logically independent of one another, a point made inadvertently by William H. Payne when he declares that "Dr. Fish is a right-wing apologist" (echoing others who accuse me of wanting to uphold the current power structure or promote a conservative political position or undo the advances of the sixties). In the context of academic disputes, "right-wing" might be a plausible description of where I am, for whether the issue is the curriculum, the scope of academic freedom, the constraints on interpretation, the requirement for tenure, or the form of university governance, I tend to be on the conservative side. But out in the world I almost always vote Democratic and support the initiatives associated with the liberal left. And I am not the only one who displays one political profile in the precincts of the university, where the issues are professional, and quite another when the school day is over and the conversation turns to what the next Congress should do. The point, again, is that the "everything is political" argument, even if it is true at some very high level of generality, in no way undermines the distinction between what is appropriate when you are speaking at a political rally and what is appropriate when you are speaking to students in front of a class.

The mistake of thinking that politics and political options are always the same no matter what the context or situation is a variant of the mistake of thinking that one's responsibility to truth is always the same no matter what the context or situation. L. A. Marland declares that "unlike Fish I believed and continue to believe in the truth." The reasoning, as I take it, is that because I urge an analysis of political controversies and inveigh against coming down on one side or the other in the classroom, I must be a postmodern relativist who disdains notions of truth and objectivity. (This is the burden of several posts put up by Christian Haesemeyer.) In fact, the heart of my position (as it has been elaborated in many writings) is that determining the truth of something—whether it be the meaning of a poem or the causes of an event or the neural mechanisms of the reading process—is the prime academic activity. It's the business we're in, and I reject the arguments of those who think we are in some other business, like the fashioning of moral character or the production of democratic citizens or the inculcation of tolerance and respect for others. These may all be worthwhile endeavors (although I have my doubts about the last one), but they are not academic endeavors, and it would be wrong, I contend, to give the classroom over to them and take precious time away from the search for truth.

But (and here's the rub) the truth you are in search of as a teacher must be an academic truth, not truth generally, or the truth about anything and everything. There are many who believe, with Saint Augustine, that the truth and meaning of any matter—scientific, literary, historical—is to be found in the fact that Christ died for our sins and redeemed us on the condition that we accept him as the foundation of our lives. For such believers, Jesus Christ is the answer to every question. But unless you teach in a sectarian college where that answer is to some extent mandated, you are committed to giving answers in the terms provided by the academic history of the question. You may be fully persuaded that it was the hand of God that gave victory to the Allies in World War II, but if you're teaching a history class on World War II, you are obliged to talk about military strategies, troop levels, supply lines, weather conditions, weaponry, and the like. Or, to take an example always in the news, you may be fully persuaded that God created the world and everything in it, but if you're teaching biology, that proposition cannot be seriously advanced; not because it isn't true—and how would an academic inquiry settle that question anyway?—but because either affirming or denying its truth would contribute nothing to the programs of research and experimentation engaged in by biologists. Just as the inevitable presence of politics in every realm of human activity does not mean that you are always being political in the same way, so does the centrality of truth to every human inquiry not mean that every truth you hold to is everywhere relevant or to the point. A commitment to truth, rather than telling against my insistence that academic work has its own integrity, provides the strongest support for it.

The last resort of those who are reluctant to leave their political positions at the classroom door is to reveal them up front in the belief that by doing so they insulate their students from any undue influence. The students, says Natika Newton, will be "reassured of a balanced presentation if the professor states her viewpoint at the beginning, and says that she will take pains to present both sides equally." Viewpoint about what? If the professor has a viewpoint about an academic question—is string theory a powerful conceptual tool or a speculative fiction that proves nothing because it can prove anything?—she should not merely state it at the beginning; she should argue for it, and work hard to persuade students of its truth. If the professor has a viewpoint about a political question—should illegal immigrants be given amnesty?—she should not state it at all because coming to political conclusions, as opposed to academic conclusions, is not what either she or her students are there for. Announcing your political views at the outset as a way of alerting students to your possible bias makes sense only if it is the business of the class to approve some or other political view at the end of the day; and if you do announce your political views, even in the spirit of full disclosure, you will be sending the message that approving a political view is indeed the business of the class. If, on the other (and better) hand, you start right out subjecting the topic to an academic interrogation—inquiring into matters of structure, history, influence, and so on—the nakedly political questions will never emerge and there will be nothing to insulate the students from. The rule is (or should be) that with respect to academic disputes, the instructor, rather than taking pains to present both sides equally, should steer students in the direction of the side she considers right; but with respect to political disputes, the instructor should bring opposing sides into the discussion only as objects of analysis and never as objects of choice. Being biased toward an academic position is a good thing. (It shows that you care.) Entering into a relationship of any affective kind with a political position is not. That has been my message from the beginning, and I declare it once again in the hope that you will keep those cards and letters coming.

8.4

The Two Languages of Academic Freedom

FEBRUARY 8, 2009

Last week we came to the section on academic freedom in my course on the law of higher education, and I posed this hypothetical to the students: Suppose you were a member of a law firm or a midlevel executive in a corporation and you skipped meetings or came late, blew off assignments or altered them according to your whims, abused your colleagues, and were habitually rude to clients. What would happen to you?

The chorus of answers cascaded immediately: "I'd be fired." Now, I continued, imagine the same scenario and the same set of behaviors, but this time you're a tenured professor in a North American university. What then?

I answered this one myself: "You'd be celebrated as a brave nonconformist, a tilter against orthodoxies, a pedagogical visionary, and an exemplar of academic freedom."

My assessment of the way in which some academics contrive to turn serial irresponsibility into a form of heroism under the banner of academic freedom has now been at once confirmed and challenged by events at the University of Ottawa, where the administration announced on February 6 that it has "recommended to the Board of Governors the dismissal with cause of Professor Denis Rancourt from his faculty position."[1] Earlier, Rancourt, a tenured professor of physics, had been suspended from teaching and banned from campus. When he defied the ban, he was taken away in handcuffs and charged with trespassing.

What had Rancourt done to merit such treatment? According to the *Globe and Mail*, Rancourt's sin was to have informed his students on the first day of class that "he had already decided their marks: Everybody was getting an A+."[2]

But that, as the saying goes, is only the tip of the iceberg. Underneath it is the mass of reasons Rancourt gives for his grading policy and for many of the other actions that have infuriated his dean, distressed his colleagues (a third of whom signed a petition against him), and delighted his partisans.

Rancourt is a self-described anarchist and an advocate of "critical pedagogy," a style of teaching derived from the assumption (these are Rancourt's words) "that our societal structures . . . represent the most formidable instrument of oppression and exploitation ever to occupy the planet."[3]

Among those structures is the university in which Rancourt works and by which he is paid. But the fact of his position and compensation does not insulate the institution from his strictures and assaults; for, he insists, "schools and universities supply the obedient workers and managers and professionals that adopt and apply [the] system's doctrine—knowingly or unknowingly."[4]

It is this belief that higher education, as we know it, is simply a delivery system for a regime of oppressors and exploiters that underlies Rancourt's refusal to grade his students. Grading, he says, "is a tool of coercion in order to make obedient people."[5]

It turns out that another tool of coercion is the requirement that professors actually teach the course described in the college catalog, the course students think they are signing up for. Rancourt battles against this form of coercion by employing a strategy he calls "squatting"—"where one openly takes an existing course and does with it something different." That is, you take a currently unoccupied structure, move in and make it the home for whatever activities you wish to engage in. "Academic squatting is needed," he says, "because universities are dictatorships . . . run by self-appointed executives who serve capital interests."[6]

Rancourt first practiced squatting when he decided that he "had to do something more than give a 'better' physics course." Accordingly, he took the Physics and Environment course that had been assigned to him and transformed it into a course on political activism, not a course about political activism, but a course in which political activism is urged—"an activism course about confronting authority and hierarchical structures directly or through defiant or non-subordinate assertion in order to democratize power in the workplace, at school, and in society."

Clearly, squatting itself is just such a "defiant or non-subordinate assertion." Rancourt does not merely preach his philosophy. He practices it.

This sounds vaguely admirable until you remember what Rancourt is, in effect, saying to those who employ him:

> I refuse to do what I have contracted to do, but I will do everything in my power to subvert the enterprise you administer. Besides, you're just dictators, and it is my obligation to undermine you even as I demand that you pay me and confer on me the honorific title of professor. And, by the way, I am entitled to do so by the doctrine of academic freedom, which I define as "the ideal under which professors and students are autonomous and design their own development and interactions."

Of course, as Rancourt recognizes, if this is how academic freedom is defined, its scope is infinite and one can't stop with squatting: "The next step is academic hijacking, where students tell a professor that she can stay or leave but that this is what they are going to do and these are the speakers they are going to invite." O, brave new world!

The record shows exchanges of letters between Rancourt and Dean Andre E. Lalonde and letters from each of them to Marc Jolicoeur, chairman of the Board of Governors. There is something comical about some of these exchanges when the dean asks Rancourt to tell him why he is not guilty of insubordination and Rancourt replies that insubordination is his job, and that, rather than ceasing his insubordinate activities, he plans to expand them. Lalonde complains that Rancourt "does not acknowledge any impropriety regarding his conduct." Rancourt tells Jolicoeur that "Socrates did not give grades to students," and boasts that everything he has done was done "with the purpose of making the University of Ottawa a better place," a place "of greater democracy." In other words, "I am the bearer of a saving message and those who need it most will not hear it and respond by persecuting me." It is the cry of every would-be messiah.

Rancourt's views are the opposite of those announced by a court in an Arizona case where the issue was also whether a teaching method could be the basis of dismissal. Noting that the university had concluded that the plaintiff's "methodology was not successful," the court declared, "Academic freedom is not a doctrine to insulate a teacher from evaluation by the institution that employs him" (*Carley v. Arizona*, 1987).

The Arizona court thinks of academic freedom as a doctrine whose scope is defined by the purposes and protocols of the institution and its limited purposes. Rancourt thinks of academic freedom as a local instance of a global project whose goal is nothing less than the freeing of revolutionary energies, not only in the schools but everywhere.

It is the difference between being concerned with the establishing and implementing of workplace-specific procedures and being concerned with the wholesale transformation of society. It is the difference between wanting to teach a better physics course and wanting to save the world. Given such divergent views, not only is reconciliation between the parties impossible; conversation itself is impossible. The dispute can only be resolved by an essentially political decision, and in this case, the narrower concept of academic freedom has won. But only till next time.

1. Erin Anderssen, "Professor Makes His Mark, but It Costs Him His Job," *Globe and Mail*, February 6, 2009.

2. Ibid.

3. Denis G. Rancourt, "Academic Squatting: A Democratic Method of Curriculum Development," *Activist Teacher* blog, April 13, 2007, http://activistteacher.blogspot .com/2007/04/academic-squatting-democratic-method-of.html.

4. Ibid.

5. Jesse Freeston, "Dismissing Critical Pedagogy: Denis Rancourt vs. University of Ottawa," *rabble.ca*, January 12, 2009, http://rabble.ca/news/dismissing-critical -pedagogy-denis-rancourt-vs-university-ottawa.

6. All subsequent quotes regarding Rancourt are from http://activistteacher .blogspot.com/2007/04/academic-squatting-democratic-method-of.html.

Are Academics Different?

FEBRUARY 15, 2009

Last week's column about Denis Rancourt ("The Two Languages of Academic Freedom" [8.4]), a University of Ottawa professor who is facing dismissal for awarding A-plus grades to his students on the first day of class, and for turning the physics course he had been assigned into a course on political activism, drew mostly negative comments.

The criticism most often voiced was that by holding Rancourt up as an example of the excesses indulged in by those who invoke academic freedom, I had committed the fallacy of generalizing from a single outlier case to the behavior of an entire class: "Is the Rancourt case one of a thousand such findings this year, or is it the most outlandish in 10 years?" (Jack, No. 88).

It may be outlandish because it is so theatrical, but one could argue, as one reader seemed to, that Rancourt carries out to its logical extreme a form of behavior many display in less dramatic ways. "How about a look at the class of professors who . . . duck their responsibilities ranging from the simple courtesies (arrival on time, prepared for meetings . . .) to the essentials (lack of rigor in teaching and standards . . .)" (h.c. ecco, No. 142). What links Rancourt and these milder versions of academic acting-out is a conviction that academic freedom confers on professors the right to order (or disorder) the workplace in any way they see fit, irrespective of the requirements of the university that employs them.

This conviction, as Matthew Finkin and Robert Post have reported, is widespread and isn't going away.[1] "[A]cademic freedom has in recent decades increasingly come to be conceived of as an individual right to be asserted against all forms of university regulation." It may be that most of those who hold this view would stop far short of the actions performed by Rancourt, but what Finkin and Post call "this antinomianism" (the refusal to accept external constraints on the promptings of conscience and the inner light) is, as they say, inherently "corrosive," and what it corrodes is any sense of responsibility to the institution.

The response many would make to this accusation is that a teacher's responsibility is to the ideals of truth and justice and not to the parochial rules of an institution in thrall to intellectual, economic, and political orthodoxies. "Democracy," insists G.Tod Slone (No. 228) "clearly depends on . . . professors willing to risk career for truth and integrity." Academics, in this view, exercise freedom only when they subject the norms of the institution to a higher standard and act accordingly. They must, says mattm (No. 247), "retain the right to ask the question of what constitutes academic freedom—without any deference to the interests of the university whatsoever." Here, nakedly, is the reasoning I attributed to Rancourt: the university may pay my salary, provide me with a platform, benefits, students, an office, secretarial help, and societal status, but I retain my right to act in disregard of its interests; indeed, I am obliged by academic freedom to do so.

It would be hard to imagine another field of endeavor in which employees believe that being attentive to their employer's goals and wishes is tantamount to a moral crime. But this is what many (not all) academics believe, and if pressed they will support their belief by invoking a form of academic exceptionalism, the idea that while colleges and universities may bear some of the marks of places of employment—workdays, promotions, salaries, vacations, meetings, and so on—they are really places in which something much more rarefied than a mere job goes on. John in Boston (No. 229) declares, "Your first move to say that the professor was hired to perform a job is evidence enough to prove that you don't understand education; it is not a path that leads in a certain direction," and certainly not a direction mandated by an administrative hierarchy.

One sees from this and similar statements that an understanding of academic freedom as a right unbound by the conditions of employment goes hand in hand with, and is indeed derived from, an understanding of higher education as something more than a job to be performed; rather, it is a calling to be taken up and followed wherever it may lead, even if it leads to a flouting of the norms that happen to be in place in the bureaucratic spaces that house (but do not define) this exalted enterprise. If that's the kind of work you think yourself to be doing, it follows that you would think yourself free to pursue it unconstrained by external impositions; you would think of academic freedom as E. Mucemn (No. 67) thinks of it: "Ultimately, academic freedom is nothing different than the freedom of human mind, as immense as the size of the universe."

The alternative is to understand academic freedom as a much more earthbound thing, as a freedom tailored to and constrained by the requirements of a particular job. And this would mean reasoning from the nature of the job to a specification of the degree of latitude those who are employed to do it can be said to enjoy. This is Finkin's and Post's position: "Academic freedom is not the freedom to speak or teach just as one wishes. It is the freedom to pursue the scholarly profession . . . according to the norms and standards of that profession."[2]

Statements like this are likely to provoke the objection that "Academe should not be a Business or a Corporation" (G.Tod Sloane, No. 228). But that is a fake issue. Saying that higher education has a job to do (and that the norms and standards of that job should control professorial behavior) is not the same as saying that its job is business. It is just to say that it is a job and not a sacred vocation, and that while it may differ in many ways from other jobs—there is no discernible product, and projects may remain uncompleted for years without negative consequences for researchers—its configurations can still be ascertained (it is not something ineffable) and serve as the basis of both expectations and discipline.

So these are the two conceptions of academic freedom that are in play: academic freedom as the freedom to do the academic job (understood by reference to university norms and requirements); and academic freedom as the freedom to chart your own way, to go boldly where no man or woman has gone before, constrained only by your inner sense of what is right and true.

It is sometimes said that the grander conception of academic freedom is as large in its scope as the freedom guaranteed to citizens by the First Amendment. In fact, as the case law shows, the scope claimed is even larger. In *United States v. Doe* (1972) a researcher argued that his academic freedom rights were infringed when a federal grand jury asked him questions about his research. He claimed "scholar's privilege," in response to which the government said that no such privilege was "to be found in the province of jurisprudence." The court agreed and declined to "make scholars a uniquely privileged class." But the decision went the other way in *Dow Chemical v. Allen* (1982) when a court ruled that University of Wisconsin researchers could not be compelled by a subpoena to disclose notes, reports, and working papers relating to a dispute about the toxicity of herbicides. The court declared that absent a compelling state interest, any such intrusion into the world of research would have the effect of "chilling the exercise of academic freedom." In response, Dow contended that "the First Amendment interests at stake at this case are no greater than those involved in the ordinary case of enforcement of a subpoena." That is, academics are citizens like any other and should not be treated as a different, special class. While that argument lost in *Dow*, it won in *Wright v. Jeep* (1982) when a professor asserted that he was exempt from a requirement to testify because as a researcher he had "a right to refuse to give or produce evidence and . . . a denial of this right would have a chilling effect." The court replied that "the possibility of being subpoenaed to testify exists for everyone" and that a professor "is no different than any other witness who may be called on to give evidence."

That, of course, is the key question. Are academics different, and if so, in what ways, and to what extent do the differences legitimate a degree of freedom not enjoyed by the members of other professions? These and related questions were debated in *Urofsky v. Gilmore* (2000). In that case professors from a number of state colleges and universities in Virginia contended that their right of academic freedom was infringed by a law requiring state employers to gain permission from a supervisor before accessing sexually explicit materials on state-owned computers. Judge Wilkins, writing for the majority, treated the complaining professors as employees rather than as possessors of a special right, and observed that "It cannot be doubted that in order to pursue its legitimate goals effectively, the state must have the ability to control the manner in which its employees discharge their duties." The professors had anticipated this reasoning and maintained that even if the law was "valid as to the majority of state employees, it violates the First Amendment freedom rights of professors at state colleges and universities." Or, in other words, we understand the legal point, but it doesn't apply to us, for we're different.

Wilkins heard this argument as a claim by professors to have a constitutional right to determine for themselves "without the input of the university (and perhaps even contrary to the university's desires)" the manner in which they would pursue their scholarship and teaching. But he found no basis in law for this view, and concluded that while academic freedom may be a "professional norm"—it represents the profession's thinking about the optimal conditions required for its members to do their work—it is not "a constitutional right," and thus it cannot be invoked or enforced in a judicial proceeding.

Chief Judge Wilkinson, concurring in the opinion but dissenting from the majority's reasoning, disagreed. He noted the scorn with which his brethren greeted the claim of "academic privilege" and the assertion that "professors possess a special constitutional right of academic freedom" because "the academy has a special contribution to make to society." Citing the many passages in Supreme Court decisions in which paeans to academic freedom were given full voice, Wilkinson finds ample evidence in the record to persuade him that "academic speech" is a matter of "public concern" and so rises to the level of constitutional notice.

What exactly would the public's interest in academic speech be? One answer is provided by law professor J. Peter Byrne, who argues in a critique of Urofsky (*Journal of College and University Law*, 2004) that a constitutional right of academic freedom exists "not for the benefit of the professors themselves but for the good of society."[3] Why? Because it is only in universities that a certain kind of speech—"serious and communal, seeking to improve the understanding"—flourishes. The special protection afforded to professors leaves them free "to articulate and critique more knowledgeable and complex assertions . . . in ways not possible on street corners or on television." Now I have my elitist moments, but this is a bit much. Only professors, we're being told, do real thinking; other people accept whatever they hear on TV and retail popular (but uninformed) wisdom on street corners. Thus, while there is no reason to extend special protections in the workplace to nonacademic speech—which is worthless—there is a good reason to extend them to the incomparably finer utterances of the professorial class.

Once again we see that the argument for academic freedom as a right rather than as a desirable feature of professional life rests on the assertion of academic exceptionalism. What I have been trying to say is that while academic work is different—it's not business, it's not medicine, it's not politics—and while the difference should be valued, academic work should not be put into a category so special that any constraints on it, whether issuing from university administrators or from the state as an employer, are regarded as sins against morality, truth, and the American Way.

It should be possible to acknowledge the distinctiveness of academic work and to put in place conditions responsive to that distinctiveness without making academic work into a holy mission taken up by a superior race of beings. One can argue, for example, that since it is the job of the academy to transmit and advance knowledge, there should be no preemptive anointing or demonizing of any particular viewpoint or line of inquiry; not because such preemptings would be an assault on truth, but because they would impede the doing of the job. Free inquiry means free in relation to the goals of the enterprise, not free in the sense of being answerable to nothing.

Those who would defend academic freedom would do well to remove the halo it often wears. Stay away from big abstractions and remain tethered to work on the ground. If you say, "This is the job and if we are to do it properly, these conditions must be in place," you'll get a better hearing than you would if you say, "We're professors and you're not, so leave us alone to do what we like."

1. Matthew Finkin and Robert Post, *For the Common Good: Principles of American Academic Freedom* (New Haven, CT: Yale University Press, 2011). I reviewed the book in my column, Opinionator, *New York Times* online, November 23, 2008, http://opinionator.blogs.nytimes.com/2008/11/23/an-authoritative-word-on-academic-freedom/.

2. Finkin and Post, *For the Common Good*, 149.

3. J. Peter Byrne, "Constitutional Academic Freedom in Scholarship and in Court," *Chronicle Review*, Chronicle of Higher Education, January 5, 2001, http://chronicle.com/weekly/v47/i17/17b01301.htm.

The Kushner Flap:
Much Ado about Nothing

MAY 8, 2011

On May 5, the historian Ellen Schrecker of Yeshiva University gave back an honorary degree she had received from John Jay College because the playwright Tony Kushner had been denied the same honor by the CUNY Board of Trustees. At the urging of a trustee who objected to Kushner's views on Israel, the nomination, which had been forwarded by the faculty and administration of John Jay, was tabled. (Kushner had been informed of the impending honor.)

Professor Schrecker explained in a letter to the board's chairman, Benno Schmidt, that she "could not remain silent when the very institution that once recognized the value of academic freedom now demeans it."[1] That doesn't sound right. Kushner is not an academic and so he has no academic freedom that can be demeaned. And his more general freedom—his freedom as an artist and a citizen—has not been infringed on by what the board did. He can still write and speak and say pretty much what he wants. He just won't be saying it at a CUNY graduation ceremony this spring.

Schrecker anticipates the point and moves to preempt it by offering an expansive definition of academic freedom: "That freedom is more than just the protection of the teaching, research and public activities of college and university teachers. It also extends to the entire campus, fostering the openness and creativity that allow American higher education to flourish." But a freedom spread so generously over the entire campus loses its contact with the limiting adjective "academic." No longer tied to the performance of specific tasks, it isn't clear what this freedom protects unless we are to understand (and this seems to be Schrecker's understanding) that it protects everything that goes on. A concept of freedom so diffuse loses its usefulness because it becomes hard to say with any precision where and when it has been abridged. What is required if the concept is to have any cogency are distinctions that allow us to say one thing is a matter of academic freedom and another is not.

The scholarly literature on academic freedom identifies four locations or arenas where it can properly be invoked: the classroom, the
research library or laboratory, off-campus pronouncements on matters of public concern (extramural expression), and on-campus criticism of the university's policies (intramural expression). Other things
that go on in a university fall under the category "extracurricular"—
that is, to the side of the core academic enterprise although related
to it. The category includes lectures by outside speakers, noontime
rallies, graduation ceremonies, athletic events, and, yes, the awarding
of honorary degrees. No doubt these extra-academic activities take
place in the context of rules and protocols, but the rules are rules of
thumb and the protocols are more prudential than principled.

Take honorary degrees. I have been fortunate enough to have received them, and I have served on a committee charged with the
responsibility of evaluating nominations. Schrecker complains that
the CUNY trustees "let extraneous political considerations override
educational priorities," but in the meetings I attended, "extraneous"
considerations governed the conversation. What sector of society
or industry has not been represented in recent years? Which of the
nominees has a connection with the university? Which are donors?
Which are politically connected in ways that might benefit the university? And which are controversial in ways that might generate unwel-
come publicity? There were, I recall, differences of opinion of the kind
that apparently marked the CUNY trustees' meetings (seven trustees
voted to approve Kushner). I remember political and ideological objections to some candidates, and in such cases the wisdom of consensus was invoked and contested candidacies were put to one side,
perhaps to be revisited in another year. The uproar surrounding the
tabling of Kushner's nominations suggests that something remarkable and untoward had been done, but my experience indicates that
there was nothing exceptional about the board's action, which, while
it may have been unwise, is pretty much business as usual.

Thinking clearly about this matter requires making the distinctions Schrecker blurs when she declares that "censoring outside
speakers, including honorary degree recipients, is like refusing to hire
instructors or firing them because of their reputed political views."
No, it isn't. Refusing to hire or firing instructors because of their political views is against the law; anyone who could show in a court
of law that he or she had been a victim of such treatment would get
both a job and a large settlement in the bargain. Refusing to award an

honorary degree even for political reasons involves no penalties—
the disappointed non-honoree doesn't have a case—except for the
penalty of looking small-minded, biased, and stupid. (More about
that later.) And besides, no honorary degree recipient has been censored. To claim that Kushner has been censored is to say that getting
an honorary degree is a right like the right of free expression and that
not getting one is a First Amendment cause of action. The only ag-
grieved parties here are the faculty and administration of John Jay,
and they haven't been censored either; they have been overridden.

Almost everything said about this brouhaha is beside the point.
Some, including Kushner, complained that he was not given a chance
for rebuttal, as if an honorary degree were something you stand for
at an open meeting. Dr. Barbara Bowen, the president of the Professional Staff Congress (PSC), calls the failure to honor Kushner "an attempt to close off and narrow public debate."[2] If that was the board's
purpose, it certainly failed; public debate now surrounds its action.
But in fact the board has no obligation to the state of public debate.
Its only obligation is to decide whom to honor, and that decision is
one it makes in private, according to criteria it alone establishes. Jeffrey Wiesenfeld, the fiercely anti-Kushner trustee, got it right when he
declared that "An honorary degree is wholly within the discretion of
the board to grant."[3]

This does not mean that the board's action is immune from criticism. A good case could be made for saying that it was dumb. It is or
should be a rule of thumb that in matters like this, you don't ask for
trouble. No recommendation by a college for an honorary degree has
been turned down in the CUNY system since 1961. Turning down this
one, especially in the explosive context of opposing views of Israel,
would seem to be courting trouble, and the courtship has been all
too successful. (Of course, approving Kushner's nomination would
have also caused a furor, but the trustees could have said they were
deferring to John Jay and thus spread the blame.) Now the board is
poised to generate additional flak by changing its mind at a meeting
called for Monday at 6:00 p.m.[4] Having offended a number of constituencies already, the trustees now have a chance to offend the rest by
flip-flopping. A lamentable spectacle may get more lamentable still.

But, someone might object, maybe they'll get it right this time.
There is no right to be gotten. To make the point once again, this is
not an academic, a moral, a philosophical, or an educational moment;
it is a moment of ceremony and self-presentation. The goal is to do

what you do with as little fuss and fallout as possible. That's getting it right, and the possibility of doing that has long since gone with the wind.

1. Ellen Schrecker, "An Open Letter to the CUNY Board of Trustees from Ellen Schrecker," *Chronicle of Higher Education*, May 5, 2011.

2. Francis Clark, "Statement from PSC President Dr. Barbara Bowen on CUNY Trustees' Decision to Table Motion on Granting an Honorary Degree to Tony Kushner," PSC.Cuny, May 4, 2011, http://www.psc-cuny.org/statement-psc-president-dr-barbara -bowen-cuny-trustees'-decision-table-motion-granting-honorary-degr.

3. New York Association of Scholars, "CUNY Trustees Stand Up Against Faculty's Anti-Israel Sentiments—In Vain," National Association of Scholars (NAS), May 11, 2011, http://www.nas.org/articles/CUNY_Trustees_Stand_Up_Against_Facultys_Anti-Israel _Sentiments_-_In_Vain.

4. Winnie Hu, "After Reversal, Honor Is Likely for Kushner," *New York Times* on-line, May 6, 2011, http://www.nytimes.com/2011/05/07/nyregion/after-reversal-honor-is -likely-for-kushner.html.

Sex, the Koch Brothers, and Academic Freedom

MAY 16, 2011

More than a few of the respondents to my column "The Kushner Flap: Much Ado about Nothing" (8.6), about CUNY's on-again-off-again-on-again awarding of an honorary degree to Tony Kushner, say that while I may be correct about the "technical" definition of academic freedom, I miss the larger point. That's because there isn't one. A board of trustees with every right to make a decision made it in a way that (a) ran counter to its previous practice (b) permitted a single member (Jeffrey Wiesenfeld) to derail a process that had seemed to be on a familiar track, and (c) put CUNY right in the middle of the briar patch called the Israeli-Palestinian conflict. Maladroit, unfortunate, and (as I said) dumb. But that's it. It was just the board screwing up with the predictable public-relations disaster as the result. No one's freedom was curtailed, no one's speech was censored, no harm—except to the board's reputation and by extension to CUNY's—was done.

Because Wiesenfeld's objections were to Kushner's views on Israel, the uproar that followed the board's decision to table his nomination quickly escalated into a shouting match between those who said that Israel was engaged in ethnic cleansing and those who replied that people who said that were anti-Semites and/or self-hating Jews. The responses to my column followed the same pattern. No one wanted to hear the topic of academic freedom "parsed" (a word used in derision by one reader, as if parsing something, trying to get it right, were a crime). MSP Shiloh complained that "Dr. Fish misdirects our attention to the arcane and off topic of the academic honorary degree process," when "[t]his was, and is, about Israel's persecution" of Palestinians. Other respondents were just as sure that "this was, and is, about" a university honoring a "self-righteous hack" (mcghostoflectricity) who spews "current-day Palestinian propaganda" (neilrobert). Both sides are wrong, not about Israel—I did not and will not come down on that issue—but about what "this" is about. It's about institutional ineptness, a relatively small matter that nevertheless can teach us some lessons. The back-and-forth trading of ritual insults is hardly edifying, but a proper understanding of what academic freedom is might be.

My general point is that academic freedom is a useful notion only if it is narrowly defined. More things escape its ambit than fall within it. Lawyerjonathan declares that "the overriding purpose of the university is supposed to be free inquiry and the pursuit of truth." Not quite. The pursuit of truth is what is done in classrooms and laboratories, and that is why those activities should be protected from outside interference. Truth cannot be pursued if constraints in the form of political or ideological preferences block the search for it. Other activities not in the pursuit-of-truth business merit no such protection because there is no specifically academic value to their being allowed to occur without constraint. Mike Munk recalls that when he was a student in the '50s, the president of his college vetoed a speaker his group had wanted to invite. He was (and remains) "outraged that our 'academic freedom' to hear and debate ideas on campus was violated." It's good that he puts academic freedom in quotes because there is no freedom to hear outside speakers; it's a nice extra, it's good entertainment, and I'm all for it, but its curtailment violates nothing.

Sasha cooke thinks that the John Jay faculty's "right to free expression" was violated because its choice of Kushner was originally disallowed. In the same vein, Joe Gould wonders "what effect the Board's decision on the academic freedom of the faculty who chose Mr. Kushner for the award." None at all. The faculty expressed itself freely and its free expression was then trumped by the free expression of a body authorized to do so, and in the future the faculty is free to express itself again.

Warren insists that "academic freedom surely extends to the process of receiving academic honors," but that is to hang too much on a word. True, the honor Kushner was at first denied and now may receive was awarded in a setting presided over by the academy, but it was not an academic honor in the sense of being awarded for academic reasons or according to academic criteria that could be the basis of an academic freedom claim; the reasons for giving honorary degrees are varied, and the criteria (such as they are) are all over the place.

Jstafura asks, "If the awarding of honorary degrees isn't academic then what is it?" As I indicated in the previous column (8.6), it's a tool for fund-raising, recruiting, payback for political help, publicity, and, occasionally, for rewarding academic or artistic achievement. A corollary question is, if the awarding of honorary degrees is not implicated in academic freedom issues, then what is?

Two examples recently in the news provide an answer. In early March, Professor John Michael Bailey of Northwestern University allowed a couple to perform a live sex act in front of the students in his course on Human Sexuality. (Attendance at the presentation was optional.) The man brought the (naked) woman to orgasm with the help of a device with a name this newspaper will not print.

Bailey defended himself by saying that such "events" provide "useful examples and extensions of concepts students learn about in traditional academic ways."[1] This statement amounts to acknowledging that the live-sex demonstration was outside the boundaries of academic practice (Bailey might respond that he was stretching the envelope), and it's an easy step to conclude that it is not protected by academic freedom, by an instructor's freedom to bring into a class whatever materials he thinks appropriate so long as they serve a legitimate pedagogical end. Bailey claims the live-sex demo did serve such an end because it was an extension of one of his course's main themes, the diversity of sexual experience.

But Northwestern president Morton Schapiro, after a brief period when the dean and a university spokesman waffled and murmured "academic freedom," declared, "I simply do not believe this was appropriate . . . or in keeping with Northwestern University's academic mission."[2] That, of course, is the question: Was the sexual exhibition staged for a valid educational purpose or was it, as researcher Robin Mathy believes, a case of confusing "voyeuristic excitement" with education.[3] If it was the first, academic freedom kicks in; if it was the second, it doesn't, and that's because academic freedom is for academic activities and not for everything that happens to go on in a university building.

The controversy continues. The Northwestern administration has assigned Bailey other courses and said that this course will not be offered in the coming academic year while the curriculum is being reviewed. Now academic freedom complaints are coming from those who say that Bailey's rights were violated by his not having been allowed to teach a particular course and that the course's rights were violated by its not being given in a particular year. The administration's action, said Simon LeVay, author of the course's textbook, amounted to "disrespecting the subject" of human sexuality.[4] Emory professor Kim Wallen, coauthor with LeVay of a letter to President Schapiro, announced, "There's great concern about academic freedom."[5]

It's hard to see why. No one owns a course; no course has a right to be given; and no subject has a claim on university time and money. LeVay and Wallen are behaving as so many in the Kushner controversy did; they are crying academic freedom whenever a university does something they don't like, and by doing so, they cheapen the concept.

In contrast, the invocation of academic freedom is certainly to the point in my second example, the controversy at Florida State University over a gift given to the Economics Department in 2008 by a foundation funded by the ultraconservative Koch brothers. The gift was given to support the creation of two new appointments. There's nothing untoward about that; it is routine for corporations and foundations to underwrite or augment the funding of faculty appointments. (At Johns Hopkins I held a Kenan chair, the support for which came from an oil fortune.) Sometimes the funds are provided without specifying a subject or a discipline; sometimes the gift is more targeted. This gift was very targeted; it was to support the teaching of free-market, antiregulatory economics.

That's where the trouble begins. Is the foundation funding the study of free-market economics—a perfectly respectable academic subject—or is it mandating that free-market economics be promoted in the classroom? Is it a gift intended to stimulate research the conclusions of which cannot be known in advance, or is it a gift intended to amplify a conclusion—free-market economics is good; regulation is bad—the philanthropists have already reached and want to broadcast using Florida State University as a megaphone? If it is the second, Florida State University courts the danger the doctrine of academic freedom was designed to avoid (see the 1915 statement of the then fledgling American Association of University Professors [AAUP]), the danger of allowing an outside constituency to take control of academic proceedings and dictate academic decisions.

Evidence that a line may have been crossed is provided by the contract between the foundation and the university. Foundation representatives serve on the search committee and have the power to veto candidates. If the selected professors fail to perform in a manner the foundations approves, it will withdraw its support. This, of course, means that the foundation in effect monitors and assesses academic performance. On the other side, the faculty has the decisive voice in making appointments; it need not accept the candidates the foundation favors, and in fact the two who were finally hired were not on the foundation's preferred list, although we can presume the foundation did not find them objectionable.

In a telephone conversation with me, Florida State University (FSU) president Eric J. Barron (who was not in office when this all went down) explained that while the foundation's representatives could have exercised a veto, it never came to that. He added that if the new faculty members ever failed to meet the foundation's expectations and its gift was withdrawn, the university would step in and provide the necessary support. He acknowledged that these arrangements might make people nervous—some administration members expressed reservations in 2008 and changes were made to the contract—but he insisted that, despite press characterizations of the situation, FSU had not sold its soul. (I am not a stranger to such situations. My first assignment as a dean at the University of Illinois at Chicago [UIC] was to finalize the details of a gift given to the university for the funding of a Catholic studies program. Many of the issues that arose at FSU arose at UIC and were negotiated.)

Barron makes a reasonable case, but it is undercut by the words of David Rasmussen, dean of the College of Social Science, a signatory to the contract, at FSU. Rasmussen is either tone deaf or disingenuous. His account of the affair is anodyne: "The Economics department says here are the two people we really like, goes to the advisory board and says, will you approve these two people, and they say yes."[6]

In short, what's the problem? The problem is that the sequence unfolds under the threat of an adverse action by a nonacademic entity. Rasmussen says he is "sure some faculty will say this is not exactly consistent with their view of academic freedom."[7] The implication is that "their view" is a minority view or an overfastidious view, but the view that university hiring and firing procedures shouldn't dance to the tune of an external constituency is absolutely mainstream and is the core of what academic freedom stands for.

Rasmussen's most egregious comments concern another matter. BB&T, the bank holding company, funds an ethics course on the condition that Ayn Rand's *Atlas Shrugged* be required reading. (That might constitute cruel and unusual punishment.) The reasoning, offered by BB&T representative John Allison, is that "most universities are dominated by liberal professors." (I have argued elsewhere that a scholar's political views and his or her disciplinary views are independent variables.) Rasmussen thinks this is just fine. "If somebody says, 'We're willing to help support your students and faculty by giving you money, but we'd like you to read this book,' that doesn't strike me as a big sin." What would be a big sin, he continues, "is saying that certain ideas cannot be discussed." No, the sin is to insist that a certain idea be discussed whether or not it has made its academic way because a few disappointed outsiders are willing to spend big bucks to get it inside. If, in the judgment of an instructor, *Atlas Shrugged* will contribute to a student's understanding of a course's subject, there is every reason to assign it. But if assigning *Atlas Shrugged* is the price for the receiving of monies and the university pays that price, it has indeed sold its soul.

The Northwestern and FSU examples help us to understand when academic freedom issues legitimately arise. They arise when the university either allows its professors to appropriate the classroom for nonacademic purposes, as some think John Michael Bailey did, or allows itself to become the wholly owned subsidiary of another enterprise, as FSU may have done.

There are, of course, other contexts in which academic freedom is at stake, but the awarding of an honorary degree to Tony Kushner or anyone else isn't one of them. You needn't take my word for it. Give yourself the pleasure of reading two learned but entirely accessible books—Matthew Finkin's and Robert Post's *For the Common Good: Principles of American Academic Freedom* (2009) and Rodney Smolla's *The Constitution Goes to College* (2011).[8]

1. "Prof. John Michael Bailey Issues Statement on After-Class Event Controversy," *Daily Northwestern* online, March 1, 2011, http://dailynorthwestern.com/2011/03/01/campus/campusarchived/prof-john-michael-bailey-issues-statement-on-after-class-event-controversy/.

2. "Statement by Northwestern President Morton Schapiro," Northwestern University, March 3, 2011, http://www.northwestern.edu/newscenter/stories/2011/03/statement-president.html#sthash.w6EwWnZ1.dpuf.

3. Patrick Svitek, "Updated: Northwestern Copes with Fallout, Attention from Sex Toy Demo," *Daily Northwestern* online, March 3, 2011, http://dailynorthwestern.com/2011/03/03/campus/campusarchived/updated-northwestern-copes-with-fallout-attention-from-sex-toy-demo/.

4. Patrick Svitek, "Human Sexuality Class Cancellation Prompts 70 Academics to Send Letter to Schapiro," May 11, 2011, *Daily Northwestern* online, http://dailynorthwestern.com/2011/05/11/campus/campusarchived/human-sexuality-class-cancellation-prompts-70-academics-to-send-letter-to-schapiro/.

5. Ibid.

6. Stanley Fish, "Sex, the Koch Brothers and Academic Freedom," *Scholars at Risk*, May 16, 2011, http://scholarsatrisk.nyu.edu/Events-News/Article-Detail.php?art _uid=2787.

7. Ibid.

8. Finkin and Post, *For the Common Good*; and Rodney Smolla, *The Constitution Goes to College* (New York: New York University Press, 2011).

To Boycott or Not to Boycott, That Is the Question

MARCH 15, 2009

I.

In response to last week's column on neoliberalism and higher education,[1] Sobriquet writes that neoliberalism, like neoconservatism, is "an opaque catchphrase coined by wannabe pundits" that doesn't "refer to anything." That judgment finds support in an essay soon to be published in *Studies in Comparative International Development*. The authors, Taylor Boas and Jordan Gans-Morse (political science researchers at UC Berkeley), report that while in recent years "neoliberalism has become an academic catchphrase," its use "remains a puzzle" because it is "left undefined . . . even by those who employ it as a key independent or dependent variable."[2]

This corresponds to what I found in my reading. It wasn't that I had been unaware of the term; it was just that it never seemed to be doing much work; its force, as a Boas and Gans-Morse remark, is often more rhetorical (take that, you accursed neoliberal) than analytic. I didn't feel I had to have a firm grasp on it in order to continue reading; that is, until I found the word being applied to me.

Boas's and Gans-Morse's other point is that neoliberalism is used in so "many different ways . . . that its appearance in any given article offers little clue as to what it actually means." This is borne out by the commentators, many of whom vehemently disagree with me and at the same time disagree with one another:

> Neoliberalism is just another word for neoconservatism; no, they're different; neoliberalism is nineteenth-century laissez-faire capitalism; no, it isn't; neoliberalism is what "new Democrats" Bill Clinton and Al Gore urge; neoliberalism is Adam Smith on steroids; neoliberalism is Marx's dialectical materialism; neoliberalism is just capitalism; neoliberalism is J. S. Mill's libertarianism; neoliberalism is plain old cost accounting; neoliberalism is Bushism;

neoliberalism is classical liberalism; neoliberalism is what Ayn Rand promoted; neoliberalism is globalism; neoliberalism is avarice; neoliberalism is Law and Economics.

The variety of views about neoliberalism was matched by the variety of views about me, which ranged from gratitude ("I enjoy running into something so calmly, methodically, and complexly reasoned in the newspaper") to admiration ("Well worth reading. The author does an admirable job") to derision ("What a massive whiff of hot air") to contemptuous dismissal ("The title of this column should be 'Think Before Writing' "). One poster even made fun of a sports jacket he says I wore forty years ago; he must have been waiting all those years for an opportunity to sneer, and he got it.

The praise and dispraise came along with opposing characterizations of my position. *I am a neoliberal; no, I'm a critic of neoliberalism. I am for American higher education. I am against it. I am an apostle of free enterprise. I make fun of it.* A.C. gets it right when he or she complains, "After reading this entry twice, I'm still not sure where professor Fish stands on this issue."

Reading it two hundred times wouldn't help, for I don't stand anywhere; that's the (non)point of most of these columns, not to endorse or reject agendas but to follow out the lines of argument that accompany them, to see how those arguments work or don't work, to see where they lead.

II.

In the last line of the column, I say that the arguments of the academic critics of neoliberalism lead straight to support for and participation in the boycott of Israeli academics. (Which isn't to say that all critics of the neoliberal university are necessarily pro-boycott, only that it is easier for them to arrive at that position because they are already halfway down the road.) Several posters wondered how I could get from here to there. Here's how, in five easy steps:

(1) The academic critics of neoliberalism complain that one effect of the neoliberalization of the university has been the retreat by faculty members from public engagement, with the result that intellectual work becomes hermetic and sealed off from political struggle. "We need," says Henry Giroux, "to link knowing with

action, and learning with social engagement, and this requires addressing the responsibilities that come with teaching . . . to fight for an inclusive and radical democracy by recognizing that education in the broadest sense is not just about understanding . . . but also about providing the conditions for assuming the responsibilities we have as citizens to expose human misery and to eliminate the conditions that produce it."[3]

(2) In the eyes of many academics, a great deal of human misery is being produced by Israel's policy toward Palestinians. Eliminating it is everybody's business.

(3) This includes academics who cannot stop at just talking about injustice, but must do something about it, must act.

(4) The political resources of academics are limited, but one way academics can show political solidarity is to put pressure on colleagues who are silent in the face of injustice: "The boycott or the divestment campaign is the mode of political protest that is left after all other forms of struggle have been tried"; it is "the politics of last resort."[4]

(5) Therefore, it is appropriate and even obligatory to boycott Israeli academics and Israeli universities "that have turned a blind eye to the destruction and disruption of Palestinian Schools."[5] "If, in the midst of oppression, these institutions do not function to analyze and explain the world in a way that promotes justice . . . but rather acquiesce in aggressive neo-colonialist practices, then others may legitimately boycott them."[6]

Nor will they be saved by the invocation of academic freedom, for rather than protecting Israeli academics, academic freedom, as the boycotters understand it, demands reprisals against them for having stood by while the freedom of Palestinians was being violated. "There is a whiff of hypocrisy," says Steven Rose, when after failing to protest against the atrocities of their government "Israeli scientists complain that those of us . . . who refuse to collaborate with them . . . are attacking their academic freedom."[7]

David Lloyd drives the point home: "Israeli institutions are complicit in immense infringement on Palestinian academic freedom, so it's really hard, it seems to me, for Israeli institutions to claim the rights of academic freedom that they are so systematically denying to their Palestinian counterparts."[8]

Lloyd's last phrase—"their Palestinian counterparts"—raises a question that helps us to see what has happened to academic freedom in these statements. Counterparts in what respect? Not, obviously, as coreligionists or citizens of the same polity, but as academics—men and women trained to engage in research and to follow lines of intellectual inquiry wherever they might lead.

Whatever their political or religious or geographical situations, scholars throughout the world are linked by a set of concerns to which they have a responsibility that is distinct from (although not necessarily antithetical to) the responsibilities they may have in other respects. The strength of an academic discipline, Murray Hausknecht observes, "depends on maintaining relationships across national borders."[9]

Academics, Hausknecht explains, "can be likened to citizens of a nation," and while they are also citizens in political units (particular nations and finally the world), if we conflate the two citizenships by making academic judgments (whether to accept a paper in a journal or invite a speaker to a conference) on political grounds, we do great damage to the scholarly community, the nature of which "is exemplified by academics who publish papers in foreign journals, attend international conferences, and collaborate with colleagues in research projects."[10]

But it is just such a conflation that the boycotters insist on, as Grant Farred makes clear when he declares that "academic freedom has to be conceived as a form of political solidarity."[11] Political solidarity, not academic solidarity. Farred denies to academic work any distinctive identity (he, of course, would receive this as a compliment, not an accusation), and insists that decisions about how to engage in it—where, in collaboration with whom—should be guided by political considerations, by a determination of whether this or that scholar is on the right side.

For the most part, opponents of the boycott do not engage on this point, but instead put forward arguments that are weak, either because they are counterproductive or merely strategic. In the counterproductive category is the charge that the boycotters are anti-Semitic. Rather than shaming or cowing those it is aimed at, this accusation only produces indignation, both on the part of those who favor a boycott and are Jewish (like its founders Steven and Hilary Rose) and those who declare that they have been fighting all forms of racism, including anti-Semitism, for their entire lives.

The charge of anti-Semitism also provokes two responses of principle: first, that one can and should distinguish between opposition to the policy of a state and prejudice against that state's racial majority (*Are you telling me I can't criticize Israel without being a racist?*); and second, that the invocation of anti-Semitism has the effect, if not the intention, of chilling speech (a First Amendment no-no). How can one "vigorously advocate the idea that the Israeli occupation is brutal and wrong . . . if the voicing of these views calls down the charge of anti-Semitism?"[12]

A second line of antiboycott reasoning invites counterresponses that merely continue the debate without in any way clarifying it. It asks, why single out Israel when European and North American academics regularly engage with researchers from countries (including, perhaps, the United States) with well-documented records of human-rights abuses? The trouble with this debating point in the guise of a question (you're supposed to realize that you'd end up boycotting everyone) is that it implies that if Israel were the only state performing bad acts it would be okay to embargo its academics.

The real question is, should the policies (whatever they are) of a country an academic happens to live in ever be a reason for denying her the courtesies academics extend to each other in recognition of the collaborative nature of the work they do? (Yes, I would include academics from the Third Reich.) That question has the advantage of facing squarely the issue of what academic work is and isn't, an issue that is obscured if you're just toting up and rank-ordering atrocities as a preliminary to determining which scholars you will or won't deal with.

Boycott opponents do no better when the focus is narrowed to just Israel and Palestine, and they argue, as Anthony Julius and Alan Dershowitz do, that it is incorrect and a suspicious distortion to regard Israel "as the pure aggressor," and the Palestinians "as pure victims."[13]

But again, the degree of culpability assigned to the two states (and of course that is a matter that will never be settled) should not yield a formula for treating its academics differently (you guys can come to our conference, but you lot can't). Even if it were agreed that Julius and Dershowitz are right and there is blame all around, that agreement would say nothing about whether or not to boycott, unless you believe that the question is an empirical one that can be answered by history and analogy.

Because antiboycotters offer arguments that trade in comparisons and calculations of relative guilt, they are vulnerable to the boycotters' trump card: If you supported the boycott of South Africa and the disinvestment by universities from companies doing business in or with that country, you are obligated, by your own history, to support the boycott of Israeli academics. Hilary and Steven Rose reported in 2002 that they knew many academics "who thought that cooperating with Israeli institutions was like collaborating with the apartheid regime."[14]

In response, antiboycotters say that (1) boycotting is a "blunt instrument" that harms individuals and institutions indiscriminately; (2) it wasn't the boycotts that brought down the South African regime; (3) the boycott against South Africa was economic and was not aimed primarily at scholars; and (4) despite the loose use of the word by boycott promoters, Israel is not an apartheid state, for it accords its Arab citizens political rights that were denied to blacks in apartheid South Africa.

But the effort to detach Israel from South Africa by claiming that the sins of the latter were much greater than the sins of the former has not been successful, in part because those who make it are trying too hard. (You can almost see the sweat on their foreheads.) The American Association of University Professors ties itself up in knots explaining that while its own history includes "support for divestiture during the anti-apartheid campaigns in South Africa," it nevertheless opposes this boycott.[15] The rationale seems to be that South Africa was a special, onetime case—"South Africa is the only instance in which the organization endorsed some form of boycott"—but that is hardly going to satisfy those who are prosecuting the "if you protested injustice then, you should protest it now" argument.

The better course would be for the AAUP and other boycott opponents to accept the equivalence of the two situations and repudiate what they did in the past. Not "what we did then is different from what we decline to do now," but "we won't boycott now and we were wrong to boycott then."

Whether or not divestiture and other actions taken by academics were decisive in, or even strongly contributory to, ending the apartheid regime is in dispute. What should not be in dispute is that those actions, however salutary and productive of good results, were and are antithetical to the academic enterprise, which, while it may provide the tools (of argument, fact, and historical research) that enable good and righteous deeds, should never presume to perform them.

1. "Neoliberalism and Higher Education," *New York Times*, March 9, 2009.

2. Taylor Boas and Jordan Gans-Morse, "Neoliberalism: From New Liberal Philosophy to Anti-Liberal Slogan," in *Studies in Comparative International Development*, 2009, http://people.bu.edu/tboas/neoliberalism.pdf.

3. Henry Giroux, *Against the Terror of Neoliberalism* (Boulder, CO: Paradigm, 2008).

4. Grant Farred, "The Act of Politics Is to Divide," *Works and Days* 26 & 27 (2008–9), http://www.worksanddays.net/2008–9/File17.Farred_011309_FINAL.pdf.

5. David Lloyd, "Boycott Promotes Debate: Protest Takes Nonviolent Approach toward Preserving Intellectual Freedom in Israel," *Daily Trojan* online, February 17, 2009, http://dailytrojan.com/category/opinion/boycott_promotes_debate-1.1482958.

6. Mona Baker and Lawrence Davidson, "In Defence of the Boycott of Israeli Academic Institutions," *Counterpunch*, September 17, 2003, http://www.counterpunch.org/2003/09/17/in-defense-of-the-boycott-of-israeli-academic-institutions/.

7. Steven Rose, "A Whiff of Hypocrisy," *Guardian*, May 26, 2004.

8. Elizabeth Redden, "Israel Boycott Movement Comes to U.S.," Inside Higher Ed, January 26, 2009, https://www.insidehighered.com/news/2009/01/26/boycott.

9. Murray Hausknecht, "Whether Academics Have Different Responsibilities than Citizens," *Dissent*, September 2007.

10. Ibid.

11. Grant Farred, "The Art of Politics Is to Divide," *Works and Days* 26/27 (2008/2009): 355.

12. Judith Butler, "No, It's Not Anti-Semitic," *London Review of Books*, August 21, 2003.

13. Anthony Julius and Alan Dershowitz, "The Contemporary Fight against Anti-Semitism," *Times* online, June 13, 2007.

14. Hilary and Steven Rose, "The Choice Is to Do Nothing or Try to Bring about Change," *Guardian* online, www.guardian.co.uk/Archive.

15. "On Academic Boycotts," AAUP, September–October 2006, http://aaup.org/file/On-Academic-Boycotts_0.pdf.

Academic Freedom against Itself: Boycotting Israeli Universities

OCTOBER 28, 2013

I hate it when I have a book in press and people keep writing about the subject anyway. You would think that they would have the courtesy to hold their fire until I have had my say. I raise the issue because my book on academic freedom (*Versions of Academic Freedom: From Professionalism to Revolution*) will be out in about a year and the on-line *Journal of Academic Freedom* (published by the American Association of University Professors) has just posted its fourth volume consisting of essays on a topic that figures prominently in my analysis—the boycott of Israeli universities by academic institutions and scholars housed in other countries.[1]

For those of you who haven't heard about this movement, let me briefly rehearse its history. Since the early 2000s a number of academics have been arguing that because Israel is a rogue state engaged in acts of oppression and apartheid, and because Israeli universities are by and large supported and administered by the state, it must be assumed that those universities further the ends of a repressive regime, either by actively supporting its policies or by remaining silent in the face of atrocities committed against the Palestinians. Accordingly, it is appropriate, and indeed a matter of urgency, for right-thinking (meaning left-thinking) academics to refuse to engage in intellectual discourse with the Israeli academy. If you have an exchange program with an Israeli university, suspend it; if you are the editor of a scholarly journal and an Israeli researcher is a member of your board, remove him.

In response to the objection that such actions violate the academic freedom of Israeli academics by singling them out for exclusion from the scholarly conversation for which they were trained (thereby making them into second-class academic citizens), boycott supporters make two points that are somewhat in tension. They say, first, that the academic freedom of Palestinian professors and students is violated daily when they are denied access, funding, materials, and mobility by the state of Israel; no academic freedom for you if you don't accord it to them. This argument, you will note, assumes that academic freedom is a primary value. The second argument doesn't. It says that while academic freedom is usually a good thing, when basic questions of justice are in play, it must give way. Here is the Palestinian researcher Omar Barghouti making that point in the current issue of the *Journal of Academic Freedom (JAF)*: "[W]hen a prevailing and consistent denial of basic human rights is recognized, the ethical responsibility of every free person and every association of free persons, academic institutions included, to resist injustice supersedes other considerations about whether such acts of resistance [like a boycott] may directly or indirectly injure academic freedom."[2]

Or, in other words, adhering strictly to academic freedom standards is okay in the conduct of academic business as usual, but when something truly horrible is happening in the world, the niceties of academic freedom become a luxury we can't (and shouldn't) afford: "[I]n contexts of dire oppression, the obligation to save human lives and to protect the inalienable rights of the oppressed to live as free, equal humans acquires an overriding urgency and an immediate priority."[3]

The repetition of the word "free" in Barghouti's statements alerts us to something peculiar in this line of reasoning: academic freedom, traditionally understood as the freedom to engage in teaching and research free from the influences or pressures of politics, is being declared an obstacle to—even the enemy of—genuine freedom, which is defined politically. You can be true to academic freedom, at least in this logic, only if you are willing to jettison its precepts when, in your view, political considerations outweigh them. David Lloyd and Malini Johar Scheuller (writing in the same volume) say as much when they describe a boycott as "a specific tactic, deployed in relation to a wider campaign against injustice."[4] Wider than what? The answer is, wider than an academic freedom conceived as a professional—not moral or political—concept. That professional conception of academic freedom, characterized by boycotters as impoverished, desiccated, and an alibi for neoliberal hegemony, must be left behind so that actions in violation of academic freedom narrowly defined may be taken in the name of an academic freedom suitably enlarged.

The formula and the rationale for this vision of academic freedom undoing itself in the service of academic freedom are concisely given in a Howard Zinn quotation Lloyd and Scheuller ask us to remember:

"To me, academic freedom has always meant the right to insist that academic freedom be more than academic." This declaration has the virtue of illustrating just how the transformation of academic freedom from a doctrine insulating the academy from politics into a doctrine that demands of academics blatantly political actions is managed. What you do is diminish (finally to nothing) the limiting force of the adjective "academic" and at the same time put all the emphasis on freedom (which should be rewritten FREEDOM) until the academy loses its distinctive status and becomes just one more location of a universal moral/political struggle. Balakrishnan Rajagopal, cited by Rima Najjar Kapitan in her essay, says it forthrightly: "[A]cademic freedom is not only an end. . . . It is also the means for realizing other important ends, including individual freedoms, that go beyond expressive freedoms to encompass all freedoms such as nondiscrimination."[5] When the means, strictly adhered to, seem to block the realization of the end, sacrifice them. (Oh, Kant, thou shouldst be living at this hour!)

As you can tell from my citations, nearly all of the essays in the new issue of *JAF* support the boycott, although the AAUP itself is against it, at least so far. Only one essay (out of nine, plus a polemical and biased introduction) and two published responses to the volume take the opposite position. Ernst Benjamin, an old AAUP hand, makes the key point when he observes that "The AAUP is not itself a human rights organization."[6] Cary Nelson, until recently the president of the AAUP, elaborates, explaining that "The focus of the AAUP's mission is higher education." It follows, he continues, that academic freedom is to be understood within the context of that focus: "[A]cademic freedom is a specialized right that is not legally implicated in the full spectrum of human rights that nations should honor."[7] (That's perfect.)

This does not mean, of course, that academics are bent on violating human rights or that they display an unconcern with them. It means, rather, that watching out for human rights violations and taking steps to stop them is not the charge either of the AAUP or the academy or the doctrine of academic freedom. Watching out for academic freedom violations—instances in which a scholar's right to pursue his or her research freely has been compromised by an overweening administration—is the charge, and it includes taking steps to stop him or her by exerting pressure or threatening legal action. As Nelson's vocabulary reminds us, this is a specialized monitoring of behavior in circumscribed educational contexts, not a monitoring of bad behavior wherever on earth it might be found. We should not, says Benjamin "compromise this principle [of academic freedom] in the name of others which, though they may be larger and even more important, are not the principles specific to our association." If we do so, and extend academic freedom only to those "found worthy" by a political measure, we shall have lost our grip on academic freedom altogether, for "[p]olitically qualified academic freedom is not really academic freedom at all." (Amen!)

Distinctions like the ones invoked by Benjamin and Nelson are likely to be waved away by those they argue against, because, as Marjorie Heins, the third dissenter, observes, in the eyes of academics "incensed at Israeli policies . . . delicate questions about the unjust targeting of innocent professors, or of imposing political tests, are minor concerns compared to the moral exigency of the issue."[8] "The issue" is, of course, the Israeli treatment of Palestinians, and while it is easy to understand how academics, among others, might find that treatment objectionable and reprehensible (and I take no position on the question here), it is not so easy to understand how moral outrage at a political action can be so quickly translated into an obligation to deny professional courtesies to people whose responsibility for that action is at best attenuated and in many instances nonexistent. And it absolutely defies understanding—except by the convoluted and loose arguments rehearsed above—that the concept of academic freedom could be used to defend a policy, the policy of boycott, that so cavalierly throws academic freedom under the bus.

A final question. What animates the boycotters? They would, I am sure, answer, we are animated by a commitment to the securing of social/political justice, a commitment that overrides lesser commitments we might have as professionals. I'll grant that as a part of their motivation, but another, perhaps larger, part is the opportunity to shed the label "ivory-tower intellectual"—a label that announces their real-world ineffectuality—and march under a more flattering banner, the banner of "freedom fighter." But the idea that an academic becomes some kind of hero by the cost-free act of denying other academics the right to play in the communal sandbox (yes, this is third-grade stuff) is as pathetic as it is laughable. Heroism doesn't come that cheaply. Better, I think, to wear the "ivory-tower intellectual" label proudly. At least, it's honest.

1. Stanley Fish, *Versions of Academic Freedom: From Professionalism to Revolution* (Chicago: University of Chicago Press, 2014); and *Journal of Academic Freedom*, vol. 4 (2013).

2. Omar Barghouti, "Boycott, Academic Freedom, and the Moral Responsibility to Uphold Human Rights," *Journal of Academic Freedom*, vol. 4 (2013), http://www.aaup .org/sites/default/files/files/JAF/2013%20JAF/Barghouti.pdf.

3. Ibid.

4. David Lloyd and Malini Johar Schueller, "The Israeli State of Exception and the Case for Academic Boycott," *Journal of Academic Freedom*, vol. 4 (2013), http://www .aaup.org/sites/default/files/files/JAF/2013%20JAF/LloydSchueller.pdf.

5. Rima Najjar Kapitan, "Academic Freedom Encompasses the Right to Boycott: Why the AAUP Should Support the Palestinian Call for the Academic Boycott of Israel," *Journal of Academic Freedom*, vol. 4 (2013), http://www.aaup.org/sites/default/files /files/JAF/2013%20JAF/Kapitan.pdf.

6. Ernst Benjamin, "Why I Continue to Support the AAUP Policy in Opposition to Academic Boycotts," http://www.aaup.org/sites/default/files/files/Response-Benjamin .pdf.

7. Cary Nelson, "Academic Boycotts Reconsidered," http://www.aaup.org/sites /default/files/files/JAF/2013%20JAF/Responses/Response-Nelson.pdf.

8. Marjorie Heins, "Rethinking Academic Boycotts," *Journal of Academic Freedom*, vol. 4 (2013), http://www.aaup.org/sites/default/files/files/JAF/2013%20JAF/Heins.pdf.

Boycotting Israeli Universities: Part 2

NOVEMBER 11, 2013

The responses to my column "Academic Freedom against Itself: Boycotting Israeli Universities" (8.9) on the call by some academics to boycott Israeli universities in the name of academic freedom were impassioned and polarized. I was pleased to find more readers than usual on my side, but one argument favored by those who agreed with my negative view of the boycott is, I think, beside the point. That is the argument that the boycott is wrong because it is selective, because it singles out Israel when there are so many other countries in the world whose policies and actions are just as bad or worse. Actually, this is not an argument; it is a debating point (as some who offer it know): it is the rhetorical trick of extending an opponent's claim until it yields an absurd result, in this case the absurd result that follows if we are required to break off relations with universities housed in nations whose human rights record we find questionable: on this reasoning, we would have to break off relationships with everyone and there would be no academic exchange at all.

The problem with this debating point is that it puts the emphasis on the wrong question—whether Israel is a good or bad country, and thereby implies that if it were clearly one or the other, the boycott would be clearly bad or good. But Israel's moral status is irrelevant to the right question, which is whether academic institutions boycotting other academic institutions can ever be an expression of, rather than an undermining of, academic freedom. Ian Maitland is exactly on target when he says that "[t]he point isn't whether the policy of boycotting universities in countries whose policies we deplore is applied consistently. It is whether it is good policy in any circumstances." Even if it were true that "Israel has no recognized moral standing in the world" (Tom Paine), that would not be a reason for engaging in an academic boycott against it, and the anointing of Israel as the beacon of freedom would not be a reason for exempting it from a boycott, should one be academically justified (as I think it could not be).

For many posters, playing the "consistency" card is merely preliminary to the accusation they really want to make, the accusation that the boycotters are anti-Semites. They are saying, if you won't follow the logic of your argument to its absurd conclusion and boycott everyone, it must be because you harbor a special animus toward Jews. But again this is a red herring, indeed the same red herring. No doubt some boycotters are anti-Semitic, while others (a vast majority, I would think) are not. But the rightness or wrongness of an action has nothing to do with the moral status of the actor who performs it. If academics boycotting other academics is wrong, it is wrong whether the boycotter is a virulent anti-Semite or someone whose heart is discrimination free.

It follows that the determination of the rightness or wrongness of the boycott should begin not with a moral calculus of either nations or persons, but with a specification of what business universities are in, which will also be a specification of what activities are appropriate to university professors and a specification of the proper scope of academic freedom. Poster Nana's understanding of what professors are supposed to do is expansive: "Part of academics' responsibility is the advancement of Justice, equality, human rights preservation." That would come as a surprise to the committee that approved my dissertation, to the departments that hired me, and to the presses that have published my work. They didn't ask me how I planned to advance justice and equality; they were concerned with the quality of my scholarship and with the contribution my analyses might make to the discipline's continuing conversations. They were concerned, that is, with my professional, not my political, performance. Of course, Nana's capacious definition of academic responsibility makes no distinction between the professional and the political. Indeed, in her account the professional is an extension of the political, and, if that is so, it makes perfect sense to regard boycotting—described by Robert Jennings as a "definitive political instrument"—as a legitimate professional act and as an expression of academic freedom, no longer understood to be "academic" in any serious sense.

Jennings derides my "narrow" and "simplistic categorical reasoning," which, he says, is not "up to the task of addressing so complex a question." By that he means that by insisting on a limited, guild notion of academic freedom—it is the freedom to pursue scholarly inquiry, not the freedom to advance justice and equality on university time—I fall short of addressing the "multilayered social milieu" in which the academy inevitably resides. I would reply that while the "multilayered social milieu" is properly the object of academic attention—it can be described, analyzed, and mapped—it is not the proper object of academic intervention. "Narrow" is an adjective the academy should not shun but embrace, for if academic activity cannot be narrowly defined, it loses its shape and becomes indistinguishable from political rallies and partisan exhortation. This, of course, is what the boycotters want. Definitions like Nana's do not enhance the academic enterprise or add a heroic gloss to the concept of academic freedom; rather, they destroy both by emptying them of any specific content.

Chris does the same thing when he declares that "it is entirely appropriate for any [academic] institution to indicate its disapproval of a political regime by refusing to establish . . . arrangements with institutions that collaborate with that regime." But nothing in the charge given to a university by the state or by a board of trustees authorizes, much less demands, the awarding of points to a political regime. It is only if universities are thought to be in the business of giving seals of approval or disapproval to sovereign states (a job reserved for organizations like the State Department and the United Nations) that arrangements with other universities can "appropriately" be conditioned on a determination of political correctness. A university is free, just as Chris asserts, not to enter into arrangements with another institution for all kinds of reasons: the curriculums may not fit, the finances may not work, the prestige of the would-be partner may be insufficient. These and other professional reasons are the appropriate ingredients of a negative decision; disagreement with the policies of the state regime is not an appropriate ingredient because it is not a professional one.

Some posters say that by focusing on neatly cabined professional issues, I display an unconcern with the "right of Palestinians not to be bombed, and killed, imprisoned, have their olive trees burned and land stolen" (Christian Haesemeyer). But if I "take no position" on these matters, it is because they are not my subject in the column, and not because I regard them as trivial or unworthy of a response. Jim R. gets it right: "Fish is writing about academic freedom. Not about boycotts, political messaging, or anything else." Posing a limited question about the nature and scope of academic freedom does not mean that one is dismissing, or saying anything at all, about other questions that are not, at the moment, on the table. It means, simply, that one is keeping to the point, a cardinal intellectual virtue.

Another version of the demand that I declare a position on everything takes the form of a series of questions: "Where were you, Stanley Fish, when Noam Chomsky was refused admission to Israel? Where were you when the University of Haifa drove the distinguished historian Ilan Pappe into exile?" (Rosa H.). "[W]here was [Fish] when Finkelstein was denied tenure at DePaul? When Shortell was pushed out of chairmanship at Brooklyn College? When the CUNY board of Trustees usurped faculty authority to institute a dumbed-down, general ed-lite curriculum ignoring the registered opposition of 92% of the faculty?" (David A.). "And what would Professor Fish say about the boycott used to deny South Africa access to . . . academics when their policy of apartheid was in full cry?" (chickenlover). "I would also ask Mr. Fish if his interest in academic freedom extended to a support of the lecture by Omar Barghouti and Judith Butler at Brooklyn College last winter?" (Mary Ann).

The last two questions are easy. I am on record ("To Boycott or Not to Boycott" [8.8]) saying that university divestment from South African–related stocks for political rather than economic reasons was wrong. And I wrote two columns in this space supporting the Barghouti-Butler lecture and excoriating those who tried to stop it. As for the other questions, that's a lot of places where I should have been instead of where I probably was, in class teaching, or in my office writing. Moreover, the examples hurled at me are not always to the point of my column. Professor Finkelstein was denied tenure, not boycotted. (No consolation to him.) The CUNY trustees may have been unwise to ignore the views of 92 percent of the faculty, but they had the right and authority to do so. Maybe they were being stupid and arrogant, as trustees often are, but they weren't boycotting anything. And what I as an American citizen have to do with the decision of the state of Israel to admit or not admit someone—even Noam Chomsky—is beyond me. It would certainly help if the parties to conversations like this one would keep to the terms of the debate and not engage in scattergun hypotheticals. But my main objection to these questions/challenges is that by demanding that one (in this case I) take up every issue that could conceivably be related to the topic under discussion, they ensure that the topic will never come into focus and that the discussion itself will be hopelessly diffuse.

Finally, allow me to comment on two criticism of my prose style. N. S. Edwards says that he has "never read such a convoluted, poorly written article." Robert, on the other hand (or is it the other hand?), complains that the column is too well written: "Am I the only one who feels exhausted after reading Fish's tight, manicured precise-to-within-an-inch-of-their-lives sentences? They seem to form granite like paragraphs all precisely metered and placed 'so'—like the foundations of a pyramid." My goal is to be guilty of this charge every time out.

So Long, It's Been Good to Know You

DECEMBER 23, 2013

In 1995 I got a call out of the blue from an editor at this newspaper who invited me to write an op-ed. "About what?" I asked. "Anything you like," she replied. That was obviously an offer I couldn't refuse, so I set about writing, schooled by my wife, who had been a book reviewer for the *Raleigh News and Observer*. She taught me to forgo the academic habit of withholding the goods until the end and explained how in this genre the main point should be announced immediately because readers might not wait around while I indulged myself in the pleasures of building a pretty argument. (This is a lesson I have hewed to only intermittently.) The result was a piece titled "How the Right Hijacked the Magic Words" (4.11). The editors liked it, readers seemed interested, and I was hooked.

In the next ten years I wrote five or six pieces a year, usually at the editors' invitation, and in 2006 I was asked to write a regular column, first under the rubric of "Think Again" (a title bestowed by the then op-ed page editor David Shipley), then as a member of the Opinionator team, and most recently as a contributing writer. Now, some three hundred essays later, the party's over and this is my last column, at least as an author whose work appears at an appointed time either once a week or twice a month.

Looking back, what I will remember most are the readers and their comments. The relationship between us was often adversarial, sometimes because of a disagreement with the views I had expressed, sometimes because of a frustration with my unwillingness to express a view at all. I explained (too often) that I was typically less interested in taking a stand on a controversial issue than in analyzing the arguments being made by one or more of the parties to the dispute. I was making an argument about the structure of argument, and the fact that I came down hard on the reasoning put forward by one side didn't mean either that I rejected its position or embraced the position of the other side.

So, for example, when I found the writings of the "New Atheists"—Richard Dawkins, Sam Harris, and Christopher Hitchens (6.1)—shallow, callow, historically uninformed, and downright silly, that didn't mean that I was a religious believer. Bad arguments can be made on behalf of a position you may well hold, and by pointing out their badness you don't (necessarily) reject the position. "I believe X, but think that the case you guys are making for X is faulty" is a perfectly reasonable thing to say. (I say that all the time about the Obama administration.) In the columns that provoked frustration, I stopped short of offering the "I believe X" part, leaving readers to wonder where I stood. I tried to stand on the side of cogency and against slipshod reasoning, which meant that I stood on neither side of a substantive question like "Is there a God?" or "Does religion do more harm than good?" I might of course have answers to those questions, but it wasn't the point of the columns I wrote to reveal them. Let me hasten to say that I wasn't trying to be objective (a label pinned on me by both my detractors and defenders) or to be above the fray; I was in another fray, making points about making points, and reserving the deeper, moral issue for another day, which usually never arrived.

I say "usually" because on occasion my anatomy of a structure of argument bled right into a substantive position. This was so recently, when I analyzed the case being made by some academics for boycotting Israeli universities. They reason that a boycott is justified because as the result of Israel's actions, "Palestinian universities have been bombed, schools have been closed, and scholars and students deported."[1] I quote from a statement by the American Studies Association, which just a few days ago endorsed the boycott and did so in the name of academic freedom, defined (correctly) by the statement as "the necessity for intellectuals to remain free from state interests and interference."[2] Yet, in the next breath, the association is busily assuming the interests of one state against another and acting accordingly, on the reasoning that the academic freedom of Palestinians has been "severely hampered" by Israel's policies. Or, in other words (my words), "the state of Israel has done things to the Palestinians and therefore we should do bad things to Israeli universities."

That's a good example of the kind of bad argument I like to skewer: the American Studies Association resolves to harm the good (academic freedom) it has pledged many times to protect in the hope that by doing so it will bring about a greater good somewhere down the line; it will misidentify the appropriate target of retaliation, because the target it has in its sights—the Israeli academy—is the only one it can hope to affect; it will compromise, indeed abandon, its principles in exchange for the (possible) furtherance of a political goal. And I would add that not only is the argument bad in this instance in the context of these particular facts; it would be bad in any instance. No matter what the motivation or the circumstances, curtailing the freedom of academics because of a political judgment—saying, as the boycotters say, "because we don't like the policies of your government, we won't have anything to do with you"—is just flat-out wrong.

Now, that's a substantive position if there ever was one, but it still stops short of answering the substantive question that will be of interest to many readers: Who, generally, is in the right or wrong, the Palestinians or the Israelis? The answer to that question has absolutely nothing to do with the question of whether a boycott of Israeli universities can be justified. One question turns on a geopolitical calculation I am not competent to make and so I don't make it; the other turns on the true nature of academic work and academic freedom, matters on which I am always ready to pronounce because they involve a professional, not a moral, judgment. Moral judgments are often necessary, but they are not always necessary, and sometimes the better part of wisdom is to refrain from making them because they get in the way of conceptual clarity.

In saying that, I find myself back at the same old stand, making a point about the kind of point I'm not making, doing what I do just after having announced that I will no longer be doing it. As John Wayne might have said, but in fact didn't, a man's gotta do what a man's gotta do. And in whatever venue (including, perhaps, this one) I continue to do it, I hope you'll be along for the ride.

1. "What Does the Boycott of Israeli Academic Institutions mean for the ASA?," American Studies Association, http://www.theasa.net/what_does_the_academic _boycott_mean_for_the_asa/.
2. Ibid.

ACKNOWLEDGMENTS

My greatest debt is to the *New York Times* readers whose comments energized me even when—no, especially when—they were less than positive. I will always be grateful to David Shipley and Andy Rosenthal for giving me the opportunity to write the "Think Again" columns. Once again I acknowledge Stephanie Dimitrakis, who rescued me from the consequences of my computer illiteracy. And I want to thank George Kalogerakis, Mary Duenwald, Peter Catapano, and Toby Harshaw for the expert editorial guidance they so generously provided.

Without the interest expressed by Peter Dougherty, director of Princeton University Press, this volume would never have gotten off the ground. Whittling it into shape was the work of Rob Tempio. Debbie Tegarden saw it through the production process with tact and patience. I am more than pleased to be a Princeton University Press author.

INDEX